The Theodosian Code

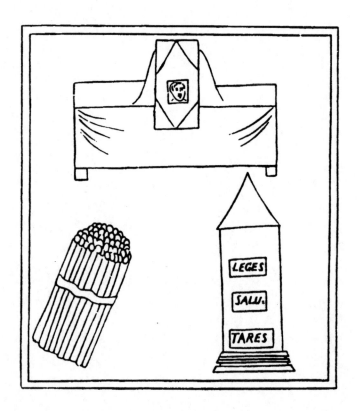

Insignia of the Eastern Quaestor, from O. Seeck's edition
of the *Notitia Dignitatum*

The Theodosian Code

Studies in the Imperial Law
of Late Antiquity

edited by

Jill Harries & Ian Wood

Bristol Classical Press

Second edition 2010
First published in 1993 by
Gerald Duckworth & Co. Ltd.
90-93 Cowcross Street, London EC1M 6BF
Tel: 020 7490 7300
Fax: 020 7490 0080
info@duckworth-publishers.co.uk
www.ducknet.co.uk

Editorial arrangement © 1993, 2010
by Jill Harries and Ian Wood

The contributors retain copyright
in their individual chapters.

A catalogue record for this book is available
from the British Library

ISBN 978-1-85399-740-2

Printed and bound in Great Britain by
the MPG Books Group

Contents

Contributors

Jill Harries is Lecturer in Ancient History, University of St Andrews.

Ian Wood is Senior Lecturer in History, University of Leeds.

Boudewijn Sirks is Associate Professor in the Faculty of Law, University of Amsterdam.

John Matthews is Professor of Middle and Later Roman History and Fellow of The Queen's College, Oxford.

Tony Honoré is Emeritus Professor of Civil Law in the University of Oxford.

Simon Corcoran was formerly a research student at St John's College, Oxford.

Judith Evans Grubbs is Associate Professor of Classical Studies, Sweet Briar College, Virginia.

David Hunt is Lecturer in Classics, University of Durham.

Mark Vessey is Professor in the English Department, University of British Columbia.

Dafydd Walters was formerly Head of the Department of Civil Law, University of Edinburgh.

Brian Croke is Director of Schools, Diocese of Broken Bay (Sydney) and Honorary Research Associate, Sydney University and Macquarie University.

Preface to the Second Edition

When this book first appeared in 1993, we were agreed that the contents were 'not the last word on the compilation of the Code' (p. 18) – or indeed on any other Code-related question. Subsequent scholarly activity has proved us right. The text is receiving fresh attention in its own right, through the Projet Volterra, based at University College London; and an ongoing French project aims to publish a French translation, based on Mommsen's text, and commentary in a series of volumes, under the overall editorship of S. Crogiez-Petrequin and P. Jaillet.

The essays contained in this volume address questions of fundamental importance as to what the code was, what it says about the nature of late Roman law and its impact on mediaeval Europe and beyond. A number of significant publications since, many by contributors to this volume, have improved understanding and stimulated further debate, both on the text itself (discussed in Part 1), its use as evidence for the history of Late Antiquity and its later place in the history of law.

On the origins of the Code, John Matthews[1] and Boudewijn Sirks[2] still adhere, in general terms, to the positions outlined in their contributions to this volume on the archival and other sources for the constitutions, which the compilers would abbreviate and rearrange in (supposedly) chronological order. The Matthews study is especially wide-ranging: although much space is devoted to more technical matters, such as the sources, editing and what to do about the seriously incomplete state of Mommsen's text (1905), he also captures the 'historical moment', when the Theodosian Code came into being (pp. 1-9), offers insights on numerous individual constitutions and (pp. 121-67) develops ideas on the Sirmondian Constitutions also addressed by Mark Vessey in this volume (below, 178-99). Since then, the *Gesta Senatus* have received detailed treatment from Lorena Alzeri,[3] who, *inter alia*, suggests that the Senate meeting at Rome, where the Theodosian Code was presented by the prefect Anicius

[1] *Laying Down the Law: A Study of the Theodosian Code* (Yale 2000).
[2] *The Theodosian Code: A Study* (Amsterdam 2007, revised 2008).
[3] *Gesta Senatus Romani de Theodosiano Publicando: Il codice Teodosiano e la sua diffusione ufficiale in Occidente* (Berlin 2008).

Acilius Glabrio Faustus, took place, not on 25 December, but 25 May (amending *VIII. K. Ian.* to *VIII.k. Iun.*). An aspect perhaps underplayed in the present volume is the importance of adducing the Code of Justinian, not merely to plug gaps, as Krueger's edition sought to do, but also to provide a setting for the Theodosian compilation in the broader framework of the Roman legal tradition.

Tony Honoré's contribution to this volume is one in a line of articles and books, notably his study of the quaestors of the Theodosian dynasty,[4] which bring to life the draftsmen of the texts, the 'mouths' of the emperor. By identifying divergences in style and legal agendas, Honoré supplements what is known already of careerists at the imperial court, who held the office, while adding, on the basis of style, several more 'anonymous' individuals, who also contributed their learning and eloquence to imperial legislation. Thanks to him, the central position of the quaestor in the legislative process is increasingly accepted as a given, although some, like one of the present editors, might quibble that some of the shorter-lived 'quaestors' identified by Honoré may in face have been *magistri memoriae*, deputising while there was a vacancy.

Increased understanding of how the texts came into being has rightly affected their use as sources by historians of Late Antiquity. For imperial constitutions were not dreamed up by emperors in isolation. They were the product of a process of dialogue and negotiation between emperors, officials and subjects. They reflect, in varying degrees, imperial preferences (even when edited, Julian the Apostate is allowed to refer to the temples and the gods in the plural); juristic tradition; and the self-interested suggestions or proposals of ambitious courtiers, provincial power-brokers and pressure-groups – even bishops. The situations on the ground, which generated the constitutions, and which were in turn affected by what the emperor decided, had their own dynamic; enforcement (e.g. of tax legislation or the criminal law) was only a small part of the emperor's legislative role.[5] Much of the *ius civile*, the law as it applied to Roman citizens, concerned dispute settlement; what emperors were asked to decide related, still, to problems faced by judges dealing with civil litigation in the courts.

Much work remains to be done on the implications of the responsive character of imperial legislation. A decision which appears, in isolation, to be radical, such as Constantine's ruling on one aspect of

---

[4] *Law in the Crisis of Empire, 399-455 AD* (Oxford 1999). His study of *Tribonian* (London 1978) is definitive for the most influential of all quaestors, the man behind the *Corpus Iuris Civilis* of Justinian.

[5] J. Harries, *Law and Empire in Late Antiquity* (Cambridge 1999). For the collective contribution of Harries (1999), Honoré (1999) and Matthews (2000), see A.D. Lee, 'De-Coding Late Roman Law', *Journal of Roman Studies* 92 (2002), 185-93.

episcopal legal hearings (*CT* 1.27.1), becomes less so, once it is appreciated that the decision was a response to a question about an existing situation. In other words, Constantine did not found or legalise bishops' judicial hearings; he merely offered assistance when problems arose. The same applies to his decisions on manumission in churches, and whether this could be done on a Sunday. Constantine did not institute manumission before bishops, nor did he make Sunday a holiday; he merely answered questions about regulations and how the holiday should be observed. The work of Caroline Humfress has analysed the importance of the responsive and negotiated nature of imperial law in relation to Christianity, heresy and court procedure;[6] she is also a leading analyst of the place of imperial law in the juristic tradition. The importance of the courts and of church councils in the formation of questions, referrals, proposals and decisions is becoming increasingly clear. Fergus Millar's work on the 'legislative' processes of the Church Councils under Theodosius II shows in detail the working of proposal and response as a means of 'persuading' (and being persuaded by) the powerful elite at the court of Constantinople.[7]

The presence of the proposer, the *consistorium*, which debated legal decisions, the quaestor who drafted them and emperors, who might have views of their own, complicates the issue of authorship; we cannot be sure whose views a given text in fact reflects (although, formally, they are those of the emperor). The Theodosian Code, therefore, is not a single text but an anthology of texts, reflecting divergent agendas and providing a snapshot of only one stage in the negotiated process of producing a 'law'. The missing voices should be acknowledged, even if we cannot identify them for sure. Nor can we be sure of the scale of the problems addressed. Large numbers of entries on a topic indicate, not that the problem was necessarily widespread, but that it was in the interest of a lot of people that the imperial line on it should be known. Still, the Code reflects the end-product of imperial decision-making and, working on that basis, two recent collections of essays on Late Antiquity drawing on the Theodosian Code as a 'source' provide diverse examples of how the Theodosian Code can be used to illuminate the history of late antiquity.[8]

As for the afterlife of the Code, that too has been the subject of

---

[6] *Orthodoxy and the Courts in Late Antiquity* (Oxford 2007).
[7] F. Millar, *A Greek Roman Empire: Power and Belief under Theodosius II (408-450)* (Berkeley, California 2006).
[8] S. Crogiez-Petrequin and P. Jaillet, with O. Huck (edd.), *Le Code théodosien: diversité d'approches et nouvelles perspectives* (École française de Rome 2009) is issued in conjunction with the French translation project. See also J.-J. Aubert and P. Blanchard (edd.), *Droit, Religion et Société dans le Code Théodosien* (Geneva 2009).

increased interest. In particular the 1500th anniversary of the promulgation of the Breviary of Alaric prompted reconsideration of the breviary itself, of its relations with the Code, and of its manuscript history – which, given the textual problems of the Code, itself casts light on the Theodosian compilation.[9]

---

[9] M. Rouche and B. Dumézil (edd.), *Le Bréviare d'Alaric. Aux origines du Code civil* (Paris 2008).

Introduction

The Background to the Code

Jill Harries

In AD 369, an anonymous petitioner to the emperors Valentinian I and Valens concluded a list of suggestions on financial, administrative and military policy with a proposition that the emperors codify the law: 'there remains one remedy needed from Your Serenity to cure the evils of the Roman state, that by the judgment of your imperial will you should reject the legal confusions caused by wicked men and cast light on the confused and contradictory pronouncements of the laws' (*De Rebus Bellicis* 21.1). The possibility that the petition may have been received and stored as part of a bureaucratic file in the imperial archives suggests that, even in the rigid and formalised structure of the Later Empire, the tradition of individual subjects' direct access to the emperor was not yet dead. However, it must be admitted that the Anonymous had no discernible influence on imperial policy. Although a precedent for a codification of imperial laws already existed in the Diocletianic compilations of Gregorian and Hermogenian in the 290s, no progress would be made with the idea for a further sixty years after the Anonymous' petition until, in March 429, Theodosius II, the Roman emperor in the East, set up the first Code commission (*CTh* 1.1.5). Eight years later, in 437, the work of compilation and arrangement had been completed and the wedding of Theodosius' cousin Valentinian III with his daughter Eudoxia was made the occasion of a formal presentation of the Code to the praetorian prefects of Italy and the East. On 15 February 438, Theodosius issued his first 'new law', *novella*, validating the Code in the East, while, in the West, the praetorian prefect who had received the Code from Theodosius presented it to the Roman Senate on 25 December of that year.[1]

The initiative was arguably long overdue. In a society governed by an autocratic emperor accountable to no one, the outcome of all legal

---

[1] Proceedings described in the *Gesta Senatus*, printed at the start of Mommsen's edition of the Theodosian Code, 1-4 and translated by C. Pharr, *The Theodosian Code* (1952), 3-7.

disputes and the character of much of the running of the Empire itself
depended on an accurate knowledge of the emperor's will. Litigation
was resolved in favour of the party which could produce the most
recent imperial opinion, often in the form of a rescript which was
relevant to their case. The incentive for forgery was always present;
even if a rescript were genuine, its authenticity could be questioned
and a case thus prolonged.[2] *Iudices* also suffered from the uncertainty
and insecurity engendered by the absence of an independent judiciary.
A judge was liable to be appealed against to the emperor, with
embarrassing consequences to himself, if he was wrong.[3] In cases of
doubt, therefore, the *iudex* might opt to consult the emperor before
passing judgment, through a *consultatio*. Constantine impatiently
objected to this, observing that *iudices* should only consult him on a
few matters, which could not be resolved by judicial sentence, as he
was a busy man who did not like being interrupted – and there was
always the option of appeal (*CTh* 9.30.1). A similar attitude was
adopted by Valens (AD 365-378), apparently at the prompting of the
praetorian prefect, Modestus; Valens avoided the hearing of legal cases
'believing that the investigation of swarms of legal disputes was
designed to humble the loftiness of imperial power' (Amm. Marc.
30.4.2),[4] a case of negligence which, according to Ammianus, vastly
increased the incidence of corruption and collusion in the system. The
problem, however, was not of Valens' creation, but derived from the
fear of the emperor's underlings over the consequences of being wrong.
The emperor, if he handled everything himself, was bound to be
overworked. Although a reduction in the number of appeals was not
made an explicit aim of the Theodosian Code project, it may well have
been a motive; only two years after its promulgation, Theodosius II
delegated his hearing of appeals from *spectabiles iudices* to a two-man
court, consisting of the praetorian prefect of the East and the imperial
quaestor (*CJust* 7.62.32).

   The establishment of the dynasty of Theodosius I in the eastern
capital at Constantinople from 395 created conditions for a stable and
settled administration capable, at last, of taking a considered look at

   [2] Courts could also reject rescripts that were 'against the law'. *CTh* 1.2.2 (29 Aug. 315)
implies fraudulent grants, 'contra ius rescribta non valeant, quocumque modo fuerint
impetrata. Quod enim publica iura perscribunt, magis sequi iudices debent.' Examples
occur at *CTh* 1.2.8 (22 Feb. 382) rescinding rescripts postponing debt repayment and
1.2.9 (24 Sept. 385), cancelling tax exemptions gained through rescripts 'elicitum
damnabili subreptione'.
   [3] The section at *CTh* 11.30, *De Appellationibus et Poenis Earum et Consultationibus*
contains 68 constitutions reflecting the importance of the subject to emperors and
iudices. The latter also risked being appealed against for political reasons, hence
Symmachus' caution in his *Relationes*, state papers addressed to Valentinian II in 384.
   [4] 'ille ad humilitandam celsitudinem potestatis negotiorum examina spectanda
instituta esse arbitratus (ut monebat), abstinuit penitus, laxavitque rapinarum fores,
quae roborabantur in dies ...'

the question of imperial law in the Empire. A long-standing tendency to accept rescripts, which were issued in response to specific queries, as in practice having universal application, which had been enshrined in the Diocletianic Codes of the late third century, was overturned by Arcadius, father of Theodosius II, in 398; thereafter, rescripts issued in reply to *consultationes* should apply only to the lawsuits for which they were issued (*CTh* 1.2.11).[5] This constitution would have had the beneficial result of cutting back on the proliferation of material, genuine or otherwise, which could be cited in trials, but did not remove the basic problem of ignorance of the state of the law itself. It also set a precedent for the Theodosian Code, which, unlike its Diocletianic predecessor, avoided the inclusion of rescripts, resorting instead to the *edicta* and *epistulae*, which could be categorised as 'general laws'.

The Code project also grew out of the character of the young Theodosius' administration in the 420s. Although much is made of Theodosius' apparent lack of personal drive, and his tendency to be dominated by the female members of his family,[6] his reign witnessed a cultural renaissance in Constantinople for which he must take some of the credit. Not only was he the dedicatee of two great historians, the pagan Olympiodorus in 425 and the Christian Sozomen in the 440s,[7] but his court was a magnet for cultured men, including those learned in the law. The same cultural interest motivated Theodosius' reorganisation of teaching in Constantinople in 425, restricting the numbers of professors in named subjects who were allowed to practise officially and allowing improved facilities to recognised teachers (14.9.3 & 15.1.53). Similar priorities emerge in the Code. The first commission, set up in 429, was instructed to preserve constitutions which had fallen into disuse and been superseded by others 'valid for their own time only' ('pro sui tantum temporis negotiis valituri'), because of the interest of learned, antiquarian *diligentiores*. In his *novella* validating the Code in the East in 438, Theodosius returned to the theme, observing that, despite the incentives available to encourage the arts and scholarly pursuits, few people existed with a full knowledge of the *ius civile*, and ascribing this dearth to the excessive numbers of books, cases and imperial constitutions.[8] Such scholars' problems were now behind them, thanks to the

[5] 'Rescripta ad consultationem emissa vel emittenda, in futurum his tantum negotiis opitulentur, quibus effusa docebuntur.'

[6] E.g. by K. Holum, *Theodosian Empresses* (1982) *passim*. The sources' focus on Pulcheria and theological disputes can be somewhat corrected by concentrating on the male, secular office-holders who actually ran the Empire.

[7] Phot. *Bibl.* 80; Soz. *HE praef.* For the date of Sozomen's *History*, see C. Roueché, 'Theodosius II, the Cities and the Date of the "Church History" of Sozomen', *JTS* 27 (1896), 130-2.

[8] *NTh* 1 *praef.* 'Saepe nostra clementia dubitavit, quae causa faceret ut tantis propositis praemis, quibus artes et studia nutriuntur, tam pauci rarique extiterint, qui plene iuris civilis scientia ditarentur ...'

'light of brevity' shed on previous obscurities by the Theodosian Code.[9]
The emphasis on scholarship was not incompatible with Theodosius'
other stated aim, that the Code was to be valid for all law-suits and
legal transactions ('codicis in omnibus negotiis iudiciisque valituri',
CTh 1.1.6, of 20 December 435), as jurisconsults were expected to put
their learning at the service of advocates and *iudices* involved in the
conduct of trials, whose own knowledge might be insufficient.
Nevertheless jurisprudence was an acknowledged separate discipline:
two official law-teachers were set up in Theodosius' reorganisation of
teaching in the capital and both Code commissions, in 429 and 435,
contained a legal expert, the *scholasticus* Apelles in the first and, in the
second, Erotius, a *iuris doctor*.

The interest of the Theodosian government in law went far beyond
its academic aspect. In November 426, an *oratio* was sent to the Roman
senate, emanating, nominally, from the four-year-old Valentinian III;
in fact, it is more likely to be of eastern inspiration. Valentinian had
been restored to the throne of the West in the previous year by his
cousin, Theodosius II, many of whose following would still have been
present at Ravenna at the time. No doubt the men from the East noted
the contrast between the disarray and disorder in the West and the
new imperial system emerging in Constantinople. Their urge to impose
order, already shown in the new rules for teaching in Constantinople,
found expression in the *oratio* of November 426. Although preserved
only in the extracts included in the Theodosian and Justinianic Codes,
it was of considerable length. As far as we know, it covered two
apparently unrelated topics: the administration of justice and the
definition and categories of imperial law;[10] and the law of succession.
Not only is the former topic a mini-code in itself and of direct relevance
to the Theodosian Code three years later, but the procedure of
addressing it to the senate is also paralleled in the setting up of the
commissions for both the Theodosian and the first Justinianic Codes,
as well as in the formal publication of the former in the West in
December 438.

In its sections on the administration of the law, the *oratio* discussed
the citation of jurists in court, the so-called 'Law of Citations', which
gave pre-eminent authority to Papinian, Paulus, Gaius, Ulpian and
Modestinus and included various provisions about the authentication
of other jurists cited by the five[11] and guidance to *iudices* about how to

---

[9] Ibid. 1, 'verum egimus negotium temporis nostri et discussis tenebris conpendio
brevitatis lumen legibus dedimus'.

[10] On administration of law: *CTh* 1.4.3, the 'Law of Citations'; *CJust* 1.14.2 and 3
(rescripts and *leges generales*); 1.19.7 (rescripts); 1.22.5 (fraudulent rescripts).

[11] The validation of Paulus' *Sententiae* at *CTh* 1.4.3.5 confirms the judgment of
Constantine at 1.4.2 (27 Sept. 327/8) that the *Sententiae* were 'libros plenissima luce et
perfectissima elocutione et iustissima iuris ratione succinctos', a pithy demonstration of
the close connection of law with *eloquentia*.

proceed, if the jurists did not agree with each other. The purpose of the law was administrative, to ensure that *iudices* knew which authorities could be cited in their courts and which could not. Such guidance was very necessary, given that *iudices* had no authority to interpret, still less to make, laws for themselves. The law should have ensured that a *iudex*, provided he acted within the rules, could not be taken to task by litigants, or a superior. Of course, the ruling that a decision should be reached by majority vote of the Big Five, rather than by considering who was right, is hardly a model of legal principle, but the aim of the law was not to establish principle but simplify the operation of the courts and, it may be inferred, reduce the volume of appeals.

The *oratio* also offered clarification on how *leges generales* issued by the emperor were to be observed and identified (*CJust* 1.14.3). What concerned the drafters of the *oratio* was the form and appearance of the constitution in question, not its content. A *lex generalis* was either (1) sent to the senate as an *oratio* or (2) qualified by the inclusion of the word *edictum*. These two principal forms of general law were not affected by the occasion to which the *lex* was a response, be it imperial initiative, petition, referral or legal dispute. Both *oratio* and *edictum* would have originated at the highest level, in the imperial consistory, where the form of the law, as well as its content, would have been decided by the emperor and his counsellors.[12] All this was also consistent with the criteria used by the Theodosian Code compilers in their selection of appropriate constitutions, as both addresses to the senate and *edicta* (or 'leges edictales') to a general audience, the People, or the Provincials, are contained therein.

Thus far, however, the authors of the *oratio* had not covered one of the most extensively used forms of legal source to be present in the Code, imperial *epistulae* addressed to various recipients informing them of the new regulation.[13] This is covered in what follows. Having repeated himself on the *edictum* label, the author of the *oratio* added further qualifications, namely that a *lex* was *generalis* also if it was published throughout the Empire, or if it was explicitly stated that decisions made in one case should apply in the resolution of all similar cases. This allows for *epistulae*, the means by which laws were communicated to the officials charged with the responsibility of their publication. There was still one snag. Not all the definitions offered would apply to every *lex generalis* issued. Thus it was possible to issue a *lex generalis*, which did satisfy some of the criteria but which had limited territorial application. Such a law was not published 'per

---

[12] Procedure discussed by Tony Honoré, 'The Making of the Theodosian Code', *ZSS RA* (1986), 136-7 and by Jill Harries, 'The Roman Imperial Quaestor from Constantine to Theodosius II', *JRS* 78 (1988), 165-6.

[13] On *epistulae* and their composition by the *magister memoriae* and in the *scrinia*, see Harries, art. cit. in n. 12, 150 and 159-64.

omnes populos', throughout the Empire, but designated as valid only in particular provinces or areas, as in, for example, the obvious cases of Rome and Constantinople, where special conditions applied. Laws therefore could be 'general' without being universal.[14]

Leges generales could also be clearly differentiated from *rescripta*. The *oratio* of November 426 (*CJust* 1.14.2) stated that *rescripta* were prompted by the *relationes* or the *suggestiones*, referrals or reports, of *iudices* (as general laws might also be) but that they were to apply only to the bodies to which they were addressed.[15] This was in accordance with Arcadius' ruling in 398, and followed him in seeking to tighten up the categorisation of laws and thus to sharpen the definition of *leges generales*, by indicating what *rescripta* were – and were not. Rescripts were not *orationes* or *edicta* and, crucially, could not be sent to provincial governors in the form of *epistulae* to be brought to the attention of all whom he governed by widespread publication. It also followed that rescripts, provided they were recognised as such, would not be included in the Theodosian Code.

The Code, then, was a natural product of its environment and of a government consistently preoccupied with seeking to systematise and to simplify the process of government, with admittedly only partial success, streamlining the teaching of the arts at Constantinople, the citation of jurists in courts and the categorisation of imperial constitutions. The compilers, part of whose task was to arrange constitutions under headings in chronological order, were concerned about the evolution of law from Constantine onwards on specific issues, but they were not worried about the possibility that they might themselves impose anachronistic concepts on their material, some of which went back more than a century. The very idea of 'general law' although it existed in practice, had not achieved the refinement of definition accorded to it in 426 for much of the fourth century; despite the theory that rescripts were specific and other forms of imperial constitution were general, the distinction was blurred in practice, until reinstated by Arcadius.

The people who were involved with the construction of the Code itself are discussed by Tony Honoré elsewhere in this volume and the

[14] See remarks of B. Sirks, 'From the Theodosian to the Justinian Code', *Atti dell'Accademia Romanistica Costantiniana* (1986), 273-5. He notes also double enactments with separate territorial application, e.g. *CTh* 6.23.2 (Ravenna, 9 March 423) applying to the West, and 6.23.4 (Constantinople, March 17, 437), confirming the law in the East; in *CTh* 10.19.7, Valentinian I confirms for Illyricum and Macedonia a law passed by Valens and applicable to the East; cf. also *CTh* 13.5.23 (East, 393) and 24 (West, 395), but note the complication caused by the usurpation of Eugenius in the West from 392 to autumn 394 and the possibility that *CTh* 13.5.24 is part of an edict to the provincials of Africa containing assurances that the policy of the new western emperor, Honorius, was a continuation of that of Theodosius.

[15] 'nec generalia iura sint, sed leges fiant dumtaxat negotiis quibus fuerint promulgata.'

difficult problems of the making, purpose and sources of the Code are considered in full, from different standpoints, by John Matthews and Boudewijn Sirks. What follows considers the texts as the products of a distinctive and complex administrative system, which requires some analysis in order to appreciate some of the true significance of the Code as an historical source.

The purpose of constitutions was two-fold, to regulate and to communicate. Students of legal history are naturally more concerned about the former, and the nature of the content of the regulations contained in the Code. However, the aim to communicate not only the will but also the character of the emperor to his subjects was an essential part of the methods by which an area extending from Hadrian's Wall to the Euphrates was kept together by concentrating attention and (it was hoped) loyalty on the central power, as personified by the emperor. The language of the constitutions was therefore expected to be, at the very least, correct and to conform to the literary criteria employed by the rhetors of Late Antiquity; thus the language of law was influenced by considerations which were not strictly legal but which derived from the nature of imperial rule.[16]

It is uncertain who composed the wording of what were technically always the emperor's pronouncements in the early part of the fourth century. However, the role of the imperial quaestor,[17] a distant descendant of the senatorial *quaestor candidatus*, who acted as the emperor's spokesman in the Senate, evolved in the reign of Constantius II (337-361) and Valentinian I (364-375) into that of the emperor's legal adviser who drafted or 'dictated' his laws, a function which was entirely his own by the time of the *Notitia Dignitatum* in the early fifth century. Analysis of known holders of the post in the fourth century suggests a considerable disparity of legal expertise as the two facets of the quaestor's persona, as imperial spokesman or legal expert, struggled for prominence: the former is well represented by Ausonius (quaestor 375-6/7), the eloquent poet from Bordeaux, whose legal knowledge seems to have been minimal,[18] the latter by Valentinian I's quaestor, Eupraxius (367-70), who had the courage to correct the irate emperor on the law of treason (Amm. Marc. 28.1.25). By the fifth century, there are signs of some divergence in this, as in so much else, between East and West. In the West, the emphasis on eloquence as the prime qualification for the emperor's spokesman was retained, to culminate in the early sixth century with Cassiodorus'

[16] Discussed by W.E. Voss, *Recht und Rhetorik in den Kaisergesetzen der Spätantike. Eine Untersuchung zum nachklassichen Kauf- und Übereignungsrecht (Forsch. zur Byzantinischen Rechtsgeschichte* 9, 1982).

[17] Harries, art. cit. in n. 12 *passim*.

[18] Ausonius is taken apart by Tony Honoré, 'Ausonius and Vulgar Law', *Iura* 35 (1984, publ. 1987), 75-85.

highly literate rendering of the wishes of the Ostrogothic king in Italy. In the better-documented East, the picture, as Tony Honoré's study below reveals, is more varied, but the primacy of the legal role of the quaestor was well-established and a group of them, drawn from the increasingly professional bureaucracy of the Eastern court, were instrumental in the creation of the Code.

The effect of the quaestor on the content of law was probably limited by the convention that officials made proposals about their own sphere of administration and did not trespass on those of others. This meant that court officials would put up proposals on matters to do with the running of the court bureaucracy, but the main source of *suggestiones* on the running of the Empire in general would be the praetorian prefects, the authorities to which all provincial governors and *vicarii* ultimately looked. This is what one would expect from the hierarchical principles on which operated the system of filtering upwards proposals that originated lower down. This consideration tends to diminish the role of the quaestor, whose legal expertise would qualify him as the maker as well as the drafter of laws. The quaestor had no *officium* or office-staff belonging to him,[19] nor was he associated with provincial government (although many quaestors went on to hold praetorian prefectures). Apart from the *laterculum minus*, the lesser register of offices (*CTh* 1.8.1-3), the quaestor had nothing to originate laws about, before he acquired appellate jurisdiction under Theodosius II in 440. This isolation also ensured neutrality: the quaestor had no departmental axe to grind.

Communication between the government and the governed was a two-way process, of which the contents of the Code reflect only the latter part, the pronouncements of the emperor to his subjects. But although emperors allowed for the operation of their own initiative ('spontaneous motus' *CJust* 1.14.3) in formulating constitutions, laws were not in fact made by emperor and consistory in splendid isolation from the world outside. The relationship between emperor at the centre and provincial officials was symbiotic. A *suggestio*, proposal, from the official backed by a report was the most common means of supplying information from below and prompting an imperial decision. 'When ambiguity emerges about a new law', states a constitution of 474 (*CJust* 1.14.11), 'which is not established by long usage, there is need both for a *suggestio* and for the the authority of the emperor's decision.'[20]

The arrival of a *suggestio* at court signalled the first stage in the production of a constitution. The document would be discussed by the

---

[19] *Not. Dig. Or*. 12 'officium non habet sed adiutores de scriniis qua voluerit' and *Oc*. 10 'habet subaudientes adiutores memoriales de scriniis diversis'.

[20] 'Cum de novo iure, quod inveterato usu non adhuc stabilem est, dubitatio emergat, necessaria est tam suggestio iudicantis quam sententiae principalis auctoritas.'

top palatine ministers and members of the consistory and, after 446, by the senate, and a constitution would then be drafted, usually by the quaestor. In the course of discussion and drafting, the nature of a proposal could have changed considerably. Many proposals must have been non-controversial and the sheer volume of work would ensure them an easy passage. In other cases, unless members of the consistory had a particular interest at stake (as was not infrequently the case), proposals from high provincial officials had the advantage of coming from men in a position to know what they were talking about. When Monaxius, the Constantinople City Prefect in 408 drafted regulations for oil distribution, they were simply confirmed by the emperor (14.17.15). Later in 427 the prefect of Illyricum, Antiochus, made a more far-reaching proposal that deputies standing in for governors of provinces should have the right to appoint guardians, and to exercise all other judicial powers held by full governors. Theodosius II and Valentinian III agreed to all this 'in accordance with the schedule of your Eminence', and the official instructions (*mandata*) were sent to Antiochus by special messenger (*CJust* 1.50.2). Antiochus had formerly been quaestor and was two years later to be on the Theodosian Code's first commission. His combination of drafting and provincial experience and interest in legal matters reflected in the constitution made him an ideal proposer of new regulations. It has to be admitted that both Antiochus and Monaxius served emperors whose delegation of power to the ministers was extensive, perhaps exceptionally so. However their employment is still a valid illustration of the respect paid to men who in areas without political connotations might be expected to know their business best.

Lesser provincial governors were not expected to contact the emperor directly but to send their proposals to the *vicarii*, who in turn would forward them to receive the approval of the praetorian prefect, whose sanction probably gave proposals of lesser people a better chance in the consistory (*CTh* 1.15.3). This filtering of proposals through the administrative hierarchy may not always have been observed. Particularly for the fourth century, there are indications that emperors were responding to proposals from *consulares* and others directly, although that of course says nothing about the route taken by the *suggestio* to the emperor's attention in the first place. Constantius II, to take one instance, sent a letter in 349 to Antonius, the *dux*, military governor, of Mesopotamia on preventing unqualified civil servants from entering the armed forces illegally; the *suggestio*, perhaps here no more than a report, had come from the *vicarius* (*CTh* 8.44). But emperors were concerned to spread their nets wide in the constant battle for reliable information and therefore tried to ensure access to the accepted channels of communication from the provinces for all who might have proposals to put.

Proposals were also put from within the palace by heads of department reorganising their staffs or seeking benefits for them and the same procedure seems to have been used. Palatine ministers were of course well placed to ensure imperial decisions in their favour – unless they were in conflict with someone else within the inner circle. Such proposals included one by the *comes sacrarum largitionum* Trifolius in 385 to Theodosius I about retirements of officials (6.30.8); a proposal about abolishing the unrestricted right of palatine officials to choose the place of trial in a lawsuit (although there were difficulties with this) in 439 (*NTh* 7.1 but see *NTh* 7.2 and 4); and a grant in 441 of privileges to the *scholae* requested by the *magister officiorum* (*NTh* 21). This last official, with his overall responsibility for the palatine civil and military services was no doubt an especially prolific source of *suggestiones*, but his subordinates could also be active. Justin and Justinian in the sixth century in a constitution to Tatian, the *magister officiorum*, agreed that clerks (*adiutores*) should be allowed to find replacements if prevented from working, but the proposal had come from Proculus, the *magister memoriae*, at the instigation of the clerks themselves (*CJust* 12.19.5.2).

A *suggestio* could also be merely a report of facts to which the emperor would react without being a proposal. Emperors would request reports, particularly in military contexts, so that the situation could be understood at court and action taken or authority given. Masters of the soldiers were on occasion asked about numbers and location of troops and supplies; such reports were especially needed by emperors absent from the armies themselves. When Honorius and Theodosius (in fact the ministers of the latter, then aged 12) wrote to the master of the soldiers in Thrace, it was in part a response to a report submitted earlier about the numbers of river craft on the Danube to be ordered. The constitution (*CTh* 7.17.1) authorised provision of these but also required a follow-up report on their requisitioning, so that if the *dux* failed in his job, he and his staff could be fined. The active supervision of military matters from the centre, albeit at long-distance, is paralleled by other requests for information sent out from Constantinople later in the century. Writing to the master of the soldiers in Illyricum, Anastasius forbade the transfer of troops from one base to another without imperial authorisation and ordered both the master and the praetorian prefect to make a report direct to the emperor (*CJust* 1.29.4). In case they were in any doubt about what to say, Anastasius told them. They were to list the places from which and the places to which the soldiers were being transferred; the names of the units; their supplies; and, most important, why they were being moved. Short of writing the report himself, Anastasius could hardly have done more. Some twenty years earlier a similar problem had arisen, this time over recruiting, and

Zeno required a report on 'who, how many, in what unit and on what frontier' these recruits were to be levied (*CJust* 12.35.17). These constitutions are both in fact requests for information: the binding regulation, not found in the Justinianic Code, would have been Zeno's and Anastasius' response to the reports, when they gave written approval to their contents.

Outbreaks of public disorder would have inspired a report from the prefect or other official in charge of law and order, as a matter of routine. A set of constitutions in the Code set a general rule in response to a known specific incident, a violent and prolonged period of sporadic unrest and rioting in Constantinople in the early 400s caused by the bishop John Chrysostom and the attempts by his enemies to get him exiled. This culminated in the burning down of John's church and the senate-house. The supporters and opponents of John blamed each other and the prefect of Constantinople, Studius, having arrested several of the clergy, held a public enquiry.[21] Despite this, he failed to identify the culprits and reported this to Arcadius. In reply, Arcadius ordered the clergy to be released but deported to their homes, a measure designed to remove them from the temptation to cause further disorders (16.2.37). Also, householders in the city would be penalised if they offered them shelter. Further regulations designed to keep the peace were introduced with a prohibition on slaves and members of guilds, the latter a traditionally fertile source of unruly mobs, from taking part in riots (16.4.4-6). All this was to be publicised in edicts to the people of the city. In this affair, Studius' report, which conveyed nothing useful, had little importance; Arcadius' response was a fairly standard set of precautions designed to prevent a recurrence of similar troubles.

Proposals could also come from anyone outside the administration who could gain the emperor's ear. Members of recognised interest groups could put their case directly. In 380 the *navicularii* (shipowners) felt that a clarification of their exemption from another public service was required, perhaps because an official or officials unknown were trying to press-gang them into serving, contrary to the principle that Romans were not expected to serve the empire in more than one (often onerous) capacity. To prove their exemption from curial burdens, the *navicularii* collected many ancient constitutions of emperors, no easy task in the fourth century when there was no Code, and submitted a well-researched petition, which the emperor granted, no doubt overwhelmed by the impressive documentation (13.5.16.1).

Many imperial constitutions are addressed to cities, whose embassies had always been admitted and allowed to speak. Sometimes

---

[21] Soc. *HE* 66.18, Soz. *HE* 8.23-4, J.H.W.G. Liebeschuetz, *Bishops and Barbarians: Army, Church and State in the Age of Arcadius and Chrysostom* (1990), 208-22.

this was without the sanction of the governor on the spot because it was to complain about his activities. In a notorious episode reported by Ammianus, the citizens of Tripolitania sent envoys to Valentinian to complain about the corruption and inefficiency of the local *comes* Romanus; their representations, which Ammianus calls a *relatio*, were frustrated by the false advice tendered to Valentinian by the *magister officiorum*, who was hand-in-glove with the corrupt *comes*, and by subsequent bureaucratic inertia (Amm. Marc. 28.6.5-30). Other attempts to by-pass officialdom were more successful. In 409 Honorius was informed 'by public attestation' that bishops in Africa had been subjected to torture and public humiliation – and that the provincial governors had not made a report about it (*Const. Sirm.* 14). These assaults took place at the height of the Donatist controversy in the province and the public representations may have emanated from a provincial council more sympathetic to the victims for religious reasons than were the delinquent officials.

For one section of the community, bishops, the innovation made by the conversion of Constantine, that bishops could approach the emperor without fear, was of enduring benefit (see Chapter 6 below). While much of the internal discipline of the church was regulated by the canons of church councils, bishops sometimes found it convenient to request the backing of the secular arm to enforce an ecclesiastical rule. In 420 a proposal which forbade clerics from cohabiting with women other than their mothers, sisters or wives married before ordination was agreed to by the emperors (*Const. Sirm.* 10.1); the same episcopal representation also requested imperial enforcement of laws against rapists of nuns. The ideas came from the priesthood but the implementation of the constitution was the responsibility of the praetorian prefect to whom the law was addressed. Assistance with policing the church was an imperial priority because of the wider duty of emperors to keep the peace in the cities of the empire. When it was reported in 405 by a deputation of bishops that some former bishops exiled by church councils had not left their cities but continued to cause trouble, it was predictable that the emperor would order the decrees of exile to be enforced (*Const. Sirm.* 2). Sometimes the prefect acted as the spokesman for the church; in 411/412 the prefect Melitius was reassured that church lands were exempt from certain forms of tax and curial burdens and that 'the privileges which ancient times granted to the churches' were guaranteed (*Const. Sirm.* 11). A constant flow of petitions could also have a cumulative effect, as when in 419 the protection of sanctuary was extended to within fifty paces of church doors and priests were assured of access to prisons to investigate cases of unlawful confinement (*Const. Sirm.* 13).

Also illustrative of the complexity of communication between subject and emperor is his relationship with the most historically important interest group, the senate in Rome. Representations from the senate on matters to do with itself were made through special delegations or the prefect of the city. Their missions were not always on points of law or even policy.[22] They were the established means of maintaining contact of the flow of information between a body based at Rome and an emperor who was almost invariably elsewhere. They carried at regular intervals messages such as congratulations on anniversaries, or gifts, all of which were designed to preserve both contact and harmony. In return the emperor also sent gifts, as at the New Year, gave entertainments to the Roman people, and entrusted the reading of his addresses to the senate to a distinguished senator of his choice: Symmachus was the lucky man to be thus honoured in 379 (Symm. *Ep.* 1.95; 3.18). Both senate and emperor used this well-tried route of contact through embassies and formal speeches for more serious matters. In 370, many senators found themselves being tried and executed on a number of charges as a result of a witch-hunt organised by the *vicarius* appointed by Valentinian, Maximinus. In the course of the judicial investigations, senators were being tortured, with the authorisation, so it was believed, of the emperor himself. An embassy of three senators, the former prefect of the city Vettius Agorius Praetextatus, Venustus a former *vicarius* and Minervius, representing the lowest of the three official ranks, was sent to protest against this policy, as senators were supposedly exempt from torture. The deputation was heard in the consistory and, thanks to the level-headed conduct of the quaestor Eupraxius, was successful (Amm. Marc. 28.1.24-5). Here, although the contact was initiated by the senate, it was in response to a vagary of imperial policy.

Symmachus' *Relationes* as prefect of the city of Rome in 384 provide the most comprehensive picture of the variety of contacts between senate and emperor. Some of these documents are referrals of cases for various legal and non-legal reasons, while others convey news, such as the death of Praetextatus (*Rel.* 10-12), or complaints about the bad behaviour of officials in Rome (*Rel.* 21) and Symmachus' political enemies at court, to whose intrigues he ascribes such diverse matters as false accusations that he was persecuting Christians in Rome and attempts by financial officials to reclaim a debt to the wine treasury allegedly due from Symmachus' by now defunct father-in-law (*Rel.* 34). Symmachus knew perfectly well that his were not the only messengers travelling the road to Milan, that the emperor was hearing about events in Rome from many sources – and that court ministers had their own aims to pursue. But, intrigue apart, senate and emperor could between them generate proposals which became law without it

[22] Note, for example, Symmachus' presence at the court of Valentinian I at Trier in 369-70, Symm. *Or.* 1, 3 and 2 (in order of delivery); *Epp.* 1.14 and 32.

being clear which side had come up with the original idea. In 384 Symmachus formally thanked the emperor for two proposed reforms (*Rel.* 8), first to limit senatorial expenditure, thus helping poorer senators who had either failed to match the extravagant ostentation of their richer colleagues or had beggared themselves trying to do so. Second, priority in making speeches in the senate was taken from those who had gained it because of wealth and generosity and restored to those who had reached the highest offices. These two proposals were made in an imperial *oratio*, which was then approved by a senatorial resolution. The emperor in his turn was then required to give his authority to the senatorial decision by the making of an imperial law.[23] In the case of the senate, whose own procedures had all the weight of a tradition going back to the Early Republic, the process of consultation and resolution was so complex that it would be difficult even for people on the spot to ascertain where the initiative lay. Symmachus' *relatio* on the expenditure proposal implies that the idea came from the emperor, but motives of tact would anyway have led him to suppress mention of an earlier senatorial approach.

The *suggestio* procedure guaranteed a constant inflow of information, ideas and proposals to be considered by the emperor and his advisers at the centre of the web. Despite the ever-growing power of the court bureaucracy and the failures of emperors after Theodosius I to travel very far or be seen by their subjects, the emperors continued to hear something of their subjects' complaints, even though direct access must have been ever more strictly limited. The initiative still came (as a rule) from outside the court but decisions on proposals were taken within a context of existing policies and practices. Dominant individuals could influence policy in the areas within their competence, which is why considerable importance must be attached to the praetorian prefects as the most prolific source of proposals affecting the provinces of the Empire. But conflicts of interest and personality inside the court and beyond meant that the process of policy-making was far more complex that any simple description of the procedural system would suggest. Emperors and their ministers set the 'tone' of an administration, but would be themselves guided by the assumptions they had inherited or helped to create.

The Theodosian Code has a distinctive place in a system of imperial rule which had evolved over four centuries and its contents must be understood within that context. Law-giving as a means of communication and control inherited from emperors of the first and second centuries AD continued to build on its heritage under the Later Empire. The process the men of Late Antiquity knew as *suggestio* was

[23] *Rel.* 8.3. 'Superest ut ea ... lex augusta confirmet.'

more formalised than before but the need of subjects and officials to communicate their concerns to the centre (which was wherever the emperor happened to be) was as imperative as in the time of Augustus. The Code, therefore, as a compendium of imperial responses to stimuli which were largely external, did not necessarily reflect the preferences of emperors, but the areas of late Roman life on which representations would most vigorously and repeatedly be made. Although some constitutions were oppressive, even violent, in tone and content, they were often evoked by some influential group, in whose interests it was that such regulations should be enforced; the extensive legislation on *curiales*, for example (*CTh* 12.1), was drafted to assist men trapped on city councils, in whose interest it was that loopholes offering escape into more prestigious careers could be blocked. Nor does the fact that laws were often repeated indicate that the laws were ineffective (although this could be the case, where all concerned agreed to ignore the imperial will); rather, reiterated requests for clarification indicate the eagerness of subjects and *iudices* to be accurately informed in cases of doubt. Thus a new emperor might be asked to confirm his agreement with the legislation of his predecessor, or a law issued in one part of the Empire would require confirmation and reissue in the other. Such a system inevitably favoured those who could muster support for their petitions; it bore heavily on the poorest sections of society and could be frustrated by corruption among the bureaucracy, as evidenced in the issue of rescripts 'against the law'. But the basic structure was, to a great extent, adapted to the expression of the priorities of governors and subjects rather than those of the emperor.

Yet, despite all these external pressures, the character of his administration and of its achievements was the ultimate responsibility of the emperor alone. Ammianus' summaries of fourth-century emperors at the end of his accounts of each reign from Constantius II to Valens assume that the character of a reign was the character of the emperor, not of his advisers, and Ammianus, as a *protector domesticus*, one of the elite corps of soldiers attached to the emperor or his chief servants, was in a position to know. The personality of the emperor interacted with his officials who made proposals; they would have taken account of imperial preferences and avoided making proposals that had no chance of success. Theodosius was married to a poetess and a patron of scholars, to whom he offered, as he said himself, 'great rewards'; his capital was a magnet for men of talent, many of whom worked on the Code; his troops had set in place in 425 in the West, the junior Augustus, Valentinian III; his reign as Augustus of nearly half a century was, despite the threats of the Huns on the Danube, and the over-mighty soldier, Aspar, and eunuch Chrysaphius at court in the 440s, an era of intense cultural activity and, on the whole, of social stability. The Theodosian Code accurately mirrored the emperor's achievement, as a work of scholarship designed for practical use and a monument to the juristic expertise and political supremacy of the eastern court.

Part I

Compilation

Introductory Note

Jill Harries

This first part addresses questions that are fundamental to the Code as a text. The three constitutions of March 429, December 435 and February 438, which initiated, continued and confirmed the Code, are tantalisingly vague about the criteria of selection and the methods of compilation employed. What was the relationship of the procedures envisaged in 429 and 435 to each other and to the finished product celebrated in the confirmatory constitution of 438? What did the compilers do between the spring of 429 and the winter of 435? Did they travel the whole Roman Empire researching in the archives of Rome, Ravenna and the provinces, as posited by Seeck, followed by Matthews (Chapter 1), as well as acquiring material from the central archives of Constantinople itself? Or were their operations based almost exclusively in the eastern capital, as Sirks believes (Chapter 2)? And what of the shadowy figures behind the Code project, the quaestors, who were instrumental in its production, and whose predecessors had drafted the originals of much of its contents?

The three essays that follow show an historian and two lawyers approaching these issues from divergent standpoints and employing different methodologies. The first two, by Matthews and Sirks, set out the arguments on the question of central versus provincial archives; both have been influenced by extensive pre-publication discussion between the two authors. Readers may judge the merits of their arguments for themselves, but the fact that the controversy remains unresolved is a comment on the complexity of the problems and the necessity for continued research. In Chapter 3, Tony Honoré employs the tools of stylistic analysis already familiar to readers of his *Tribonian* and his earlier work on the Theodosian Code, to bring to life the quaestors of Theodosius II. While his method is innovative and, for some, controversial, his conclusions are important for the administrative background not only of the Code but of the eastern court in general.

The chapters in this part seek to promote and stimulate debate. They are not the last word on the compilation of the Code but together they show the importance of continuing inter-disciplinary dialogue and co-operation which may result in further advances in the future.

1. The Making of the Text

John Matthews

The Theodosian Code was promulgated in the West at a meeting of the Roman senate held on 25 December 438. The record of the proceedings, as published by Fl. Laurentius, *exceptor amplissimi senatus*, whose subscription appears at the end of the document, is preserved in a single manuscript of the eleventh century from the Ambrosian Library at Milan.[1] Also preserved in this sole manuscript is a law of 23 December 443, from which it appears that the proceedings, described as 'senatus amplissimi gesta', were submitted to Valentinian III by the praetorian prefect Faustus, in support of his request for confirmation that exclusive rights in and responsibility for the preparation of copies of the Code be vested in the *constitutionarii* Flavius Anastasius and Hilarius Martinus, to whom the emperor's reply, the law of 443, was addressed. On pain of a fine (the crime was that of sacrilege) no persons other than the *constitutionarii* should involve themselves in the publication or manufacture of copies for sale: 'nec habeant [*sc.* unauthorised persons] vel de editione vel de confectione commercium.'

The situation revealed by the law is one of some interest, evidence of the popularity and usefulness of the Code; it would appear that demand already outstripped the rate of production, and even competent judicial authorities were forced to seek pirate copies. This may be inferred from the text of the law itself: 'sacrilegii poena constringi *tam cognitionale officium quam eos*, qui nostris minime paruerunt constitutis' – where the italicised words refer to officials and their departments. The *Gesta Senatus* were meticulous and emphatic on the question of maintaining the authenticity of the text of the Code and the authority of the *constitutionarii*; it was no doubt the latter who ensured the preservation of this confirmation of their rights, by appending the *Gesta* and the imperial law to copies of the Code

---

[1] Cf. Mommsen's ed., Prolegomena, pp. LXXXIII-IV; the MS is that known as *A* (Ambrosianus C.29 inf.). The epitaph of Laurentius, describing him as 'scriba senatus', survives as *CIL* 6.33721. He was buried on 12 March 451 (the epitaph was later used as building material in the church of St Maria Trastevere); *PLRE* II, p. 659 (Laurentius 11). The meeting of the senate was held in the private house 'quae est ad Palmam' of the praetorian prefect; on the significance of this, see below, n. 63.

subsequently produced by them, one of which descended to the manuscript in the Ambrosian Library. To the *constitutionarii*, therefore, and to the praetorian prefect Faustus, we owe the survival of a unique and fascinating document, priceless evidence for the conduct of an actual meeting of the late Roman senate. Among the many opportunities which the *Gesta* provide, I shall concentrate in this chapter on their evidence on the definition and initial procedures envisaged by the editors of the Theodosian Code. I shall then look at some anomalies and idiosyncrasies in the published text of the Code, which may throw light on the manner in which the editors set about their task.

*

The *Gesta Senatus* begin by naming the consuls, the Emperor Theodosius (for the sixteenth time) and Anicius Acilius Glabrio Faustus. The full name of Faustus, 'tertio expraefecto urbi, praefectus praetorio et consul ordinarius', also heads those of the three high officials present at the meeting: the others, mentioned in order of seniority, are Fl. Paulus, *v.c. et inl(ustris) urbis praefectus*, and Iunius Pomponius Publianus, *vir spectabilis vicarius urbis aeternae*. Then follow the 'proceres amplissimique ordo senatus'. The senators, having assembled, had some discussion, the nature of which is not recorded, and then there joined the meeting by invitation ('ingressique ex praecepto') the *constitutionarii* Anastasius and Martinus; these are the Fl. Anastasius and Hilarius Martinus to whom, still at their work five years later, Valentinian's law of 23 December 443 was addressed. The *constitutionarii* were not senators, and it was necessary by ancient convention that they should be formally invited to attend the deliberations.

Anicius Acilius Glabrio Faustus then addressed the meeting. He began by reminding his audience of the circumstances. He recalled his attendance the year before at the wedding of the young Valentinian III to Theodosius' daughter Licinia Eudoxia. He does not name them, nor the place and date of the wedding, which was in fact at Constantinople on 29 October 437.[2] Faustus was one of the *legati* sent by the Roman senate to attend the occasion: a colleague on the embassy was Rufius Antonius Agrypnius Volusianus, *praefectus urbi* in 417-18 and *praefectus praetorio* in 428-9.[3] In earlier years Volusianus was a famous correspondent of Augustine, and he is mentioned as a newly-appointed urban prefect in the poem of Rutilius Namatianus, *De Reditu Suo*; his illness and late baptism, and his death on the day of

[2] Mommsen, *Chron. Min.* II, p. 79.
[3] Chastagnol, *Fastes*, No. 125 (pp. 276-9).

Epiphany (6 January) 438 while on an embassy to Constantinople, are described by the biographer of his niece, the younger Melania, who had travelled from the Holy Land to visit him. It was surely the same embassy as that now described by Faustus; an absence of a year or more on such a mission, with all its ceremonial as well as practical implications, would not be unusual, and the participation of a senator of Volusianus' distinction and seniority would well suit the importance of the occasion.[4]

After the completion of the wedding ceremonies (continued Faustus), Theodosius had announced his intention to present to the world a compendium of imperial law, to be called after himself: and this project Valentinian, 'loyal as a colleague, loving as a son', had approved: 'quam rem aeternus princeps dominus noster Valentinianus devotione socii, affectu filii conprobavit' (*Gesta Senatus*, 2). Needless to say, the project was already completed; when it was begun, in 429, Valentinian had been just ten years old.

At this point Faustus paused, while his words were greeted with acclamations of approval of their eloquence: 'nove diserte, vere diserte.' When these were over (unlike the more elaborately orchestrated series of acclamations later in the meeting, there is no indication of the number of repetitions) he continued by describing how Theodosius had summoned to his presence Faustus himself and the *praefectus praetorio* of the East at that time, and had personally given to each of them – or, more accurately, had 'ordered to be conveyed to them from his divine hand' – a copy of the new *codex*: we may indulge ourselves for a moment by imagining the scene, as an imperial functionary advances, takes the splendidly bound copies of the Code from the emperor and solemnly presents one to each of the prefects in turn. It may be that it was on this very occasion that Faustus received promotion to the praetorian prefecture of Italy, Illyricum and Africa, indeed that this was his first official act in that capacity. An inscription from Aricia in Latium, on which the promotion is mentioned, records it as an expression of the judgment of each part of the Empire: 'utriusque inperii iudicii(s) sublimitato.' We may well see this, from a western perspective, as a promotion to a western prefecture taking place at the eastern court.[5] So Faustus had received the Codex, given with the

---

[4] *Vita Melaniae* (Greek version), §§50-6; ed. D. Gorce, *SChr* 90 (1962), 224ff. The *Vita* mentions the wedding as the occasion for the embassy; it is not impossible that it concerned an earlier stage of the planning, but more likely that it was the same embassy as that undertaken and described by Faustus. For the date of Volusianus' death (438, not 437), I accept the arguments of Kenneth Holum, *Theodosian Empresses: Women and Imperial Dominion in Late Antiquity* (1982), p. 183 with n. 39.

[5] *ILS* 1283 = *CIL* 14.2165; Faustus had rescued the town of Aricia 'ab into[le]rabilibus necessitatibus'. Despite the comment in *CIL*, ad loc., the phrase cited in the text should refer to the appointment to the praetorian prefecture rather than to the unspecific 'tertio praefectus urbi' which precedes it. Cf. *PLRE* II, p. 453 (Faustus 8).

direction ('praeceptione') of each emperor, and he completed his initial statement by acknowledging the presence in the senate of the *constitutionarii* and proposing the reading out of the law (he actually says 'leges') by which the emperors had brought all this about.

Again follow acclamations of approval – 'aequum est, placet, placet' – and Faustus, presumably taking the copy from the *constitutionarii*, proceeded to read out the law of 26 March 429, addressed to the senate of Constantinople, by which the entire project was initiated.[6] The law is cited by Faustus 'ex codice Theodosiano, libro primo, sub titulo "de constitutionibus principum et edictis" '; it is 1.1.5 in the edition of Mommsen and Meyer and is the fundamental evidence for the manner in which the Theodosian Code was compiled, and for its purpose. What now follows is a close summary of what it said.

The Theodosian Code was to be a successor to and to complement the earlier (late third-century) codes of Gregorius and Hermogenianus, and would follow the same pattern of composition. It would include all imperial constitutions possessing the force of edicts or of general application issued by Constantine and his successors down to the present day: 'omnes constitutiones, quas Constantinus inclitus et post eum divi principes nosque tulimus edictorum viribus aut sacra generalitate subnixas.' The laws were to be arranged by titles (or subjects), with the proviso that extended texts containing material relevant to more than one subject were to be divided, and the separate parts classified under the titles to which they individually applied; and, whether intact or as the separate parts of divided laws, they were to be entered under their titles with their dates, and in the sequence in which they were originally issued. In this way the actual ordering of the material would make clear which constitutions on any particular subject were the later and therefore the more valid: 'ipsius etiam compositione operis validiora esse, quae sunt posteriora, monstrante.' Extraneous matter not relevant to the point of substance in a law was to be omitted – a stringent, and in a way disappointing requirement, given the vigorous rhetoric habitually used to enhance the force of late Roman legislation:[7] and the Code was to be complete, even to the

---

[6] For the presumed connection of the project with the 'establishment of the law school of Constantinople' in 425, see the references cited by Boudewijn Sirks in the next chapter, n. 69.

[7] W. Turpin (cf. n. 9) writes (p. 628) of the elimination of extraneous matter as intended 'to cut down on the talking which went on in the law courts', but it is better understood as referring to superfluous words in the *written* laws (so Turpin, at 628). Boudewijn Sirks, Chapter 2 §7 below writes of the matters 'ad vim sanctionis non pertinentia' as meaning that 'a rule, no longer in use, has no force any more. Therefore this prescription implies that obsolete rules have to be omitted.' I do not think that this was in the emperor's mind in issuing this instruction to the editors. What is to be omitted is superfluous wording, i.e. rhetoric, with no intrinsic legal force. This further affects the view one takes of the development of the project between 429 and 435, see below, n. 18 and pp. 24f., 30.

extent that earlier laws clearly superseded by later were nevertheless to be included.[8] It would be more convenient, the emperor admitted, if only currently relevant law were to be codified, but the Theodosian Code, like its predecessors, was to be as complete as it could be made. It was to be a work for specialist scholars and practitioners ('diligentiores'), whose professional interest ('scholastica intentio') would wish to know even of laws valid only for their own time and now obsolete. (It should be remembered that the term 'scholasticus' indicates in this period, not simply an academic, but an advocate or pleader at law).[9] A further volume was promised for the future, in which the Gregorian, Hermogenian and new Theodosian Codes, together with the opinions of jurists on the subjects in question ('per singulos titulos cohaerentibus prudentium tractatibus et responsis'), would contribute to a compilation of law free of error and ambiguity, setting out definitively for all 'what is to be followed and what avoided': 'sequenda omnibus vitandaque monstrabit.' Although this volume, combining 'leges' and 'ius' in a critical digest, would also be published by Theodosius, it was a project for the future. The law of 429 looked forward to it, and indeed envisaged that the same panel of experts would be responsible for it,[10] but did not set out to encompass it.

The constitution of 429 went on to nominate an editorial panel of nine persons with powers to co-opt experts ('eruditissimum quemque adhibituros confidimus'), and it concluded with a provision, in effect a limiting clause, on the relevance in either part of the Empire of laws issued in the other: such law was only to be valid if it was officially directed to, and accepted and published in, the part in which it was received.[11]

With these instructions, we may suppose that the editorial panel of nine, with their co-opted assistants, had enough guidance to set about their task. However, the emperors returned to the subject in a law issued at Constantinople on 20 December 435, which again, with some

[8] Cf. Turpin, 621f. The idea that old law may still be valid 'in affairs [i.e. outstanding cases] dating back to the time when the obsolete legislation had been issued' ('pro sui tantum temporis negotiis valitura') is only naturally relevant to the more recent superseded law, and cannot be a general interpretation of this provision. It is more natural to think of a legal historian's interest in older cases and their solutions in law than in current legal practice or issues.

[9] W. Turpin, 'The Purpose of the Roman Law Codes', *ZSS RA* 104 (1987), 620-30, at 621-2. Turpin argues convincingly that the Codes were not just scholastic enterprises, but were intended to clarify the law for practical use.

[10] *CTh* 1.1.5; 'eorundem opera, qui tertium [*sc.* the Theodosian Code] ordinabunt'. My point is, that this next stage constitutes a separate *editorial* process from that visualised in 429.

[11] See on this general issue of validity between East and West of individual laws, and of the Theodosian Code itself, A.J.B. Sirks, 'From the Theodosian to the Justinian Code', *Atti dell'Accademia Romanistica Costantiniana: VI Convegno Internazionale* (1986), 265-302.

repetition, defines editorial procedures (*CTh* 1.1.6). Again we find the instructions to collect all laws issued by Constantine and his successors up to the present day, to arrange by titles, dividing laws where necessary, and to omit material not relevant to the substantive point at issue. A new editorial panel is appointed, this time of sixteen persons, only three of whom are inherited from the previous panel.

It has sometimes been argued that the new arrangements represent a substantial amendment, or even a cancellation, of those of 429. Mommsen thought that the law of 435 indicated an abandonment of an earlier plan that had turned out unsuccessful, a view expressed also by Gaudemet, and by Jolowicz, who wrote of 'a new commission with different instructions' set up by the law of 435.[12] Wolfgang Kunkel supposed that 'the commission appointed by the emperor [*sc.* in 429] ... evidently produced nothing', and that a 'second commission called into being six years later' completed in two years a modified version of the initial project of Theodosius.[13] A closely similar view was expressed by A.H.M. Jones.[14] Archi, whose discussion of the relevant evidence is the most subtle and perceptive known to me, still writes of an 'old' and a 'new' programme, and of 'saving what could be saved of the project of 429'.[15]

I am convinced that these interpretations involve a misreading of the evidence.[16] The constitution of 26 March 429 stated clearly that the project of a critical digest that would contain only currently relevant law was one set aside for the future. It was indeed contingent upon the publication of the Theodosian to add to the Gregorian and Hermogenian Codes ('ex his autem tribus codicibus ... noster erit alius', etc.), but was not in editorial terms a part of the current project. Jolowicz's observation, again echoed by Jones, that 'the project of including juristic writings was abandoned [*sc.* by the law of 435]' is also misconceived. It was only later that it was envisaged that the writings of the jurists would be included, to produce a definitive, critical compilation of Roman law, both 'leges' and 'ius'. This too was part of

---

[12] Cf. Mommsen in his ed., Prolegomena, p. IX; J. Gaudemet, *Institutions de l'Antiquité* (2nd ed., 1982), 738; H.F. Jolowicz, *Historical Introduction to the Study of Roman Law* (1952), 483. See too L. Wenger, *Die Quellen des römischen Rechts* (1953), 536.

[13] W. Kunkel, *An Introduction to Roman Legal and Constitutional History*, tr. J.M. Kelly (2nd ed., 1973), 158, cf. F. Schulz, *History of Roman Legal Science* (1946, rev. ed. 1967), at 286 ('the plan failed') and 315 ('more ambitious plans having come to naught...').

[14] A.H.M. Jones, *The Later Roman Empire* (1964), I, 475; 'they apparently failed to complete even their first task' (viz. the collection of imperial constitutions, the second task being the collection of the opinions of jurists); cf. *PLRE* II, pp. 102-3 (Antiochus 6 & 7).

[15] G.G. Archi, *Teodosio II e la sua codificazione* (1976), 33, 37.

[16] See also, in agreement with the view expressed here, Tony Honoré, 'The Making of the Theodosian Code', *ZSS RA* 103 (1986), 133-222, at 166-7.

the next phase of the project. The constitution of 429 gives no guidance on that subject, nor was it ever meant to.

It is also clear that the process of compilation and editing set out in 429 would in the best of circumstances, and with the best will in the world, take a long time, as the editors and their co-opted assistants applied themselves to recovering imperial constitutions from what, at least on my view of their methods (see below), were widely scattered sources, in both eastern and western Empires, as well as from whatever central and provincial archives were available: and, when this stage was complete, to a detailed process of editing. We ought not to be surprised if such a project were not brought to completion in all its stages in the 6¾ years from March 429 to December 435. Conversely, it is beyond belief that, as the views of Mommsen and others just quoted would imply, the project should have been rescued from failure, revived and completed, even in a modified form, in less than two years between December 435 and its publication as a complete text in October 437. We may add that, by the mere fact of its being read out, the senatorial meeting of 25 December 438 was invited to look back to the law of 429 as initiating a process brought to completion without interruption. Indeed, unless, as is unlikely, something has gone wrong with the text of the *Gesta Senatus*, the law of 435 was not even read to the senate.[17]

It is more convincing to see the law of 435 as in part reiterating, in part refining the principles laid down in 429, *at a specific point in the editorial process*; that is to say, at the moment when the task of collecting the laws was complete and that of organising and editing the material could begin. This conclusion is supported by certain differences between the laws of 429 and 435, which I would suggest are better seen as refinements of an existing method than as definitions of a new one:[18]

(i) The constitution of 429 had defined the laws to be collected as those 'with edictal force or [i.e. in other ways] of general application': 'constitutiones ... *edictorum viribus aut sacra generalitate* subnixas.' The constitution of 435 repeats this provision in the phrase 'omnes

[17] Cf. Honoré, 166; Sirks, Chapter 2 §7 below and op. cit. (n. 11 above), at 277 on the (non)-reading of *CTh* 1.1.6.

[18] Cf. also Honoré, 165f.; Sirks, Chapter 2 §7 below: 'It seems as if the design of 435 concerning the editing of the constitutions is more detailed than that of 429, or even replaces it.' I agree with the first of these statements (insofar as they are intended as alternatives); and further, '[the] design did not abrogate that of 429, but elaborated upon it'. My view of what happened between 429 and 435 differs however from that of Sirks, who sees a shift from a more scholarly emphasis in 429 to a forensic/administrative one in 435, which 'found its expression in the exclusion of obsolete rules' (p. 58; cf. above, n. 7). I regard the constitution of 435 as an internal stage in the process of editing rather than as reflecting any change of circumstances or policy. See below, n. 52 for a striking example of editorial completeness.

edictales generalesque constitutiones', but adds the apparently radical, one might even think contradictory, amendment that laws valid or published in particular provinces or places were also to be included: 'vel in certis provinciis seu locis valere aut proponi iussae' (1.1.6). In formal, juristic terms, this is not as surprising as it looks, once we set it in the context of what is meant by a law of 'general' application. The best and most relevant definition of 'generalitas' is given in *Codex Justinianus* 1.14.3, part of a long constitution addressed to the senate on 6 or 7 November 426, of which this particular paragraph is either for some reason not excerpted, or does not survive, in the Theodosian Code.[19] According to this text, which must have been known to the editors of the Code, 'generalitas' consists of pronouncements sent to the senate in the form of imperial *orationes* or issued by the emperors as *edicta*, whatever the specific situation that might have occasioned them; and, more broadly, of imperial pronouncements made public by provincial governors which had relevance to other cases. 'Generalitas' is also defined by limitation, to exclude rescripts issued to individual litigants,[20] and 'interlocutiones', or legal rulings made in the course of specific proceedings without the intention that they should be applied more generally.

All this seems in formal terms comprehensible, and certainly should have been so to the editors of the Theodosian Code. The difficulty was that the formal definition does not comprehend the varied nature of the actual material which the compilers turned up. This was by no means primarily 'juristic' in character, nor on a commonsense view defined by its general relevance, but covered any subject, large or small, upon which the emperors had made pronouncements. This was remarked upon by Gibbon as he 'gratefully remembered' how, in studying the Code with the commentary of James Godefroy, he had found it far more than a book of law in any narrow sense: 'I used it (and much I used it) as a work of history rather than of Jurisprudence: but in every light it may be considered as a full and capacious repository of the political state of the Empire in the fourth and fifth centuries.'[21]

If Gibbon's remark is welcome support for the historian's rights of settlement in the territory of Jurisprudence, it also highlights the difficulties of selection and judgment faced by the editors of the Code. Even if they began their work by applying the most formal understanding of *generalitas* – that is, by excluding all rescripts and

---

[19] For the law, sometimes known as the 'law of citations', cf. Mommsen's ed., Prolegomena, p. CCCI; Seeck, *Regesten*, p. 352 (dated 7 November). It survives in seven citations from *CTh* and five from *CJust*. See esp. on these laws, in relation to the issue of *generalitas*, Sirks (n. 11 above), at 286-91.

[20] A brief statement of Arcadius restricting the validity of 'rescripta ad consultationem emissa vel emittenda' to the proceedings ('negotia') in respect of which they were issued survives as *CTh* 1.2.11; 6 December 398. See Harries above, p.13.

[21] *Memoirs of My Life* (ed. G.A. Bonnard, 1966), p. 147.

interlocutiones – they must often have found their material very difficult to classify. They will have found many cases where principles which clearly *could* have possessed force as general laws were enshrined in pronouncements addressed to individual officials and posted in particular places; it cannot always have been clear whether any general force was intended, particularly in cases where such pronouncements had been superseded by later ones addressed, it might be, to superior officials. The editors would appreciate that even in their most specific pronouncements the emperors often gave general reasons for acting as they did; it was simply not the case that points of general application were only ever embodied in laws of a formally general character. They must also have realised that many of the laws recovered were versions addressed to particular officials, of laws originally more general in scope which had *not* been recovered. They would know too that the distribution of late Roman legislation was sometimes a very complicated process. As laws passed down the line from emperor to praetorian prefect to provincial governor to local community, they underwent changes in form – as from imperial *epistula* to prefect's or governor's *edictum* – and acquired commentary by intermediate authorities; a law brought to the attention of the compilers of the Code might in principle belong to any of its various phases, and might not be directly from an emperor at all. *Codex Theodosianus* 7.13.11, for instance, issued on 15 May 382 'at Tyre the metropolis' and posted at Beirut, cannot derive from an imperial letter but must be part of an edict of the praetorian prefect of the Orient sent on to a provincial governor, and there are other such cases.[22] The Gregorian and Hermogenian Codes, cited as precedents in the law of 429, further confused the issue, since these earlier collections, though much more 'juristic' in character than the texts which now lay before the editors, consisted almost entirely of rescripts. These, as we have seen, were together with *interlocutiones* specifically excluded from the category of *generalitas*.[23]

Formal assumptions made by the editors about the character of

---

[22] See Mommsen in his edition, ad loc. (p. 339), Seeck, *Regesten* 11; the other cases include *CTh* 5.14.34; 8.1.8, 4.6; 16.2.12, 15. An excellent example of documentary proliferation in legislation is provided by the edict of toleration issued by Galerius at the end of the Great Persecution; cf. Stephen Mitchell, *JRS* 78 (1988) 105-24, at 113; below, n. 60. Galerius' edict was posted at Nicomedia on 30 April 311 (Lactantius, *De Mort. Pers.* 33.11-35.1). It was followed by a letter to the rest of the Empire, and in its own text refers to other letters to judges about the rules to be applied, presumably in the restoration of property to Christians. However, Maximinus, who occupied Asia Minor after Galerius' death a week later, did not wish to end the Persecution, and merely issued verbal instructions to his praetorian prefect Sabinus to send out letters to provincial governors. These letters (Eusebius, *HE*. 9.1.3-6) 'enjoined on governors the task of writing to *logistai, strategoi*, and those who had charge of the *pagi* of each city to ignore "that [an earlier] letter" and implement the new policy'.
[23] Tony Honoré, *Emperors and Lawyers* (1981), esp. at 33-41 and 104-6.

generalitas in the law must repeatedly have clashed in common sense with the specific character, and often the sheer oddity, of the situations in which their ever-conscientious emperors had expressed themselves. Considering such a law as that which appears as *Codex Theodosianus* 7.1.13, instructing that horses be washed downstream out of sight of military camps, so that drinking water was not polluted by mud and sweat (and worse), nor the eyes of beholders by the sight of naked grooms splashing about in the river, the editors might have inferred a general principle relating to public health and propriety. The law stated a comprehensible general benefit to the public, and one could readily see why, in its necessarily particular circumstances, it should always be observed. A more elusive principle lay in such a provision as that expressed in a law of 355 addressed to the praetorian prefect: 'Henceforth, whenever cured pork, or perhaps fresh meat, is issued to soldiers stationed in Africa, We command that only the hoofs and tips of the noses of the animals shall be cut off and removed, so that all the pork shall not be separated but shall serve in the issue of the food supplies' (7.4.2; transl. Pharr). The *generalitas* of this regulation lay, not in its wide reference to all sorts of situations, but in the fact that it was formally stated to be applicable to any similar situation in the future.[24] One could readily accept that it was wrong for the recipients of exported meat to be deprived of part of their rations by cunning suppliers who had the carcases divided before they were dispatched, and sometimes 'lost' joints of meat to their own advantage, but this principle is implied rather than stated in the text of the constitution. In any case, it hardly belongs to the juristic heights of Roman law. The better-known law of 397, posted at Rome in the Forum of Trajan and on pain of exile and confiscation of property banning the wearing of Oriental and Germanic trousers in the streets of the venerable city, derives its *generalitas* from the categorical nature of the ban and from the fact of its address to the people, rather than from the universality of the situation envisaged; this could only, by definition, affect the city of Rome.[25]

We have to imagine our editors, confronted with cases like this, constantly attempting to reconcile juristic notions of *generalitas* with

[24] Pharr's 'Henceforth, whenever ...' is a little too strong for the Latin 'cum ... deinceps', but makes it clear that, however specific the situation, the rule that applied to it was always to be observed. The law is addressed to Taurus without designation of office, but he is known to have been praetorian prefect of Italy in 355-61; *PLRE* I, pp. 879-80 (observing that the law 'refers to the military *annona* in Africa'; hence it was a matter of concern to the praetorian prefect).

[25] *CTh* 14.10.2. Does the phrase 'usum tzangarum adque bracarum ... nemini liceat usurpare' imply that some (*bona fide* Orientals and German visitors, perhaps, or members of the military) had the *right* to wear this garb? The three laws here discussed all address specific situations, the latter two in specific places. Their *generalitas* lay in the fact that they were applicable whenever the situations envisaged might recur.

the actual content of the laws which they discovered. Were they really to suppose that the washing of horses, the snouts and hoofs of slaughtered pigs, or the wearing of trousers at Rome, were issues involving *generalitas*, just because the emperors had pronounced upon them?

In view of such considerations I suggest that we might see in the phrase 'vel in certis provinciis seu locis valere aut proponi iussae' not an amendment of their original instructions but a definition made to help the editors of the material as they contemplated their task, and as the book of law on which they were engaged looked progressively more unlike any other book of law which they knew. It responds to queries raised by the editors as they began their work of excerpting and classifying the material they had collected, this material having proved much more varied in character than was allowed for in their original instructions. The tendency of the definition would be to increase the scope of what was included in the Code by subjecting the editors' material, often against the apparent implications of its actual content, to the most formal definition of *generalitas*. Without its guidance, the editors might well have been tempted to omit the snouts of slaughtered pigs.[26]

(ii) Editorial considerations also explain a second innovation in the constitution of 435. The editors were now empowered not merely, as in 429, to abbreviate laws by omitting extraneous matter but, in order to ensure the clarity of the published texts, to expand where necessary, to alter what was unclear and to emend what did not make sense: 'et *adiciendi* necessaria et *demutandi* ambigua et *emendandi* incongrua.'[27] Again, this looks like a response to a request from the editors, based upon inspection of the material they had collected, that they be given these powers. It was prudent to settle this point, since even the most obscure words of the emperors issued from their divine mouth (which is, indeed, sometimes called an 'oracle'). As Symmachus learned as *praefectus urbi* in 384, to question the emperor's judgment in making appointments was an act of sacrilege, which might cost the offender ten pounds, and his *officium* five pounds of gold in fines.[28] To amend the emperor's utterances might be no less hazardous than to question his judgment; it was as well to be careful.

---

[26] It is again worth emphasis that the problems sketched here confronted the editors *at the outset* of their work, when the full range of imperial conscientiousness had become apparent to them but before they had had much time to digest it.

[27] Cf. Honoré, *ZSS RA* 103 (1986), 165f. on these powers and their restrained use by the editors. Turpin (n. 9 above), at 622 n. 7 regards this clarification of the meaning of texts by altering their wording as the 'principal difference' in the law of 435 as compared with that of 429.

[28] *CTh* 1.6.9 (28 December 384), taken with Symmachus, *Relatio* 17; see my 'Symmachus and his enemies', in *Colloque Genevois sur Symmaque* (1986), at 165-6.

(iii) These new editorial powers are assigned to those *'about to begin* this work'; *'adgressuris* hoc opus'. I would suggest that this phrase be understood as referring to the stage of production that had now been reached, that of editorial ordering, in the manner described in the constitutions both of 429 and 435, of the material that had been assembled.[29] The enlargement of the editorial panel from nine to sixteen members and the replacement of most of its personnel were other appropriate steps to take at this stage: a recognition, not of failure, but of the fact that the project had reached a specific point at which the nature of the work had changed, from one of collection to one of classification and editing, at which the true extent of its scale and variety was beginning to be realised, and it was convenient to review the size and composition of the panel that would now be required to supervise a very different kind of work.

If these arguments are valid, and the law of 435 represents, not the initiation of a new project but a specific stage in the development of the original one, then we have here important information on the progress of work on the Code in its different phases. The period from 26 March 429 to 20 December 435 will be that in which the work of assembling the primary material for the compilation was taking place; the recovery of the original texts of imperial constitutions. By late 435 the compilers had inspected their source material sufficiently and had done enough preliminary work to pose the further questions of editorial policy that I have been discussing. It would be unrealistic to claim that it had not begun at all, but the editorial process proper – the division of the material under titles by subject, the extrapolation of points of substance and the elimination of superfluous matter, the arrangement in chronological order, and so on – all this could now take place in earnest, and occupied the much shorter period until late summer or autumn of 437. The completed Code, set out in two copies of an authoritative *codex*, was, as we saw, handed to the praetorian prefects of East and West after the marriage of Valentinian and Eudoxia on 29 October of that year. It was given authority in the eastern provinces by a constitution of 15 February 438 (*NTh* 1) and presented to the Roman senate on 25 December. Its acceptance by that body, at the instigation of the praetorian prefect who had received it from Theodosius, and the prefect's acceptance of the senate's instructions for the diffusion of copies, constituted its publication in the West.[30]

---

[29] Honoré, *ZSS RA* 103 (1986), at 162 n. 4.

[30] Sirks, op. cit. (n. 11 above), at 275-84, argues that the Code was 'never confirmed in the West', a *senatus consultum* being in his view not sufficient for this purpose. I doubt this; the *acta senatus*, that is the *Gesta* of 438, were submitted to the emperor for his acceptance; cf. A. Chastagnol, *La Préfecture urbaine à Rome sous le Bas-Empire* (1960), esp. at 67.

*

This interpretation of the procedures employed by the editors of the Theodosian Code is of course connected with, indeed is one way of viewing, the question of the actual, physical sources from which they recovered the texts of their laws. This question is discussed by Boudewijn Sirks in Chapter 2 of this book, with a preference for central archives – in particular copy-books (*Registerbücher*) in which the emperors entered copies of the legislation they issued – over the provincial archives favoured by Seeck.[31] A consequence of this theory is that the first stage of editing I have been describing, based, in this case, merely on the recovery of imperial copy-books and such provincial archives as are required to explain the 200 *proposita* datings relied upon by Seeck as indicating provincial origin, would have been a relatively compact and painless operation, and one that can hardly without good excuse have taken 6¾ years; other causes for what now appears as a delay between 429 and 435, such as a change of policy or emphasis, have to be postulated.[32]

My own view is that we should not work with too restrictive a conception of the sources available to the compilers of the Code. It would be absurd to deny in principle the use of imperial and provincial archives if these existed, whether in the form of copy- or day-books, select *commentarii*, or in whatever form they may have been kept. On the other hand, the idea that central archives in any sort of continuous form were the main or essential source for the compilers of the Code fails sufficiently to explain the discrepancies between laws, and between different versions of the same laws which can be found, and which seem most easily explained on the assumption that their texts were derived from different sources. It would clearly be dangerous to assume that all such discrepancies indicate provincial or local origin and then to assign all laws that do *not* show them to central sources, since not all discrepancies may be apparent to us. We also have to account for the omission from the Theodosian Code of laws which are known to have existed from literary sources such as Eusebius' *Vita Constantini*, independent collections like the *Fragmenta Vaticana* and the *Sirmondian Constitutions*, from occasional inscriptions, and from references to lost earlier legislation made in surviving texts of the Code itself.[33] It is of course possible to postulate whatever incompleteness in or damage to archives as is required to explain the omissions in the

[31] Sirks, Chapter 2 §4 below.

[32] Sirks, Chapter 2 §7 below. For my reservations on these, cf. above, nn. 7, 18. See below, nn. 53, 62 for indications of recovery from local sources; *proposita* datings are not always required to establish this.

[33] E.g. to laws of Constantine; *CTh* 13.5.26, 9.3; 14.3.12; 16.10.2; to Gratian's law on temple property, 16.10.20. Wenger, op. cit. (n. 12 above), 537, emphasises the 'Unvollständigkeit der kaiserlichen Archive'.

Code that are found or may be suggested,[34] but this can be a rather tautological procedure. In general it seems more likely, not that the 'missing' laws were found but omitted from the Code, as suggested by Sirks, but that they were never found.[35] Indeed, if there were substantial central archives at the disposal of the compilers, one might have expected far more laws to have been found than seems to have been the case. The total of 2,700 'basic texts' postulated by Sirks (plus whatever, on his view, was omitted by the editors) does not seem an especially impressive haul of legislation if the originals survived in central archival sources approaching anything like completeness over the whole period 311-437.[36] It is much more impressive if central sources were very incomplete and the laws had to be recovered from a range of diverse provenances. Furthermore, the argument that laws were recovered from officially maintained copy-books, whether central or provincial, leaves out of account one of the most obvious and important ways in which law is known to have been preserved in the Roman Empire; by the copying down by interested parties of publicly posted texts. I will briefly return to this below.

I believe, therefore, that no single or narrow range of possibilities relating only to officially preserved versions of imperial legislation explains the discrepancies and anomalies that do in fact occur in the published texts of the Code. The answer to the question of the sources of the Theodosian Code lies not at one or two, but at many points in the very wide area between the central records perhaps consulted in the case of some recent laws issued in the East, and the diverse and scattered locations, especially in the West,[37] in which the laws recovered were originally received. Given the wide variety of individual anomalies that may be found, in what follows I shall proceed by the illustration of possibilities rather than by general analysis, and will begin with two cases of relatively recent eastern legislation where it seems clear from the edited protocol, either that

[34] As a matter of interest and indirect relevance, B. A. van Groningen, *A Family-archive from Tebtunis* (1950), at 44-62 and 85-108 provides a fascinating account of a dispute over (i.e. avoidance of) the municipal duty of maintaining the public archives; cf. esp. (among many other difficulties), p. 56 on '[documents] missing for the greatest part the beginning, some also, as is usual, in a damaged condition ... [some] lost, being torn and worn by age, others also have been partly damaged and several have been eaten away at the top because the places are hot'. Cf. E. Posner, *Archives in the Ancient World* (1972), at 151f.

[35] Sirks, Chapter 2 §7 and his n. 74 below. Sirks' view is linked with a different understanding from mine of the phrase 'ad vim sanctionis non pertinentia' as a criterion for editorial exclusion in the constitution of 429, and in general about what was going on between 429 and 435.

[36] Sirks, Appendix 1; to the basic 2,700 texts Sirks adds [y], the number of constitutions collected but omitted by the editors of the Code. It will be clear that we take different views of [y], cf. nn. 7, 52.

[37] The predominance of western legislation collected in the Code, pointed out by Seeck, *Regesten* 2, does require explanation (cf. n. 62 below).

the compilers had found various copies or versions of laws, which they gave in a single text while indicating the alternative sources that had come to their notice, or that they found a single copy already annotated in the fashion shown. Both laws are discussed in much the same sense by Seeck.[38]

(1) 1.8.1: IMPP. HONORIUS ET THEODOSIUS AA. FLORENTIO MAGISTRO MILITUM. Viro illustri quaestore Eustathio suggerente, etc. ... DAT. ID. OCT. CONSTANTINOPOLI HONORIO X ET THEODOSIO VI AA. CONSUL. SCRIPTA EODEM EXEMPLO SAPRICIO MAGISTRO MILITUM, HELIONI MAGISTRO OFFICIORUM ET EUSTATHIO QUAESTORI [15 October 415].

(2) 11.28.9: IDEM AA. ANTHEMIO PP. ... DAT V ID. APRIL. CONSTA(NTI)NOP(OLI), CONSTANTIO ET CONSTANTE CONSS. DE EADEM RE SCRIBTUM EDICTUM AD POPULUM: AD MARCIANUM COM(ITEM) S(ACRARUM) L(ARGITIONUM): MUSELLIO PRAEPOSITO SACRI CUBICULI DE TITULIS AD DOMUM SACRAM PERTINENTIBUS: AD RECTORES PROVINCIARUM: ET DE METALLARIIS EDICTUM AD POPULUM PER PROVINCIAS ILLYRICI ET AD RECTORES PROVINCIARUM [9 April 414].[39]

The first of these laws concerns what Honoré (p. 77 below) calls 'an item of official infighting', the restoration of certain military appointments (*praepositurae*) to the *laterculum minus* or 'lesser register' maintained by the quaestor, from the *magistri militum* who had taken them over. For this purpose copies would have to be sent 'eodem exemplo' to all the relevant officials, including the *magister officiorum*, who had general supervision of all court arrangements; any one of these copies might in principle have been recovered. The law is also a modest bureaucratic success for the influential quaestor Eustathius who 'suggested' it. It does not follow that it was in his department that it was found, but a central archive, whether his or that of the *magister militum*, might be the best interpretation of the

[38] *Regesten*, 4f. In these and the other examples that follow, the argument is developed from the recorded protocols of the laws rather than the content, which is indicated by dots (...) without any indication of the length of the text. The phrases POST ALIA and ET CETERA are original editorial indications of omitted matter. The presentation of the names of emperors, either in full (as IMP. HONORIUS ET THEODOSIUS AA.; laws were issued in the names of all reigning emperors) or as abbreviated (IDEM AA.), again follows the fifth-century editors' practice. The presence of an abbreviation is of no significance for my argument, showing only that the same emperors' names had occurred earlier in the same title.

[39] 'On the same matter an edict was issued to the people; to Marcianus, Count of the Sacred Imperial Largesses; to Musellius, Grand Chamberlain, with reference to accounts pertaining to the sacred imperial household; to the governors of the provinces; and, with reference to the miners, an edict to the people throughout the provinces of Illyricum and to the governors of the provinces' (transl. Pharr).

text and style of annotation of this recent law.[40] In the case of 11.28.9 it might be a valid deduction from the reference to the publication of a *part* of the text as an 'edictum ad populum per provincias Illyrici et ad rectores provinciarum', that the document was recovered as annotated at an early stage from the archive of a central official, possibly that of the praetorian prefect who had responsibility for its further diffusion. Had this 'edict concerning mineworkers' been recovered only in the version received and published in Illyricum, it would not have been defined in this way. Like the 'edict to the people', and the section to Musellius referring to 'accounts pertaining to the sacred imperial household', it would have needed amendment and commentary in order to be intelligible by itself.

We might similarly view as deriving from central sources certain very late inclusions in the Code, of laws issued in the period between the revised instructions issued to the editorial panel in December 435 and the completion of the text in late 437. Since the last dated laws in the Theodosian Code, from summer 436 and spring 437, were addressed to successive praetorian prefects of the Orient, Isidore and Darius, we might assume that these laws – one of those to Isidore, of 4 June 436, being edited in six extracts, three of them in succession (12.1.189-191)[41] – were made available to the editors of the Code from sources close to the centre of power. In a further example from this late period, however, three edited laws deriving from a single pronounce-ment of 3 April 436 were addressed to the praetorian prefect Isidore, two of the extracts but not the third preserving the annotation that the same law was also issued to the praetorian prefect of Illyricum:

(3) 8.4.30: IDEM AA. ISIDORO PPO. POST ALIA: EODEM EXEMPLO EUBULO PPO ILLYRICI ... DAT. III NON. APRIL. CONST(ANTINO)P(OLI) ISIDORO ET SENATORE CONSS.

(4) 12.1.187: IDEM AA. ISIDORO PPO ... ET CETERA. DAT. III NON. APRIL. CONSTANT(INO)P(OLI) ISIDORO ET SENATORE CONSS. EODEM EXEMPLO EUBULO PPO ILLYRICI.

The interest in this group of laws lies partly in the fact that the prefect of Illyricum mentioned, Eubulus, was a member of the editorial panels both of 429 and of 435 but had evidently been promoted from his work

[40] According to the *Notitia Dignitatum* (*Or.* 12.6, cf. *Occ.* 10.6) the quaestor, like the *magistri scriniorum* (*Or.* 19.14), had no established *officium* but drew 'adiutores' from the *scrinia* as desired; the *primicerius notariorum* was in a similar position (*Or.* 18.6; *Occ.* 16.6): cf. Jill Harries, 'The Roman Imperial Quaestor from Constantine to Theodosius II', *JRS* 78 (1988), 148-72, at 159. The efficiency and completeness of the archives maintained by these departments remains an open question; those of the *primicerius notariorum* at least should have been extensive (since he maintained the *Notitia Dignitatum* itself).

[41] The others are 11.5.3; 14.26.2; 14.27.2.

on the Code to take up the prefecture;[42] he, if anyone, was *au fait* with the proceedings of the panel and in a good position to ensure that the commission received contemporary legislation in its best and most authentic state. Despite this, the third version of this law (12.1.188), largely duplicates, but also differs in detail from, 8.4.30, and in its protocol makes no mention of the prefect of Illyricum. It seems clear that in this very recent case the compilers of the Code recovered and worked with not one, but at least two copies of the law.

If this is so even for the most recent eastern legislation, the situation for the more distant past, and especially for the western Empire, is much more complicated. Here we find anomalies that are very difficult to reconcile with the notion of a single archive maintained, in whatever form, at the centre of power.[43] By what process of editorial recovery, for example, do we possess the text of a single law of Constantine 'accepted' at Hispalis (Seville) on 18 April 336, apparently a full four years after it was issued at Constantinople?[44]

(5) 3.5.6: IDEM A. AD TIBERIANUM VICARIUM HISPANIARUM ... DAT. ID. IUL. CONSTANT(INO)P(OLI). ACCEPTA XIIII K. MAI. HISPALI NEPOTIANO ET FACUNDO CONSS.

A four-year gap between issue and acceptance is excessive on any assumptions of bureaucratic delays or difficulties in communication between East and West in the time of Constantine, and it may be that this is a special case, to be solved by a more radical approach than any so far thought of to problems of textual transmission or fourth-century prosopography. A convincing historical context can however be found for discrepancies in a law of Valens addressed to the *comes sacrarum largitionum*, which survives in two fragments of what – given the diversity of subject-matter in the two fragments – was clearly a much longer law issued at Noviodunum on 3 or 5 July 369. One fragment and

[42] *PLRE* II, p. 403; Eubulus is not among those thanked on the occasion of the publication of the Code in the East on 15 February 438; *NTh* 1.

[43] An interesting test case might be the comparison of Constantine's law preserved as *CTh* 16.2.7 (5 February 330) to the *consularis* of Numidia, with the paraphrase, including additional provisions not mentioned in the Code, given by Constantine himself in his letter to the African bishops; Optatus, *Appendix* X, in C. Ziwsa, *CSEL* 26, p. 215; cf. Mommsen, ad loc. (p. 837). Constantine recalls his own words closely, but not exactly, and, where they differ, in less technical language.

[44] T.D. Barnes, *NE*, 145 & n. 17. The question of the date of issue of the law turns on the date, or dates, on which Tiberianus can have held office as *vicarius* (or *comes*) of Spain. *PLRE* I, p. 911 (Tiberianus 4) has him as *comes Hispaniarum* in 332 (17 October), replaced by Severus in 333-5, and returning as *vicarius Hispaniarum* in 335 (taking this to be the date of *issue* of *CTh* 3.5.6, which would then have been addressed to Tiberianus one year, and not four years, before it was posted). But (i) *CTh* 13.5.8 to Severus has him still in office on 19 May 336 (*PLRE* solves this by moving the law to 335), and (ii) setting aside this problem, a return of Tiberianus to be *vicarius* of Spain does not seem likely. Seeck, *Regesten*, 183, lists 3.5.6 under 335, but offers no comment or argument.

not the other of this law is (with other variations in the protocol) recorded as 'accepted' at Marcianopolis on 18 July:

(6) 10.16.2: IDEM AA. ET GRATIANUS AD ARCHELAUM COM(ITEM) OR(IENTIS) [*sc.* COM. S. L.] ... DAT. III NON. IUL. NOVIODUNO VAL(ENTINI)ANO N(O)B(ILISSIMO) P(UERO) ET VICTORE CONSS.

(7) 10.21.1: IMP. VAL(ENTINI)ANUS ET VALENS AA. ARCHELAO COM.S.L. ... DAT. V NON. IUL. NEVIODUNI; ACC. XV KAL. AUG. MARCIANOPOLI VAL(ENTINI)ANO NOB. P. ET VICTORE CONSS.

It is not difficult to work out what has happened here. In 369 Valens made Marcianopolis his base for his third campaigning season against the Goths, advancing to Noviodunum on the lower Danube for the conduct of hostilities. It looks from 10.21.1 as if the emperor left behind his court administration at Marcianopolis, and addressed this law to his *comes sacrarum largitionum* there from his campaign headquarters.[45] The text clearly derives not from the original version issued by the emperor and copied into some central file, but from that received by the *comes sacrarum largitionum*. The different protocol of 10.16.2 (with the correct inclusion of the name of Gratian), the transmitted discrepancy in the date, and the error in the office of the recipient, make it clear that this part of the law was recovered from a different source, which again is unlikely to be a central archive; had it been so, the compilers would have found both laws together as part of the same text, without the discrepancies between them that we find in the published versions. The compilers have here recovered two partial, already separated, versions of the same law but because of the differences in dating and protocol did not realise that they were dealing with a single pronouncement.

In another example, subtly different versions are found of a law addressed to the *vicarius* of Africa on the evasion of municipal duties under the assumed guise of high office. One law is recorded as 'accepted' at Carthage on 12 December 338, the other as 'posted' somewhere unspecified (not at Carthage, since the date is earlier) on 27 November and 'accepted' at Timgad on 15 December:[46]

---

[45] Amm. Marc. 27.7.5f. In 378, by contrast, Valens took with him to Hadrianople 'thesauri ... et principalis fortunae insignia cetera cum praefecto et consistorianis' (31.12.10, cf. 31.15.2, 'potestatum culmina maximarum et fortunae principalis insignia thesaurosque').

[46] Pharr's translation of 6.22.2 is the more effective of the two [an additional phrase found only in 12.1.24 is shown in square brackets]: '... to which we add that if any person should attempt to evade the duties of his municipal council and should seek to obtain the shadow and the name of high rank, [even though he should be deceived of his hope of this false honour], he shall be compelled to pay thirty pounds of silver ...'

(8) 12.1.24: IDEM A. ACONIO CATULLINO VIC. AFRIC. Quicumque fugientes obsequia curiarum *affectaverint adumbratae nomina dignitatis*, etsi eos spes falsi honoris inluserit, XXX argenti libras inferre cogantur. ACC. KARTHAG. PRID. ID. DEC. URSO ET POLEMIO CONSS.

(9) 6.22.2: IMP. CONSTANTIUS A. ACONIO VIC. AFRIC. ... cui addimus, ut quicumque fugientes obsequia curiarum *umbram et nomina adfectaverint dignitatum*, tricenas libras argenti inferre cogantur, etc. PP. V KAL. DEC., ACC. XVII IAN. THAMUGADI URSO ET POLEMIO CONSS.

The second of these versions, in which the recipient's name is also transmitted incompletely, perhaps represents a copy sent on by the *vicarius* to the city of Timgad, improved by someone in the *vicarius'* office who fancied his hand at re-touching the style (perhaps he thought that he was simplifying it). In any event, it is clear that the compilers of the Code recovered two versions of the law and not a single, authoritative copy from some central archive. It is also of interest that *CTh* 12.1.25 & 26, issued respectively on 28 October and 1 November (the latter also to Catullinus), nevertheless follow 12.1.24 in the published text of the Code. The editors must have realised that, although the recorded date of *acceptance* at Carthage of 12.1.24 was later, it was *issued* earlier than its successors. That this was an editorial inference is clear, since the date and place of issue of the law are not recorded at all.[47]

At 16.1.4 the Theodosian Code preserves one of the most widely-reported of late Roman laws, that issued by Valentinian II at Milan on 23 January 386 permitting the free assembly of Arian congregations. The circumstances which led up to and the consequences which followed the publication of the law are described by various writers, including Ambrose bishop of Milan (*Ep.* 20) and Augustine, who was in the city at the time as professor of rhetoric (*Conf.* 9.7(15)), and the church historians Rufinus (11.16) and Sozomen (7.13.5ff.). From Rufinus and Sozomen, and from Gaudentius bishop of Brescia, we hear about the latter's parishioner the *magister memoriae* Benivolus, who resigned his office rather than draft the legislation:[48]

(10) 16.1.4; IMPPP. VAL(ENTINI)ANUS, THEOD(OSIUS) ET ARCAD(IUS) AAA. AD EUSIGNIUM PPO. ... [scituris] his, qui sibi *tantum* existimant colligendi copiam contributam, *quod*, si turbulentum quippiam contra nostrae

[47] On this particular point, it is of course possible that the date of issue of 12.1.24 was lost at a later stage in the transmission of the text. I would assume that 12.1.24 (+ 6.22.2) and 12.1.26, also addressed to Catullinus, form part of a long law addressed to the *vicarius* (12.1.25, with no named addressee, is on the same subject but was issued by Constantius II at Emesa in Syria). If so, the discrepancies between them fortify the inference that its separate parts were recovered separately and not simply divided in the editing.

[48] Cf. for a brief account of the circumstances and Benivolus' exploit my *Western Aristocracies and Imperial Court, AD 364-425* (1975, repr. 1990), 185, 189 and (on Augustine), 221; and esp., on the technical aspects, Jill Harries, *JRS* 78 (1988), at 162f.

tranquillitatis praeceptum faciendum esse temptaverint, ut seditionis
auctores pacisque turbatae ecclesiae, *etiam* maiestatis capite ac
sanguine sint supplicia luituri [manente nihilo minus eos supplicio, etc.]
... DAT. X KAL. FEB. MED(IOLANO) HONORIO NOB.P. ET EUODIO CONSS.[49]

That the circumstances of this law concern Milan and the relations of
the imperial court, influenced by the Arianism of the empress and her
supporters, with the Catholic community of the city and its bishop is
beyond any doubt. It is puzzling, therefore, to find at *CTh* 16.4.1 a
single sentence of the law cited almost (not exactly) verbatim and with
the same date as 16.1.4, but presented as if issued at Constantinople:

(11) 16.4.1; IMPPP. VAL(ENTINI)ANUS, THEOD(OSIUS) ET ARCAD(IUS) AAA.
EUSIGNIO PPO. His, qui sibi *tantummodo* existimant colligendi copiam
contributam, si turbulentum quippiam contra nostrae tranquillitatis
praeceptum faciendum esse temptaverint, ut seditionis auctores
pacisque turbatae ecclesiae, maiestatis capite ac sanguine sint supplicia
luituri. DAT. X KAL. FEB. CONSTANTP. HONORIO NOB.P. ET EUODIO V.C. CONSS.

The textual differences in this version are slight but from an editorial
point of view significant. Apart from the different place of issue,
'Eusignio' is read for 'ad Eusignium',[50] and the consul Euodius is given
his rank 'v(ir) c(larissimus)'; Euodius was the consul of the western
usurper Magnus Maximus, and his name is here recorded, as in many
laws, in the year in which he was recognised by Theodosius.[51] The
minor discrepancies of phraseology do not suggest that the shorter text
was edited from the longer, or either text from a common original;
compared with 16.1.4, 16.4.1 omits the words 'quod' and 'etiam' but on
the other hand reads the longer 'tantummodo' where 16.1.4 has merely
'tantum'. Although it is true that it concerns the most general aspect of
16.1.4, it is hard to see how 16.4.1 ever became connected with the
eastern Empire; for present purposes, it is relevant only to observe
that the editors of the Theodosian Code must have acquired these two
laws from different sources. Had they extrapolated 16.4.1 from 16.1.4

[49] 'If those persons who suppose that the right of assembly has been granted to them
alone should attempt to provoke any agitation against the regulation of Our
Tranquillity, [they shall know that,] as authors of sedition and as disturbers of the peace
of the Church, they shall also pay the penalty of high treason with their life and blood.
[Punishment shall also await those persons, etc.] ...' (transl. Pharr). In my text above,
discrepancies between this law and 16.4.1 are italicised.
[50] This difference of style was thought by Seeck to be an indicator of the origin of texts
(*Regesten*, 17); but cf. Sirks, Chapter §2, below. The 'dissertatio' of Maximinus (n. 52
below) transmits the address as 'ad Eusignium pf. pretorio'. The discrepancy between
the two forms of address also occurs in 10.16.2 and 10.21.1, discussed above (p. 36).
[51] *Western Aristocracies and Imperial Court*, 179.

they would not have incorporated the discrepancies in the protocol that I have described.[52]

In similar fashion, the only likely explanation of a law addressed to the *consularis* of Campania *or* the *consularis* of Picenum is that the compilers recovered two copies of a law originally issued more widely, perhaps to all provincial governors, to all governors of Italian provinces, or to a praetorian prefect with the instructions to forward it to them:[53]

(12) 12.1.71: IDEM AA. ET GR(ATI)ANUS A. AD AMPHILOCHIUM CONS. CAMPANIAE SIVE AD SOFRONIUM CONS. PICENI ... DAT. III NON. MAI. TREV(IRIS) VAL(ENTINI)ANO ET VALENTE III AA. CONSS. [5 May 370].

The same explanation might hold for a law addressed to the proconsul *and* the *vicarius* of Africa but beginning with a phrase in the singular, and so clearly addressed to them separately:

(13) 1.12.6; IDEM AA. VICTORIO PROCONSULI AFRICAE ET DOMINATORI VICARIO AFRICAE. Apparitioni *tuae* et legatorum quadringentos de his dumtaxat, quos rei publicae membra non querentur sibi esse detractos, etc. [including also the phrases 'arbitrii tui' and 'officii tui'] ... DAT. XII K. IUN. MED(IOLANO) HONORIO A. IIII ET EUTYCHIANO CONSUL. [21 May 398].[54]

In another instance of a single law preserved in two versions addressed to the same official, the Theodosian Code and an independent source, the *Collatio Legum Mosaicarum et Romanarum*, derive from copies of a law posted in different places and at different dates in the city of Rome:

[52] The law is also summarised, from the fuller version at *CTh* 16.1.4, by Sozomen, *HE* 7.13.7, and cited in full (including protocol) from the shorter version at 16.4.1, hence with the place of issue given as Constantinople, by the fifth-century Arian bishop Maximinus, in his so-called 'dissertatio' on the council of Aquileia, §95 (ed. R. Gryson, *CC* 87 [1982], p. 195f.); cf. on this text Peter Heather and John Matthews, *The Goths in the Fourth Century* (Liverpool, 1991), at 145f. It is of course remarkable enough that a law in favour of Arian congregations was included in the Theodosian Code at all, and shows how strictly the editors observed their instructions to 'record *cunctas/omnes* constitutiones' (laws of 429 and 435). The Arian Maximinus actually fails to realise that 16.4.1 was originally *in favour of* the Arians, as he would have done had he made the connection with 16.1.4.

[53] For this and the following case, cf. Seeck, *Regesten*, 6. In Seeck's words, to say that a law was issued to one *or* another of two officials is 'nonsense' ('Unsinn'). The compilers clearly had two copies, which they combined 'in jener wunderlichen Weise'! It is worth noting (cf. above, n. 32) that the text preserves no date or place of acceptance.

[54] 'For your office staff and that of the legates, [We decree] that four hundred apparitors shall be assigned from those persons only whom the members of any municipality do not complain of as having been withdrawn from them', etc. (transl. Pharr).

(14) 9.7.6; IDEM AAA. ORIENTIO VICARIO URBI ROMAE. ... PP. IN FORO TRAIANI VIII ID. AUG. VALENTINIANO A. IIII ET NEOTERIO CONSS. [6 August 390].

(15) *Collatio* 5.3 (Riccobono, FIRA², p. 557): IMPP(P). VALENTINIANUS THEODOSIUS ET ARCADIUS AUGGG. AD ORIENTIUM VICARIUM URBIS ROMAE ... PROP. PR. ID. MAIAS ROMAE IN ATRIO MINERVAE [14 May, *sc*. 390].

It would in principle have been possible for the compilers of the Code to have recovered either of these, or indeed other, copies of the law, which the *vicarius* of Rome would have had posted in public places in the city in order (see below) that they might be read and copied by interested parties. An additional benefit in this case is that the version in the *Collatio* (the subject is male prostitution) preserves the original rhetoric that the editors of the Theodosian Code, following their editorial instructions concerning 'matters not relevant to the force of sanction' ('ad vim sanctionis non pertinentia'), omitted.[55] It is enough for legal purposes that burning alive be prescribed as the sanction. It is not necessary from a legal or editorial point of view also to evoke the improving effect of this procedure upon onlookers, vividly expressed in the longer version of this law.

　　Particularly intriguing, to return in conclusion to purely technical considerations, is the varied collection of dates and recipients presented by the group of laws in the Code which are textually related to – though not derived from – the law preserved to us as the the the sixth of the *Sirmondian Constitutions*:[56]

(16) *Sirm*. 6: IMPP. THEODOSIUS ET VALENTINIANUS CAESAR AMATIO V.I. PRAEF. PRTR. GALL. ... DATA VII IDUS IULIAS AQUILEIAE D.N. THEODOSIO A. XI ET VALENTINIANO CONSS. [9 July 425].

This version of the law preserved in the *Sirmondian Constitutions* restores legal privileges and benefits to the clergy in the aftermath of the usurpation of Iohannes at Ravenna, making particular reference to the treatment of heretical bishops in Gaul. The prefect is also instructed to convey the imperial commands to the knowledge ('notitia') of the provinces under his jurisdiction. It is evidently from such further instructions sent on to governors and officials, in this case in Italy and Africa, that the compilers of the Theodosian Code derived their corresponding material:

(17) (i) 16.2.47: IDEM A. ET CAES. BASSO C(OMITI) R(EI) P(RIVATAE) ... DAT. VIII ID. OCTOB. AQUIL. D.N. THEOD. A. XI ET VAL(ENTINI)ANO CONSS. [8 October].

　　(ii) 16.5.62: IMP. THEOD. A. ET VAL(ENTINI)ANO CAES. AD FAUSTUM

---

[55] Cf. above, n. 7 for the meaning of this phrase.
[56] Seeck, *Regesten*, 5.

P(RAEFECTUM) U(RBI) ... DAT. XVI KAL. AUG. THEOD. A. XI ET VAL(ENTINI)ANO CAES. CONSS. [17 July].

(iii) 16.5.64: IDEM A. ET CAES. BASSO C.R.P. POST ALIA ... ET CETERA. DAT. VIII ID. AUG. AQUIL. D.N. THEOD. A. XI ET VALENTINIANO CAES. CONSS. [6 August].

(iv) 16.2.46: IMPP. THEOD. ET VALENTINIANUS CAES. GEORGIO PROC. AFRIC. POST ALIA ... ET CETERA. DAT. PRID. NON. IUL. AQUIL. D.N. THEOD. A. XI ET VAL(ENTINI)ANO CAES. CONSS. [6 July].

In addition, 16.5.63 (cf. 16.5.62 and 64 above) seems likely to be connected in some way with the same pronouncement:

(v) 16.5.63: IDEM A. ET CAES. GEORGIO PROC. AFRIC. ... ET CETERA. DAT. PRID. NON. AUG. AQUIL. D.N. THEODO. A. XI ET VAL(ENTINI)ANO CAES. CONSS. [4 August].

The fragments of the law preserved in the Theodosian Code clearly derive from versions issued to officials working under the praetorian prefect of Italy (the *comes rei privatae*) or as part of separate jurisdictions (the urban prefect and the proconsul of Africa) in the area of the Italian prefecture;[57] there is no textual dependency between these versions and the separate tradition relating to Gaul preserved in the *Sirmondian Constitutions*. Nor, apparently, was the corresponding version of the full text of the law, which we can assume to have been addressed to the praetorian prefect of Italy, available to the compilers of the Code. These derived their texts from partial versions addressed on five different transmitted dates to three different officials operating within the Italian prefecture. Yet this is a recent law, which would surely have been preserved in full in imperial copy-books, had these been available.

*

Such cases as these pose endless problems in the detailed interpretation of the Theodosian Code, many of which are discussed, with due regard for the uncertainties, in the pages of Seeck's *Regesten*, in *The Prosopography of the Later Roman Empire*, and in T.D. Barnes' *The New Empire of Diocletian and Constantine*. My purpose is rather different; it is to argue, following in this respect Seeck and A.H.M. Jones, that the compilers of the Theodosian Code cannot have worked with systematic access to central archives or registers of legal sources; had that been the case, there would be more laws, fewer discrepancies between different versions of the same laws, fewer indications too of the circumstances in which laws were received, read out, and posted in public places. This returns us to the very important point mentioned

---

[57] The prefect of Rome and proconsul of Africa stood outside the hierarchy headed by the praetorian prefect, and reported direct to the emperor; cf. A.H.M. Jones, *The Later Roman Empire* I, pp. 374f. with n. 22.

earlier. It was by hearing the law announced in public places and reading it when posted on notice-boards, usually in ephemeral form – only a very small proportion of imperial legislation achieved the permanent status of being engraved on bronze or marble tablets[58] – that the populations of the Empire were expected to have knowledge of it, and legal authorities to take note by making copies for themselves. I need here only illustrate this very common practice of copying down imperial legislation: from criticism of the Emperor Caligula because he imposed new tax laws and had them engraved in very small letters and in an awkward corner, so that they could not be copied,[59] to the quotation by Eusebius, in a Greek translation of a Latin original, of Galerius' edict of toleration; and, later, from the copy engraved (again in Latin) at Tyre, of Maximinus' rescript against the Christians, a document also known from two inscribed copies from Asia Minor.[60] Of the two versions of the so-called 'Edict of Milan' of Constantine and Licinius offering toleration and rights of ownership of property to the Christians, one was cited by Lactantius from the copy posted at Nicomedia, which is where he was living at the time (*De Mort. Pers.* 48, cf. Eusebius, *HE* 10.5.2-14); it was in that city, as Lactantius also records, that an angry Christian had torn down an edict against the Christians from the board where it was posted, declaring sarcastically that victories over Goths and Sarmatians were being promulgated (*De Mort. Pers.* 13). The text of one of the most important of all Roman legal enactments, the so-called 'Constitutio Antoniniana' of AD 212, survives because it formed part of a dossier of legal documents assembled by an individual who wished to use it to support his title to residence at Alexandria, or some other question of social status or immunity to which the 'Constitutio' was relevant.[61]

[58] E.g. for engraving on bronze, *CTh* 12.5.2 (given as 'pp. Karthagine', so not recovered from an engraved version), 'quod ut perpetua observatione firmetur, legem hanc *incisam aeneis tabulis* iussimus publicari', cf. 14.4.4; for engraving on bronze or painting on wooden tablets or linen posters, 11.27.1, '*aereis tabulis vel cerussatis aut linteis mappis scribta* per omnes civitates Italiae proponatur lex'; for posting in public places, 16.5.37, 'proposito programmate *celeberrimis in locis volumus anteferri* et gesta, quibus est huiuscemodi allegatio inserta, subnecti'. The instruction to display legislation in public places and legibly is a common provision recorded on inscriptions, cf. esp. Callie Williamson, 'Monuments of Bronze: Roman legal documents on bronze tablets', *Classical Antiquity* 6.1 (1987), 160-83.

[59] Suetonius, *Caligula* 41.1: 'minutissimis litteris et angustissimo loco, uti ne cui describere liceret.'

[60] Eusebius, *HE* 9.7.3. For this and the epigraphic evidence, adding a new Latin inscr. from Colbasa (on the road Antalya-Burdur) to the Greek inscr. already known from Arykanda in Lycia, see the fundamental and fully-documented discussion by Stephen Mitchell, 'Maximinus and the Christians in AD 312: a new Latin inscription', *JRS* 78 (1988), 105-24. For Tyre as the metropolis of Phoenicia, see above, p. 27.

[61] *P. Giss.* 40; cf. F. M. Heichelheim, 'The text of the *Constitutio Antoniniana* and three other decrees of the Emperor Caracalla contained in Papyrus Gissensis 40', *JEA* 26 (1940), 10-22, esp. 21-2. See also Callie Williamson (n. 58 above), 165f. for the copying of military *diplomata*.

Between the extremes of centrally maintained archives and ephemeral display on the notice-boards of the cities of the Later Roman Empire, there existed an array of opportunities for recovery from intermediate sources, particularly from law schools (Berytus, where fourteen laws in the Theodosian Code are recorded as 'posted', is an obvious example, though it is in a way surprising that there were not more),[62] and other places where lawyers practised and made working collections of imperial enactments, but also from individuals and groups who had an interest in copying and preserving the law on particular subjects; and one may add to these the possibility countenanced by Seeck and A.H.M. Jones, of the recovery of legislation from the family papers of individuals, primarily aristocratic, who had kept them after their departure from office.[63] On the assumption, however, valid on any of these grounds, that the recovery of so large a proportion of western laws was not achieved without some actual visits, at least to major centres in the West at which laws might have been collected and made available for later recovery, it is worth reflection that the period in which the recovery took place, 429-435, was the last in which such a project, involving travel in an increasingly insecure western Mediterranean, could easily have been envisaged. In conclusion it is therefore worth pausing for a few moments on the political context in which the project was conceived and implemented.

On 23 October 425 an era of co-operation between eastern and western governments had been inaugurated by the installation by the generals of Theodosius of the child emperor Valentinian III, and by the restoration to Ravenna of his mother Galla Placidia, for the past two years a refugee at the court of Constantinople.[64] The marriage of Valentinian and Licinia Eudoxia in October 437 was the culmination and symbol of the unity of the imperial house achieved in this period. If the process of accumulation of the law that was achieved in the years 429-435 is a tribute to the actual possibilities of travel and communication in the Mediterranean world achieved by the political unity of the imperial house, the publication of the Code, coinciding with the

---

[62] See the *proposita* datings listed by Seeck, *Regesten*, 12, of which the four most frequent are: Rome 70, Carthage 38, Berytus 14, Constantinople 12. There is then a drop to Hadrumetum 5. Three other places are mentioned four times, four places three times, six places twice, and twenty-six places (only seven of them eastern) once each.

[63] Seeck, *Regesten*, 11, citing the family of the great senator S. Petronius Probus, to whom a very large number of surviving laws were addressed. Cf. A.H.M. Jones, *JRS* 54 (1964), at 79, citing John Lydus, *De Mag.* 2.20: until 471 'the man administering the office [*sc.* the praetorian prefecture] conducted business in his own premises'. It is relevant that the senatorial meeting of 25 December 438 was held in the private house 'ad Palmam' of the praetorian prefect Faustus; *Gesta Senatus* 1. Without excluding any possibility, whether the private papers of senators or imperial archives where they existed, I would still regard earlier collections made by lawyers and other interested parties as the commonest general source of laws.

[64] See my *Western Aristocracies and Imperial Court*, 381ff.

marriage of Valentinian and Eudoxia, was a corresponding symbol of this political unity.

But we have only to glance at the immediate future to see what a narrowly-achieved symbol it was. In 430, just a few months after the Theodosian Code received its impetus from the imperial government, the Hippo of St Augustine came under Vandal siege. In a process that coincides almost exactly with the stages of editing and publication of the Code, the Vandals were conceded settlement in north Africa by a treaty concluded at Hippo on 11 February 435, and in October 439 took possession of Carthage. In Gaul, Gothic settlement in Aquitania, and later Burgundian settlement in the Rhone valley, began to break the hold of the government of Ravenna on all but the Mediterranean seaboard of the north-western provinces of the Empire. The preservation of the Theodosian Code in just these areas of Germanic occupation of Gaul reflects a very different historical phase from that in which the accumulation of the primary material for the Code had taken place. It was a period of political uncertainty in the western Mediterranean world, in which the actual compilation of the Theodosian Code, seen, in part at least, as a physical process of travel and access to widely scattered sources, can begin to seem not only a supremely optimistic, but even a modestly heroic, activity. The Theodosian Code, the first fully official attempt since the publication of the Twelve Tables by a Roman government to collect its own legislation,[65] is one of the last expressions, as well as one of the last symbols, of Roman imperial unity.[66]

---

[65] This is to evoke the opening words of Mommsen's Prolegomena, p. IX; though cf. (emphasising the officially sponsored character of the Gregorian and Hermogenian Codes), Turpin, op. cit. (n. 9 above), at 625f.

[66] The final version of this chapter owes much to the criticism of Boudewijn Sirks, both at the St Andrews Colloquium and in conversations and correspondence since then. There remain differences of emphasis and interpretation between us, but we are agreed both that the discussion is productive, and that much remains to be done.

2. The Sources of the Code[1]

Boudewijn Sirks

1. This chapter examines the way in which the Theodosian Code was compiled and the effect of this on its structure, particularly of the texts contained therein. Here we inevitably encounter Seeck, whose theories still dominate the field. Far more than any other author before or since, Seeck was engaged in elucidating the dates of the constitutions of the Theodosian Code, beginning with his *Die Zeitfolge der Gesetze Constantins (Zeitfolge)* in 1899[2] and culminating in his *Regesten der Kaiser und Päpste (Regesten)* in 1919.[3] Seeck set out to ascertain the dates and the locations mentioned in the texts of the Theodosian Code. In the course of his research he soon realised the need first to examine the way the Theodosian compilers had gathered and used their material.[4] It is this preparatory work which is of interest for us: namely, Seeck's theories concerning the sources and collection of the basic texts, and how the compilers dealt with them; his dating of the constitutions has received ample criticism, first by Mommsen and most recently by Voss.[5] I shall first discuss Seeck's methodology (which did not undergo any change between 1899 and 1919), then proceed to deal with the differences between the designs of 429 and 435 and the way the compilers may have worked, and conclude by looking at the Theodosian Code from another perspective.

2. Seeck's view of the legislative process of the Empire was that

---

[1] I wish to express my sincere gratitude to Prof. Dr Roger S. Bagnall, the Dean of Columbia Law School and Columbia University in New York for a Visiting Scholarship which enabled me to embark on the research for this contribution. I further want to thank Dr K. Worp and Prof. N. van der Wal for their remarks on a draft of this, and Andrew Lewis for his correction of my English.

[2] Seeck, 'Die Zeitfolge der Gesetze Constantins', *ZSS RA* 10 (1889), 1-44, 177-251; reprinted in *Materiali per una Palingenesia delle Costituzioni Tardo-Imperiali* 2 (Milan, 1983).

[3] Seeck, *Regesten der Kaiser und Päpste* (1919).

[4] *Zeitfolge; Regesten* vii-viii.

[5] Mommsen's criticism was devastating (in 'Das theodosische Gesetzbuch', *ZSS RA* 21 (1900), 179-90). W.E. Voss, in his review of the re-edition of *Zeitfolge, ZSS RA* 106 (1989), 632-45, underlines Seeck's imprudence. This lies, however, outside the scope of this chapter.

imperial enactments were made in the form of a letter (leaving aside the far less numerous imperial edicts and the letters to the senate).[6] The emperor had a letter containing a regulation written to a magistrate, including an order to promulgate it, and then signed the letter. The magistrate received the letter and promulgated its contents by means of an edict (if necessary he ordered a lower magistrate to promulgate; this alters nothing).[7] It was only by the promulgation (*propositio*) that the rule became legally valid.[8]

From this procedure three dates emerge, and three locations: date (the day and month, D1, and consulate, C1) and place (P1) of the imperial signing, date (D2, C2) and place (P2) of the acceptance by the magistrate, and date (D3, C3) and place (P3) of the promulgation. Since the consulate was put after the location, we will refer to these entries as D1-P1-C1, D2-P2-C2 and D3-P3-C3.[9] These three dates were all registered on the imperial letter kept in the archives of the receiving magistrate: the first as part of the text after the entry of data or a similar entry, the second and third noted down in the margin after the entries of *acc(epta) and p(ro)p(osita)*, or similar entries.[10] Seeck refers to *NVal* 1.3 (of 450) as a splendid example of this.[11]

Between D1 and D2 or D3 several days, and often longer, might elapse.[12] The annotated letter remained in the archive of the magistrate.

Thus the text the compilers found in the addressee's archives had the following structure:

<text>-data-(D-P-C)1-acc-(D-P-C)2-pp-(D-P-C)3

Seeck considered that the letters in the archives of the receiving magistrates were the primary source of texts used by the compilers. The archives furnished the majority ('die grosse Masse') of the texts, a proportion which became larger the older the texts were.[13] The

---

[6] *Regesten* 2.28-4.9. For the latter it sufficed to record it in the archives of the senate.

[7] *Regesten* 10.19-26; in that case *data* may refer to the letter sent by the magistrate (*Regesten* 11.1-3).

[8] *Regesten* 9.27-8.

[9] (1)The emperor writes a letter: <text> *data* <D(ate)1> <P(lace)1> <C(onsulate)1>: <text>-data-D1-P1-C1; The text includes the name of the addressee in the dative.
(2)The magistrate receives the letter and adds in the margin: *acc(epta)* <D(ate)2> <P(lace)2> <C(onsulate)2>: acc-D2-P2-C2;
(3)The text is promulgated by an edict, which is mentioned in the margin: p(ro)p(osita) <D(ate)3> <P(lace)3> <C(onsulate)3>: pp-D3-P3-C3.

[10] *Regesten* 10.27ff.

[11] *Regesten* 2.27, 4.12-15.

[12] *Regesten* 10.27.

[13] *Regesten* 2.12, 2.16-17, 2.24, 2.25. In *Zeitfolge* 6-7 Seeck states that the *proposita* present reflect the state of the archives. Where the barbarians had roamed around, archives had been destroyed and indeed we find no *proposita* there. For the rest, unlike

imperial archives in Constantinople were used for the texts of the laws issued in the West and sent to the East, and for those laws which had been sent to a collective body of magistrates.[14] Geographically the West contributed more than the East; another argument for a provincial provenance.[15]

Further, according to Seeck, the addressed magistrates kept an 'Aktenbuch', a record of, *inter alia*, the letters sent or received. (Seeck is not clear on this: beginning with a record of letters sent, he changes to a record of letters received; moreover, he does not make clear whether his 'Aktenbücher' were *commentarii* with excerpts or *acta* with integral copies, although he suggests the former.)[16] These have the following structure. At the beginning of every year the consulate was recorded (if the names were not yet known, a postconsulate was used). All the entries then were recorded with the name of the magistrate to whom it was addressed in the accusative, preceded by *ad*, then the day and month, and the place; after which the text of the letter was copied (including the D1-P1-C1 in the letter received).[17] In these cases the addressee would be identified in the accusative with a preceding *ad*, contrary to the dative of the letter. Where the compilers found the original letter, according to Seeck, they would always take over the dative.[18] In all cases they had to add the function of the addressee.[19]

The compilers used primarily the original letters in the archives of the high Constantinopolitan and provincial officials, but if these were not available, they had recourse to the *commentarii* (sent to

---

the emperors the provincial magistrates had uninterruptedly kept a permanent residence and consequently their archives were good (*Zeitfolge* 13-14). *Zeitfolge* 17: 'So sahen die Quellen des Codex Theodosianus aus: ein buntes Gemisch von Büchern, Rollen und einzelnen Blättern, aus allen Teilen des Reiches zusammengeschleppt, keine der andern an Art und Gestalt vollkommen gleich. Und was sie vereinigen und ordnen sollte, war nicht Wille und Verstand Eines Mannes, sondern die vielköpfige Weisheit einer Beamtencommission, der die allgemeinen Regeln ihres Verfahrens zwar durch eine einheitlichen Instruction vorgeschrieben waren, doch ohne dass dadurch die Willkür jedes Mitglieds verhindert wurde, sich in tausend kleinen Einzelheiten zu äussern.'

[14] *Regesten* 17.10-11, 25.13-15. However, apart from possible incidental dispatches this does not seem to have been the custom. If this had been the case, why the future tense used in the end of *CTh* 1.1.5?

[15] *Zeitfolge* 7-8; *Regesten* 2.

[16] *Regesten* 13.13-15. Seeck seems to confuse the *acta* and the *commentarii*. On 13.13-15 he speaks of 'Aktenbücher' known as *commentarii*, in which letters sent away were 'eingetragen' (registered). The provincial 'Urkundensammlungen' were modelled on these. Yet in 14.6 he speaks of 'Akten' and in 14.7ff he speaks of the archive of the Proconsul of Africa and texts ('Abschrift') of letters received.

[17] *Zeitfolge* 15; *Regesten* 14.21, 14.32-3. Such recording would have this structure: New Year: <consulate = C2> (or postconsulate) *ad* <name of addressee> <D2><P2> <text letter, incl. D1-P1-C1> *ad* etc.

[18] *Zeitfolge* 42-3; *Regesten* 17.1-8.

[19] *Zeitfolge* 43.

Constantinople by order of the emperor – thus Seeck, but this order is unsubstantiated).[20] Although Seeck cannot prove this, according to him the proposita and postconsulates retained in the Code provide an argument in favour.[21] A copy from such an archive would have the structure:

$$actum\text{-}<\!D2\!><\!P2\!>\text{-}<\!text\!>\text{-}<\!C2\!>[22]$$

This form is suggested by the postconsulates.[23]

The Theodosian compilers had to incorporate *valid* laws and to arrange these in chronological order. But since the moment of validity differed from province to province,[24] they realised that this was an impossible task. For that reason they took D1 as the distinguishing date, because there is only one D1 for the entire Empire, and left D2 and D3 out.[25] Consequently if we find a text with only a *propositum*, it is certainly taken from a local archive.[26]

Despite this, errors were still made (according to Seeck, who did not have a high opinion of the compilers). If there was no D1 the compilers took D3 for the *data*-date; sometimes they mechanically copied both the dates of *datum* and *acceptum* or *propositum*;[27] or merely the *proposita*-date since the *data*-date was missing.[28] With such an abundance of dates scribal errors were also made; and Seeck assumed that this happened often. The places were not essential and therefore often omitted. For that reason they are the more reliable when included.[29] Further, the *commentarii* gave occasion for wrong consulates: postconsulates were taken from the heading and placed with texts which had been received at a time when the new consuls were already known; a later correction would often produce a consulate one year too early or one year too late.[30] Then the fact that the same law was often found in several archives could (and would) cause confusion in the addressee, date and entry.[31]

After the constitutions had been collected and, if necessary, split up, the compilers corrected the consulates, using the consular *fasti* of Constantinople.[32] Then the names of the emperors were added with

[20] *Zeitfolge* 16.
[21] *Regesten* 15.2-30.
[22] *Regesten* 13.32-9.
[23] *Regesten* 15.2-30.
[24] *Regesten* 11.36-8, 80.16-18.
[25] *Zeitfolge* 16, 28-9; *Regesten* 11.21-4, 11.27-31.
[26] *Regesten* 11.38-41.
[27] *Regesten* 81.11-19.
[28] *Regesten* 11-31-5, 80.18-21.
[29] *Zeitfolge* 41; *Regesten* 106.3-5.
[30] *Zeitfolge* 26-8; *Regesten* 68.13-15.
[31] *Zeitfolge* 18; *Regesten* 7.
[32] *Regesten* 19.13, 22-7, 23.1-3, 73.44-74.2.

the use of the same fasti (in *commentarii* these were usually absent, the emperor being cited like this: Idem A). Divergences with the *fasti* appear more often in older laws.[33] Similarly postconsulates were corrected.[34]

3. This is how Seeck thought the collection of the basic texts took place. His views correspond with those previously formulated by Mommsen.[35] Later authors conform, with some variations.[36] Only Van der Wal has stressed that the Theodosian compilers used none other than the integral texts of the imperial constitutions since they were not allowed to use anything less, and he has rejected the idea that excerpts from *commentarii* were used. The Imperial *acta* furnished these integral texts. They were kept next to *commentarii*, and both records were divided according to subject-matter or category.[37]

4. It is indeed remarkable that Seeck in his *Regesten* almost completely leaves aside the question whether the emperors kept an archive or a copy book of letters sent, and whether, if extant, the compilers may have used these. In *Zeitfolge* he had, however, dealt extensively with this question.

In an article published in 1885 Bresslau had examined the origin of the papal recording books ('Copialbücher', 'Registerbücher', i.e. systematically arranged copy books of outgoing letters). He concluded that these had been modelled after the only existing records of that time: those of the Roman emperors and their officials. Bresslau next examined the form of the records: were these (a) (loose) copies of drafts, (b) (loose) copies of the final documents, or (c) books in which authentic copies of the final documents were entered ('Registerbücher')? Bresslau determined on the latter on the basis of several arguments – for

---

[33] *Regesten* 21.30-1, 23.3-5.

[34] *Regesten* 22.30-4, 66.17.

[35] Mommsen presumed the eastern constitutions to have been taken from the archives at Constantinople, and rather from the archives of the high officials than from the emperor's. Some had been proposed in Berytus and thus had been collected by the law professors there. The western constitutions had been collected in their place of promulgation (*ex propositione earum publica*), with the exception of a private collection, prepared by a lawyer in Carthage (Mommsen, *Prolegomena*, xxix, under reference to his earlier article in *ZSS RA* 21 (1900), 164-75).

[36] Gaudemet mentions as sources next to the local archives collections of chronologically ordered constitutions in the central archives, referring to Volterra: J. Gaudemet, *La formation du droit séculier et du droit de l'église au IVe et Ve siècles* (1979), 58-61. Honoré, in accordance with the goal of his research, restricts himself to giving a detailed picture of the legislative process, which ended in a text read aloud before and signed by the emperor, after which promulgation followed: T. Honoré, 'The Making of the Theodosian Code', *ZSS RA* 103 (1986), 136-7; the compilers had to ferret the laws out of central and provincial archives (161-2).

[37] N. van der Wal, 'Die Textfassung der spätrömischen Kaisergesetze in den Codices', *BIDR* (1986), 1-27.

example that books were more convenient to keep and were indeed used, and that loss of a book led to the loss of texts over a period, for instance one year (attested for the Gregorian Code). Further he found similar editing marks ('Kanzleivermerke', such as *eodem exemplo*) in both imperial and papal texts, and this in the fourth, fifth and sixth centuries. These 'Registerbücher', which contained the full text with *inscriptio* and *subscriptio* in often abbreviated form, thus formed a uninterrupted source for the compilers of Theodosius' and Justinian's Code and were indeed their main source. *Proposita* noted down in the margin may have been drawn from the answers of the addressees (this is, however, not probable).[38] We will refer to these books as copy books, as distinct from the *commentarii* which contained mere excerpts.[39]

Seeck admitted that such copy books had existed, and conceded that, where such editing marks were found, the text had to derive from the imperial archive. However, he rejected Bresslau's conclusion that these were copies of the final documents, maintaining that copies of drafts were involved.[40] According to him many copy books were lost once Diocletian started to travel around the Empire. By the time Arcadius and Honorius took up permanent residence again, the habit of copying had been lost.[41] Only in the provinces had the custom remained.[42] Had all these books not been lost, the compilers would certainly not have had to resort to the provincial archives, as it would of course have been easier to use the 'Copialbücher'.[43]

Seeck's argument is not convincing, since it is conditional upon the extent to which he can prove that the compilers used provincial archives. The only arguments he adduces for this are the *proposita* and similar entries (merely *c*. 200 out of more than 2,300). Yet Seeck, while

---

[38] H. Bresslau, 'Die Commentarii der römischen Kaiser und die Registerbücher der Päpste', *ZSS RA* 6 (1885), 242-60. The argument against the provenance of the *proposita* from reply letters is that there would have been as many *proposita* as there were provinces, theoretically. There is no trace of this.

[39] Bresslau identifies these 'Registerbücher' with the imperial *commentarii*, although these are supposed to have contained mere excerpts. There is, however, no need to make this step. *Commentarii* may well have been used in combination with copy books with the integral texts (such as *acta*), providing quick access to the latter.

[40] *Zeitfolge* 9; *Regesten* 4.

[41] *Zeitfolge* 10-11; *Regesten* 13.13-15.

[42] *Zeitfolge* 13: 'Nennt umgekehrt die Ueberschrift einen afrikanischen Beamten, so muss das Exemplar des Gesetzes, welches die Compilatoren des Codex benutzten, entweder dem Hofarchiv oder einem der afrikanischen entnommen sein. Im ersteren Falle wird das Propositum ganz fehlen, im zweiten kann es zwar auch weggelassen sein, doch falls es vollständig erhalten ist, so wird es Karthago oder Hadrumetum oder irgend eine andere Stadt Afrikas nennen. Für das Hofarchiv haben wird die Führung von Copialbücher leugnen müssen; doch der Grund, welcher zum Aufgeben diesen alten und trefflichen Kanzleigewohnheit führte, machte sich nicht in den Provinzen geltend. Der Kaiser zog immerfort im Reiche umher; der Proconsul von Afrika bereiste zwar auch von Zeit zu Zeit seinen Verwaltungsbezirk, doch seine ständige Residenz blieb zu allen Zeiten Karthago.'

[43] *Zeitfolge* 11-12.

admitting the existence of copy books, did not prove that the imperial chancelleries stopped keeping them. For instance the Novels of Theodosius, which the emperor sent in 447 to the West, are an argument that the habit had remained in existence. These Novels will have been copied from his own copy books (Bresslau mentioned two entries, in *NTh* 7.4 and 26, as proof for this).[44] We often find emperors referring to previous regulations. How could they do this, if they had no access to them in their own archives? Even the famous *c.Sirm.*1 of AD 333, often cited as an example of the disorganisation of archives in the Empire, presupposes an organised imperial archive.

Seeck took *NVal* 1.3 as the model of the basic text the Theodosian compilers used. But how do we know that their sources had this structure and not, for example, that of the Novels of Theodosius?[45] Moreover, Seeck's argument that the copies used must have come from provincial archives in view of their structure is not compelling. A copy in the imperial copy books will have carried the date $D1$-$P1$-$C1$, and no signature (the consulate being taken from the text itself and not from the heading; see §6 below). But such a copy would be identical to the copy of the letter in the provincial archive as usually rendered in the Theodosian Code: with the subscription $D1$-$P1$-$C1$ taken from the full subscription and the signature being left out. Consequently we may not assume that a text in the Code with the mark *data* necessarily came from the archive of the addressee. Since there are good reasons to assume the existence of such imperial copy books, we may only do so if we have evidence of a provincial provenance; for instance, an accompanying *acceptum* or *propositum*, or a date that fits better an *acceptum* or *propositum*. Conversely, if only *data* is present we may assume the obvious, namely an origin in those central archives.

Another argument against Seeck's propositions is of a practical nature. If the letter actually sent was the primary source for the compilers, is it not likely that they would first have recorded all laws sent out, and then checked these in the provincial archives? Thus they would have been certain (at least to the extent that the imperial archives were complete) that they had collected all laws enacted. Yet if one proceeds in this way, and if one realises that the date of the signing of the law is the date to be used, then there is no further need to run a check in the other archives (except for filling lacunae).

The consequences of this are that *data* now refers to an origin in the archive of the sender and *accepta* and *proposita* to an extraction from the archive of the addressee, unless arguments for a different interpretation can be adduced. The statistical evidence corresponds

[44] See further §6 for these Novels.

[45] According to Liebs the compilation of the Valentinian Novels, based on a collection of Theodosian Novels, was done in Rome in 460 or 461; see D. Liebs, *Die Jurisprudenz im spätantiken Italien (260-640 n. Chr.)* (Berlin, 1987), 188, 190.

much better with this. 85 per cent of the basic constitutions (i.e. the texts before the dividing process) carry merely *data* with one date. According to Seeck these basic constitutions with *data* (or a similar entry) were for the greater part or all copies from (provincial) archives where D2-P2-C2 and D3-P3-C3 had been left out; this notwithstanding the fact that in only 6 per cent of these 85 per cent could he demonstrate such an origin,[46] and that he states that in three-quarters or four-fifths of these laws with *data* the dates were correct.[47] Now, however, we may assume that these came from the imperial archives. In the end we may suspect for 9 per cent at most an origin other than the imperial copy books (in Constantinople, Rome or Ravenna), private collections (such as the Italian or African, as suggested by Mommsen), or law schools (such as those in Berytus or Constantinople).[48] This confirms Van der Wal's postulate (see above section 3).

Besides, Seeck's own attitude to the dates and places of the constitutions is revealed in the way he assumed that the compilers deviated from the basic pattern. Elsewhere he remarked with regard to the way the addressee is formulated that there are anomalies which indicate that the dative was also used in the *commentarii*; he explains this by referring to a difference between sources of recent and older date.[49] His methodological assumptions left him, one has to say, considerable scope for adaptation of the date or place.

5. We return for one moment to the difference in the mode of address. Seeck used this to support his theory of provincial provenance. *Ad* with the accusative would indicate an extraction from the *commentarii*, the dative a copy from the original letter. This would also explain why we find the former more frequently among the older constitutions. Lacking the originals in their sources, the compilers had recourse to the *commentarii*. It is certain, however, that we should not attach any

---

[46] He counted 49 cases of deleted *proposita*, 201 cases of *proposita* or a similar entry, and *c.* 70 cases of a erroneously substituted postconsulates (on a total of 2777 fragments or *c.* 2300 basic constitutions) (*Regesten* 82.27-30; previously in *Zeitfolge* 4-5). Yet Seeck based himself on *c.* 200 out of *c.* 2300 or *c.* 2500 texts, and for the addressees on the defective first books. This is really no basis for Seeck's contention.

[47] *Regesten* 1.12-15 and n. 1.

[48] Of the remaining 15 per cent 5 per cent have no entry at all, and 6 per cent *proposita*. The combination of *data* and *proposita* or *accepta* accounts for 1 per cent. Yet of these 7 per cent more than half come from Rome, Constantinople, Carthage and Hadrumetum, or Berytus and might be drawn from private collections. Therefore the compilers will have used the imperial archives in Rome or Ravenna and private collections may have supplemented this, subject of course to examination of their authenticity. The Italian or African collection, suggested by Mommsen, and probably taken to Rome after the invasion by the Vandals in 429, or that of the law school of Berytus may have been such ones, and there may have been others. All this does not mean that still other archives or collections were not used in addition to the imperial copy books.

[49] *Regesten* 17.15-16, 23-4.

significance to this difference: both forms were used in correspondence during the entire Empire (so Kühner, Gaudemet).[50]

Moreover, the statistical evidence points to another conclusion.[51] Seeck linked the use of the dative with Theodosius I taking up permanent residence in Constantinople (while his predecessors used to travel permanently). As a result the laws enacted, including those sent over from the West, could now be collected at a permanent place. This archive enabled the compilers to use originals from that period onwards.[52] Yet closer examination of the data, distinguished according to eastern and western origin, shows that before 379 *ad* with the accusative dominated both in East and West.[53] With Theodosius' accession in 379 the dative became preponderant in the East,[54] while in the West *ad* with the accusative continued to be generally used until Theodosius went to the West in 388. From then on, and certainly after his return to Constantinople in 394, both in East and West the dative became paramount (see Appendix 2). The obvious conclusion is that Theodosius or his aides had a preference for the dative which both of the chanceries followed after Theodosius took charge of them.[55]

6. Seeck assumed that the compilers corrected the dates by means of the eastern *fasti consulares*.[56] Did they in fact need to do this? They had to cite the dates (day, month and consulate) of the laws included, since the laws would otherwise lack force as a result of the prescript of *CTh* 1.1.1 (322). The reason for this requirement is unknown. It may have been introduced to make verification possible in proceedings. Yet it is not specified which date is intended and apparently D1, D2 or D3 sufficed. Consequently copying the date found would have sufficed for

---

[50] R. Kühner/F. Holzweissig, *Ausführliche Grammatik der Lateinischen Sprache* (Hannover, 1912), II.1, 519; Gaudemet, op. cit. (n. 36) 59.

[51] As we find the division between the two everywhere in the Theodosian Code, in every book and title, we may assume that the division already existed prior to the distribution over the rubrics. Otherwise the compilers would have homogenised the titles. The difference thus existed either in the sources or came into existence during the copying from the sources. The first is Seeck's position. The second possibility assumes a convention or a prescript with the copyists. This, however, is also open to objections. Is it possible to distinguish clusters, attributable to one copier? If this were possible, it might also indicate a single source, but not necessarily: various persons may have worked from one source. And the change under Theodosius would have to be explained as being the result of the copying of one person, or of an imposed prescript. Since this all is at the moment impossible to examine, and since there is a good explanation offered in the text, this second possibility is to be left aside.

[52] *Regesten* 17.8-13. It is true that for 311-385 the dative is present in *c*. 25 per cent of the cases, and for 386-437 in *c*. 8 per cent.

[53] For the period 313-378, there are 771 constitutions with ad with the accusative and 194 with the dative, which is certainly a predominance of *ad* with the accusative.

[54] As a result of hypercorrection?

[55] If Seeck had been right, the change would have occurred simultaneously in East and West.

[56] Similarly *CLRE*, 77-8.

the compilers (it is hardly conceivable that the compilers would invent dates).[57] There is indeed no order for the compilers to do what Seeck wanted them to do and in fact Seeck did not always find the eastern version of a consulate.

Seeck's argument for his assumption is that the dates should be easily recognisable, viz. by making them identical to the official *fasti*. In this way the users of the Code could distinguish between the earlier and the later constitutions, whether these were in the same title or not.[58] Apart from the fact that this would not make sense in a code containing only valid laws (see §7 below),[59] if the compilers and the prospective users disposed of *fasti* it is still not certain that these were impeccable.[60] Certainly the compilers will have used a consular list, and occasionally they or the copyists may have 'corrected' a date; but this may also have been the source of text corruption.

The question becomes acute when dealing with the postconsulates. Seeck assumed that these were corrected, sometimes wrongly, while some were overlooked. In many cases Seeck thought he could discover such a correction. The authors of *CLRE* deny the use of postconsulates at the imperial court since the emperor would always know the consul he had designated himself and therefore preferred to use the *et qui fuerit nuntiatus*-formula in which the designated consul is mentioned.[61] They doubt Seeck's reconstructions and try to explain the remaining postconsulates (not always convincingly).[62] Yet, like

[57] *Zeitfolge* 20-2: if the date was missing, this was due to a copyist's error, which led the compilers to invent a date in order not to have to go to the archive again. Yet, in view of the care for a good text (see the example of the Gesta Carth., mentioned by Seeck himself), may we suppose this? In our opinion not. *CLRE* 75 n. 14 cites Maas (P. Maas, 'Besprechung Theodosianus cum const. Sirmondianis et leges novellae, edd. Th. Mommsen – P.M. Meyer', *147te Göttingische gelehrten Anzeigen* (1906), 641-62; repr. in P. Maas, *Kleine Schriften* (München, 1973), 608-28) approvingly, who posited that a group of nine fragments originally did not bear a day-date. To include them nevertheless the compilers invented these. They all vary. Yet: if this were true, they would have added the day-date to the basic constitution, thus generating the same day-date. Moreover, the consulates also differ. It seems more probable that we are dealing here with several laws and corrupted dates.

[58] *Zeitfolge* 26; *Regesten* 18.30-9, 66.19-20.

[59] The argument has sense for a Code of the first design, but not for the final Code of the first design, nor for a Code of the second design, since in these only rules still valid would be included.

[60] *CLRE* 28, 48.   [61] *CLRE* 28.

[62] *CLRE* 79ff. states that the *e.q.f.n.*-formula was current at court itself up till the latest date in the year it is attested, but that the same does not hold for the postconsulates, contrary to what Seeck assumed. Of the 41 fragments with a postconsulate (some stemming from the same basic constitution) 19 may derive from a collection made in Africa. This leaves 22 fragments which are eliminated on the basis of a hypothesis offered by the authors of *CLRE*. Mostly the hypothesis sounds attractive, but for the postconsulate of *NTh* 22.2 [443] the explanation given cannot hold. According to the authors of *CLRE* the (western) postconsulate is an *accepta*-date added in the West, after the law was dispatched late in 442. Yet this *novella* was sent, with others, in Oct. 447 by Theodosius to the West (see *NTh* 2) and their promulgation there was ordered in

postconsulates, these *e.q.f.n.*-formulas then should have been corrected, but we find them often, and neither Seeck nor the authors of *CLRE* can explain this.[63]

The Novels of Theodosius furnish the answer. In these we see for the first months of the year merely the eastern consul mentioned, sometimes with the addition of *e.q.f.n.* In one case, where there were two western consuls to be appointed, we find a postconsulate.[64] Thus it would seem that only when both consuls were appointed by the emperor of the other half would a postconsulate be used until their names had been communicated, and that otherwise the name of one's own consul would be used until the other's name arrived; the addition of *e.q.f.n.* was not necessary. Since *e.q.f.n.* is sometimes missing, we may conclude that the consulates were entered at the end or beginning of the copies and re-copied with these and not from the heading of the copy book. Moreover, these dates were not corrected by either Theodosius' or Valentinian's clerks. There was indeed no reason to do so. The laws carried a day and identifiable consulate and this was enough. The same applies to the laws that the Theodosian compilers collected. Although we may be quite sure that, for example, for the year 435 they or their clerks will have known both consuls' names, the *e.q.f.n.*-formula was retained.[65] Apparently there was no order to 'correct',[66] and since the consulate as dating system was less venerated than it used to be[67] they did not feel any obligation to do so.

June 448 (see *NVal* 26). It is not probable that the law was sent separately to the West, in view of the text of *NTh* 2 (it rather is more probable that we lost some of the Novels, now known via Justinian's Code). Besides, *NVal* 11 of four days later was already dated after the (western) consuls of 443, who would have been known in Rome already in January. It is therefore highly unlikely that the date refers to an acceptum in the west. It is more probable that the date is a postconsulate of the form *PC SS*, since in that year both consuls were appointed by the West and their names might not have arrived in March 443. With *SS* the consuls of 442 mentioned in the preceding *novella* (*NTh* 22.1) were meant (cf. the manuscript Delta, which has *cons. supra scribt.* under *NTh* 10.1). This abbreviation would then have been written out in the West in the western form of that consulate.

[63] *CLRE* 78 states that this formula often was corrected. But why not the examples below?

[64] For the year 438: lastly in February; 439: in April; 444: in July; in 443 a p.c. in March.

[65] Four constitutions, of respectively 29 January, 12 March, 3 August and 9 October, all carry *e.q.f.n.* A fifth constitution, of 14 November, has the full consulate. The addressees were officials, certainly or almost certainly residing in Constantinople. The year is 435, and the clerks who copied the constitutions for the Code will have known the consuls; they may actually have copied these in that year. Moreover, the dissemination of the missing consul, the emperor of the other half, cannot have been here that slow, certainly not in Constantinople. Why, then, is the consulate not corrected, if not for the reason that there was no obligation to do so?

[66] Since the consulate was correct, but not complete.

[67] *CLRE* 28 observes that by the beginning of the fifth century neither imperial courts bothered whether the announcement of the new consul of the other court took a long time.

Consequently the cases in which consulates are 'corrected' may have occurred by accident or where a consulate was unintelligible. It is true that the compilers will have needed *fasti consulares* in order to put the laws in chronological order.[68] Yet the laws they utilised had a date and consulate and this sufficed.[69]

7. If we may assume that the compilers used basically the imperial copy books in Constantinople and Rome (or Ravenna), and a few reliable private collections, and kept to the dates found with the texts, i.e. the dates as entered at the moment of copying, the picture of how the Code was assembled changes. The six years between 429 and 435 are often assumed to have been used mainly or entirely for gathering the constitutions in far-away provinces. Now we may assume that this was a relatively simple task, soon finished, and that the delay may have been due to other factors.

It lies outside the scope of this chapter to enter substantially into the purposes Theodosius had in the design of 429 or of 435, the relation between these and the reasons why the 429 plan was not completely executed. It suffices here to state briefly our understanding in order to support the rest of our argument.[70]

It seems as if the design of 435 concerning the editing of the constitutions is more detailed than that of 429, or even replaces it. Such a labour was perhaps not yet foreseen, but it was inevitable: although in 429 only the elimination of the *inanis verborum copia* is mentioned, this will have borne – *vide* Van der Wal – upon the phrasing of the main text. It must have posed a problem for the compilers, judging from the prescripts of the 435 design which imply

---

[68] *Regesten* 18.30.

[69] Some may have been corrupt, but – if we keep to Seeck's own figure – not more than in a quarter or a fifth of the cases, and even in these cases it does not usually seem to have mattered that much. For Seeck 'corrupt' means different from the real date. Yet how could the compilers know this? It did not matter to them, as long as they could establish whether the rule was still in force or not.

[70] The link between the establishment of the law school of Constantinople in 425 and the plan of 429 is obvious, but does not need to be the sole reason. Of the abundant literature on this, see *inter alia*: B. Albanese, 'Sul programma legislativo esposto nel 429 da Teodosio II', *APal* 38 (1975, 251-69; A.D. Manfredini, 'Osservazioni sulla compilazione teodosiana (*CTh* 1,1, 5.6 e *NTh* 1), in margine a *CTh* 9,3,4 (*de famosis libellis*)', *Atti Accademia Costantiniana* 4 (1981), 385-428; G.G. Archi, *Teodosio II e la sua codificazione* (Napoli, 1976), with other literature; Gaudemet (n. 36) 48-52; id., 'Aspects politiques de la codification théodosienne', *Atti di un incontro tra storici e giuristi Firenze 2-4 maggio 1974* (Milano, 1976), 261-279 (repr. in J. Gaudemet, *Études de droit romain* (Camerino, 1979), I, 349-69; T. Honoré (n. 36) 168-89 discusses four factors (166-7 on the discussion whether or not the design of 435 is the continuation of that of 429 (he and Archi consider it to be); S.-A. Fusco, '*Constitutiones principum* und Kodifikation in der Spätantike', *Chiron* 4 (1974), 609-28.) See for this, *inter alia*, G.G. Archi, op. cit. with other literature and also Manfredini, above. A reason for the change may have been that it required good editions of the jurists. This may have taken too much time to prepare.

questions arising from this work. So the second design may be regarded as a more detailed formulation of the first, changing the order of work and solving questions that had apparently arisen.[71] Such questions could have been thrown up during the first stages of the 429 plan. The design of 435 would have answered them, and therefore this design did not abrogate that of 429, but elaborated upon it.

As constitutions might be split up into fragments after 435, the initial concept (of 429) of reproducing the original constitutions completely (except for the preface and conclusion)[72] was abandoned: now the actual rules became central. This becomes more evident when we perceive that the compilers not only made a division when they attributed the rules of a constitution to different titles, but even when they were placed in the same title. Often we see fragments of the same constitution successively placed in one title. Fusco has observed that this is less harmless than it seems: stripped of its context a rule may gain a wider application.[73] Yet this may have reflected an already existing interpretation. The systematisation of Justinian's Code was to go a step further again. Here the compilers added fragments of one constitution to other constitutions (or fragments), thus creating a composite rule (*sanctio*).[74] Although in all three instances the validity of the rule depended upon its original promulgation, in the case of such a composite rule only one date was taken.

Did the compilers exclude from the compilation rules abrogated by later constitutions or no longer observed? The *ad vim sanctionis non pertinentia* were to be deleted. A rule, no longer in use, has no force any more. Therefore this prescription implies that obsolete rules have to be omitted. And what would the use of editing obsolete rules have been? In practice it appears indeed that the compilers, if not everywhere, at least for the greater part omitted rules no longer valid or applied, or which are restated by later laws.[75] Repetitions appear to be illusory, reducible to

[71] Such questions would have been, regarding the differences between the texts of 429 and 435: (a) Had a constitution to be universally valid, or were those with a regionally limited validity to be included too? (The administrative division of the Empire would give to this problem.) (b) Putting a constitution on more than one subject only in one title was unpractical, and duplicating it added unnecessarily to the volume of the code: so would it not be better to divide such constitutions according to the subject-matter covered? (c) Should not the texts be edited in order to clarify the remaining rule, actually in force? (Van der Wal observes that the mere removal of preface and conclusion would anyway necessitate an adaptation of the text.)

[72] The systematical concept of, presumably, the Gregorian and Hermogenian Codes and the first design, in which rescripts and constitutions in their entirety had been collected in the most apt titles.

[73] Fusco (n. 70) 614-16.

[74] *C.Deo 9; c.Summa 1: colligentur, efficientur.*

[75] We often find references in the Theodosian Code to laws not incorporated in the Code but which should have been incorporated were the Code of 438 to have contained also obsolete laws; for example *CTh* 13.5.26; 13.9.3, 14.3.12.

rules for different regions.[76] *CTh* 1.1.5.pr. mentions such regional validity. This actually renders the chronology obsolete (as it is in Justinian's Code). The principle of *lex posterior derogat legi priori*, once applied in a codification, leaves no traces and is no longer of use.[77] This had been foreseen, perhaps, for the final code and consequently it would have been no real change of policy. The result is, however, that a title now represented the current state of the law, in as far as laid down in legislation from between 311 and 437 (every law still deriving its authority from the enacting emperor). Besides, the original plan to include obsolete laws was aimed at scholarly use. The present code was still usable for the law schools, but we find forensic and administrative practice expressly mentioned in *NTh* 1.3. We may suspect that this change in objective occurred between 429 and 435 and found its expression in the exclusion of obsolete rules.[78]

The design of 435 also changed the order of work. In 429 editing was foreseen in the second phase, after the insertion of the Gregorian and Hermogenian Codes and the legal writings. Now this was to be done at the end of the first stage. Theoretically the compilers could still have started, upon completion of this part, with the insertion of the constitutions of the Gregorian and Hermogenian Codes, and the

[76] Such in any case is the outcome of our research into the law on the *navicularii, pistores, suarii* and some other *corpora*, published in *Food for Rome* (Amsterdam, 1991); a similar phenomenon is distinguishable with the decurions. On the other hand, a rule in the Theodosian Code did not have universal validity by the very fact of its inclusion. So there would be a difference in this respect between the ultimate goal of the 429 design and the 435 design. The ambiguity with regard to application within a certain territory is lifted, but the differences of territorial validity have been maintained. Limited validity can be deduced from the addressees and the place of enactment or promulgation.

[77] If only valid law is to be included, then there has to be a concept of the law presently valid. On basis of this obsolete rules are omitted. The remainder may be ordered according to preference. In the Theodosian Code it is a combination of systematic order (headwords, *tituli, quae sunt vocabula negotiorum*), with some relation to the order of the Perpetual Edict, and chronology within the titles. The chronology was probably retained since this was prescribed in the first phase. See also A.J.B. Sirks, 'Observations sur le Code Théodosien', *Subseciva Groningana* 2 (1985), 30-1.

[78] And thus useless for practice. A consequence of this is that we may not presuppose that the Code contains repetitions (except for some errors in the compilation). Secondly, if the Code would contain all legislation still valid of the period 311-437, this would amount to *c.* 2,700 constitutions, i.e. an average of 21 per annum. Exclusion of the obsolete laws raises this figure. It depends on one's appreciation whether this output of legislation is to be considered high, low or normal. (On the basis of Seeck's *Regesten* and without the missing constitutions: for 361-437 the average for the entire Empire is 24 per annum; in 364-389 for the West 17 per annum, for the East 11.5 per annum and for the entire Empire 28.4 per annum; for 395-437 for the entire Empire 17 per annum. There are considerable variations per year. Yet it is impossible to conclude anything from this. All our figures come from the Theodosian Code. Therefore any statement based on it is invalid. We cannot compare with a complete year, independent from the Code. There are constitutions known which are not included in the Code, but they may have been left out because they were not *leges generales*. The variations over the years can to a great extent be connected with certain emperors like Valentinian I and Theodosius I.)

jurists' writings. Since the collection of post-Constantinian constitutions was to acquire the name of Theodosius, this second phase was apparently discarded or not proceeded with further. But since the constitutions in the Code had been weeded out and edited with these texts in mind, their insertion was no longer necessary. Thus the code supplements these earlier collections with the law produced over the last 137 years. The goal, set in 429, was realised, albeit in a restricted sense in regard to the time-span covered. This would explain why in the Roman senate's meeting of 438 the constitution of 429 was recited. The plan of 429, supplemented with details on the execution by the order of 435, had been successfully completed for its first stage: the constitutions of the (Christian) emperors.

Although a formal universalisation of the rules collected was lacking, despite Theodosius' intentions,[79] legal practice apparently was to harmonise divergent rules on the same subject, if they clashed.[80] It will not have been too difficult in many cases. On the one hand, most of the law was common to both parts and remained unchanged or involved only slight differences. On the other hand, how much do we know of local customs already recognised in law? Part of the divergence may be ascribed to this.

8. Some of Seeck's assumptions have been scrutinised and found wanting. This cannot diminish the greatness of a man who produced such a work as *Untergang der antiken Welt*. Yet, with all respect, did Seeck not expect too much from the compilers? His scathing remarks seem to suggest that in his view the compilation should have been a work of much higher precision as regards dates and places.[81] That was exactly what he needed, but it is not what the compilers set out to achieve. It is a clash of different goals and standards, a wrong methodology.

To elucidate this point let us look at the Code from a different point of view: not as a precursor of Justinian's Code, but as the latest in a series of unofficial or official compilations of imperial constitutions. As such the Theodosian Code stands in an intellectual tradition maintained by

[79] *CTh* 1.1.5 *in fine*. Since each administration already knew which rules applied in its territory, there was no need to indicate this in the Code, nor was this apparently considered to be necessary. It is, however, not to be excluded that the compilers originally had the intention that the laws should be unified. But this is not visible in the Code we have.

[80] A constitution could be applied, by way of interpretation or straightforwardly, in the other half of the Empire. The end of *CTh* 1.1.6 hints at such practices, which are attested in other places: *CTh* 12.1.158 [398, W]; *CJust* 6.61.5 [473, E].

[81] Several remarks: 'immer nachlässiger' (23.5), 'stumpfsinnige Kopisten' (14.23), 'Inkonsequenz und Liederlichkeit' (66.18), 'in keiner Beziehung Sorgfalt' (66.29), 'ihre große Nachlässigkeit' (81.10), 'im Fortgang ihrer Arbeit immer nachlässiger' (82.1), 'in gewohnter Flüchtigkeit' (115.43). See also n. 13 for Seeck's depreciatory opinion of the Theodosian compilers.

lawyers. What intellectual standards do we see applied?

9. An early compilation such as Papirius Iustus' *constitutiones libri XX* (*c.* AD 170)[82] merely mentions the emperors and gives an account of the rescript. Other authors sometimes mention the addressee and give quotations. The exact date apparently did not matter. Since these were not official collections, their reliability will have depended upon the author and the sources he used. Presumably collections gained authority in practice, which would suggest a check by the judges. The various additions might have facilitated such a check. But, as Volterra observed, as the imperial constitutions gained importance as a source of law, so did collections of them, and we see some uniformity emerge.[83] The Gregorian Code usually mentions the emperor and the addressee, and sometimes a date (of the *propositio*), although dates may have been lost in the textual tradition.[84] Likewise the Hermogenian Code.[85] Conventions were thus established. In 322 Constantine decreed that all constitutions and edicts should bear a day and a consulate, viz. when cited in proceedings. Otherwise they would lack force. This may have been done in order to make checking easy; Constantine's decision will have fitted into an existing convention.

The Fragmenta Vaticana is a collection made after 317. It consists not only of rescripts, but also of constitutions in the form of letters to officials and of excerpts from writings of jurists.[86] Why the letters and not the edicts? Since the position of the emperor had become dominant in the second century, it was inconceivable that the senate would make amendments in an *oratio* delivered to the senate by the emperor or his representative. Consequently the text of the *oratio* became more important than the subsequent senatusconsult. The same occurred with the edicts of the provincial governors. They would receive a letter from the emperor (either directly or by way of a high official), with the order to promulgate the contents in an edict. Again it is inconceivable that they would alter the contents, and consequently the text of the original letter became the more important. This importance is acknowledged by its designation as *lex edictalis*, which put it on the same legislative level as an imperial edict.[87] Publication remained

---

[82] Liebs (n. 45) 134.

[83] E. Volterra, 'Il problema del testo delle costituzioni imperiali', *Atti II Congr. Intern. soc. ital. del diritto* (Firenze, 1971), II, 948, 1094-7.

[84] On this Code: Liebs (n. 45) 134-7. Published probably in 291, divided in 15 or 16 books, each numbering 15-20 titles, containing rescripts over the period from Hadrian to Diocletian.

[85] Liebs (n. 45) 137-43. Published in 295 and containing rescripts over the period 293-April 295, divided into *c.* 100 titles.

[86] On this work Liebs (n. 45) 150-62. The inscriptions and subscriptions do not follow the patterns of the Gregorian and Hermogenian Code and seem to have been done casually.

[87] See N. van der Wal, *'Edictum und lex edictalis.* Form und Inhalt der Kaisergesetze

important as regards the moment the edict took effect in province or Empire, but not as regards the authoritative text. The rescripts in the Fragmenta Vaticana always bear a date, sometimes the date of a *datum*. The same goes for the other constitutions. Since the Fragmenta Vaticana most probably date from after Constantine's decree and will have complied with it, it follows that any plausible date sufficed. As far as the structure of the collections is concerned, the early ones were sometimes subdivided into books, the Gregorian Code into books and titles, the Hermogenian Code and the Fragmenta Vaticana into titles. In all cases the inscriptions are usually adapted by the authors.

We find variations, but what remains is the text which should be rendered faithfully. Textual corruption was public enemy number one, so to speak, in an era when texts were multiplied by manual copying and in a profession where much depended on their reliability. We see this care expressed several times: in the prohibition on using *notae* and the confirmation of the validity of all Paul's writings (*CTh* 1.4.1 [321] and 2 [327]), in the so-called Law of Citations (*CTh* 1.4.3 [426, W]), which in reality gives criteria for establishing textual reliability,[88] in the re-editing of the classical writers during the second half of the fourth century, in the wishes of the Roman senate in 438[89] and, lastly, in the plans for the Theodosian Code.[90]

How did the design of 429 for the Theodosian Code differ from this? In fact, the entire concept and structure does not differ from what we find in the Fragmenta Vaticana, except for the prescribed chronological order in the first version and the elimination in the final Code of diversity and repealed rules. Thus the Theodosian Code of 429 may be viewed as an improved collection within the tradition of legal collections. Nor is there any reason to suppose that the standard for the required date was suddenly set higher than before. After all, we can only surmise why Constantine required this. The compilers will have used the date probably as randomly – in our eyes – as the compiler of the Fragmenta Vaticana did. There was no need to check the publication date. There was no need to check the date in any case, as long as it was a plausible date. The important thing was the text

---

im spätrömischen Reich', *RIDA* 3e s. 28 (1981), 277-313, and the observation of G. Vidén, *The Roman Chancery Tradition* (Göteborg 1984), 73 n. 63 on this. Further on the law sources of the Romans, M. Kaser, *Römische Rechtsquellen und angewandte Juristenmethode* (Wien/Köln/Graz, 1986), 17-18, 20-1, 41; although not on the Late Roman Law.

[88] See A.J.B. Sirks, 'From the Theodosian to the Justinian Code', *Atti Accademia Costantiniana* 6 (1983 [1986]), 287-8.

[89] *Gesta Senatus* 5: 'Ne interpolentur constituta, plures codices fiant. Ne constituta interpolentur, omnes codices litteris conscribantur. Huic codici, qui faciendus a constitutionariis, notae iuris non adscribantur.' Other remarks concern the accessibility and dissemination of the Code.

[90] Even if the texts were to be adapted to present interpretation (i.e. practice), they should still be as much as possible identical to the original phrasing.

itself: this should contain no false words, and of course it should not be a falsification. For this purpose they would have checked the text and as soon as that had been done (preferably by comparing with the official copy, if not already copied from it) and the text had been found correct, the date was unimportant. Since rules rendered obsolete by disuse should be left out in the final Code, and diversity should be removed, the Code was even modern in this respect.

Yet the compilers encountered some difficulties during their work. What about restricted validity? The administrative division of the Empire? What about the adaptation of texts? Since the Code was to be used in the courts, should rules which had been repealed or which had passed into disuse nevertheless be included? Perhaps some of these questions had already been posited before 429. Practitioners of law will not have been interested in abolished laws. Nor will a final Code as envisaged by Theodosius have figured high on their list of requirements. The Gregorian and Hermogenian Codes were reliable editions, the major legal writings existed in reliable editions. The only thing needed right away was a good edition of laws enacted since the two Codes and still valid. In 435 the emperor took several decisions (no invalid rules; both eastern and western laws, without a decision about precedence; splitting, editing and adapting of the texts)[91] and the result was a Code of lesser ambition, with a definite bias towards legal practice and its demands, but also a Code in which actual rules systematised according to subject-matter are central. In this respect the Code as realised represents a change in the concept of collections of constitutions.

10. It appears that Seeck attached too great a significance to the texts of Theodosius' and Justinian's Code as sources of historical knowledge. In his view these texts were basically the final laws as promulgated, which meant that they represented the exact wording of the law and their dates the exact moment of application. Corruption had, however, set in as soon as the compilers amassed the texts and edited them. Yet Seeck, as a true nineteenth-century historian, attached too much importance to the texts as objective source.[92] The problem that the Theodosian Code and other collections of legal texts were designed to remedy was a lack of convenient access to reliable editions of legal texts. For this the legal texts as established in an *oratio* or an imperial letter sufficed. The date was an addition, prescribed by law but not regarded as important. Seen in the light of this, the Theodosian compilers did a good job, since their textual work is generally considered favourably.

---

[91] It appears from this that the dates as such did not pose a problem.
[92] And probably to the promulgated text as the actual law source. Yet see Kaser (n. 87) 10-11, 41 on this.

Postscript

In the light of Matthews' comments on the propositions made above, I would suggest for the reader's consideration the following questions. Any resolution of the problems raised will need to take account of these.

Matthews cites Gibbon, who used the Code rather as a work of history than of law, and of course historians have as much right to the Code as anyone else. However, the Code is and remains in the first place a lawbook and the compilers will have viewed it from a different perspective from modern historians. They were, as we are not, acquainted with the law in which the rules of the Code were embedded, and with its relation to the rules collected in the Gregorian and Hermogenian Codes. It is the same when legal historians use a literary source like Ammianus: no one can teach them the dangers inherent in too legal an approach to such a source better than Matthews.

It is as well to remember that legal historians such as Mommsen were so interested in the actual publication because of the rules: that would be the only valid text. For that reason Seeck proposed the idea that most of the constitutions had been stripped of *proposita* etc. Yet the collection of the novels of Theodosius II shows that the Romans themselves thought differently about this. For them the letter of the emperor was an adequate statement of the law, as was also the copy preserved in the file of the promulgators. Matthews doubts a systematic access to central archives. Otherwise there would have been more laws collected than there are now (the amount of basic laws not being impressive), there would be fewer discrepancies between different versions of the same laws, fewer indications of the circumstances in which the laws were received etc. (p. 41 above). How many more laws? How many discrepancies or indications otherwise? And on what basis may we assume that there would have been more of the earlier laws and fewer of the later? We do not even know any year's output of laws. What about the fact that some 80 per cent of all basic constitutions of the Code do not pose any discrepancy at all and merely have the mark *data*? Indeed, there are many references in the Code to laws which are apparently not included (they cannot all have been in the missing parts). How many laws might not have been included? 25 per cent? 50 per cent? This is important. We may assume that the compilers had a good knowledge of the law existing at that moment. So laws still in force will certainly have been included. If not, they would have been abolished by *NTh* 1, and it is unlikely that the compilers would have resigned themselves to this. As for the rest, everything depends on the question how many general laws were issued in 311-437, to which there is as yet no answer. Yet the greater this number, is it not the more probable that those omitted were left out on purpose? The argument that the older constitutions were more difficult to trace so that fewer were recovered is not watertight: they may just as well have been supplanted by newer rules. The variations in the figures of laws over years can be connected with known periods of higher legislative activity.

True, private persons copied laws of publicly posted texts. Yet is not the success of the Gregorian and Hermogenian Codes due precisely to the fact that they were collections made by an official close to the emperor and thus near the imperial archives, and for that reason undoubtedly much more complete than collections made in the provinces?

It would be interesting to see statistical evidence pointing to a predominant use of local archives. Since the reverse is the case, should we not assume, so long as there is no good argument to the contrary, that most of the constitutions were taken from central archives (whether the emperor's or the prefects')? It would be interesting to know whether, and if so why, my arguments against Seeck's methods and presumptions do not hold. Do we have reasons to assume that the provincial archives were in such a bad shape? How, for example, are the barbarian invasions in Gaul, Italy, Spain and Africa consistent with the so-called predominance of western constitutions? Would not the compilers have had knowledge of this?

Undeniably there are cases which are puzzling and Matthews is right to draw attention to them, but we should always keep in mind that contemporaries did not intend to use the Code to reconstruct imperial itineraries, Regesten or consulates, but to find the law.

Appendix 1. The fragments and basic constitutions of the Theodosian Code

The fragments of the Theodosian Code are found in three sources: manuscripts of the Code itself, the Breviarium Alaricianum, and Justinian's Code. There are references in other sources. The first two sources supply fragments, in principle authentic, the last supplies fragments which in some 50 per cent of the cases were re-edited by the Justinian compilers.[93] But such re-edition does not have to affect the inscription and subscription, except when the fragment is inserted into another fragment.[94] The references in other sources should not be

---

[93] Based on the first seven books of the Theodosian Code: of 338 *CJust* versions, 172 were altered, while 111 were not or fractionally changed. Krüger did not find it right to omit them merely on the ground of a possible alteration (P. Krüger, 'Über Mommsens Ausgabe des Codex Theodosianus', *ZSS RA* 26 (1905), 316-31, here 328; P. Krüger, 'Beiträge zum Codex Theodosianus V', *ZSS RA* 38 (1917), 21-2).

[94] Of the 757 fragments we can use for recomposing constitutions, 258 have a counterpart in Justinian's Code. Of these 11 are inserted; of the remaining 247, 233 had the addressee in the same form as their 'mother' (yet it is not impossible that there may have been reconstructions in Krüger's edition on the basis of the Theodosian text).

used for speculations on the form of the addressee etc.

The total of the fragments Mommsen took from the manuscripts and the Breviarium is 2,509, to which he added seven cases of references to fragments (one of which is probably confirmed by a *CJust* version). Of the 2,509 fragments two merely have a (partial) inscription or subscription.[95] In this way we possess books 7 to 16 almost complete, book 6 for the greater part and a lesser part of books 1 to 5.[96] This lack is partly made good by Justinian's Code. In this 261 fragments, originating in the Theodosian Code, figure without their version in the first two sources.[97] The total of known fragments is then 2,777 (2,509 + 261 + 7). However, a number of these fragments derive from the same constitution, as divisions according to different subjects or as *leges geminatae*. It is doubtful whether there is a real difference between these. Gaudemet has examined the *leges geminatae* and concluded that in most or all cases it is probable that they imply slightly different rules.[98] We therefore treat the 39 fragments of the *leges geminatae* as pertaining to 19 constitutions. By subtracting those 'extra' fragments of combinations, we obtain a figure of 2,307 constitutions (since 750 fragments constitute 283 constitutions). This figure includes 10 fragments or constitutions of uncertain date which should be excluded when examining the textual variations. Of these 2,307 (or 2,297) constitutions, 283 (*c.* 12 per cent) covered more than one topic (since they were split up).

We see that the basic collection the compilers used consisted of 2,307 constitutions, plus [x] constitutions of which fragments were included in the Theodosian Code but not in Justinian's Code (or are irretrievably inserted in other constitutions of the latter Code) and thus are lost to us (65 of these are indicated by PA or ETC in a fragment without a corresponding fragment), plus [y] constitutions of which no use at all was made since they were no longer in use (in total: 2307 + [x] + [y]).

After the splitting up the Code contained 2,777 fragments plus the [x] fragments. Mommsen estimated [x] at *c.* 480, on the basis of the word density in Vat. 886. If he is right, then the total number of fragments would amount to *c.* 3,250.[99] This would mean that we dispose of more than 80 per cent of the Theodosian Code, including the part supplied by Justinian's Code; and of more than 75 per cent of the Theodosian Code in its original version.[100] And if we assume the missing part to have been fragmented in the same proportion as the rest, then the basic collection would have been *c.* 2,700, not taking [y] in account. Of that 2,700, some 350 (265 + 61: *c.*13 per cent) covered multiple topics. Of course it is not claimed that Mommsen's total of fragments or his combination of fragments are final. Krüger suggested four additions and Maas mentioned other combinations; yet since these differences are marginal, it will not affect the

---

[95] Referred to with rendering of contents: *CTh* 3.1.10; 3.5.14; 3.18.2; 4.20.4; 4.24.0; 5.17.3; 5.19.2 (of which *CJust* 11.50.2 is probably the text). Original, with merely (partial) inscription or subscription: CTh 3.5.10; 4.12.2.

[96] See n. 100.

[97] According to Mommsen 260. He considers *CJust* 6.3.1 as derived from the Hermogenian Code. Seeck includes the fragment and couples it with *CTh* 4.12.4 [314]. Our version of Justinian's Code lacks a few constitutions, but this is of no consequence here.

[98] See J. Gaudemet (n. 36) 63 n. 4.

[99] This is less than Haenel's 3,400, cited by Karlowa and later L. Wenger, *Die Quellen des römischen Rechts* (Wien, 1955), 556 n. 271.

[100] Mommsen, Prolegomena XXXVIII and Krüger (n. 93) 'Über' 320: of the part between the beginning and *CTh* 6.2.12 two-thirds is missing; also Krüger (n. 93) 'Beiträge V', 21: more than 80 per cent remains.

outcome of the statistics as long as we adhere to a reasonable rounding up or down.[101]

Appendix 2. The distribution of the dative and *ad* with the accusative in the inscriptions of constitutions

On the basis of Mommsen's Prolegomena, for the years 375-400 ('East' and 'West' refer to the part of the Empire the constitution was sent to, '/d' refers to basic constitutions with the dative, '/a' to basic constitutions with *ad* and the accusative):

Year	East/d	East/a	West/d	West/a
366	–	3	–	13
367	2	1	–	18
368	1	3	4	32
369	4	4	2	28
370	1	9	–	18
371	1	4	2	15
372	1	5	–	17
373	–	2	–	4
374	2	1	2	10
375	1	1	1	2
376	–	2	2	8
377	3	4	2	8
378	–	–	–	8
379	3	–	1	15
380	20	5	1	12
381	18	7	1	12
382	28	4	1	15
383	22	6	1	13
384	19	4	–	7
385	17	–	6	21
386	27	2	–	14
387	7	1	1	6
388	9	–	3	–
389	13	–	10	4
390	13	–	9	1
391	8	1	4	3
392	30	2	1	–
393	38	1	3	–
394	8	–	–	–
395	18	1	28	1
396	38	5	15	1
397	19	1	16	2
398	19	2	17	–
399	14	2	30	1
400	3	–	26	2

[101] Maas's suggestion takes 27 fragments more to produce 263 combinations, while this reduces the *leges geminatae* to 18 (37 fragments). In that case there would have been 2,520 fragments, 281 combinations comprising 779 fragments; the basic collection would have contained 2,357 constitutions, i.e. 2 per cent more.

On the basis of Seeck's *Regesten*, for the years 375-400 for East and West, for the dative and *ad* with accusative respectively:

East – 375: 1-1, 376: 0-2, 377: 3-4, 378: 0-0, 379: 5-0, 380: 25-5, 381: 17-6, 382: 27-3, 383: 26-6, 384: 16-5, 385: 14-0, 386: 30-2, 387: 9-1, 388: 10-0, 389: 17-3, 390: 14-0, 391: 7-1, 392: 29-2, 393: 33-1, 394: 10-0, 395: 17-0, 396: 40-6, 397: 19-1, 398: 19-2, 399: 11-3, 400: 3-0.

West – 375: 2-1, 376: 2-9, 377: 1-10, 378: 1-10, 379: 1-11, 380: 1-11, 381: 1-10, 382: 0-16, 383: 2-13, 384: 0-8, 385: 5-22, 386: 0-13, 387: 1-6, 388: 0-0, 389: 3-1, 390: 7-3, 391: 2-3, 392: 2-0, 393: 5-0, 394: 1-0, 395: 26-1, 396: 13-1, 397: 17-1, 398: 19-0, 399: 34-2, 400: 22-2.

East and West – 390: 2-0, 391: 2-1, 392: 0-1, 393: 1-0, 394: 0-0.

3. Some Quaestors of the Reign of Theodosius II[1]

Tony Honoré

This chapter[2] has a number of connected aims. One is to confirm the view that the general laws[3] of the Later Empire, enacted in the imperial consistory, and in particular those excerpted in the Theodosian Code (henceforth the Code)[4] were mainly drafted by quaestors[5]. During or near the reign of Theodosius II the sources agree that it was the quaestor's duty to act as the emperor's legal adviser and to speak on his behalf, in particular by drafting laws.[6] Symmachus,[7] Claudian,[8] the *Notitia Dignitatum*[9] (395 to 421 for the West, before 413 for the East), Zosimus,[10] Corippus,[11] Cassiodorus[12] and the *Anthologia*

---

[1] References to the Codex Theodosianus, Novellae Theodosianae and Codex Justinianus include a line number, lines being counted according to the Mommsen edition of *CTh* and the Krueger edition of *CJust*. The counting is continuous, so that if the text as printed runs over to a second page, the number of lines on the first page is added to the number on the second page up to and including the reference.

[2] I am grateful for Professor Wulf Eckart Voss for his detailed and helpful comments on an earlier version of this paper. This is not the place to discuss the respects in which our views diverge.

[3] *CTh* 1.1.5.3-4 (26 March 429), 1.1.6.1 (20 Dec 435, both Constantinople) cf *CJust* 1.14.3 (Ravenna 6 Nov 426).

[4] In relation to the Code I call *CTh* 1.1.5 the first directive, and the commission it set up the first commission; *CTh* 1.1.6 the second directive and the commission it set up the second commission; and *NTh* 1 of 15 Feb 438 the confirming law.

[5] Viz by the official called *comes et quaestor* or *quaestor sacri palatii*, perhaps dating from Constantine (see Zosimus n. 10); P. Noailles, *Les collections de Novelles de l'empereur Justinien* (1912), 2f; W.E. Voss, *Recht und Rhetorik in den Kaisergesetzen der Spätantike* (1982), 33-9.

[6] Good account by J. Harries, *JRS* 78 (1988), 148-72.

[7] *Ep.* 1.23: 'concilii regalis particeps ... precum arbiter, legum conditor ...'

[8] *Paneg. dict. M Theod. cons.* 17.34: 'terris edicta daturus, supplicibus responsa venis.'

[9] *Not. dig. Or.* 12.3-5; *Occ.* 10.3-5: 'sub dispositione viri illustris quaestoris: leges dictandae, preces.'

[10] Zosimus 5.32: 'ho ta basilei dokounta tetagmenos hupagoreuein.'

[11] *Paneg. in laud. Anastasii quaest. et mag.* 26f: 'principis auspicio leges et iura gubernans, iustitiae vindex.'

[12] *Variae* 6.5.1,2: 'quaesturam ... quam nostrae linguae vocem esse censemus ... armarium legum ... qui ore principis populos noscitur admonere' and cf 6.5.6: 'necesse tibi

Palatina,[13] all say much the same thing. But the quaestor thesis, as it may be called, needs stressing. Scholars have so far been reluctant to accept and act on its corollary, that we can in favourable circumstances hope to discover which texts were drafted by which quaestor, and to group laws according to the quaestor responsible for them.

The quaestor thesis fits the view that in the Later Empire government was specialised. It is not true that emperors did everything themselves. They did not normally decide questions of law; even if the decision was technically theirs, they deferred to the opinion of competent lawyers. Emperors left the drafting of general laws to quaestors. So to understand the system of government we need among other things to build up a portrait gallery of quaestors and lawyers. This is my second aim, and leads in this essay to a listing of twelve quaestors of Theodosius II, six or seven of whom were directly concerned with the Code project (429-438), while two others played a role in preparing the ground for it. For convenience these quaestors are numbered chronologically from 1 to 12 (see Table on p. 71). In the last part of this essay seven of them are discussed in more detail, including Antiochus Chuzon, who was the central figure in the project.

Their role depended to some extent on the importance, somewhat neglected, of constitutional convention in the imperial government. One must not be bemused by the doctrine, which legal historians overplay, that sole legislative power rested with the emperor. Not only did political realities count, but the emperor's sovereignty, like that of the British Parliament, was limited by procedure and custom.

The reign of Theodosius II, which ran for our purposes from 408, when his father Arcadius died, to 450, suits these themes because in it we know the names of ten quaestors, often the rough dates at which they held office (which in several instances this study makes more precise) and sometimes other details. His extended reign straddles the Code which bears his name. My last four quaestors were in office after it was promulgated in 438, but as two or three of them served on the second Code commission their careers bear on it.

The arguments deployed are mainly based on style and vocabulary.[14] These are likely to convince those who, reading the texts

---

est omnibus sufficere, quantos a nobis contigerit legum remedia postulare.'

[13] *Anthologia Palatina* 16.48 ('stoma basileos').

[14] On which see G. Vernay, 'Note sur le changement de style dans les constitutions impériales de Dioclétien à Constantin', *Etudes d'histoire juridiques offerts à P.F. Girard* II (Paris 1913), 263-74; A.J. Fridh, *Terminologie et formules dans les Variae de Cassiodore: Etude sur le développement du style administratif aux derniers siècles de l'antiquité* (Stockholm 1956); W. Ax, 'Probleme des Sprachstils als Gegenstand des lateinischen Philologie', in C.J. Classen, A. Heuss, K. Nickau, W. Richter and P. Zanker, *Beiträge zur Altertumswissenschaft* (Hildesheim, New York 1976); G. Viden, *The Roman Chancery Tradition: Studies in the Language of Codex Theodosianus and Cassiodorus'*

chronologically, will see why certain sequences appear coherent in style and why some seem to have been drafted by lawyers and others not; but there is no sure way of convincing others. Warnings are of course needed about the scope of the quaestor thesis. Not all laws which can be termed 'general' were the work, or wholly the work, of the quaestor in office at the time. Some did not go through the consistory. Sometimes the office of quaestor was vacant. Sometimes the holder was ill or absent or for some other reason not available or competent to deal with a particular subject. He had no administrative staff of his own and no deputy, so that in his absence the drafting of new laws might be put off until he was available. There is an interesting legislative gap in the summer of 440 between 20 May and 21 September (see n. 109) which can plausibly be accounted for by the absence of the quaestor Epigenes on a mission to the Huns.[15] But if the matter was urgent enough, someone else, perhaps an ex-quaestor or the head of one of the departments of state (*scrinia*), was called on to stand in for him. The quaestorship of Cynegius under Theodosius I offers an example. While he was quaestor the emperor sent him away on an autumn mission for a couple of months in 383;[16] during this period laws continued to be enacted, but in a different style,[17] after which Cynegius resumed his duties.

An emperor might draft a law himself, if he was determined to do so or fancied his literary talent, but between Julian and Justinian[18] emperors seldom did. A text drafted by the quaestor might of course contain phrases taken from the proposal of an official, *suggestio*, or from materials supplied by officials whom he could call on in the various imperial departments (*scrinia*), especially the office of petitions (*libelli*), which possessed legal expertise and could apprise him of the existing state of the law and the relevant precedents. But a broad distinction must be made between substance and style. Thus Nestorius, having become bishop of Constantinople, boasts of his influence on the anti-heretic law of 30 May 428.[19] But this does not mean that he composed it, merely that he pressed for it and perhaps supplied the extended list of heresies which appear in it (*CTh* 16.5.65.10-27). Quaestors varied in the use they made of the available materials. Some like Ausonius put their stamp on every text.[20] Others were more reticent, but the quaestor was not expected merely to rubber-stamp even a document submitted by a praetorian prefect.

Variae (Gothenburg 1984).

[15] *PLRE* II 396; Priscian fr 1.

[16] Honoré, *ZSS RA* 103 (1986), 133, 151-4, 220.

[17] Ibid.

[18] Honoré, *JRS* 65 (1975), 107-23.

[19] *CTh* 16.5.65; *ACO* 1.4.16: 'qui certe legem inter ipsa meae ordinationis initia contra eos qui Christum purum hominem dicunt, et contra reliquas haereses innovavi.'

[20] Honoré, *ZSS RA* 103 (1986), 133, 203-10; *IVRA* 35 (1984/1987), 75-85.

Another warning must concern the texts of the Theodosian Code in which the second commission made certain changes, as the directive of 435 told them to,[21] some the inevitable result of shortening, others in the interests of clarity. But the extent of these changes should not be exaggerated. Wherever we can judge, they turn out to be no more than the substitution of an odd word here and there. No one lightly tampered with imperial constitutions.

Despite the undoubted pitfalls, a reader who troubles to read the texts chronologically will find that he encounters groups of texts coherent in style and vocabulary. If read consecutively for this period the constitutions in the Code and Theodosian Novels yield at least twelve chronological groups of texts which appear to be by the same hand. These are now set out in a table, to which the reader is asked refer from now on. In it a member of the first Code commission is marked by p, of the second by s; one thanked in the confirming law by t; a lawyer by *, a likely Christian by †.

No	Dates	Name	Laws
1	19 Jan 409 to 4 Sept 410	Unknown A	34
2	7 Aug 412 to 27 Apr 413	Unknown B	16
3	13 Dec 414 to 10 Apr 417*†	Eustathius	37/38
4	6 Nov 422 to 14 Nov 424*†	Sallustius	36
5	1 Feb 425 to 1 June 426p†	Antiochus senior?	15
6	16 March 427 to 16 Apr 430pst*†	Antiochus Chuzon	31/33
7	27 Nov 434 to 14 Nov 435pst*	Eubulus	7
8	8 March 436 to 28 Aug 436st	Maximinus	13
9	31 Jan 438 to 6 Dec 439st*†	Martyrius	29
10	22 Jan 440 to 30 Dec 440st	Epigenes	11
11	6 March 441 to 21 Aug 442	Unknown C	16
12	28 Dec 442 to 19 Feb 445st*	Procopius?	23/24

A. The quaestor and legislation

Before we come to individuals some general remarks about the office of quaestor and the procedure for enacting general legislation will help. The office was a high one and quaestors were members of the imperial consistory, but their political influence varied. On the whole the praetorian prefects were the emperor's most powerful ministers, and one test of a quaestor's political standing is whether he is later promoted praetorian prefect, either of Illyricum (PPO Ill) or, still more prestigious, of the Orient (PPO Or). There seems to be some correlation between a powerful style and political power, but this cannot be pressed very far. In assessing styles it has to be remembered that the Code texts lack the preambles and epilogues which the Theodosian Novels possess, so that they appear less rhetorical than they would if

[21] *CTh* 1.1.6.7-10 (20 Dec 435)

the whole law survived. Making allowance for this, styles divide not only into the more and less forceful but also into genres: literary, bureaucratic and legal, with various hybrids. The literary quaestors aim at rhetorical elegance, employ unusual words and constructions, avoid technical terms and plain speaking. The bureaucrats like their modern counterparts are pedants but aim to be accurate and comprehensive.[22] The lawyers are marked off from the non-lawyers by the use, when the law calls for it, of technically correct language, which the non-lawyers avoid.[23] In other respects their style may incline either to the literary or the bureaucratic. Some quaestors, including six of the twelve on our list (nos 3, 4, 6, 7, 9, 12), seem to have been lawyers, the rest not. To act as the emperor's legal adviser a quaestor did not have to be a lawyer but merely to have access to legal expertise. Ausonius for example, though he had some court experience, was no lawyer.[24] Four or five of our quaestors may have been Christians, to judge by the fact that instead of distancing themselves from the dominant religion, by referring to 'Christiani' they identify themselves with it, ('nostra fides', 'vera religio').[25] By this test several of the lawyers of this period write as Christians. Is this merely a camouflage? I am inclined to think that it is, on the contrary, a significant development.

In what follows an attempt is made to match the ten names of quaestors to the twelve stylistic groups and to say something about the career and outlook of some of those who can be thus matched. No fewer than seven of the ten names, perhaps as many as nine, can plausibly be thought to fit one of the twelve groups. The minimum number of texts treated as forming a group is, apart from one instance, eleven, the maximum thirty-eight. The maximum simply reflects the longest coherent sequence of texts, and extends for just over three years.[26] To fix a minimum is harder, and depends on striking a balance between the number of texts and the period they cover. The minimum period covered by the groups selected is just under six months,[27] which is on the short side. Still shorter periods, say of a month or two, are rejected because they raise a doubt whether the person concerned held office as quaestor or merely as a stand-in. The smallest number of texts in a group is eleven,[28] apart from one group of seven, which is however spread over

---

[22] *CTh* 5.3.1 (15 Dec 434: Eubulus) 'Si quis episcopus aut presbyter aut diaconus aut diaconissa aut subdiaconus vel cuiuslibet alterius loci clericus aut monachus aut mulier, quae solitariae vitae dedita est, nullo condito testamento decesserit nec ei parentes utriusque sexus vel liberi vel si qui agnationis cognationisve iure iunguntur vel uxor extiterit ...'

[23] Voss, op. cit.

[24] *Praef.* 1.17: 'nec fora non celebrata mihi.'

[25] pp. 76, 81, 82, 87-8, 92.

[26] no. 6 (March 427 to Apr 430).

[27] no. 8 (8 March to 28 Aug 436).

[28] no. 10 (Jan to Dec 440).

a whole year.[29] On average a group extends over seventeen months, and runs to twenty-two laws, a decent length and quantity. The actual number and period will be a bit greater, since the quaestor may have drafted laws outside the period of those that survive. There are 341 laws of this period in the Code and the post-Theodosian Code Novels (*NTh*), an average for 42 years of just over eight a year. Of these 78-79 per cent (between 268 and 272) are attributed to one or other of the twelve quaestors. This reveals a contrast between what seem productive and lean times: an average of nearly sixteen texts a year for the seventeen years when the twelve quaestors were in office, against just under three a year for the rest. Either chance has cut down the number of laws for the apparently lean years or, more likely, vigorous lawmaking alternated with fallow periods.

The dates of the first and last laws in a stylistic group suggest that a quaestor often took office on 1 January, or in the last weeks of the previous year after the wine harvest was in. An attractive hypothesis is that he normally took office on 5 December, the date Mommsen gives for the beginning of the quaestor's term in both Late Republic and Empire,[30] the continuity of the late imperial quaestorship with its forerunners being greater than is sometimes supposed. The quaestor was meant to hold office for not less than a year from the date of appointment and was sometimes renewed for a further year or years.[31] Of the stylistic groups seven (nos 1, 5, 6, 8, 9, 10, 11) begin with the first surviving law of a calendar year, whose dates range from 19 January to 16 March. Two of them (nos 3, 12) begin with a law dated after 5 December of the previous year which is the last law of that year. Two others (nos 4, 7) begin in November, which might be accounted for if by arrangement with his predecessor these two quaestors-elect began to draft laws a little in advance of formally taking office. In only one case (no. 2) does the first law of a group fall at another time of year, August. A tenure of office also tends to finish with a calendar year or at the wine harvest period (nos 1, 4, 7, 9, 10 with dates ranging from 4 September to 30 December), one of them (no. 10) later than the Mommsen date of 5 December, or with the last law of the year in question (nos 8, 12) or the last before the wine harvest (nos 3, 6, 11). When the stylistic date changes after 5 December one has to bear in mind the possibility that the new quaestor was working on a draft made by his predecessor. But all the evidence suggests a changeover towards the end of a year or the beginning of the next. Only once or twice have we evidence of a change of office in the middle of the year (no. 5, June 426; no. 3/4, between April and November 417).

To understand the quaestor's role, it is useful to bear in mind the

[29] no. 7 (Nov 434 to Nov 435).
[30] *Staatsrecht* II[1] (Leipzig 1874) 500.
[31] One year: nos 7, 8, 10; two years: nos 1, 4, 9, 11; more than two years: nos 3, 6, 12.

process of legislation.[32] The best description comes in an eastern law of 446 (*CJust* 1.14.8, 17 Oct) which brought the senate into the legislative process by requiring that it should discuss and approve any proposed new general law before enactment. From this we can see what the procedure was previously, when the consistory alone was consulted. A proposal for a new law having emerged, for example in a proposal from an official ('suggestio'), it is discussed ('tractari') in the imperial consistory or a restricted group of its members (called variously 'proceres', 'iudices', 'consistorium'). If after discussion it emerges that a new general law is needed a draft proposal (in modern terms a bill) is formulated ('tunc allegata dictari'): in one of its uses 'allegare' means 'to put a case or proposal'.[33] At a second meeting the consistory or the inner group discusses the matter, including the draft, a second time ('denuo recenseri'). If after discussion unanimous agreement is reached on the draft, if necessary as amended,[34] the text is finally read out ('recitari'). The emperor validates it by subscribing it, ('firmari'), after which it is promulgated.[35]

Hence for general legislation either two or three meetings were needed, depending on whether one assumes an interval between the second meeting, at which the draft is discussed, and the final stage at which the agreed text is read out and subscribed by the emperor. The quaestor's role fits into the procedure in the following way. He has (i) to formulate the proposal approved at the first meeting by drafting the new law ('allegata dictari'), (ii) to read out the draft at the second meeting, (iii) to incorporate in it any amendments agreed at that meeting and (iv) to read out ('recitari'), the final text to the consistory. I think we should postulate three meetings, in view of the wording of the 446 law and the requirements of orderly deliberation.

The need for unanimity ('cum omnes consenserint': 'omnes' can hardly mean both consistory and senate considered as bodies) is important, because it shows that the legal doctrine that the emperor has exclusive power to make laws is modified by convention. The opinion of each member of the consistory counted. If at the end of the second meeting opinions were divided, members in the minority might defer to the majority and in particular to the emperor, even so weak a

[32] For a slightly different account see J. Harries, op. cit. 165-6.

[33] *Dig.* 3.1.1.6 (Ulp. 6 ed); 22.3.26 (Pap. 20 qu); 46.1.71 pr (Paul 4 qu); 48.1.13.1 (Pap. 13 resp).

[34] Often by a final sentence, as in *CTh* 16.8.25 (15 Feb 423).

[35] *CJust* 1.14.8 Ad senatum: (my subdivision into stages) 'Humanum esse probamus, si quid de cetero in publica vel in privata causa emerserit necessarium, quod formam generalem et antiquis legibus non insertam exposcat, (i) id ab omnibus antea tam proceribus nostri palatii quam gloriosissimo coetu vestro, patres conscripti, tractari, et, si universis tam iudicibus quam vobis placuerit, tunc (ii) allegata (legata) dictari et sic ea denuo omnibus collectis recenseri et, cum omnes consenserint, tunc demum (iii) in sacro nostri numinis consistorio recitari, ut universorum consensus nostrae serenitatis auctoritate firmetur.'

one as Theodosius II. But they need not and, if they did not, the matter might properly be deferred or lapse.

B. Individual quaestors

There follow some remarks about the style and careers of seven quaestors who held office between 414 and 439 and who were either members of one of the Code commissions or are significant figures in the run-up to it. They consist of one major figure, Antiochus Chuzon, the main architect of the Code, and six lesser but not insignificant ones. Want of space obliges me to pass over the rest without comment.

no. 3. *CTh* 1.7.4 (13 December 414) to *CTh* 16.9.4 (10 April 417): Flavius Eustathius[36]

This group of 37 or 38 texts[37] is marked by technically correct legal language: 'corporalis traditio', 'ususfructus exceptio', 'imperfecta donatio', 'nullius momenti esse' (8.12.8.2,3,5,14), 'filii legitimi', 'in sacris patris', 'ut sui' (3.12.4.5,6), 'testamenti factio', 'per interpositam personam', 'ab intestato venire', 'legitimas intestatorum deferre hereditates' (16.5.58.14,18,20-1), 'species traditionis', 'retentio ususfructus' (8.12.9.2,3). The drafter was clearly a competent lawyer.

His texts are polished and, especially in the earlier part of his tenure, forthright. Here are some examples: (on confirming title to loot) 'nec enim crimen dissimile est rapere et ei, qui rapuerit, rapta servare' (9.28.2.4); (on the abuse of tax and debt remission) 'in suum compendium rapinamque convertere, ut fierent privata debita, quae fuerant publica' (11.28.10.3-4); (against Eunomians and double baptism) 'in modum semel nati hominis semel a deo conceditur; pares ceteris sint, qui pares sunt in dogmatis pravitate' (16.5.58.3,15-6); (on undeserving *agentes in rebus*) 'quos vita culpabiles et origo habet ignobiles' (6.27.18.2); (on combining senatorial and municipal duties) 'nec enim credimus utrumque per unum, prout convenit, posse compleri' (12.1.180.4-5); (on by-passing written wills) 'nemo scriptis proprium auferat robur et non scriptis sub praetextu nostri vel

[36] *PLRE* II Fl Eustathius 12 p. 436.
[37] *CTh* 1.7.4 (13 Dec 414), 6.27.18 (20 Jan 415 Seeck, *PLRE* 416), 3.1.9 (17 Feb 415), 9.28.2 (5 March), 8.1.15 (16 March), 8.12.8 (23 March), 3.12.4 (16 May), 11.28.10 (11 July), 10.10.26? (25 July), 5.12.2 (5 Aug), 7.7.4,5 (5 Sept), 1.8.1 (15 Oct), 16.8.22 (20 Oct), 6.23.1 (31 Oct), 16.5.57 (31 Oct), 16.5.58 (6 Nov), 11.24.6 (3 Dec), 16.10.21 (7 Dec), 6.26.17 (6 Feb 416), 6.32.1 (8 Feb), 12.1.180 (17 Feb), 4.4.5 (13 March), 7.9.4 (10 May), 6.30.21 (29 June), 14.16.2 (23 July), 12.1.182 (26 Aug), 9.40.23 (30 Aug Seeck Sept) 11.28.11 (9 Sept), 16.2.42 (29 Sept 416 Seeck 5 Oct), 12.12.15 (5 Oct), 6.33.1 (4 Nov), 6.25.1 (11 Nov), 6.27.17 (11 Nov 416 MS 415), 6.24.8 (17 Nov), 6.24.9 (18 Dec), 8.12.9 (14 March 417), 16.9.4 (10 Apr).

potentium nominis ingerat firmamentum' (4.4.5); (on security of tenure for agentes in rebus) 'nam probata schola et animadversionem vereri iudicis et nullam debet timere contumeliam vilitatis' (6.27.17.5); (on relaxing formalities in donations) 'cum observationem iuris contrahere potius quam propagare debeamus; idem sit in his causis usumfructum retinere quod tradere' (8.12.9.4,8-9). He can use strong language, for example in condemning looting and heresy: 'contagium quoddam funestae pestis' (9.28.2.4); 'execrabilia mysteria' (16.5.57.6); 'servilis faex' (6.27.18.3); 'nefanda superstitio; caeno propriae sectae' (16.9.4.6,8). His direct, concrete manner impels him to begin two-thirds of his laws with a sentence in the indicative.[38]

His texts are not free of superfluous duplication: 'pari et simili ratione' (3.12.4.3), 'spoliatio ac direptio' (16.5.57.13), 'sponte atque ultro' (16.5.58.7), 'salva atque intemerata' (6.26.17), 'militiam vel sollicitudinem' (6.32.1). His forceful style recalls Nicomachus Flavianus, western quaestor in 388-390,[39] with whom he shares the phrase 'nihil commune habere'.[40] But a reference in one of his laws to 'right religion', 'recta religio', in contrast to Judaism, points to his being a Christian (16.9.4.5-6).

The style described begins in December 414.[41] The five earlier laws of 414 are ponderous, with elaborate sentences marked by the use of 'nec non et/etiam' (11.28.9.6; 13.3.17.3) and 'sit/sitque/sint' (9.40.22.4; 6.2.23.6; 13.3.16.10). The new manner persists, though with diminishing vigour, up to 10 April 417. The next two laws, of 28 July (7.11.2.4) and 27 September (15.11.2.2,5) deploy a rather mechanical formula ('comperimus ... ideoque praecipimus') which does not comfortably fit the preceding laws, though continuity is not entirely ruled out. After that there is a clear change, with a group of five laws in a more bureaucratic manner, three of them introduced by 'no one' or 'none'.[42]

The quaestor responsible for the group of 37 or 38 texts between 13 December 414 and 10 April 417 can be identified as Flavius Eustathius. He is cited as quaestor in two of them, dated 15 October 415 (1.8.1.2) and 6 February 416 (6.26.17.1). Given that the first text is from December 414, Eustathius was appointed not long after the

---

[38] Twenty-four out of 37 or 38: *CTh* 1.7.4, 3.1.9, 9.28.2, 8.1.15, 8.12.8, 11.28.10, 10.10.26, 7.7.5, 7.7.4, 1.8.1, 6.23.1, 6.27.18, 6.26.17, 4.4.5, 6.30.21, 9.40.23, 11.28.11, 16.2.42, 12.12.15, 6.27.17, 6.24.8, 6.24.9, 8.12.9, 16.9.4.

[39] T. Honoré *ZSS RA* 103 (1986), 210-16; (with J.F. Matthews), *Virius Nicomachus Flavianus* (Konstanz 1989)).

[40] *CTh* 16.2.42.5 (29 Sept 416) cf 16.5.17.9 (4 Apr 389); 16.5.18.5 (17 June 389).

[41] *CTh* 1.7.4 (13 Dec 414: 'minime oportebit'), 3.1.9 (17 Feb 415: 'praecipimus infirmari'), 9.28.2 (5 March: 'non est sanctitatis negotium'), 8.1.15 (16 March: 'penitus convenit inhiberi').

[42] *CTh* 8.1.16 (24 Oct 417: 'nemo'), 6.27.19 (27 Nov), 16.2.43 (3 Feb 418), 12.1.183 (17 Apr: 'neminem'), 13.1.21 (21 Aug: 'nemo').

influence of Theodosius' austere sister Pulcheria supplanted that of Anthemius, who had been prefect of the Orient from July 405 to April 414. Eustathius took office as quaestor in December 414[43] at about the same time as Aurelian, who had been prefect of the orient in 399,[44] returned to that office in place of Monaxius. Aurelian, perhaps Pulcheria's choice as prefect, had been quaestor himself much earlier, about 393[45] and remained prefect at least until 10 May 416 (7.9.4).

Eustathius' quaestorship went on into 417, so that the last months of his term were concurrent with Monaxius' return to office as prefect from 26 August 416 to 27 May 420.[46] Did the change of prefect account for the repeal of a law earlier in Eustathius' quaestorship inspired by legal purism? Property given as a gift must henceforth be physically transferred to the donee if ownership was to pass. If the donor retained a life interest and remained in physical control, a common practice, the ownership would not pass to the donee. After Monaxius returned as prefect this inconvenient law was effectively repealed (8.12.9), with apologies, Eustathius drafting the repeal. The laws he addresses to Monaxius as prefect, though recognisably his, are flatter than his earlier compositions (12.1.182, 9.40.23, 11.28.11, 16.2.42, 12.12.15, 6.25.1, 6.24.8, 6.24.9, 8.12.9, 16.9.4). This may show that their text was influenced by Monaxius' proposals. Eustathius went on, after a gap of three years from April 417, to succeed Monaxius as prefect of the Orient between 18 September 420 (7.16.3a) and 19 June 422 (8.4.27). He was consul in 421.[47]

This lawyer-quaestor who went on to be prefect of the Orient was clearly a figure of some weight. Like other officials a quaestor might propose a new law. The suggestion for the law of 15 October 415 (*CJust* 1.8.1) came from him, and he is naturally one of those to whom it is addressed. The subject is an item of official infighting. Command posts on the military establishment, *praepositurae*, had been removed from the lesser register, *laterculum minus*, under the quaestor's charge and taken over wholly or for the most part[48] by the army office, *magistri militum*. Forty of these posts are now restored to the lesser register and commissions for them are henceforth to be issued by the third clerk in the department of records, *scrinium memoriae*,[49] who acted on the quaestor's instructions. Eustathius had won a notable though incomplete victory against the army office, which Sallustius later exploited.[50]

---

[43] After 30 Nov 414 (*CTh* 13.3.16) and not later than 30 Dec 414: *Chron. Min.* II 71; *PLRE* I Aurelianus 3.

[44] *PLRE* I Aurelianus 3 PPO Or (1) 399 (11) from 30 Dec 414 to 10 May 416.

[45] Synesius, *De Prov.* 92A.

[46] *PLRE* II Fl Monaxius pp. 764-5.

[47] *PLRE* II Flavius Eustathius 12 PPO Or 420-2

[48] 'universae vel mediae': *CTh* 1.8.3, 29 Apr 424.

[49] Called *laterculensis* (*CJust* 12.19.13.1, 518-527; Nov. 35 1, 535).

[50] p. 81.

Eustathius' texts display lawyerly values. He is hostile to petitions to the emperor for benefits or exemptions (1.7.4, 5.12.2), and to the circumvention of the law by the emperor (4.4.5, 14.16.2), soldiers (7.7.5, 7.7.4, 7.9.4) or magnates (3.1.9, 11.28.10, 4.4.5). The very first text of his tenure says that the staff of the army office are not to be dragged by imperial rescript before any court other than that of the master of soldiers, 'even if someone has by disclosing or suppressing the truth obtained a rescript from our clemency to that effect'.[51] This is strong meat. But most and perhaps all of these texts of high propriety belong to the period when Aurelian was prefect.

Since Eustathius proceeded in due course to be prefect of the Orient it is worth asking whether the texts of his prefecture show any parallels in style or substance with those of his quaestorship. I have not been able to detect any. From his period as prefect only three scattered texts survive in 420 (7.16.3; 10.1.17) and 421 (16.8.21 Mommsen 412 = 16.2.45 & in part *CJust* 11.21), then six in a consistent style during the first half of 422.[52] They have none of Eustathius' sharpness, even when the subject is the technical one of a soldier's or office holder's service fund, *peculium castrense* (1.34.2 cf. *CJust* 1.51.7). So far as conclusions can be drawn from this instance, a prefect could influence the substance of legislation; but of the three prefects considered (Aurelian, Monaxius and Eustathius) only Monaxius perhaps influenced the tone of the laws addressed to himself.

The career of the lawyer/quaestor/prefect Eustathius marks the arrival on the scene of a type of public figure who was to be central in the composition of the Code, though he himself was to have no part in it.

no. 4. *CTh* 6.8.1 (6 November 422) to *CTh* 2.12.7 (14 November 424): Sallustius[53]

A roughly equivalent group of 36 laws in a consistent style runs from November 422 for two years.[54] The quaestor responsible for these was also a lawyer, as his technical correctness shows: 'praedium urbanum

[51] *CTh* 1.7.4.4-5 (13 Dec 414: etiamsi quis id <sacrum rescriptum> a nostra clementia vel exposita vel suppressa veritate meruerit).

[52] *CTh* 6.32.2 (12 Jan 422), 7.8.13 (3 March), 1.34.2, 2.10.6 (23 March), 6.30.23 (29 Apr = ? *CJust* 12.46.4: *PLRE* II Nestorius 4), 8.4.27 (19 June).

[53] *PLRE* II Sallustius 4 p. 972.

[54] *CTh* 6.8.1 (6 Nov 422), 7.4.35 (14 Feb 423), 16.8.25, 15.3.6 (15 Feb), 7.15.2 (7 March, 7.6.5 (9 March), 4.18.2, 11.30.67 (30 March), 11.31.9 (30 March 423 Seeck 424), 16.8.26, 16.10.22, 16.5.59, 16.9.5 (9 Apr), 8.4.28, 6.35.14 = in part 12.1.184 (18 May), 1.34.3 (31 May), 16.5.60, 16.8.27, 16.10.23, 16.10.24 (8 June), 16.5.61 (8 Aug), 12.3.2 (9 Aug), *CJust* 4.63.6 (23 Aug), 8.10.11 (29 Sept 423), *CTh* 15.1.52 (9 Jan 424), 10.21.3 (16 Jan), 4.4.7 =

aut rusticum cuiuscumque condicionis' (12.3.2.5-6: viz 'res mancipi' or 'nec mancipi'), 'agere ex testamento', 'fideicommissi persecutio', 'bonorum possessio secundum/contra tabulas', 'edictum divi Hadriani', 'de inofficioso agere', 'vis codicillorum', 'gradus agnationis et cognationis', 'in iure praetorio sive civili' (4.4.7.1-3,7-9,12-14,22-4,26-7,35), 'donationis titulo', 'dominus constitutus possessionis', 'non vendita sed legitime donata vel iure successionis adquisita possessio' (11.20.5.8,11), 'personales actiones', 'actione vel persecutione', 'triginta annorum praescriptio', 'pignus vel hypotheca', 'petitio finium regundorum', 'post litis contestationem in iudicium actione deducta', 'pupillaris aetas', 'actiones perpetuae', 'legis ignorantia' (4.14.1.3,5-7,9,17-18,21,25-6,41), 'dominus causae', 'iudicati actionem in dominum dari vel domino', 'procurator vel cognitor in rem suam' (2.12.7.2,3-4,7,8-9,11). He was a first-rate jurist, as capable of dealing with awkward problems of costs and 'res judicata' (4.18.2) as of turning the classical law of robbery against Christians, true or so-called, who despoil temples and synagogues (*CTh* 16.10.24). His greatest claim to distinction is to have introduced a decisive aid to security of title, the thirty-year period of prescription (*CTh* 4.14.1) against 'perpetual actions', in a complex law which paid due regard to the transition from the previous state of the law and to existing litigation.

The quaestor insists on strict procedures.[55] Periods of time (11.30.67.7-8; 11.31.9.6,8-9,11,13; 8.4.28.8; 6.35.14.4,9; 1.34.3.6; 11.20.5.4-7,12,29; 4.14.1.3,6,11,19,25-6,32,34-5,37-38,40), degrees (4.4.7.26,28), amounts (7.6.5.3, *CJust* 8.10.11.3,5-7, *CTh* 11.1.33.4-5) and numbers (4.4.7.40,43) are carefully specified. So is the scope of the law, the moment at which it is to take effect and the problem of retrospectivity (6.8.1.11-20; 16.8.25.1-5,7-8; 4.18.2.1-2; 6.35.14.11-18; 12.3.2.12-19; 10.19.15.17-22; 10.20.14.6-9). The laws seem to rest on a policy of future strictness, but with this goes some willingness to relax the existing rules, for example as regards practising pagans (if any), though they should be put to death (16.10.23.2-3): and past alienations of curial land in Osroene, though strictly speaking invalid (12.3.2.13). The usual rule of law values are in evidence: emphasis on general laws (16.5.59.4-5; 12.3.2.5), opposition to derogations from them by rescript (4.18.2.2), the pursuit of certainty of title and status, which calls for fixed prescriptive periods (4.14.1, 8.4.28, 6.35.14) and clarity (11.31.9.18), which may call for repeating or explaining a previous law (16.8.27, 16.5.61). If any scholar still believes in the existence of an imperial vulgar law[56] he will rapidly be cured by reading this group of texts.

2.19.7 (14/24 Feb 424 = *CJust* 6.13.2, 6.35.8), 15.5.4 (22 Apr), 1.8.2 (26 Apr MS 25 Apr = *CJust* 1.30.1), 1.8.3 (29 Apr), 11.20.5 (13 May), 10.19.15 (11 July), 11.1.33 (10 Oct), 10.20.14 (16 Oct), 4.14.1, 2.12.7 (14 Nov).

[55] *CTh* 4.18.2: claims for costs; 11.31.9: appeals; 4.4.7: formalities for wills.

[56] As in G. Stühff, *Vulgarrecht im Kaiserrecht, under besondere Berücksichtigung der*

The quaestor's style flows evenly, his prose more rounded than that of Eustathius. There are some good phrases: (of one who has made good the transition from local to imperial service for ten years) 'minime conveniatur ulterius, sed privilegia et praemia viri fortis expectet' (8.4.28.10-11); (of Jews buying Christian slaves) 'nefas enim aestimamus religiossissimos famulos impiissimorum emptorum inquinari dominio' (16.9.5.23-30); (of those who lose money through the ban on trading in purple etc.) 'nec est, ut quisquam de abiurato pretio conqueratur, quia sufficit calcatae legis impunitas, nec vacet illi curare de quaestu, cui sua salus esse non debet in pretio' (10.21.3.10-12); (on the right to claim under a trust) 'non enim par eademque ratio videtur amittere debita et lucra non capere' (4.4.7.33-4); (on the restoration to the quaestor of his former powers) 'placuit nunc clementiae meae vetusti temporis more renovato ad prisca deinceps iura revocare' (1.8.3.4-5).

His writing proceeds at an even pace with well-balanced clauses. Doublets are common, like 'sedibus et consessu' (6.8.1.9), 'pro cupiditate ac libidine' (7.4.35.3-4), 'cedant ac deserant' (7.15.2.2), 'absolutum dimissumque iudicium' (4.18.2.5-6), 'spiritum audaciamque compressimus' (16.8.26.3), 'sine inquietudine et intermissione' (6.35.14.10), 'execrabilium religionum et professionum' (16.5.61.3), 'ieiunis et desertis possessionibus' (11.20.5.14), 'propriae originis stirpem laremque' (10.19.15.6), 'tradita oblivioni et diuturno silentio, otioso nimis ac desidi' (4.14.1.20,31). He often inverts constructions with the verb 'esse': 'sunt praediti' (6.8.1.4), 'sunt ereptae/sublata/dedicata' (16.8.25.3,5-6), 'erit dilatione obnoxius' (16.9.5.4), 'erunt obnoxii' (16.5.60.6), 'sunt apparitionibus obligati' (16.5.61.4-5), 'erit venditio' (12.3.2.10), 'esse promissum' (11.1.33.2), 'esse subeunda' (10.20.14.8), 'erit praescriptio metuenda' (4.14.1.6), 'est ordinatus' (2.12.7.2). Like some other jurists he is free with future tenses: note the examples of its inversion just given and 'conveniet' (15.3.6.12, 4.14.1.29,36), 'damnabuntur' (16.8.26.8), 'cohercebit' (16.10.23.3), 'sustinebit' (10.21.3.14), 'licebit' (4.4.7.30), 'debebit' (11.20.5.22,25, 11.1.33.9), 'non valebit, amittet' (11.20.5.27,30), 'probabuntur', 'subiacebunt', 'constabit' (10.19.15.9-10,13,21), 'durabit', 'videbuntur', 'oportebit' (4.14.1.10,36,39), 'sufficiet' (2.12.7.9).

The quaestor responsible for these thirty-six laws from 6 November 422 to 14 November 424 was Sallustius, who is referred to as quaestor in a text of 26 April 424 (1.8.2 = *CJust* 1.30.1). In the surviving laws there is a gap between June 422[57] and Nov 422, so that he probably began to draft laws after the wine harvest of 422 and went through almost to the end of 424, with a steady output of laws, broken by winter

---

Gesetzgebung Konstantins der Grossen: Forschungen zum römischen Recht 21 (Weimar 1966)

[57] n. 51.

gaps of two months in 422-3 and three in 423-4. His quaestorship begins soon after Eustathius' prefecture ends,[58] both being lawyers who improved the quaestor's status. When did his term of office end? The last three laws of 424, in December, are by a verbose and awkward writer, whose texts lack proper connectives, possibly a stand-in during what would otherwise have been another winter gap (*CTh* 7.4.36, 11.21.3, 1.6.12). His appointment may have been for the calendar years 423-4. By 1 February 425 a more competent quaestor (no.5) is in office. During most and perhaps all of Sallustius' tenure the prefect of the Orient was Asclepiodotus,[59] who served from 14 February 423 (7.4.35) to 1 February 425 (15.5.5) and was consul in 423. As a maternal uncle of the empress Eudocia, daughter of a pagan philosopher, he was attacked for sympathy to pagans and Jews (16.8.25; 16.8.27; 16.10.22; 16.10.24.4-13). Several laws of this period evince a dislike of Christians who use religion as an excuse to attack Jews and pagans. The names of heretical sects are boring.[60] Despite this, Sallustius seems to have been a Christian, speaking of 'our faith' ('nostra fides': 16.8.26.8), the first appearance of this phrase in a general law.

The law of 26 April 424 (1.8.2) shows that Sallustius was capable of extending Eustathius' victory over the army office[61] and repatriating to the quaestorship all the posts attached to the lesser register 'in accordance with ancient custom' ('iuxta consuetudinem priscam'), for which commissions are henceforth to issue 'at your discretion' ('tuo arbitratu': 1.8.2.2,5). Three days later a pithy law (1.8.3), which Sallustius must have enjoyed drafting, informs Helio Master of Offices[62] of the reversion to former practice. Justinian preserves these texts (*CJust* 1.30.1,2) but eliminates Eustathius' law of 415 (*CTh* 1.8.1) which had now been overtaken.

We do not know how his career ended. He was not on the first Code commission of 429-35 (1.1.5), though he would have been an obvious choice. The laws of his quaestorship show that in 422-4 a strong current was flowing in favour of rule of law values.

no. 5. *CTh* 15.5.5 (1 February 425) to *CTh* 12.12.16 (1 June 426): Antiochus senior?[63]

The next quaestor, able and forceful but with different habits of composition, is the author of fifteen laws between 1 February 425 and 1

---

[58] Last surviving law addressed to him is *CTh* 8.4.27 (19 June 422).

[59] *PLRE* II Asclepiodotus 1 p. 160.

[60] *CTh* 16.5.60 (8 June 423: quorum sectas piissimae sanctioni taedet inserere).

[61] p. 77.

[62] *PLRE* II Helion 1 p. 533.

[63] *PLRE* II Antiochus 6 pp. 102-3.

June 426.[64] In literary talent he outdoes Eustathius and Sallustius; on the other hand there is no sign that he was a lawyer. Those who want theatre and circus on Sundays are admonished: 'aliud esse supplicationum noverint tempus, aliud voluptatum'. It is more vital to honour God than the emperor, 'cum virtutibus dei omnipotentis ac meritis universi obsequium orbis impenditur' (15.5.5.12-13,17-18) or again 'excedens cultura hominum dignitatem superno numini reservetur' (15.4.1.6). It is likely that the quaestor, who speaks of 'Christianorum ac fidelium mentes' (15.5.5.9), was a Christian, since though a pagan would talk of 'Christiani' the reference to the faithful implies a commitment. He was a cultivated man, able to cast in appropriate terms the law which reorganised higher studies in Constantinople (14.9.1).

Though the editorial process makes such inferences fragile, it is notable that his laws often begin with nouns or noun equivalents (*CTh* 15.5.5, 15.1.53, 14.9.3, 6.21.1, 10.10.32, 6.22.8, 6.30.24, 12.12.16). He likes doublets in which the constituent elements are separated in the following manner: 'virtutibus dei omnipotentis ac meritis' (15.5.5.17-8), 'humiliores aliquanto atque angustiores, ministris eorumdem locorum desit aut populis' (15.1.53.6-8), 'discipuli sibi invicem possint obstrepere vel magistri, vocum aures quorumdam aut mentes' (14.9.3.20-2), 'ad quaestus eius compendiumque devenerit' (10.10.32.7), 'ut non culmine distinguantur aequali sed tempore' (6.30.24.7). There are striking separations of adjective and noun: 'maiore quadam imperialis officii necessitate' (15.5.5.14), 'ex ipsa ubi versatur inlicite urbe' (14.9.3.6), 'laudabilem in se probis moribus vitam' (6.21.1.8), 'efficax quod postulaverat postulatum', 'ex aequa cum aerario dividere parte', 'in eius procul dubio societate', 'suam a petitore vindicaturo aerario portionem' (10.10.32.4-5,7-8,17), 'ad summum praefecturae pervenisset usque fastigium', 'aliquibus professionum et militae meritis' (6.22.8.3,13), 'ad inlustrem meruerint magistri a vigiliis atque laboribus procedere summitatem' (6.10.4.2-3), 'in summa administrationis sunt positi potestate', 'tristi liceat proscriptionis tempestate' (9.41.1.2-3,5-6), 'ipsis quodammodo amplissimae tuae sedis obtutibus' (10.20.16.6), 'imperalis officium pertinuisse responsi' (12.12.16.2-3). Two-word phrases are linked in chains: 'si docendi peritiam facundiamque dicendi, interpretandi subtilitatem, copiam disserendi se habere patefecerint' (6.21.1.9-10); 'ad nos insimulationum genera, quaestionis ordo, criminum moles, documentorum probationumque pensanda libramenta mittantur' (9.41.1.6); 'civitatum

---

[64] *CTh* 15.5.5 (1 Feb 425), 15.1.53, 14.9.3 (27 Feb), 6.21.1 (15 March), 15.4.1 (5 May), 10.10.32 (13 May), 10.20.15 (24 May), 6.22.8, 6.10.4 (22 Sept), 6.30.24 (17 Nov), 5.16.34 (13 Dec), 9.41.1 (23 Jan 426 MS 425), 9.42.24 (23 Jan), 10.20.16 (23 Feb), 12.12.16 (1 June).

postulata, decreta urbium, desideria populorum' (12.12.16.1). Four of eight instances of 'modis omnibus/omnibus modis' in the Codex fall in these laws (14.9.3.10; 10.10.32.17; 6.22.8.6-7; 10.20.16.5).

This tenure of the quaestorship begins after the three clumsy laws of December 424. The end comes between 1 and 22 June 426, when a more pedantic style takes over for the eight laws which survive from June to December of that year.[65] The prefect of the Orient during the tenure was first perhaps Aetius (May 425[66]), then from September 425 to the end Hierius.[67]

Unlike Eustathius and Sallustius, this quaestor cannot be identified with certainty, but he may well have been the senior member of the first Code commission of 429: 'Antiochus vir illustris exquaestor et praefectus' (1.1.5.23-4), who is attested as a praetorian prefect on 14 October 427.[68] As Hierius was prefect of the Orient at this time,[69] Antiochus must have been prefect of Illyricum. The law in question is a set of instructions, *mandata*, addressed to him at his own instance setting out certain powers of deputy governors of provinces. Since it was not a general law enacted in the consistory (and not drafted by the quaestor of October 427[70]) it was not included in the Theodosian Code. The text may include elements of Antiochus' proposal. In it the phrase 'ad alienandas minorum similiumque eis personarum seu curialium facultates' presents a parallel to 'ad inlustrem meruerint magistri a vigiliis atque laboribus procedere summitatem' from our quaestor's law of 22 September 425 (6.10.4.2-3).

The argument for the identity of our quaestor with Antiochus senior is not conclusive. But the latter must have been quaestor before 429, indeed before October 427 when the younger Antiochus is drafting laws.[71] What slots are available? Apart from the groups of laws composed by Eustathius and Sallustius none, apart from this sequence of 425-6, displays the talent one would expect of the senior member of the first Code commission. That post, if not held by a skilled lawyer, should go to someone who combined literary talent with administrative experience.

Antiochus senior was not a member of the second Code commission of 435 (1.1.6.10-6) and is not heard of after 429.

---

[65] *CTh* 8.7.21 (22 June 426), 8.7.23, 11.8.14, 8.7.22 (1 July), 6.26.18 (25 Nov), 6.27.20, 21 (23 Dec), 2.7.5 (26 Dec).

[66] *PLRE* II Aetius 1 pp. 19-20; CTh 15.4.1 (5 May 425).

[67] *PLRE* II Hierius 2 p. 557; CTh 6.10.4 (22 Sept 425), 12.12.16 (1 June 426).

[68] *CJust* 1.50.2.2.

[69] *CTh* 6.10.4 (22 Sept 425) to 2.3.1 (20 Feb 428); *PLRE* II Hierius 2.

[70] no. 6 (Antiochus Chuzon).

[71] p. 84.

no. 6. *CTh* 6.24.10 (16 March 427) to *CTh* 6.27.23 (16 April 430): Antiochus Chuzon[72]

The next coherent group of constitutions stretches from 16 March 427 to 16 April 430, a full three years, and comprises between thirty-one and thirty-three texts, including the first Code directive of 26 March 429.[73] After a gap of nearly three months between the last pedantic law of the second half of 426 a vigorous and lawyerly quaestor comes on the scene from March 427 and continues until April 430, but at a reduced rhythm after March 429 when the Code project was set on foot.

He was an accomplished lawyer, who uses technically correct language: 'donationum ante nuptias vel dotis instrumenta', 'iura legitimorum' (3.7.3.1-2,4); 'rei mobilis vel immobilis dominum', 'iusti liberi' (4.6.8.3,5); 'non impetratae actionis exceptio' (2.3.1.2-3); 'donationis instrumentum ante nuptias', 'de traditione minime perquiratur', 'etsi ... rerum offerandarum in dotem habeat donatio mentionem' (3.5.13.2-3,6-7); 'capere ab intestato hereditatem', 'ab intestato venire', 'ab intestato hereditas' (5.1.9.3,13,16); 'ad exactionem dotis ... dictio vel stipulatio' (3.13.4.2-3); 'ante nuptias donatio', 'potestatis iure ad parentes revertere', 'fructu atque usu ... dominum' (*CJust* 6.61.2.5,8,9-10); 'iure frui dominii, potestatis iure frui' (15.8.2.5); 'nullo donationis faciendae invicem nullo testamenti aut voluntatis ultimae ... iure concesso', 'procuratore qui hoc nesciente domino fecerit' (16.5.65.29-31,40); 'ineundi contractus vel dissolvendi obligationis causa' (*CJust* 10.34.2.3-4); 'sive ex asse sive ex parte heres sit bonorumve possessor' (*CJust* 10.35.1.2-3); 'validiora esse quae sunt posteriora', 'in desuetudinem abierunt', 'prudentium tractatibus et responsis' (1.1.5.8,13,15). His texts like those of other lawyers of the age are hostile to derogations from the general law: 'cessante omni beneficio principali' (7.8.14.8); 'omne beneficium omnisque adnotatio ... nullam habeat firmitatem' (6.2.26.11-13); 'etiamsi obtinuisse eam speciali adnotatione nostra indulgentiae videantur' (8.4.29.4). But the attempt to apply this principle ran into opposition from pressure groups and met the snag that it is often not obvious how in a given instance to apply the rule that later laws repeal inconsistent earlier ones. Thus *CTh* 13.3.18 of August 427 upholds a law on compulsory hospitality expressed in very general terms (7.8.14) less than two

---

[72] *PLRE* II Antiochus (Chuzon 1) 7 pp. 103-4.

[73] *CTh* 6.24.10 (16 March 427), 10.20.17 (23 March), 7.8.14 (22 June), 13.3.18 (19 Aug), *CJust* 1.8.1 (21 May), *CTh* 6.2.26. 6.27.22, *CJust* 12.5.2, 12.23.13 (31 Jan 428), *CTh* 3.7.3, 4.6.8, 2.3.1, 3.5.13, 5.1.9 (20 Feb), 3.13.4 (20 Feb MS 21 Feb), *CJust* 6.61.2 (20 Feb), *CTh* 15.8.2 (21 Apr), *CJust* 8.53.29 (21 Apr), *CTh* 16.5.65 (30 May), 12.4.1, *CJust* 10.34.2, 10.35.1 (9 June), *CTh* 8.4.29 (10 July), 13.3.19 (13 July), 5.16.35 (428), *CJust* 6.62.4 (11 March 429), *CTh* 1.1.5 (26 March), *CJust* 1.19.8 (27 March), 16.8.29 (30 May), *CJust* 1.3.22? (11 Feb 430), *CTh* 10.10.34 (22 Feb), 6.27.23 (16 Apr), *CJust* 11.78.2? (Theo et Val AA) cf *CTh* 1.1.6 (20 Dec 435).

months before but makes it subject to exemptions granted by earlier laws to doctors and the liberal arts professions. 13.3.19 later the next year makes another exception in favour of doctors. 10.10.34 exempts those on the emperor's domestic staff who bid for forfeited property from the requirement that half all such property should go to the fisc. These difficulties help explain why the Theodosian Code directive of 26 March 429 (1.1.5.8) did not instruct the commissioners to omit laws which conflicted with later laws. To do so would have invited endless disputes, and it was better to leave judges, officials and citizens to work out for themselves how to apply the rule that the later law has priority. Thus, though 4.6.8 reverted to an earlier law on succession between parents and natural children and rejected the 'asperity' of a recent western one, 4.6.7, the latter was kept in the Code. 5.1.9 repealed a very recent law of Theodosius II (not traceable) as too favourable to the succession of spouses on intestacy.

The laws of this quaestorship favour informality in private transactions, such as marriage (3.7.3: valid by the parties' consent and on the evidence of friends despite the absence of dowry or a marriage ceremony), giving dowry (3.13.4: once agreed, any words suffice) and making gifts (*CJust* 8.53.29: they can be made to people unknown to the donor and, if there is no deed of gift, they can be proved in other ways).

The quaestor's style is clear, accurate and adapted to the subject-matter. It is marked by a construction in which adjectives, participles, verbs and prepositions precede the noun to which they relate but are separated from it by intervening words, typically two, sometimes one, three or more. The examples which follow are mainly of two intervening words: 'praedictum suo ordine numerum locumque' (6.24.10.6); 'promulgatum super hoc cognoverint legem' (10.20.17.3-4); 'felicibus pro salute reipublicae expeditionibus' (7.8.14.2-3); 'secundo nostrae maiestatis oraculo' (13.3.18.3-4); 'praeclaro sunt sacrati collegio', 'delatis sibi senatoriis dignitatibus' (6.2.26.2,5-6); 'senatoriis se aestimant functionibus eximendos' (6.27.22.4); 'hac nostrae mansuetudinis aeterna lege', 'in qualibet alia positas civitate' (*CJust* 12.5.2.1-2,8); 'iniungenda publica vel privata necessitate' (*CJust* 12.23.13.6 Euxodio csl); 'deesse recte alias inito matrimonio firmitatem' (*CTh* 3.7.3.3); 'intra ducentorum solidorum est quantitatem' (3.5.13.4); 'conductisve pro paupertate personis' (15.8.2.10-11); 'adhibitis aliis idoneis documentis' (*CJust* 8.53.29.3); 'abreptas tenent ubicumque ecclesias', 'si alios sibi adiungant clericos', 'omnis innovationis adimatur licentia', 'ad imam usque sceleris nequitiam', 'in certas vix concessa personas', 'delatum ad se crimen' (*CTh* 16.5.65.2-3,5,15,21-2,51-2,61-2); 'ad praediorum iubemus comparationem expendi' (*CJust* 10.34.2.4-5); 'non praeiudicante eis novella lege' (13.3.19.4-5); 'in utramque dici partem', 'pro sui tantum temporis negotiis valitura', 'coharentibus prudentium tractatibus et responsis', 'in coniunctissima parte alia valebit imperii', 'in alterius quoque recipiendum scriniis' (1.1.5.6,14,15,30-2); 'solis cum necessitas exegerit verbis precibus inserendis' (*CJust* 1.19.8.5); 'si qua per calumniam postulatio' (*CJust* 1.3.22.1); 'cum impetrabile huius fuerit postulatum' (*CTh* 10.10.34.2-3); 'memoratum statutorum numerum', 'concessa potiantur militia' (6.27.23.6-7). A related construction consists of doublets separated by intervening words, as in: 'aut patre conchyliolegulo geniti probabuntur aut matre' (10.20.17.6-7); 'otii tempore et quietis' (*CJust* 12.5.2.6-7); 'aut extantibus iustis liberis aut etiam non extantibus' (*CTh* 4.6.8.5-6); 'praeter cohortalinem in provinciis et castrensem' (16.5.65.27-8); 'sequenda omnibus vitandaque monstrabit' (1.1.5.17). There are some good examples of chiasmus: 'aptam rei et proposito negotio competentem' (2.3.1.3: this text is notably succinct and elegant); 'ad priorem statum et condicionem pristinam revocentur' (8.4.29.4-5); 'edictorum viribus aut sacra generalitate subnixas', 'non fide dubia nec privata adsertione nitatur' (1.1.5.3,31). There are also some inversions of *esse*: 'sunt sacrati' (6.2.26.2); 'est testandi occasio' (*CTh* 5.1.9.5); 'est reprimenda insania', 'si sit ingenuus', 'sunt haereticis promulgata', 'sunt initiati mysteriis' (16.5.65.2,41-2,52-3,56); 'privilegia ... sunt praestita' (*CJust* 1.3.22.5).

The quaestor responsible for these was the junior Antiochus, the second senior member of the first Code commission.[74] He is referred to in the first directive as 'Antiochum virum illustrem quaestorem sacri palatii' (1.1.5.24). He may have held the quaestorship for four full years 427-30 or, on Mommsen's view of the normal date of appointment, from 5 December 426 to 5 December 430. During his tenure first Hierius,[75] then Florentius[76] were prefects of the Orient. On the last day of 430 Antiochus had himself already become prefect in succession (11.20.6). He continued as such into March 431 (9.45.4), and corresponded as prefect with Nestorius in September of that year,[77] when he was also consul. The law of 31 December 430 addressed to him as prefect (11.20.6) effects an important reform of the land tax, with the aim of substituting objective criteria of liability to tax for haphazard privileges.[78] When this reform was later amended in 444 (*NTh* 26.13) Antiochus was treated as its author. Although couched in a more bureaucratic style than his, phrases in it echo his favourite separated constructions: 'a principio imperii divae recordationis Arcadii', 'pro aestimatis per singulos annos habitis', 'pro rata partis dimidiae portione', 'ex quarta decima feliciter futura indictione' (11.20.6.3,7-8,16,23-4). This is a good example of a law on a technical

---

[74] *PLRE* II Antiochus 7.
[75] *PLRE* II Hierius 2.
[76] *PLRE* II Fl Florentius 7 pp. 478-80.   [77] Below n. 82.
[78] *CTh* 11.20.6.35-6: neque penitus ullo sub quocumque privilegio dispositione hac eximendo.

subject in which the text follows a draft submitted by the praetorian prefect, perhaps with little amendment.

Clearly a powerful figure, Antiochus' year as prefect and consul, 431, was that of the Council of Ephesus. He corresponded in September with Nestorius about the bishop's return to his monastery after his defeat at the Council,[79] treating him gently, and also, perhaps later, with Theodoret,[80] who praises his choice of provincial governors. He seems also to have sent documents to Pope Celestinus.[81] But his praetorian prefecture was short,[79] whether for reasons connected with the turbulent Council and its theology is uncertain: it would not be surprising if a scholar from Antioch had some sympathy with Antiochene theology. By 28 March 432 Hierius had again become prefect of the Orient.[83] If Rufinus came between them[84] he had a very short prefecture.

In any event Antiochus remained an active member of the Code commission, since when Theodosius reorganised it and told the revised commission to begin editing the texts in December 435 he made Antiochus its senior member: 'Antiochus amplissimus atque gloriosissim(us) praefectorius ac consularis' (1.1.6.10-11). As such he presided over the completion of the Code and in the confirming law of 15 February 438 Theodosius thanked him for the consistently high quality of his work: 'Antiochus cuncta sublimis' (*NTh* 1.7.38-9). He is the first of three commissioners to be singled out for special praise, the others being Maximinus (no. 8) and Martyrius (no. 9), whose quaestorships are discussed below.

John Malalas (346), who mixes up the reigns of Theodosius I and II, says that Antiochus was a native of Antioch, gives his nickname 'Chuzon', a name which stuck in the family, since his grandson[85] also had it, and calls him 'the great'. He may have rebuilt the city walls of Antioch.[86] Before the end of November 444 he was dead.[87]

He stood to the Theodosian Code much as Tribonian did to Justinian's larger-scale compilation: as the main organiser of the enterprise and its dominant legal expert. Each of these entrepreneurs had great talent, but neither was the senior member of the first commission set up by their respective emperors. In both cases a senior non-lawyer was chosen for that role. Organising ability and intellectual power gave Antiochus and Tribonian their chance; they

---

[79] Above n. 77.
[80] *Ep.* XXXIII, XXXIX
[81] E. Schwartz, *ACO* 1.2.8.
[82] Letters between him as prefect and Nestorius are attested in September 431: E. Schwartz, *ACO* 1.4.64.
[83] *CTh* 9.45.5; *PLRE* II Hierius 2.
[84] *PLRE* II Rufinus 8 p. 953.
[85] *PLRE* II Antiochus (Chuzon II) 10 p. 104.
[86] Malalas 346. Tree conservation in Antioch: *CJust* 11.78.2.
[87] *NTh* 26 (29 Nov 444) refers to the 'dispositio amplissimae recordationis Antiochi'.

differed in that unlike Tribonian Antiochus was probably a Christian.[88]

It is worthwhile trying to see how Antiochus' career relates to the Code project. He became quaestor very soon after the important series of laws enacted at Ravenna in November 426[89] under the aegis of Helion, master of offices, and Galla Placidia, who had been dispatched from the East in 425 to bring some order and co-ordination into the western administration. Thus the 426 legislation defined 'general laws' (*CJust* 1.14.2,3) and listed the lawyers whose writings had authority (*CTh* 1.4.3). Presumably the western government did this along lines broadly approved by the East. But the eastern legislation of 427, with Antiochus as quaestor (above pp. 84-5), brings out some of the pitfalls inherent in trying to run the Empire on the basis of general laws, given the opposition of vested interests,[90] and of harmonising the laws of East and West. In one case at least a western law of 425-6 (4.6.7) was disapproved by an eastern law of 427 (4.6.8).

How could derogation from general laws be prevented? How could conflicts between East and West be avoided? By February 428 at latest, it seems to me, Constantinople had resolved that a Code was needed. This would (i) not merely say what amounted to a general law but set out the text of all such laws since Constantine, eastern and western, in a single volume, (ii) abrogate laws not included in the volume, (iii) allow conflicts between the laws included to be settled on the basis that the later prevails over the earlier, and (iv) provide some machinery to avoid future conflicts between East and West. The prospect of a Code made it urgent to undertake such further law reform as was necessary before the Code was enacted. This explains the legislation of 20 February 428.[91] Though on a small scale, this legislation parallels Tribonian's *Fifty Decisions*.

It is impossible to know to what extent the Code project as a whole rested on Antiochus' initiative, but the detail of the scheme does seem to bear his imprint. A small point to end this assessment of a major figure in the history of the time. Sallustius, composing a bold text about decurions etc. who improperly join the imperial service, writes that all previous laws are repealed and first ('primum'), decurions are not to join but second ('dein'), if they do and the local council takes no steps for ten years, they are not to be hauled back (8.4.28.3,6). Antiochus goes one better. In the Nestorius-inspired law of May 428 against heretics he has three steps: first, ('ante omnia'), churches are to

---

[88] *CJust* 1.8.1.3 (21 May 427: 'signum salvatoris Christi'), *CTh* 16.5.65.12-13,32 (30 May 428: 'fons veritatis; qui nostrae fidei refragantur').

[89] *CTh* 1.4.3, 4.1.1, 5.1.8, 8.13.6, 8.18.8, 8.18.10, 8.19.1, *CJust* 1.14.2, 1.14.3, 1.19.7, 1.22.5, 6.30.18.

[90] Above pp. 84-5.

[91] *CTh* 3.7.3, 4.6.8, 2.3.1, 3.5.13, 5.1.9, 3.13.4, *CJust* 6.61.2.

be returned to the orthodox; secondly ('dein'), there are to be fines for creating heretical priests and officials; thirdly ('post haec'), different classes of heretic are distinguished and different disabilities imposed on each (16.5.65.2,5,8-9). This structure recurs in the first directive on the Code. First ('et primum'), laws and parts of laws are to be arranged under title headings; second ('dein'), within titles the texts are to be arranged in order of date so that inconsistencies can be settled on the basis that later laws prevail; third, ('post haec'), unessential parts of laws are to be omitted. The type of mind that sets out what is to be done in a series of steps – something unprecedented so far as the record goes – is exactly what was needed for an enterprise like the Code.

no. 7. *CTh* 14.16.3 (27 November 434 MS 26 November) to *CTh* 16.10.25 (14 November 435): Eubulus.[92]

Little legislation survives from 431 to 433. In 434 after a gap of five months from 18 June (5.12.3, 11.28.15) we have a group of seven laws which run from November 434 to the same month in the following year.[93] There follows a gap of three months to March 436, when a different style emerges (see no. 8). There are signs that the drafter of these seven texts was a lawyer: 'mutui nomine dare' (14.16.3.6-7), 'condere testamentum', 'agnationis cognationisve iure', 'censibus adscripti vel iuri patronatus subiecti' (5.3.1.5,6,10), 'iure iurando obstricti' (*CTh* 10.8.5.4), 'caduca/vacantia vel caduca', 'iure possidere vel vindicare' (10.8.5.1,8,11). One text shows a typically legal concern with the relation of present to past laws (5.3.1.13-14; 7.8.16.8). He was probably not a Christian.[94]

Bureaucratic (5.3.1.2-5) yet at times vehement (14.16.3.8,11; 16.10.25.2), his laws, like those of Sallustius, favour inversions of 'esse': 'sit perpetuo dedicata'; 'sit solvendum' (14.16.3.2,7); 'fuerat destinatus'; 'fuerat adscriptus' (5.3.1.8,13); 'fuerint ante perfuncti'; 'fuerint versati' (6.28.8.3,10); 'fuerint delatae' (7.8.16.4); 'sunt imitati'; 'esse sortiti' (16.5.66.5-6); 'fuerit admissum' (10.8.5.18); 'esse multandum' (16.10.25.7).

The author of these texts is almost certainly Eubulus, a member of the second Code commission, who was quaestor at the time of the second directive of 20 December 435: 'inlustris ac magnificus comes et quaestor noster' (1.1.6.11-12). The directive was issued five weeks after the last text in the present group, but though Eubulus is the main draftsman ('sit divisa capita, fuerit abstractus negotio, fuerit visum':

[92] *PLRE* II Eubulus p. 403.
[93] *CTh* 14.16.3 (27 Nov 434 MS 26 Nov), 5.3.1 (15 Dec), 6.28.8 (29 Jan 435), 7.8.16 (12 May), 16.5.66 (3 Aug), 10.8.5 (9 Oct), 16.10.25 (14 Nov).
[94] *CTh* 16.5.66.2,7; 16.10.25.4: are there still any temples? 'Christian religion'.

1.1.6.5,17-18), the law, as one would expect, also bears traces of Antiochus Chuzon, now called on to preside over the editorial process.[95] The first directive had listed among members of the Code commission a Eubulus *vir spectabilis ex magistro scrinii*, no doubt the same person. He held the quaestorship, I suggest, to the end of 435 and went on to the prefecture of Illyricum in 436 (8.4.30 = 12.1.188, 187). So he did not see the Code commission's labours through to the end and was not thanked in the confirming law of 15 February 438. His is a standard lawyer/head of department/quaestor/prefect's career. During his tenure of the quaestorship the prefect of the Orient was first Taurus (to 15 December 434), then from 29 January 435 Isidorus.

no. 8. *CTh* 10.20.18 (8 March 436) to *CTh* 11.5.4 (28 August 436): Maximinus.[96]

After a gap from November 435 (see no. 7) a further group of thirteen[97] laws between March 436 and 28 August 436 fall at a time when Isidorus, consul in 436, was still prefect.[98] There follows a further gap of seven months before an isolated law of 16 March 437 (6.23.4). These thirteen laws are the most elegant of the period: 'Alexandrinis principalibus, etsi advocatione fungantur, nihilo minus pergrinatio ne incumbat' (12.1.189.1-2). Their deft constructions and subtle play of sound can best be appreciated by reading aloud. Nothing shows their composer to have been a lawyer or a Christian. Insistence on fixed periods of prescription is relaxed (8.4.30), but retrospection avoided (8.4.30; 12.1.188; 11.1.37.1-2).

This quaestor is fond of the construction by which an adjective or participle precedes the relevant noun, typically with only one word intervening – a lighter version of the figure favoured by Antiochus Chuzon.[99] Examples are: 'trecentas paene libras', 'innumeris sint constitutionibus prohibitae', 'recenti quoque interminatione', 'quaesitis multo sudore stipendiis' (10.20.18.1,5-6,12-13) 'ullam posthac adspiraverit dignitatem', 'omnibus impetrati honoris insignibus', 'in tali eius condicione', 'urbano profitetur iudicio', 'latarum pridem constitutionum'

---

[95] e.g. *CTh* 1.1.6.3,17 (20 Dec 435: 'tulimus, aliqua rei publicae detentus sollicitudine') cf *ZSS RA* 103 (1986), 184-5.

[96] *PLRE* II Maximinus 6.7 p. 742.

[97] *CTh* 10.20.18 (8 March 436), 8.4.30 = in part 12.1.188, 12.1.187 (3 Apr), 14.26.2, 12.1.191, 11.5.3, 14.27.2, 12.1.190, 12.1.189 (4 June), 11.28.17 (14 July), 12.1.192 (4 Aug), 11.1.37, 11.5.4 (28 Aug).

[98] *PLRE* II Fl Anthemius Isidorus 9 pp. 631-3: PPO Or 29 Jan 435 (*CTh* 6.28.8) to 4 Aug 436 (*CTh* 12.1.192).

[99] In which two or three words intervene between participle or adjective and noun, as in: 'praedictum suo ordine numerum locumque' (*CTh* 6.24.10.6, 16 March 427); 'promulgatum super hoc cognoverint legem' (10.20.17.3-4, 23 March 427).

(8.4.30.3-5,9-10) 'parto semel honore', 'senatoriam suscepti dignitatem', 'laborioso administrationis actu', 'suarum periculo facultatum' (12.1.187.2,5-7,9); 'ullam affectare militiam', 'talem ipsius statum' (12.1.188.4-6,8); 'diurnos centum et decem modios' (14.26.2.1-2), 'civilibus inhaesit muneribus' (12.1.191.2); 'ad omnium perveniat notionem' (11.5.3.7); 'pecunariis coherceri dispendiis' (12.1.190.3-4); 'in sua tantum civitate', 'ad summum pervenerit gradum', 'senatoriis minime functionibus' (12.1.189.3-7); 'ad publicas nominaverint functiones', 'non expectandum esse consensum' (12.1.192.4); 'contra generalem huiusmodi sanctionem' (11.1.37.2-4); 'particulari delegationum notitia', 'singulis transmissa provinciis' (11.5.4.1-2).

One figure he practises to good effect is the chiasmus: (of privileges in Alexandria) 'ut hoc bene cogniti privilegium consequantur nec eo passim fruantur indigni' (12.1.191.3-4). We also find a sort of alliterative chiasmus: 'cohortalis apparitor aut obnoxius cohorti' (8.4.30.2-3); 'a corporalibus iniuriis immunes esse censemus' (12.1.190.2); 'Cyro reverentissimo Afrodisiensium civitatis episcopo' (11.1.37.3); 'devotioni solitae, non subitis calumniis' (11.5.4.3).

This quaestor is probably the first Maximinus mentioned in the directive of 20 December 435, 'vir illustris insignibus quaestoriae dignitatis ornatus' (1.1.6.12). This phrase could be taken to mean that in December 435 when Eubulus was still quaestor Maximinus had been already designated as his successor from 1 January 436. The alternative is to identify our quaestor with the second Maximinus, junior to the first, the senior of four 'spectabiles comites et magistri sacrorum scriniorum' (1.1.6.14-15), hence presumably head of the department of records, *magister memoriae*, at the time. In the confirming law of 15 February 438 only one Maximinus is mentioned. An ex-quaestor and literary eminence, 'vir inlustris ex quaestore nostri palatii eminens omni genere litterarum', his work for the commission is singled out for praise (*NTh* 1.39-40). Though doubt has been expressed,[100] the text of the directive of 435 in which mention of the first Maximinus follows immediately on that of Eubulus points to the first as the quaestor of 436. Moreover the laws of 436 fit a man of literary talent. This quaestor could, unlike Eubulus whose duties in 436 took him to Illyricum (8.4.30 = 12.1.188), have continued to work on the Code commission to the end.

no. 9. *NTh* 3 (31 January 438) to *NTh* 18 (6 December 439): Martyrius[101]

After the isolated *CTh* 6.23.4 of 16 March 437 follows a hiatus of ten months before a group of twenty-nine laws between January 438 and

[100] As in *PLRE* II Maximinus 7 p. 742.
[101] *PLRE* II Martyrius 2 pp. 731-2.

December 439.[102] Given the firm command of classical terms which they display their author was steeped in the law: 'sine liberis vel legitimo herede decesserit non condito testamento' (NTh 6.15); 'conductor/locatori ... locator/conductori'; 'non solum inutilia sed pro infectis habeantur'; 'nec stipulationem nec mandatum ullius esse momenti'; 'fideiussorem/locatori' (NTh 9.20-1,28-9,37-9); 'civitas Romana' (CJust 2.15.1.6); 'pupillis vel minoribus'; 'sive ab intestato sive iure substitutionis'; 'legitima liberorum tutela'; 'bona iure pignoris obnoxia' (NTh 11.4-5,12-13,15-16,23-4); 'consensu matrimonia contrahere'; 'mittere repudium' (NTh 12.2); 'matrimonio dissoluto'; 'donatio ante nuptias'; 'pro marito donationem ante nuptias vel pro muliere dotem offerre'; '(res) extantes/consumptas'; 'iure hereditatis/iure peculii' (NTh 14.4-5,20-1,31-2,66-70); 'testibus septem numero civibus Romanis puberibus'; 'uno eademque die nullo actu interveniente'; 'per nuncupationem'; 'extranei scripti'; 'legata ac directae hereditates tutores etiam' (NTh 16.23-4,42-3,52,77-8,81-2); 'servi quasi nec personam habentes' (NTh 17.1.17); 'sive per se sive per interpositam in fraudem legis personam aut donationis venditionisve titulo' (CJust 9.27.6.6-7). He is interested in interpretation ('verba/voluntas': NTh 9.2-7,22-32), and drafts several reforming laws,[103] often reviving classical rules. For example it is harsh to impose greater restraints on divorce than did classical law: 'in repudio mittendo culpaque divortii perquirenda durum est veterum legum moderamen excedere' (NTh 12.5). Indeed proportionality and a sense of limits are the hallmarks of good law: 'maxime moderamen desideratur in legibus' (NTh 11.2). Rule of law values, in particular favour for general rules and hostility to derogations from them by rescript or adnotation,[104] prevail (NTh 6.25-6, 8.11-12, 5.2.14). The first three instances of 'regula legis/legum' in the legal sources are found in this tenure (NTh 8.12, 10.1.36, 16.3 cf 9.36). As Martyrius speaks of 'vera religio' and 'fides noster' he may well, despite his legal classicism, have been a Christian.[105]

His compositions flow freely, and his accomplished rhetoric rises at times to splendour, notably in the law on Jews, Samaritans, heretics

[102] NTh 3 (31 Jan 438), 1 (15 Feb)?, 4 (25 Feb), 5.1 (9 May), 6 (4 Nov), 7.1 (20 Jan 439), CJust 1.51.10 (20 Jan), 1.2.9 (23 March), 11.18.1 (23 March), 1.24.3 (3 Apr), NTh 8,9 (7 Apr), 10.1,2 (19 Apr), CJust 1.52.1 (30 May), NTh 5.2 (8 June), 11,12 (10 July), CJust 2.15.2 (17 July), NTh 13 (13 Aug), 14 (7 Sept), 15.1,16 (12 Sept), 17.1 (20 Oct 439), CJust 8.11.20 (1 Nov), 9.27.6 (26 Nov), NTh 18 (6 Dec), CJust 12.23.14 (Florentio PPO 438-9), 11.43.5 (Cyro PPO cf NTh 18, 6 Dec 439).
[103] NTh 11 (tutorship), 12 (10 July 439: divorce), 14 (7 Sept: parental property), 16 (12 Sept: formalities for wills).
[104] W Turpin, RIDA 35 (1988), 285-307
[105] NTh 3.3,20-8,63: 'vera religio/nefas quippe credimus, ut supernae maiestati et Romanis legibus inimici ultores etiam nostrarum legum subreptivae iurisdictionis habeantur obtentu et adquisitae dignitatis auctoritate muniti adversum Christianos et ipsos plerumque sacrae religionis antistites velut insultantes fidei nostrae iudicandi vel pronuntiandi habeant potestatem.'

and pagans of 31 January 438 (*NTh* 3) and the confirming law of 15 February 438 (*NTh* 1). A prominent feature of his style is an asyndeton in which the first word of a phrase is quickly repeated: 'tanti secreti, tantae fabricae ... auctorem'; 'neminem Iudaeum, neminem Samaritam'; 'non promulgatarum legum ... non denuntiati exilii'; 'quamquam ... quamquam'; 'in fortunas eius, in sanguinem' (*NTh* 3.10,17,66-7,70-1,73-4); 'si copia immensa ... si actionum diversitas ... si denique moles'; 'quo pondere ... qua actione ... quibus verbis'; 'magis imperatorium magisque credidimus gloriosum'; 'in omnium populorum, in omnium provinciarum' (*NTh* 1.6,13-14,27-8,46-7); 'neminem ducianum, neminem limitaneum'; 'scilicet opperiri, scilicet optare' (*NTh* 4.11,30); 'fundis ... sitis per Asianum diocesim, sitis per Ponticam'; 'nequaquam ulterius ... nequaquam utriusque obsequiis'; 'securus vomerem, securus falcem'; 'etiamsi domum, etiamsi domicilium' (*NTh* 5.1.6,9-10,15-16,21); 'hoc enim armat, hoc nostrum ornat exercitum'; 'ab eorum facultatibus, ab eorum patrimoniis'; 'non sacra adnotatio, non divina pragmatica' (*NTh* 6.3-4,22-3,25-6 cf *NTh* 5.2.14); 'omnes conductores, omnes qui per provincias otiantur' (*NTh* 7.1.30-1); 'nulla divinae domus patrocinio, nullo sacrosanctarum ecclesiasum reverentia, nullo qualibet vel cuiuslibet se potentia excusante' (*CJust* 11.18.1.15-16); 'contra ius contrave utilitatem publicam' (*NTh* 8.14); 'nullum enim pactum, nullam conventionem, nullum contractum' (*NTh* 9.22-3); 'nulla eis inspectio, nulla ingeratur peraequatio, nulla instructio, nulla discussio, nullum ratiocinium imponatur, nihil denique aliud eis mandetur' (*NTh* 10.1.27-32); 'licet non dominus, licet iniustus possessor'; 'contra fas contraque leges' (*CJust* 2.15.2.3-4,9); 'nunc maritum, nunc mulierem' (*NTh* 12.6); 'nullam iniunctionem, nullam sollicitudinem'; 'omni necessitate omnique fatigatione' (*CJust* 12.23.14.7-9); 'quid in publicis thermis, quid in nymphaeis ... quid his personis' (*CJust* 11.43.5.7-9). Seven of eleven instances of 'quam ob rem/quamobrem' in the Code and Novels come from this tenure (*NTh* 3.14; 1.18; 4.10,32; 5.1.18; 10.1.25; 15.1.6).

These laws fall in large part at the time when Florentius[106] was prefect of the Orient for the second time, from 31 January 438 (*NTh* 3) to 26 November 439 (*CJust* 9.27.6), but by the time of the last law (*NTh* 18) Cyrus[107] had succeeded him.

The quaestor responsible for these twenty-nine laws is Martyrius, who appears in the directive of 20 December 435 as the second of seven 'spectabiles comites consistoriani' (*CTh* 1.1.6.13), and in the confirming law of 15 February 438 as 'vir illustris comes et quaestor' (*NTh* 1.40-1). He is there thanked as the emperor's faithful interpreter, 'nostrae clementiae fidus interpres', the third member of the commission, after

---

[106] *PLRE* II Fl Florentius 7 pp. 478-80.
[107] *PLRE* II Fl Taurus Seleucus Cyrus 7 pp. 336-9.

Antiochus and Maximinus, to receive a special commendation.

The confirming law of 15 February 438 falls in the quaestorship of Martyrius, and we need not doubt that the draft is basically his, as is shown by touches like 'nulli retro principum aeternitas sua detracta est, nullius latoris occidit nomen'[108] and the use of 'quam ob rem' (*NTh* 1.18). Other parts of the text however ('tanto lucubrationum tristi pallore', 'compendiosam divalium constitutionum scientiam', 'Theodosiano non referuntur in codice': *NTh* 1.4,19-20,35-6) point to the hand of Antiochus Chuzon.

The quaestorship of Martyrius ran to the end of 439. He was succeeded in 440 by Epigenes, who was responsible for between ten and twelve laws in 440,[109] but of whom space does not permit a detailed account.

The seven quaestors discussed include five eastern lawyer-quaestors (Eustathius, Sallustius, Antiochus Chuzon, Eubulus and Martyrius) three of whom became prefects, and five quaestors who write as if Christians (Eustathius, Sallustius, both Antiochi and Martyrius). They mark the emergence in high office certainly of lawyers and perhaps of Christian lawyers who, without being fanatics (for the Code avoids doctrinal controversy by including general laws whatever their doctrinal tendency), found it not merely expedient but natural to combine pagan learning with the new faith. Even if many or most lawyers were still pagan, the gradual fusion of these traditions is an important element in the movement for legal unity, reform and codification which issued in the Theodosian Code. For a parallel, note the very different way in which Antioch received the Homeric allusions of the empress Eudocia[110] in the spring of 438 from its reception of Julian in 362-3.[111] It is perhaps not irrelevant to the background of the Code that Antiochus Chuzon certainly and Eudocia possibly had connections with Antioch.[112]

---

[108] *NTh* 1.23-4 cf p. 93.

[109] *CJust* 8.11.21 (22 Jan 440), 1.14.7 (5 Apr), *NTh* 19 (17 May), *CJust* 3.4.1, 7.62.32, 7.63.2 (20 May), *NTh* 7.2,20 (21 Sept), 7.3 (29 Dec), *CJust* 2.7.8 (30 Dec), 12.8.2? (Cyro PPO), 12.57.13? (Thomae PPO Seeck, *PLRE* 442)

[110] Evagrius 1.20. But Eudocia may have come from an Antioch family: K.G. Holum, *Theodosian Empresses* (1982), 117.

[111] J. Matthews, *The Roman Empire of Ammianus* (1989), 408-13, 439-41.

[112] Eudocia: above n. 110; Antiochus: J. Malalas 346, 362.

Part II

Constantine, Christianity and the Code

Introductory Note

Jill Harries

The Theodosian Code began with the legislation of Constantine and the three chapters in this part all reflect that emperor's influence. One unacknowledged historical difficulty confronting the compilers, who were researching on material more than a century old, was that, for much of his reign, Constantine had not ruled alone but as part of a college with colleagues accepted at the time of their legislation as legitimate. Simon Corcoran's Chapter (4) on the legislation of Licinius, who shared responsibility with Constantinian as joint Augustus for all imperial laws from 313 down to 324, shows how the enactments of a man categorised as a 'usurper' *after* 324 could nevertheless find their way into the Code as Constantinian legislation. The compilers themselves, however, may have been both unaware of and unworried by the difficulty; although preoccupied by chronological exactness in arranging laws, they were not concerned with the historical processes which had brought them into being.

No explicit justification is offered by Theodosius' Code commissioners for beginning with Constantine. The existence of the Gregorian and Hermogenian Codes of the 290s provided a pretext: the Theodosian Code was a continuation. But, unlike its predecessors, Theodosius' Code carried the emperor's name, it excluded rescripts, its copyright was rigorously protected and constitutions excluded from it were invalid. All this indicates a project more explicitly the expression of the imperial monopoly on legislation than the earlier Codes had been. The significance of the decision to begin with Constantine is thus enhanced. Book 16 is a monument to the process of legislation on Christianity set in motion by him, although, as David Hunt explains below (Chapter 6) imperial legislation tended to 'lead from behind', while over-simple notions of Christianisation are 'a snare and very probably a

95

delusion as well'. Equally complex is the related question of how far Constantinian legislation reflected Christian, or generally accepted, moral values, as Roman law moved into its 'post-classical' phase, and Judith Evans Grubbs demonstrates (Chapter 5) how a search for simple 'Christian' influences is likely to mislead.

Thus, while Part I highlighted the problems of the Code as text, Part II reveals pitfalls in its use. Behind the Code was a world of social fluidity and diversity, of tradition interacting with change and of complexities which could not be encompassed by 'general' rules. The contents of the Code provide details from the canvas but are an unreliable guide, in isolation, to the character of the picture as a whole.

4. Hidden from History: the legislation of Licinius[1]

Simon Corcoran

The fate of the legislation of the emperor Licinius poses peculiar problems for the historian, which need to be considered in two stages. First, how was he depicted in the sources, especially the Theodosian Code? Second, how is the presence of possible Licinian laws in the Codes to be detected? The answers to these questions may help to illuminate the fate of unsuccessful emperors in the historical record and highlight a perhaps unforeseen difficulty confronting the compilers of the Theodosian Code.

First, a brief account of the emperor himself and his reign.[2] Licinius was a close associate of Diocletian's Caesar, Galerius, and served under him in the Persian war which ended in a decisive Roman victory in 298. Later, he accompanied the expedition led by Galerius (now Augustus) to Italy in 307, which aimed to unseat the usurper Maxentius and was sent on an unsuccessful embassy to the latter in Rome.

Following the failure of this Italian expedition, Galerius convened an imperial conference in Carnuntum in November 308, where in the presence of the retired Augusti, Diocletian and Maximian, he appointed Licinius as Augustus. Licinius was thus one of the few emperors of the time not to hold the lesser rank of Caesar, before becoming a full Augustus. It seems to have been Galerius' plan that Licinius should drive Maxentius out of Italy and replace him there. This Licinius never did. Instead, when Galerius died in 311, he took over all his European territory, while Maximinus in the East took his Asian territory, the two of them regarding each other with suspicion across the Bosphorus.

---

[1] I should like to express thanks for help and advice in writing this paper to Professor F.G.B. Millar, Professor T.D. Barnes and Dr. T. Wiedemann.

[2] The most accessible modern narrative can be found in Barnes, *CE* chapters 3 and 5, with further summary information in Barnes, *NE* pp. 43-4 & 80-2.

In 312, Constantine defeated Maxentius, occupied Italy and was granted rank as senior emperor by the senate in Rome. Licinius then cemented an alliance with Constantine by marrying the latter's sister at Milan in February 313. When Maximinus proceeded to invade Licinius' dominions, Licinius hurried East and defeated him near Adrianople in April 313. By the end of that summer, Maximinus was dead and Licinius master of the East. At Milan, Licinius and Constantine had discussed policy towards the Christians. Persecution had already ceased in their territories and Licinius appeared in the East as a liberator from the persecution that Maximinus had only relaxed at the very end.

Relations between the two remaining emperors were soon marked by conspiracy or suspicion of conspiracy. In 315, a son was born to Licinius, providing an heir for the East. In October 316 Constantine attacked and defeated Licinius and this led to a negotiated settlement.[3] Licinius lost nearly all his European territory, while his son and Constantine's two sons were proclaimed Caesars in March 317. Relations deteriorated again after 321, when Licinius refused to recognise Constantine's consuls. Affairs reached fever pitch when Constantine violated Licinius' territory while dealing with a barbarian incursion in 323.

Since Constantine was openly and clearly Christian, Licinius perhaps regarded Christians as potentially treacherous and he now started to take measures against them, though these never amounted to a full persecution. It was enough, however, to provide Constantine with the role of crusading liberator, and he defeated Licinius in July 324 at Adrianople and again at Chrysopolis opposite Byzantium in September. Licinius surrendered, being promised his life, and was sent into custody in Thessalonica. The following spring, from real or fabricated fears of conspiracy, he was executed.

Thus it was the victorious and Christian Constantine who dominated the historical record. Even though Licinius was the saviour of the East from Maximinus, he never gained the accolades given to Constantine. As an avowed Christian favouring Christianity, Constantine naturally received the overwhelming support of Christian writers. Licinius, however, also failed to win a glowing press from pagan sources.[4] Zosimus, who is consistently hostile to Constantine and brands him an oath breaker both over the first civil war against

---

[3] Seeck, *Regesten* p. 163 followed the view that placed the first civil war in 314. The later date is now firmly established. See T.D. Barnes, 'Lactantius and Constantine', *JRS* 63 (1973), pp. 36-8.

[4] For Licinius in the Latin sources, see R. Andreotti, 'L'imperatore Licinio nella tradizione storiographica latina' in *Hommages a Leon Herrmann* (1956), pp. 105-23. In Greek, the Anonymous *post-Dionem* (Muller, *FHG* 4 p. 199) is described as having 'una certa simpatia' by G. Brizzi, 'La vittoria sarmatica di Costantino e la propaganda liciniana', *Alba Regia* 17 (1979), p. 59.

Licinius and for the execution of Licinius after his fall,[5] avoids the chance to paint a glowing picture of Licinius to set against Constantine. Even in the pages of Lactantius, where Licinius is shown as blessed with an angelic visitation from God before his victory over Maximinus, he still emerges in a rather sinister light as both miserly and cruel.[6] Finally, his record as a persecutor himself in Eusebius' account pales beside that of Galerius or Maximinus.[7] Lacking passionate commitment to either side, he is pushed into the background.[8]

Reconstructing his activities as emperor is not easy. The fullest account of his government is provided by Eusebius in the *Ecclesiastical History* and *Life of Constantine*. Eusebius, of course, is concerned to show Licinius changed by madness into a persecutor.[9] But the depiction of his misrule extends further. He is charged with a variety of standard crimes such as cruelty, greed and lust.[10] But he is also portrayed as the ungrateful junior, plotting against his benefactor and relative.[11] Most significantly, however, he is attacked as an innovator in various matters of marriage and the rights of the dying and as a deviser of harsh taxation.[12]

Constantine, in retrospect, called his defeated rival 'the common enemy of the world'[13] and in the legal texts branded him as a 'tyrant', a term which in Latin carries the meaning of usurping or illegitimate ruler.[14] Thus in December 324, not long after the final defeat of Licinius, Constantine says:

> Let all know that, with the constitutions and laws of the tyrant Licinius rescinded, they should observe the sanction of ancient law (*vetus ius*) and of our statutes.[15]

[5] Zosimus 2.18.1 and 2.28.2

[6] Lactantius, *De Mort. Pers.* 46.3 (visit from an angel), 46.12 (miserly), 50.5 (cruel).

[7] In the *Ecclesiastical History*, Eusebius concentrates upon Galerius, Maximinus and Maxentius. The description of the Licinian persecution is an afterthought, only added following Licinius' overthrow. In the *Life of Constantine*, however, more space is devoted to the anti-Christian activities of Licinius than of the other persecuting emperors.

[8] One more recent writer characterised Licinius as 'a barbarous old heathen soldier as ignorant of religion as possible' (H.M. Gwatkin, *Studies of Arianism* (1882), p. 31).

[9] Eusebius, *HE* 9.9.12, 10.8.8-9, 10.8.14, 10.9.2-3, *VC* 1.56.1-2.

[10] Eusebius, *HE* 10.8.11-13, *VC* 1.54.2-55.3. Variations upon these charges are made against many contemporary emperors, mostly the persecutors.

[11] Eusebius, *HE* 10.8.2-6, *VC* 1.49.1-50.2.

[12] Eusebius, *HE* 10.8.12-13 = *VC* 1.55.1-3.

[13] Constantine's letter to Alexander and Arius at Eusebius, *VC* 2.66

[14] Such a ruler may be seen as additionally possessing the cruelty and capriciousness which we associate with the word tyrant. The most important Theodosian title in this regard is *CTh* 15.14, *de infirmandis his quae sub tyrannis aut barbaris gesta sunt*.

[15] 'Remotis Licini tyranni constitutionibus et legibus omnes sciant veteris iuris et statutorum nostrorum observari debere sanctionem' (*CTh* 15.14.1). The manuscript date is 16 May 324 (*xvii kal. Iun.*), emended by Seeck, *Regesten* pp. 99 & 174 to 16 December (*xvii kal. Ian.*), so as to follow the defeat of Licinius.

This is as unequivocal a statement as one could desire. But a later text says:

> Though the acts of the tyrant and his judges are annulled, let no one wish to overturn through trickery what he himself has voluntarily done or what was lawfully executed.[16]

The two succeeding texts under the same Theodosian title (*CTh* 15.14.3-4) carry manuscript dates of July 326, and the Code compilers must have taken these as also referring to Licinius. Both, however, can be convincingly emended to January 313, when Constantine was still in Rome, dealing with the aftermath of the overthrow of Maxentius.[17] Nevertheless, the content of *CTh* 15.14.3 is important for Constantine's attitude towards the question of the legislation of usurpers:

> We direct that what the tyrant replied by way of rescripts contrary to law (*contra ius*) is not valid, but his legally correct rescripts are not to be opposed.[18]

The aftermath of the violent overthrow of a ruler is a dangerous time. The victor will wish to establish himself by damning his predecessor's government, perhaps conducting a purge. But the accusations and counter-accusations need to be held in check, and delators have to be restrained.[19] Total abolition of the acts of a ruler renders all legal and administrative processes during his reign open to question. This is a recipe for chaos. Pronouncements by the victor, therefore, try to temper *damnatio memoriae* with stability.

The emperor is a source of law and precedent, but a 'tyrant' emperor is seen as constitutionally illegitimate and his acts cannot be accepted as enjoying a validity emanating from himself as usurper.[20] Therefore the ability for him to make law is denied, but law already exists outside

[16] 'Tyranni et iudicum eius gestis infirmatis nemo per calumniam velit quod sponte ipse fecit evertere nec quod legitime gestum est' (*CTh* 15.14.2, February 325).

[17] See Seeck, *Regesten* pp. 64 & 160. *CTh* 15.14.3 is addressed to the *praefectus vigilum* at Rome; 15.14.4 is addressed to the senate and deals with the restitution of senators forced to serve as *navicularii*, which is clearly a matter concerning the city of Rome. This should have arisen from Maxentius' justifiable concern over the corn supply, once the revolt of Domitius Alexander in Africa had impressed upon him the importance but precariousness of the shipping of corn to the city. For the famine probably caused by the revolt, see *Pan. Lat.* 9(12).4.4 and the Chronographer of 354 in *MGH AA* IX p. 148.

[18] 'Quae tyrannus contra ius rescribsit non valere praecipimus, legitimis eius rescribtis minime inpugnandis.'

[19] Contrast the reprisals and accusations in Africa after Maxentius' suppression of Alexander (Zosimus 2.14.3-4) with Constantine's restraining of delators after the fall of Maxentius (*CTh* 10.10.1-2; *Pan. Lat.* 9(12).20.4).

[20] For a discussion of the problems associated with *recessio actorum* in the Later Empire, covering most of the points mentioned here, see G. Sautel, 'Usurpations du pouvoir imperial dans le monde romain et *rescissio actorum*' in *Studi in Onore di Pietro de Francisci* 3 (1956), pp. 480-91.

and independently of him. The concept of *vetus ius* is therefore very useful (though, as we shall see, it is not an inviolable shibboleth). Where the 'tyrant' conforms to it, his actions should not be challenged. The majority of private legal actions under his rule are therefore safeguarded. Indeed, even Constantine admits that rescripts emanating from himself can be *contra ius*. Thus he says:

> Rescripts contrary to law are not to be valid, in whatever manner they have been obtained. For the judges should rather follow what the public laws command.[21]

We must remember that, unlike imperial edicts and letters which are often described as laws, private rescripts are not strictly speaking laws.[22] Rather they are supposed to be authoritative statements explaining what the law already is. Many rescripts point out to the petitioner what a rescript cannot do. Thus Diocletian tells one petitioner:

> A document, which does not accord with law or statute, this it is not fitting for us to confirm; for we are not at all accustomed to grant benefits to petitioners without regard to the injury caused to anyone else.[23]

Any rescript that attempted to do so, whether through corruption, error or ignorance, would be *contra ius*.[24] Such a situation would be the enslavement of the freeborn under a tyranny, noted by Constantine as a product of the rule of Maxentius.[25]

As the safeguards in Constantine's laws seem to cover only rescripts, it is clear where abolition would be directed in the case of Licinius.

---

[21] 'Contra ius rescribta non valeant, quocumque modo fuerint inpetrata. Quod enim publica iura praescribunt, magis sequi iudices debent' (*CTh* 1.2.2, August 315). This text and the difficulties of interpretation over rescripts *contra ius* are discussed by D.V. Simon, *Konstantinisches Kaiserrecht. Studien anhand der Reskriptenpraxis und der Schenkungsrecht* (1977), pp. 11-16.

[22] The only description of a private rescript as a law is in trial proceedings of 340, where a rescript of Constantine is described in Greek as *nomos* (*FIRA*² 3.101 p. 321).

[23] 'Scriptura, quae nec iure nec legibus consistit, nec a nobis hanc confirmari convenit, quippe cum beneficia citra cuiusquam iniuriam petentibus decernere minime soleamus' (*Consultatio* 6.17). For other Diocletianic texts telling petitioners what rescripts cannot do, see *CJust* 2.4.16, 2.9.3, 3.32.12, 4.44.3, 4.54.7, 5.3.9, 6.23.10, 8.4.3, 8.55.5. Note that *CJust* 8.47.5 restates the legal position that women cannot adopt, and grants an *adnotatio* to allow it as an exception in this particular case. It does not change the law. See W. Turpin, '*Adnotatio* and imperial rescript in Roman legal procedure' *RIDA* 3rd series 35 (1988), pp. 296-7.

[24] This attitude lies behind the probably apocryphal anecdote that Macrinus rescinded all previous rescripts as being the products of *imperiti* or juristically ignorant emperors (*SHA, Macr.* 13.1). See D. Liebs, 'OM 13,1 und das Reskriptenwesen in der Historia Augusta' in *Historia-Augusta-Colloquium Bonn 1982/3* (1985), pp. 221-37.

[25] *CTh* 5.8.1 (314); cf. *CJust* 7.14.4 (293) for someone enslaved under the Palmyrene regime *c.* 270.

Major edicts of Licinius, containing unwarranted innovations, would appear to be the most vulnerable form of his enactments. Eusebius protests:

> Why is it necessary to record singly and severally the deeds of the God-hater and how this man, who was the extreme opposite of lawful, invented lawless laws?[26]

He charges Licinius with altering the ancient, wisely established laws of the Romans with respect to marriage and the rights of the dying.[27] Yet in 320, Constantine himself issued an edict that fundamentally altered marriage and testamentary law,[28] the most famous part of this being the annulment of most of the provisions against celibacy in the *Lex Papia Poppaea* of AD 9, a law which Constantine himself calls *vetus ius* (*CTh* 8.16.1).[29] Eusebius praises both the celibacy and testamentary dispositions of Constantine for rectifying the defects of the original laws and using reason to make them more righteous (Eusebius, *VC* 4.26.2-4).[30] It is remarkable to find the same author, who does not allude to any interrelationship between the two sets of imperial laws, nevertheless directing criticisms at Licinius for apparently enacting new legislation on precisely the same topics and at the same time as Constantine. We cannot know whether either emperor acted in knowledge of or in reaction to the other's legislation. Thus *vetus ius* is a useful concept to employ, whether an emperor cites it as precedent, claims to improve upon it or is criticised for contravening it.[31]

[26] Eusebius, *HE* 10.8.11.

[27] Eusebius, *HE* 10.8.12.

[28] This is an edict of Constantine *ad populum*, given at Serdica, 31 January, posted at Rome 1 April 320 and made up of the following excerpts: *CTh* 3.2.1 (*CJust* 8.34.3), 4.12.3, 8.16.1, 11.7.3, *CJust* 6.9.9, 6.23.15, 6.37.21 (Seeck, *Regesten*, p. 169). The *CJust* extracts are dated in the subscripts to 339, but a reference in a law of Justinian supports the attribution to Constantine (*CJust* 5.70.7.3). The Constantinian dating is demonstrated by B. Albanese, 'L'abolizione postclassica delle forme solenni nei negozi testamentari' in *Sodalitas: Scritti in Onore di Antonio Guarino* 2 (1984), pp. 777-92.

[29] The panegyrist before Constantine and Maximian in 307 had praised just this law (*Pan. Lat.* 6(7).2.4). Another part of the edict of 320 (*CTh* 4.12.3) cites *vetus ius* with approval.

[30] Sozomen, *HE* 1.9 discusses this reform in a similar vein. However, he also states that Constantine gave additional testamentary privileges to those embracing a life of continence and virginity, and supports Constantine's action by citing ancient Roman practice in regard to the Vestal Virgins.

[31] In addition to the examples already mentioned from the edict of 320, Constantine cites *vetus ius* as precedent at *CTh* 9.1.5, 9.24.1, 12.11.1, but improves on it at *CTh* 11.39.1. Note the same dichotomy for Diocletian, who modifies *vetus* or *priscum ius* (*CJust* 8.54.3, 9.9.27), while appealing to it repeatedly in the Damascus incest edict (*Collatio* 6.4). It is ironic that Constantine's own statutes were regarded as unwarranted innovations by his nephew, Julian, who styled him *novator turbatorque priscarum legum et moris antiquitus recepti* (Ammianus 21.10.8) and repealed some of his laws, re-establishing *antiquum ius* or *vetus ius* (*CTh* 2.5.2, 3.1.3).

The same Theodosian title (*CTh* 15.14) that contains the three laws I have cited, records other similar legislation by later emperors on the aftermath of the overthrow of a 'tyrant' or usurper. Arcadius and Honorius state that the time of the tyranny (of Eugenius, 392-4) shall be considered as though it had not been (*CTh* 15.14.9,395), although safeguards for certain private legal acts are provided with respect to the usurpations of Magnentius (350-3), Magnus Maximus (383-8) and Eugenius (*CTh* 15.14.5,8,9). However, in combining Constantine's annulment of Licinius' laws with texts dealing with later usurpers, the Code compilers did Licinius an injustice. Unlike Magnentius, Magnus Maximus, and of course Maxentius, who had received only brief and uncertain recognition, if at all,[32] Licinius was no usurper. His appointment as Augustus by Galerius at Carnuntum in November 308 was as legitimate as could be. He had shared rule with Constantine, though sometimes in conflict, for over a decade after the overthrow of Maximinus in 313.

This leads to another problem. Constantine clearly differentiates between the laws of Licinius and his own (*CTh* 15.14.1). But Licinius was a tyrant only in retrospect. All imperial pronouncements will have included the names of both emperors as joint issuers. In the theory of imperial collegiality, the action of either was the action of both. Therefore, Constantine's own legitimate acts would have to be emended to remove Licinius. And the abolition of Licinius' acts would involve the invalidation of texts bearing Constantine's name as well.

This creates complications of titulature. Eusebius could emend passages in the *Ecclesiastical History* where he was favourable to Licinius.[33] But although Licinius was deleted from the heading of Galerius' toleration edict (Eusebius, *HE* 8.17.5),[34] he remained embedded in the so-called 'edict of Milan', a letter to the governor of Bithynia posted at Nicomedia in June 313.[35] It is the only document of

---

[32] Constantine sufficiently recognised Maxentius as to have some (extremely rare) coins minted in his name at Trier (*RIC* 6 pp. 41, 156, 158, 217). Constantius II never recognised Magnentius. Magnus Maximus enjoyed brief and temporary recognition from Theodosius I (see J. Matthews, *Western Aristocracies and Imperial Court AD 364-425* (1975), p. 179).

[33] Eusebius, *HE* 9.9.1, 12. The principal variants are listed by T.D. Barnes, 'The Editions of Eusebius' *Ecclesiastical History*', *GRBS* 21 (1980), pp. 196-7.

[34] No edition of the *Ecclesiastical History* includes Maximinus in the edict heading, presumably a deliberate omission by Eusebius. It may also be wondered whether, conversely, Eusebius disassociated Constantine and Licinius from Maximinus' pronouncements by omitting them from the two texts in which the name of Maximinus alone appears in the heading (Eusebius, *HE* 9.9a.1 & 9.10.7). Note that the petition against the Christians sent to Maximinus in 312 from Lycia and Pamphylia was addressed to Maximinus, Constantine and Licinius (*CIL* 3.12132). The reply to them and the similar reply to Tyre, which Eusebius, *HE* 9.7.2-3 ascribes to Maximinus alone (though without directly quoting the opening formula), should have included all three emperors as issuers.

[35] Lactantius, *De Mort. Pers.* 48.2-12. Eusebius' version, presumably the copy sent to

the period where the anonymity of collegiate plurals gives way to the naming of both emperors as they agree on the measures to be taken.[36] This surviving mention of Licinius is only to be expected, as any of his legislation in favour of the Christians would be that most likely to be left untouched.[37]

A case of the certain survival of a Licinian enactment is the Brigetio Tablet.[38] This contains a letter on military privileges to an unknown Dalmatius, possibly *praeses* of Valeria.[39] It was originally issued from Serdica on 10 June 311 and therefore by Licinius.[40] The heading bears the names of Constantine and Licinius, with the name of Licinius erased. It clearly remained valid after his fall. Thus a pronouncement of Licinius survived. Note, however, that this text comes from territory already under the rule of Constantine from 316, and therefore long before any *damnatio memoriae* of Licinius.[41] It is possible that the fate of Licinius' enactments in the territories he lost in 316 differed from what happened after 324.

By contrast, where Licinius had not been so generous in his dispositions, they were revoked in no uncertain terms. Thus, in *CTh* 8.4.1, dealing with the liturgical immunity of *cohortales*, Constantine abolished what the tyrant decreed (*iniquissime tyrannus constituit*) and enacted more favourable rules of his own.[42] Thus the good

---

the governor of Palestine, occurs at *HE* 10.5.2-14.

[36] Lactantius, *De Mort. Pers.* 48.2; Eusebius, *HE* 10.5.4. The emphasis may also be designed to underline the dropping from the imperial college of the defeated but not yet dead Maximinus.

[37] As noted for Maxentius by T.D. Barnes, 'Lactantius and Constantine', *JRS* 63 (1973), p. 46. Note that, in another Christian context, Licinius is preserved in the inscription to a letter of 315 from Constantine to Probianus in Africa (Augustine, *Ep.* 88.4 = *Contra Cresconius* 3.70.81). Both Maximinus and Licinius are implied by the address *A. GGG. NNN.* in the letter of Anullinus to Constantine at Augustine, *Ep.* 88.2.

[38] *FIRA*[2] 1.93.

[39] He is often supposed to be praetorian prefect, *dux* or at least vicar. See variously D. van Berchem, *L'Armée de Dioclétien et la Réforme Constantinienne* (1952), pp. 80-1, *PLRE* vol. 1 p. 240 and Barnes, *NE* p. 232 n. 28. However, the conjunction of the forms of address *tua dicatio* and *tua devotio* and the question of military, specifically veteran, privileges, occur in another text certainly addressed to a *praeses* (Florianus) at *CTh* 7.20.1 (dated 318 in the manuscripts, but to 326 by Seeck, *Regesten* p. 176).

[40] For some inexplicable reason, the original publication renders the date *IIII idus Iunias* as 9 June (I. Paulovics, 'Una legge di Costantino e Licinio in una tavola di bronze recentemente scoperta in Ungheria' in *Atti del Congresso Internazionale di Diritto Romano 1933, Rome* vol. 1 (1934), p. 548 and *A Sznyi Törvénytábla: La Table de Privilèges de Brigetio* (1936), pp. 10-12 & 40-2), followed by *AE* 1937.232, *FIRA*[2] 1 456, D. van Berchem, *L'Armée de Dioclétien et la Réforme Constantinienne* (1952), pp. 75, 80 & 83 and Barnes, *CE* p. 40 and *NE* pp. 81, 137, 143 n. 13 & p. 232. The date is correctly noted at *PLRE* 1, p. 240.

[41] W. Seston, 'Recherches sur la chronologie du règne de Constantin le grand', *REA* 39 (1937), pp. 212-14 argues that the titulature of Constantine shows that the imperial titles on the upper band of the tablet frame were added *c.* 317-21.

[42] The manuscript date is 315, but is emended by Seeck, *Regesten* p. 176 to 326. There is also a papyrus edict which appears to show Constantine in 325 reversing an increase

regulations of Licinius survive quietly, while the bad are undone with a flourish.

Moving now to the second main topic of this chapter, how are Licinian constitutions to be identified? When Theodosius II ordered the compilation of his Code, he chose to start with the first Christian emperor.[43] Except as a tyrant, Constantine's colleague Licinius is not acknowledged. Only for the purposes of consular dating does he survive, but with the *A* for Augustus removed.[44]

Elsewhere, he is not entirely forgotten. Four constitutions in the *Fragmenta Vaticana* have headings implying two Augusti at this time, though without naming names, and only one is strictly accurate.[45] A further three give Licinius as Augustus in the consular date.[46]

Justinian's code is even more informative. Four constitutions give Constantine and Licinius as the issuing emperors as follows:

CJust 3.1.8. *Impp. Constantinus et Licinius AA. ad Dionysium.* 15th May 314.

CJust 6.1.3. *Impp. Constantinus et Licinius AA. ad Probum. Sine die et consule.*[47]

CJust 7.16.41. *Impp. Constantinus et Licinius AA. ad Titianum praesidem Cappadociae.*[48]

CJust 7.22.3. *Exemplum sacrarum litterarum Constantini et Licinii AA. ad Dionysium vice praefectorum agentem.* 29 April 314.

The origin of these constitutions is uncertain. The *Codex Justinianus* was supposedly compiled from the Gregorian, Hermogenian and Theodosian Codes plus the later novels. However, it

---

in the age-limit for immunity from liturgies or poll tax made by Licinius (Barnes, *NE* pp. 234-7).

[43] On the importance of Constantine both as cited in the Code and as its starting point, see E. Volterra, 'Sul contenuto del Codice Teodosiano', *BIDR* 3rd series 23 (1981), pp. 103-12.

[44] The sole exception is *CTh* 11.27.1, where the date is probably wrong in any case. The law is addressed to Ablabius (no office given) from Naissus with the manuscript date 315. Seeck, *Regesten* p. 179 placed the law in 329. 319 is also quite plausible, with Ablabius as a vicar in Italy, and would harmonise with Constantine's other known movements in 319 as given in Barnes, *NE* p. 74.

[45] *FV* 33-6. The headings read *Augg et Caess*. This is inaccurate except for *FV* 36, dated 317/9. A Constantinian plurality of Augusti and Caesars occurred only from 317-24. Such headings, however, may suggest that *FV* was compiled at precisely this time, shortly before 324. I think that F.G.B. Millar, *The Emperor in the Roman World* (1977), p. 244 n. 30 is wrong to doubt the date of *FV* 34 by supposing that the heading implies the first tetrarchy, since the *FV* employs some strange styles in its inscriptions and nowhere else uses this heading for the first tetrarchy.

[46] *FV* 32, 33, 274.

[47] This heading is also preserved as *Imp. Constantinus et Licinius C.*

[48] This constitution lacks any subscript. A papyrus fragment of *CJust*, which includes this passage, preserves only indecipherable traces where the subscript should be, which in any case might have been just the formula *sine die et consule* (*PSI* XIII 1347).

contains some 240 constitutions from the period of the Theodosian Code not found in that Code. Now, the Theodosian Code has a number of lacunae and gaps. Some of the unallocated Justinian constitutions may derive from these gaps, though no complete attempt has been made to correlate the subject matter of these Justinian texts with incomplete or missing titles in the Theodosian Code.[49]

There is a more plausible source for the joint Licinian-Constantinian constitutions. One of our texts opens with the words *exemplum sacrarum litterarum* (copy of the sacred letters, *CJust* 7.22.3), while a second ends with the phrase *sine die et consule* (without diurnal and consular date, *CJust* 6.1.3). The first formula occurs once[50] and the second not at all in the Theodosian Code. Indeed, a constitution of Constantine from 322 denies validity to any imperial pronouncement that lacks day and year (*CTh* 1.1.1). Even the Theodosian laws before this date carry a fully dated subscript. These constitutions are, therefore, unlikely to derive from the Theodosian Code.

Both these formulae, however, occur elsewhere in Justinian's Code in material of Diocletianic date.[51] They are therefore typical of the Gregorian and Hermogenian Codes.[52] These codes were probably published c. 292 and 295 respectively[53] and both were subsequently expanded. The Gregorian Code cannot be shown to have material after the abdication of Diocletian in 305.[54] However, seven constitutions of Valentinian and Valens are attributed to the Hermogenian Code in the *Consultatio*, a late fifth- or sixth-century work from the West, giving imaginary answers and explanatory discourse as though from the consultation of a jurist.[55] If the Hermogenian Code was expanded as late as the 360s, additions may also have been made on previous occasions. The presence of the name of Licinius as emperor in the constitutions under discussion implies that one such expansion took

[49] The closest to this is Krüger's incomplete edition of the Theodosian Code, Books 1-6 (Berlin, 1923) and 7-8 (Berlin, 1926).

[50] *CTh* 16.5.20 (391).

[51] *Exemplum sacrarum litterarum* – *CJust* 3.3.3, 7.16.40, 9.2.8, 9.41.8, 10.1.5, 10.32.2, 10.42.10 & 11.55.1, with specific Gregorian Code examples at *Collatio* 1.10 and 6.4. *Sine die et consule* – *CJust* 3.38.10, 5.59.1, 5.62.19, 6.2.10, 6.19.1, 6.26.6, 6.36.4, 7.4.11, 7.53.8, 7.62.6, 9.2.8, 9.41.8, 10.32.2 & 11.55.1 (*sine die* at 4.2.14).

[52] This is the view of Th. Mommsen in his edition of the *Codex Theodosianus* (Berlin, 1905), vol. 1(1) p. CLX.

[53] The fullest account of the dating is still G. Rotondi, 'Studi sulle fonti del codice giustinianeo' in *Scritti Giuridici I* (1922), pp. 111-46.

[54] The latest item is *Collatio* 15.3, probably of 302.

[55] *Consultatio* 9.1-7. This attribution is open to doubt. It appears in the original edition of the *Consultatio* by Cujas in 1577, based on the only known source, an apograph in his possession since 1563. However, Cujas showed no knowledge of the Hermogenian attribution, when he placed all seven texts in his 1566 edition of *CTh*, at the same time omitting them in his assemblage of Hermogenian Code fragments. See E. Volterra, 'Le sette costituzioni di Valentiniano e Valente contenute nella *Consultatio*', *BIDR* 3rd

place before the overthrow of Licinius and the expunging of his name in 324.

Further, these additions were probably made to the Hermogenian Code in Licinius' eastern territory. One of these texts is a letter to Titianus, *praeses* of Cappadocia (*CJust* 7.16.41).[56] This at least must be a true constitution of Licinius, since it concerns his part of the Empire. If the other texts derive from the same source, we may suppose that they too genuinely belong to Licinius. Hermogenian is said to have produced three editions of his Code.[57] It could be that after the initial publication in 295, a second version appeared *c.* 305 and a final one before Licinius' fall in 324, though neither of these revisions could have been very extensive.

Let us now move on to the Theodosian Code. Here there are no headings that include Licinius. Indeed, very few even acknowledge the existence of Constantine's sons as Caesars, namely Crispus (317-26), Constantine II (from 317), Constantius II (from 324) and Constans (from 333).[58] The constitutions from 313 to 337 appear to emanate from Constantine alone.

How is Licinius to be found, if at all? The simplest criterion is one of geography. *A priori*, any constitution that has a place of issue in its subscript that is in Licinius' territory, must be seen as his enactment. And any law with a destination in the East must be similarly regarded. There are over twenty such texts. Most have had their transmitted manuscript date or place emended by various scholars. Thus Licinius all but disappears.

Can he be saved? I do not want to consider all of these texts. Most of the emendations have been made for unimpeachable reasons.[59]

---

series 24 (1982), pp. 171-204.

[56] This text is undated. It is a rescript to the governor on a specific case. Identification with the Titianus of *CTh* 8.5.2 (see below) would suggest a date of 316. Barnes, *NE* p. 154 n. 40 suggests it could also be 310-12, presumably therefore a law of Galerius or Maximinus. However, the two texts of Constantine and Licinius to Dionysius (*CJust* 3.1.8, 7.22.3) are dated to April and May 314, after the fall of Maximinus. A positive attribution to Licinius is the most convincing solution.

[57] Sedulius, *Epistola ad Macedonium (altera)* in *CSEL* vol. 10 p. 172.

[58] The heading *Constantinus A et C* occurs at *CTh* 2.22.1, 3.17.1, 3.17.2, 7.1.1, 7.12.1, 9.16.3, 10.1.1 and 11.39.2. A Caesar is actually named at *CJust* 5.1.2 (Constantius) and 5.34.11 (Constanti(n)us). In addition to the Vatican Fragments already cited, the Caesars also occur at *FV* 249, 273 and 287. Crispus is nowhere named as an issuing Caesar in our surviving legal sources, though some laws in the fifth century still bore his name, as seems to be implied by Sozomen, *HE* 1.5.2. Crispus does get one mention in the Theodosian Code, other than from consular dating, in an amnesty granted for the birth of his child (*CTh* 9.38.1, 322).

[59] Emendations that I do not discuss are listed here. On account of the confusions over many subscripts, I have not included every text for which one variant reading could give a theoretical Licinian provenance. The manuscript date and place are given, followed by proposed emendations with their sources in brackets. *CTh* 2.16.2, July 315, Naissus (319; Seeck, *Regesten*, p. 168). [footnote 59 continues on p. 108]

However, I do want to discuss a few, where the attribution to Licinius need not be discounted automatically. These are as follows:

CTh 10.14.1. Constantine to Mygdonius, *castrensis palatii*. 21 March 315, Antioch.

CTh 8.4.3, 10.7.1, 10.20.1, 12.1.5. Constantine *ad Bithynos*. 21 July 317 (Nicomedia?).

CTh 1.27.1. Constantine (recipient lacking). 23 June 318, Constantinople.

CTh 11.30.12, 12.1.8. Constantine to Florenti(n)us. 13 April 323, Constantinople.

CTh 8.1.1. Constantine to Leontius. 9 June 319, posted at Hierapolis.

CTh 2.30.1. Constantine *ad universos provinciales*. 2 June 315, Sirmium.

CTh 11.16.3. Constantine *ad edictum Calchedoniensium et Macedoniensium*. 24 April 324.

Considering first the more plausible Licinian laws, let us start with *CTh* 10.14.1, addressed to Mygdonius, *castrensis sacri palatii* on 21 March 315 from Antioch. The presence of Licinius in Antioch is not incompatible with what little we know of his movements between 314 and 316.[60] After the fall of Maximinus, he visited Antioch, where he gained unpopularity by not distributing largesse.[61] He may have campaigned on the Persian front in 314. So, he could still have been in Antioch in spring 315, although there also has to be time for some Danube campaigning.

The recipient is also quite plausible. The late Roman imperial court was characterised by the presence of eunuchs as *cubicularii*, though quite how far this had been established by Diocletian is unclear.[62] Eunuchs are already described as powerful at his court,[63] though

---

7.20.3, October 320, Constantinople (325; Seeck, *Regesten* p. 175).

8.7.1, March 315, Thessalonica – to *consularis aquarum* (324; *PLRE* 1 p. 371).

8.12.2, April 316, Serdica – to Africa (317; Seeck, *Regesten* p. 165).

11.1.1, June 315, Constantinople (Jan. 360; Seeck, *Regesten* p. 207).

11.27.1, May 315, Naissus – to Ablabius, referring to Italy (329; Seeck, *Regesten* p. 179).

13.5.3, May 319, Constantinople – to Africa (Trier, June 314; Seeck, *Regesten* p. 162).

14.8.1, September 315, Naissus (339; Seeck, *Regesten* p.189. 329; *PLRE* 1 p. 285).

14.25.1, December 315, Sirmium – to Africa (318; Seeck, *Regesten* p. 167).

16.8.1, October 315, Bergule/Mursella? (339; Seeck, *Regesten* p. 187. 329; Barnes, *NE* p. 78 and A. Linder, *The Jews in Roman Imperial Legislation* (1987), pp. 124-32).

[60] See Barnes, *NE* pp. 81-2.

[61] See G. Downey, *A History of Antioch in Syria from Seleucus to the Arab Conquest* (1961), p. 335. This is based on Malalas 12.314, whose account of the tetrarchic emperors is extremely garbled.

[62] See comments of W. Ensslin in *The Cambridge Ancient History XII* (1939), p. 388.

[63] Lactantius, *De Mort. Pers.* 15.2, probably to be identified with Dorotheus 2 (*PLRE* 1 p. 270) and Gorgonius 1 (*PLRE* 1 p. 398).

specific titles such as *praepositus sacri cubiculi* and the more junior *castrensis* are not yet attested. It is easy to imagine Mygdonius as born near Nisibis and named for the river there; then being castrated and imported into the Empire. Perhaps he was even among the booty of legendary scale taken by Galerius when he defeated Narses in 298.[64] He could then have passed into the entourage of Licinius from the court of Galerius or Maximinus.[65]

There is, therefore, nothing exceptional about the circumstances of this law to demand emendation. Seeck, however, chose to identify Mygdonius with the recipient of two letters of Libanius in 357.[66] This man was powerful and influential and had taken Libanius under his protection both in Athens and at Constantinople in the 340s. He survived to be able to deliver letters to Julian in 362. The texts that mention him do not indicate what posts he held. He does not sound like a eunuch palace official of Constantius II, of the type so disliked by Ammianus.[67] However, there is no positive evidence that at this period the *castrensis* was a eunuch.[68]

Identifying the two Mygdonii, Seeck proposed to emend the date 315 (Constantine and Licinius both cos. IV) to 346 (Constantius IV and Constans III). Confusion between imperial consular dates is the most likely source of incorrect subscripts, and this choice fits in with Constantius' itinerary.[69] Seeck had an additional assumption underlying his emendation. He believed that the first civil war between Constantine and Licinius took place in the autumn of 314;[70] thus Licinius would hardly have retired so far from his rival so soon after his defeat, even though he could have reached Antioch by 21 March 315. We have seen above, however, that, as the civil war occurred in 316-17, the date and place are compatible with Licinius' movements. The need for emendation therefore disappears. The identification of the two Mygdonii, though still plausible, is not

---

[64] For the booty, see Ammianus 22.4.8. K. Hopkins, *Conquerors and Slaves* (1978), pp. 192-3 suggests that it was this victory which led to a proliferation of eunuchs at court.

[65] Licinius served in the Persian War and could have presumably shared directly in the booty himself (Eutropius 10.4.1).

[66] O. Seeck, *Die Briefe des Libanius* (1906), p. 219 and *Regesten* pp. 38 & 194. For full ancient references, see *PLRE* 1 p. 614.

[67] For Ammianus on eunuchs, see J. Matthews, *The Roman Empire of Ammianus* (1989), pp. 274-7. For Libanius' own view, see *Or.* 62.9.

[68] E.A. Costa, 'The office of the *Castrensis Sacri Palatii* in the IVth century', *Byzantion* 42 (1972), pp. 358-87. He argues that no fourth-century *castrensis* can be shown to be a eunuch and that they were not initially *cubicularii*, but rather superior to the *praepositus*.

[69] It is thus used in the reconstruction of Constantius' movements by T.D. Barnes, 'Imperial Chronology, AD 337-350', *Phoenix* 34 (1980), p. 164.

[70] Seeck, *Regesten* p. 163.

imperative. It is therefore possible that the subscript date could be left unaltered, thus providing a law of Licinius.[71]

Next we come to a set of Theodosian extracts that are normally assigned to Licinius. Four passages regulating the possession of equestrian ranks constitute part of an edict issued to the Bithynians on 21 July 317 (*CTh* 8.4.3, 10.7.1, 10.20.1, 12.1.5). Given that Licinius' main residence from 317 was Nicomedia, it is even possible that this law implies his presence there at this time.[72]

It is surprising, in view of the tendency to emend away Licinian laws, that the consular date Gallicanus and Bassus (317) has not yielded to Gallicanus and Symmachus (330), thus making it an edict of Constantine.[73] Alternatively, did Licinius here merely follow a constitution of Constantine from January 317 (*CTh* 12.1.4), that precedes one of the extracts from this edict, as was the view of Seeck?[74] After the death of Galerius, Maximinus had claimed the title of senior emperor, but this was voted to Constantine by the senate after the defeat of Maxentius in 312 (Lactantius, *De Mort. Pers.* 44.11). Licinius was therefore constitutionally subordinate, as Eusebius stressed by portraying him as an ungrateful junior. Just as Maximinus at least pretended compliance with the authority of Constantine over the Christians in 312 (Eusebius, *HE* 9.9.13), so, it is supposed, Licinius repeated his senior's legislation in this matter. It has even been thought that he could not issue his own edicts.[75]

This argument does not hold in this case. Although both constitutions concern the status of decurions, their juxtaposition in the Code is misleading. In fact, they approach the question from different angles. Constantine is concerned to safeguard the due status of decurions and prevent usurpation of their privileges. Licinius is only mentioning decurions among a number of other groups whose entitlement to the prefectissimate and other ranks needs to be strictly regulated. If this is an edict of Licinius, there is no need to deny him the initiative for issuing it. Indeed, even the Caesars in the tetrarchic

---

[71] The case of Constantius and 346 is strengthened, if the almost identical law at *CTh* 10.14.2 (348) is seen as an imitative measure by Constans for the West. See P. Voci, 'Il diritto ereditario romano nell'età del tardo impero, 1: Le costituzioni del IV secolo' *Iura* 29 (1978), p. 25. Note that Constans refers to *pater noster* (Constantine), while the text under discussion does not – if it did, attribution to Constantius II would be certain, as Licinius did not have an imperial father.

[72] For Licinius at Nicomedia, see Barnes, *NE* p. 80.

[73] This idea is noted in passing by O. Seeck, 'Die Zeitfolge der Gesetze Constantins', *ZSS RA* 10 (1889), p. 219.

[74] Seeck, *Regesten* pp. 54 & 165.

[75] C. Habicht, 'Zur Geschichte des Kaisers Konstantin' *Hermes* 86 (1958), pp. 369-70 suggests that Licinius lost the power to legislate (other than repeating Constantine's western laws in the East) after his defeat in the civil war of 316/7.

system had some legislative competence.[76]

Moreover, the ability of a senior emperor to enforce his legislative will was severely limited. Even Diocletian could not force Constantius to implement the great persecution with eagerness.[77] With the breakdown of the settlement after the abdication in 305, the rulers probably went their separate ways, whatever the constitutional theory. Maximinus and Licinius split Galerius' dominions in 311, almost going to war and then concluding a peace treaty with one another.[78] Only in 313 did Licinius enter Constantine's territory, invited in peace to confer at Milan, and he was not pleased when Constantine violated his territory in 323. Of course, this does not preclude the possibility that Licinius might voluntarily imitate Constantine's legislation, though the similar problems facing any emperor make similar legislation inevitable.[79]

We now come to laws, whose ascription to Licinius is less likely. *CTh* 1.27.1, granting jurisidiction to Christian bishops, lacks any recipient in its heading and has a corrupt subscript, which appears to state that it was given at Constantinople in June 318. It has been suggested that Licinius issued this law from Byzantium, soon to be Constantinople.[80] Could this pagan have legislated so favourably for Christians?

Licinius conquered the East as a liberator from tyranny and persecution, bringing toleration to Christians. The 'edict of Milan' granted full toleration and restitution to the church. It is an even-handed pronouncement, specifying religious tolerance not just for Christians but for all – that it is not more favourable to Christians may represent the less enthusiastic attitude of Licinius, as opposed to that of Constantine, who was already extending immunities to clerics in

[76] The most clear example of this is a rescript of 305 from Maximinus as Caesar to Verinus, probably governor of Syria (*CJust* 3.12.1). See Barnes, *NE* p. 66. Note also *FV* 282 (*CJust* 8.53.6 and 3.29.4), a private rescript of Maximian in February 286, shortly before his elevation to Augustus on 1 April. This is more problematic as the dates for Maximian's elevation as Caesar and Augustus are not beyond dispute.

[77] Lactantius, *De Mort. Pers.* 15.7 says that he complied only as far as pulling down churches. Eusebius, *HE* 8.13.13 & *VC* 1.13.2 tries to deny that he did even that much.

[78] Lactantius, *De Mort. Pers.* 36.1-2. For a more favourable view of Maximinus as trying to uphold the tetrarchic system, see D. de Decker, 'La politique religieuse de Maxence' *Byzantion* 38 (1968) pp. 544-6 and P. Bruun, 'The Heraclean coinage of Maximinus Daza. A drastic proposal' in *Studies in Ancient History and Numismatics presented to Rudi Thomsen* (1988), pp. 179-94.

[79] For some unconvincing attempts to explain problems of dating in inscriptions and subscriptions of laws, by presuming legislative correspondence between Licinius and Constantine, see C. Castello, 'Rapporti legislativi tra Costantino e Licinio alla luce dell' *inscriptio* e della *subscriptio* di *CTh* 8, 18, 1' in *Accademia Romanistica Costantiniana, Atti: Il Convegno Internazionale 1975* (1976), pp. 399-47; and M. Sargenti, 'Contributi ai problemi della palingenesi delle costituzioni tardo-imperiali (*FV* 35 e *CTh* 3.1.2)', in *Accademia Romanistica Costantiniana, Atti: V Convegno Internazionale 1981* (1983), pp. 311-28.

[80] F.G.B. Millar, *The Emperor in the Roman World* (1977), p. 591 n. 7.

Africa.[81] But it is possible that Licinius extended immunity to clerics in imitation. This is inferred because the forcible appointment of clerics to town councils was one of the marks of his later persecution, implying the abolition of previous immunity.[82]

Licinius' wife, Constantine's sister, Constantia, was Christian[83] and close to Eusebius of Nicomedia, who had chosen the episcopal see where the power was; that is, one of the main imperial residences.[84] There were thus powerful Christian voices close to the emperor.[85] Could Licinius have listened to them? If Jews enjoyed certain rights of separate jurisdiction,[86] why not Christians? This was some time before tension between the two Augusti led Licinius to take action against the Christians at some point after 321. The Council of Nicaea in 325 called Licinius' rule a tyranny,[87] and after its conclusion, Eusebius was accused of abetting the tyrant.[88] Could the persecution of Licinius, localised and uneven as it was,[89] have selected its targets carefully? Perhaps the ban on synods of bishops was designed to hinder the meetings of Eusebius' opponents in the developing Arian controversy.[90]

Interesting though this scenario is, there are too many arguments against it. If Licinius had really helped the Arians, the ammunition would have been too good for Athanasius and other anti-Arian writers to ignore. In any case, the law is in keeping with Constantine's attitude. It is most likely this passage that he refers to in a letter addressed to the praetorian prefect Ablabius in 333 (*Const. Sirm.* 1), where he refers to such a law as already in existence. He criticises

[81] Eusebius, *HE* 10.7.2, winter 312/13; cf. *CTh* 16.2.1-2, from October 313 (Seeck, *Regesten* p. 161).

[82] Eusebius, *VC* 2.20.2, 2.30.1.

[83] On the Christianity of Constantia, see S. Gero, 'The True Image of Christ: Eusebius' letter to Constantia reconsidered', *JTS* 32 (1981), pp. 460-70.

[84] Barnes, *CE* p. 70. Eusebius of Nicomedia was related to Julius Julianus, Licinius' praetorian prefect.

[85] For influential pagans, note Hermogenes, who was supposed to have been a moderating influence upon an emperor usually identified as Licinius (F.G.B. Millar, *The Emperor in the Roman World* (1977), p. 100); and an unidentified correspondent of Iamblichus, who apparently delivered orations before Licinius (T.D. Barnes, 'A Correspondent of Iamblichus', *GRBS* 19 (1978), pp. 99-106).

[86] For discussion of a near contemporary rescript (*CJust* 3.13.3, 293), which appears to deal with Jewish jurisdiction, see A. Linder, *The Jews in Roman Imperial Legislation* (1987), pp. 114-17.

[87] *Canon* 11.

[88] In a letter to the church at Nicomedia, Constantine accused Eusebius of helping Licinius both in the persecution and the civil war (Gelasius, *HE* 1.11.22-3 = 3 *App.* 1.9-10 and Theodoret, *HE* 1.20.1-2).

[89] Socrates, *HE* 1.3.

[90] The ban may be quite late, shortly before the final civil war. See R. Williams, *Arius: Heresy and Tradition* (1987), pp. 49-50 and p. 268 n. 12.

Ablabius for not knowing his original disposition.[91] This neatly highlights the problem of dissemination of imperial pronouncements, where even a high official is in ignorance.

This law, therefore, need not be attributed to Licinius. The subscript of the constitution has been sufficiently explained by Seeck, who demonstrates how the consular date for 318 became corrupted to give Constantinople.[92] Any subscript mentioning Constantinople before the date of its founding is suspect. Two laws of 323 from the code also mention Constantinople (*CTh* 11.30.12, 12.1.8) and Seeck took these to refer to Constantine in Byzantium, at the time when he had to violate Licinius' territory in the emergency of a barbarian incursion,[93] although it might equally well mean Licinius in Byzantium.[94] However, I think it more likely that Constantine's name was transposed into the consular date, even though this was a year when Constantine as consul was not in the subscript, and that the name was then corrupted to Constantinople. The only emperor found issuing laws at Byzantium in this period is Diocletian in the 290s.[95]

The subscript of *CTh* 8.1.1 states that it was posted at Hierapolis on 9 June 319. If correct, this would have to be a law of Licinius, although as it was only posted, not issued, at Hierapolis, it does not provide evidence of Licinius' movements in a year for which there is no specific attestation.[96] Seeck, however, proposed that the recipient, Leontius, whose office is not given, should be identified with Constantius II's praetorian prefect of the east and redated to 343.[97] Constantius is otherwise attested issuing a law to Leontius at Hierapolis in June 343 (*CTh* 12.1.35) and was still in the city in July (*CTh* 15.8.1).[98] Against this, Jones argued that the use of the term *tabularii*, to denote financial officials of provincial governors, supports the manuscript date. Examination of the other laws under the same Theodosian title shows that the term *numerarii* was employed in 334 (8.1.4), but that the emperors ordered the term *tabularii* to be used again from 365 (8.1.9).[99] However, this presses too far an imperfectly understood terminology. The coincidence of Leontius and Hierapolis is far more convincing in supporting an attribution to Constantius II.

It is more difficult to identify the issuer of our next constitution, *CTh*

[91] Seeck, *Regesten* p. 7; cf. *Const. Sirm.* 4 (336), which is another re-enactment. For the whole question of legislative repetition in the Theodosian Code, see J. Gaudemet, 'Recherches sur la législation du Bas-Empire', in *Studi in Onore di Gaetano Scherillo* 2 (1972), pp. 693-715.

[92] Seeck, *Regesten* p. 57.   [93] Seeck, *Regesten* pp. 110-11 & 172.

[94] Barnes, *NE* p. 82 is tentative on this point.   [95] Barnes, *NE* pp. 50-4.

[96] See Barnes, *NE* pp. 80-2. Licinius' main residence at this time was Nicomedia.

[97] Seeck, *Regesten* p. 192.

[98] All these texts are used in the reconstruction of Constantius' movements by T.D. Barnes, 'Imperial chronology, AD 337-350', *Phoenix* 34 (1980), p. 163.

[99] A.H.M. Jones, 'The Roman Civil Service (clerical and sub-clerical grades)', *JRS* 38 (1948), p. 47 nn. 98-9. This is accepted by *PLRE* 1 p. 499 (Leontius 3).

2.30.1, an edict addressed to all the provincials on 2 June 315 from Sirmium. Here the choice is between keeping Sirmium and assigning the law to Licinius, or changing it to Sirmio (near Verona) to suit Constantine's movements, as is done in the case of another constitution.[100] The law seeks to prevent goods being seized as pledges for debt in civil cases, this being seen as detrimental to the collection of taxation for the fisc. It would press the content of this law too far to see this concern as a mark of the rapaciousness of Licinius, rather than as a typical imperial worry about the unhindered collection of taxes. It is as likely to be an edict of Constantine as one of Licinius.

The last puzzle of geography is a text of April 324 with the inscription giving the mysterious wording *ad edictum Calchedoniensium et Macedoniensium* (*CTh* 11.16.3), apparently mixing territories of Constantine and Licinius. There seems to be no ready explanation for the form or content of this heading.[101] Emendation of the date seems the least problematical solution.[102]

This completes the roll call of possible Licinian laws in the code based on the premises of geography. They can all be challenged with a degree of plausibility.

Licinius may still lurk elsewhere. Titianus, governor of Cappadocia, the recipient of *CJust* 7.16.41 from Licinius, discussed above, may be the same as the recipient of a letter on the abuse of the beasts of the *cursus publicus* (*CTh* 8.5.2).[103] Less certainly, the Probus of *CJust* 6.1.3 has been identified with the recipient of *CTh* 4.12.1, and both these with the praetorian prefect of Licinius, consul in 310.[104] But there is more to this argument than thus identifying an otherwise unknown recipient. The Theodosian title under which this text comes is concerned with the *Senatus Consultum Claudianum* and the question of women who cohabit with slaves. The code did not set out to provide a consistent body of constitutions, and under this title there are reversals of attitude towards the *senatus consultum*. Three of these laws plus the *interpretatio* of a fourth are attributed to Constantine, from the years 314, 317, 320 and 331, giving respectively a severe, then a lenient, another lenient and finally a severe approach (*CTh* 4.12.1-4). The solution of this imperial changeableness is seen to be to attribute the first law to Licinius, thus allowing Constantine to undergo only a

[100] *CTh* 7.22.1. Both options are mentioned by Barnes, *NE* p. 72 n. 113. P. Bruun, *Studies in Constantinian Chronology* (1961), p. 33 prefers to change the year to 319.

[101] For discussion of possible explanations for headings *ad edictum*, see J. Gaudemet, *La Formation du Droit Séculier et du Droit de L'Eglise aux IVe et Ve Siècles*, 2nd edition (1979), pp. 32-3.

[102] Seeck, *Regesten* p. 174 proposes the year 325.

[103] Seeck, *Regesten* p. 164. *PLRE* 1 p. 917 (Titianus 1 and 2) is more cautious.

[104] For the identification, see Seeck, *Regesten* pp. 53 & 162. For Probus, see Barnes, *NE* p. 127, who is against identifying him as recipient of the second letter and suggests that the *CJust* text dates from 310/11.

single change of mind.[105] Coincidence also lends plausibility to this idea, in that three of the four Licinian texts in the *Codex Justinianus* are concerned in various ways with slavery; the one to Probus, for instance, decrees amputation and other penalties for those slaves trying to flee to the barbarians. Thus severity in such matters is seen as a mark of Licinius' attitude. Cruelty, however, is a consistent trait in late Roman legislation, and there are plenty of harsh punishments in Constantine's own laws.[106] There also seems no particular need to eliminate imperial changes of mind, and such inconsistencies may in any case reflect changes in the advice offered by the *magistri epistularum* or other officials concerned with composing pronouncements. It does, however, seem to be a dangerous precedent to set, that Licinius should become a dumping ground for problematical Constantinian legislation.[107]

Epigraphy provides us with a further salutary warning. A letter of 314 (*CTh* 9.5.1) is addressed to Maximus, urban prefect at Rome, whose period of office (319-23) does not coincide with the subscript date, making emendation of the date the likeliest solution of the inconsistency.[108] But this text is also known as part of a larger edict inscribed on stone, the *Edictum de Accusationibus*. All five surviving copies of the edict come from Licinius' dominions (Lyttus, Tlos, Padua (but probably from Asia), Sinope and Pergamum)[109] and the Lyttus copy is headed with the words *exemplum sacri edicti*. At the very least then, what appears in the Code as an undoubted letter of Constantine went out as an edict in Licinius' territory. Sentiments of hostility to informers are found in other Constantinian texts (*CTh* 10.10.1, 2,312/13), shortly after the fall of Maxentius, the mark of an appropriate desire to limit the dislocation of a change of ruler and to suppress what every ruler professed to loathe. Likewise, the edict issued early in 314 would be appropriate action by Licinius following the death of Maximinus in the summer of 313; although Licinius himself went further than Constantine by conducting an extensive purge of Maximinus' supporters, including the elimination of seven

[105] Thus R. Andreotti, 'L'imperatore Licinio ed alcuni problemi della legislazione costantiniana' in *Studi in Onore di Emilio Betti* 3 (1962), pp. 45-7. Constantine thus comes to adopt the stance of Licinius in this matter.

[106] See R. MacMullen, 'Judicial savagery in the Roman Empire', *Chiron* 16 (1986), pp. 157-8.

[107] In another example of this type of argument, apparent differences of approach to the question of the sale of children and variations in style have been used to assign *FV* 33 to Constantine and *FV* 34 to Licinius. This is discussed and rejected by D. Nardi, 'Ancora sul *ius vendendi* de *pater familias* nelle legislazione di Costantino' in *Sodalitas: Scritti in Onore di Antonio Guarino* 5 (1984), pp. 2287-2308.

[108] Thus Seeck, *Regesten* pp. 75 & 169.

[109] *Inscr. Cret.* 1.18.188 (Lyttus); *CIL* 3.12133 (Tlos); *CIL* 5.2781 (Padua); *AE* 1957.180 (Sinope); C. Habicht and P. Kussmaul, 'Ein neues Fragment des Edictum de Accusationibus', *Museum Helveticum* 43 (1986), p. 136 (Pergamum).

left-over wives and children of former emperors.[110] The fate of these lofty unfortunates aside, imperial providence on behalf of the provincials was not geographically limited, since the edict was published even in Crete, which had not been under the rule of Maximinus. The initiative of Licinius in this matter is made more likely by the presence of crucifixion in the text as one mode of punishment for slave informers. Constantine abolished crucifixion out of respect for its Christian associations, though it is not clear when he did so.[111]

The law appears to exist as a letter in the Code and an edict on stone. The end of the edict talks of *scripta* with more details being sent to the praetorian prefects (theoretically of both emperors), governors and the *rationalis* and *magister privatae* (presumably just of Licinius).[112] These *scripta* might be what we find in the Code. With a small emendation to the heading, the recipient could become the praetorian prefect of Licinius (i.e. *pu* changed to *pp*).[113] The wording in the Code is so close that it would seem odd if it represents the emperor sending what is an identical text masquerading as an amplification. However, the Code extract is very short. We may possess only the overlap between two different but complementary parts of the same administrative act. What this law does demonstrate is that when the emperor performs a single act of legislation, multiple copies of several different texts are involved. Unfortunately, we do not possess for this period all the parts involved in any act of imperial legislation, so as to be certain of any interrelationship between texts.[114] The closest

---

[110] Lactantius, *De Mort. Pers.* 50.2-51.2. The victims were Candidianus (son of Galerius), Severianus (son of Severus), the wife and two children of Maximinus (all killed during summer and autumn 313) and Valeria and Prisca (daughter and wife of Diocletian), who were not executed till the summer of 314. For the execution of Maximinus' partisans, see Eusebius, *HE* 9.11.3-7. For a similar contrast of purge and restraint, note that after the defeat of Magnentius in 353, Constantius II granted an amnesty (*CTh* 9.38.2), but also hounded suspected supporters of the usurper (Amm. Marc. 14.5).

[111] Aurelius Victor 41.4, who uses the same terminology as the law (*patibulum*); Sozomen, *HE* 1.8.13.

[112] An acephalous edict from Lyttus (or perhaps Hieropytna) in Crete (*Inscr. Cret.* 1.18.189) ends in much the same way, with instructions for copies of letters to the same selection of officials to be published, 'ut isdem quoque omnibus cognitis provinciales nostri per benivolentiam nostram consultum sibi esse laetentur'. This is an interesting document, with language very close to that of other tetrarchic legislation. Comparison to the edict *de accusationibus* suggests it might indeed be an enactment of Licinius. It seeks to restore property wrongly seized by agents of the fisc or *privata*, in particular the *Caesariani*. The emperors of the period are consistent in their attempts to restrain the *temeritas Caesarianorum*, whose fraudulence is a basic assumption; thus, Diocletian (*CJust* 10.1.5), Gelerius (*CIL* 3.12134 = *IG* II/III² 1121), Constantine (*CTh* 9.42.1, 10.1.5, 10.8.2, *CIL* 5.2781 lines 31-4) and Licinius (*CTh* 10.7.1).

[113] This is proposed by T.D. Barnes, 'Three Imperial edicts', *ZPE* 21 (1976), pp. 275-7; also *NE* pp. 127-8.

[114] Galerius' recantation edict talks of further explanatory letters to governors (Lactantius, *De Mort. Pers.* 34.5). The only cases where we have parts of more than one

available are the edicts of governors used to publish imperial edicts; namely the edicts of Aristius Optatus in 297,[115] Fulvius Asticus in 301[116] and Clodius Culcianus *c.* 305.[117]

Whatever the exact relationship between the letter in the Code and the epigraphic text, it looks as if Licinius may have survived in the Code, perhaps due to a combination of inadvertence on the part of the compilers and textual corruption.[118]

One last Theodosian problem should be mentioned. In 336, a son of Licinianus was reduced to slavery and condemned to the gynaecia at Carthage (*CTh* 4.6.2-3). His legitimacy derived from a *rescriptum sanc[tissi]mum*. This person used to be identified as Licinius Junior,[119] now more recently as an unknown illegitimate son of Licinius.[120] However, it seems most unlikely that this sacred rescript would be a phrase applied to a legitimising act of Licinius for his bastard son. But it also seems unlikely that Constantine would have legitimised his deceased rival's son, unless, perhaps, Constantia desired to adopt the child, as Valeria had adopted Galerius' natural son Candidianus.[121] The easiest solution is to suppose that the son of Licinianus is no relation of Licinius at all.

---

document are: (a) the Aphrodisias Currency Decree of Diocletian, which appears to contain both an edict and a letter. However, the text is too fragmentary to be certain of the exact nature and relationship of the documents concerned (see J. Reynolds in C. Roueché, *Aphrodisias in Late Antiquity* (1989), p. 263); (b) the Orcistus dossier (*FIRA²* 1.95), containing two letters and what may be an *adnotatio* (see W. Turpin, 'Adnotatio and imperial rescript in Roman Legal Procedure', *RIDA* 3rd series 35 (1988), pp. 300-2). The *adnotatio* and one of the letters contain considerable verbal parallels; (c) *CIL* 3.578, which contains fragments of what may be two imperial texts, although these might represent petition and reply.

[115] *P. Cair. Isid.* 1.

[116] M.H. Crawford and J. Reynolds, 'The publication of the Prices Edict: a new inscription from Aezani', *JRS* 65 (1975), pp. 160-3 and J.H. Oliver, 'The governor's Edict at Aezani after the Edict of Prices', *AJPh* 97 (1976), pp. 174-5. This is the only case where we have both published and publishing pronouncements preserved in full.

[117] *P. Oxy.* 2558.

[118] A problem that should be acknowledged is a difficulty with the Padua copy of the edict, which concludes with part of a letter restraining the audacity of the Caesarians in *urbs Romana*, presumably Rome (*CIL* 5.2781 lines 31-4). Since the Padua stone originated from Asia, it is not clear why this text referring to Rome (and which should, therefore, have emanated from Constantine) was considered a relevant addition to the inscription. This problem has led some scholars to keep Seeck's attribution of the edict to Constantine in 320. For a recent exposition of this view, see R. Delmaire, *Largesses Sacrées et 'Res Privata'. L' 'Aerarium' Impérial et son Administration du IVe au VIe Siècle* (1989), p. 29 n. 7.

[119] Thus *RE* vol. 13 (1927), col. 231. Inscriptional evidence shows that Licinius Junior was beyond doubt the son of Licinius and Constantia. See *PLRE* 1 p. 510 and M. Christol and T. Drew-Bear, 'Documents latins de Phrygie', *Tyche* 1 (1986), pp. 43-51.

[120] *PLRE* 1 p. 510 and Barnes, *NE* p. 44.

[121] Lactantius, *De Mort. Pers.* 50.2.

Now, we have seen how some acts of Licinius survived via the Hermogenian Code, precisely because they were collected before his fall, and were not subsequently emended to eliminate his name. Why then should any be found at all in the Theodosian Code, which itself contains laws annulling his constitutions?

I do not believe that Constantine's sweeping pronouncement of abolition cited above (*CTh* 15.14.1) signifies a policy of search and destroy. Such a short extract from what may have been a longer law lacks the full context. It may have originated from a specific problem. In any case, implementation would probably be difficult, lacking in both efficiency and thoroughness, just as Licinius' name was not comprehensively erased form all inscriptions.[122] Where laws were headed with the names of both emperors, it might soon be unclear who really did issue them, especially since the simple removal of Licinius' name could hide for ever his connection with the law.

As I have already noted, any startling innovations, especially if unpopular, would be likely to be known and abolished easily. If Licinius' enactments were brought forward to support a petition or were cited in court, or if there were appeals against them, all these would bring them to notice and expose them to invalidation. Several tyrant texts already noted are quite specific in this manner, those relating to the freeborn enslaved, the *cohortales* deprived of privileges and senators forcibly made *navicularii* (*CTh* 5.8.1, 8.4.1, 15.14.4).

Failing this, the constitutions of tyrants could survive quietly and then unwittingly be included in collections of laws, even if on no great scale. After all, the Theodosian Code also includes one eastern law to be ascribed to Maximinus, a letter to the governor of Lycia and Pamphylia on the immunity of urban populations from the poll tax.[123] This must have survived whatever *damnatio memoriae* that Licinius decreed for him.[124] And Licinius too, in however minimal a fashion, has survived in the later Codes. But he provides a salutary warning for users of the text. Nearly all enactments that might be attributed to him on reasonable grounds are vulnerable to challenge, but the law *de*

[122] R. Andreotti, 'Licinius (Valerius Licinianus)' in *Dizionario Epigrafico di Antichità Romane* vol. 4.32 (1959), pp. 1027-30 lists all inscriptions of Licinius then known, followed by a much shorter list of those with his name erased.

[123] *CTh* 13.10.2 = *CJust* 11.49.1 (June 313). Seeck, *Regesten* p. 159 ascribed it to Maximinus in 311. S. Mitchell, 'Maximinus and the Christians in AD 312: a new Latin inscription', *JRS* 78 (1988), pp. 122-3 proposes Maximinus in 312. The date and place of *CTh* 10.4.1 (March 313 at Heraclea) suggest Maximinus, but the recipient (the vicar of Rome) demands that the date be emended (Seeck, *Regesten* p. 176 places it in 326).

[124] For the *damnatio memoriae*, see Eusebius, *HE* 9.11.2. Maximinus survived, presumably via the Gregorian or Hermogenian Codes, in the headings of *CJust* 3.12.1, 5.42.5 and 6.9.7. The first of these at least originated from Maximinus in Egypt (Barnes, *NE* p. 66). The recipient, Verinus, may also be the addressee of two further texts, which may therefore be from Maximinus (*CJust* 2.12.20, 7.16.40; *PLRE* 1 p. 950). This is made more plausible, if the place of issue of *CJust* 2.12.20 (*Demesso*) is identified as Damascus.

accusationibus, which would not otherwise have been considered, is shown by epigraphic evidence to be his. The Theodosian compilers, however, had no idea that a tyrant lurked anonymously among their collected constitutions.

5. Constantine and Imperial Legislation on the Family

Judith Evans Grubbs

Constantine's nephew, the future emperor Julian, is said to have described his uncle as an 'innovator and disturber of ancient laws and of custom received long ago' (Amm. Marc. 21.10.8). Many scholars have agreed with Julian and have held Constantine responsible for the introduction into Roman law of fundamentally non-Roman customs derived from Christian and eastern sources. It is time to reassess this view of Constantine's legislation.

As the longest reigning emperor since Augustus, Constantine was in a better position to influence Roman law than most other emperors. The remains of about 330 constitutions attributed to him survive in the legal sources, most of them found in some form in the Theodosian Code. Approximately 25 per cent of these laws in some way concern the family or sexual relationships.[1]

Constantine could claim plenty of imperial precedent for his legislation on marriage and the family. Roman emperors had been attempting to regulate the private morals of their subjects ever since Augustus had sought to promote marriage and procreation and curb immorality with his laws on marriage and adultery. Under Augustus, a wife's adultery, which had been a matter handled in private by her family, became a public offence involving criminal penalties. Augustus also penalised the unmarried and childless by restricting their ability to receive legacies from those outside the sixth degree of kinship, and gave preference for senatorial and municipal posts to those with children. The Augustan legislation was still on the books at the

[1] J. Gaudemet, 'Les constitutions Constantiniennes du Code Theodosien', *Accademia Romanistica Costantiniana: Atti V Convegno 1981* (pub. 1983), 136-55, at 139, finds the remains of 276 different constitutions (often represented by more than one excerpt) in *CTh*; cf. Mommsen's list of Constantine's legislation on pp. ccix-ccxxiv of vol. 1.1. There are also 56 texts in *CJust* not found in *CTh*, six private rescripts in the *Vatican Fragments*, and *Sirmondian Constitution* 1. This chapter is in a sense a synopsis of my book, *Law and Family in Late Antiquity: the emperor Constantine's legislation on marriage* (forthcoming), where the laws discussed here are treated in greater detail.

beginning of the fourth century, as were other laws on the family enacted under his successors.[2]

Most of this legislation is known only from citations in the Digest or references in ancient literature, but we do have preserved in full an imperial edict on marriage enacted under Diocletian. Issued from Damascus in 295, this edict condemned in no uncertain terms all close-kin marriages contrary to Roman law, which are compared to the matings of wild beasts 'without any regard for modesty (*pudor*) or even piety'. Henceforth all Roman citizens were to obey the ancient laws of the Romans and to know 'that only those marriages are legitimate which have been permitted by Roman law'. Only in this way, declared the emperors, could the Roman people hope to keep the favour and good will of the gods.[3]

The edict of 295 against incestuous marriages should be kept in mind when examining Constantine's legislation on marriage and sexual mores. Many of Constantine's laws also display self-righteous wrath and indignation at the audacity of subjects whose behaviour runs counter to the imperial concept of morality and piety. This tone has often been attributed to Constantine's conversion to Christianity, which allegedly instilled in him a strong concern for sexual chastity. But if such expressions of moral outrage can be found also in a law of Diocletian, that most pagan of emperors, their appearance in Constantine's legislation cannot be explained as simply the result of his adoption of Christian ideology.

There is of course the question of how much of this legislation really can be called 'Constantine's' and how much is in fact the work of imperial secretaries or of members of Constantine's consistory, particularly the quaestor, whose office was apparently created by Constantine himself.[4] The amount of an emperor's responsibility in making the laws of his reign would depend on the individual ruler. By all accounts Constantine was very much a 'hands-on' emperor and I assume that he had control over what his legislation said and approved its wording, whether or not he had a hand in its composition. This does not mean that Constantine was responsible for *initiating* all his laws; on the contrary, the emperor was often reacting to reports or requests

[2] For pre-Constantinian legislation on the family, see P.E. Corbett, *The Roman Law of Marriage* (1930) and J. Gardner, *Women in Roman Law and Society* (1986). On the Augustan legislation, see R. Astolfi, *La lex Julia et Papia* (2nd ed. 1986), and P. Csillag, *The Augustan Laws of Family Relations* (1976); also n. 7 below.

[3] Text found in *Mosaicarum et Romanarum Legum Collatio* VI.4, in *Fontes Iuris Romani Antejustiniani* 5.2 (2nd ed. 1940, hereafter *FIRA*[2] 2), 558-60. T.D. Barnes has suggested that the Caesar Galerius was responsible for this law: Barnes *NE*, 62-3, n. 76.

[4] According to Zos. 5.32.6, although no quaestor is attested until 354. On the quaestor, see T. Honoré, 'The Making of the Theodosian Code', *ZSS RA* 103 (1986), 133-222; J. Harries, 'The Roman Imperial Quaestor from Constantine to Theodosius II', *JRS* 78 (1988), 148-72.

from magistrates to resolve disputes arising from private cases. Though the Code's abbreviated versions rarely reveal the underlying motivation for imperial legislation, traces of the original *suggestio* or legal case do survive in some Constantinian constitutions.[5]

Constantine's legislation on the family can be divided into five general categories (which are not mutually exclusive). This is not to imply that Constantine himself employed such a classification: this legislation is spread over a period of twenty-five years, and is only part of a large body of laws enacted on many different matters. This chapter briefly surveys the legislation on marriage and the family as a whole, focussing on some of the more interesting and innovative laws.

A. Inheritance and the transmission of property

The financial aspects of matrimony, especially questions of inheritance, dowry and gift-giving, had always been of great interest to classical jurists and to the upper-class elite for whom they wrote. This was still the case in the Late Empire, and Constantine was responsible for several reforms of the Roman laws of succession making the transferral of property easier and less encumbered by legal constraints. Of the twenty-six extant Constantinian laws on the transmission of family property, more than three-quarters date from the first decade of his reign, among them the famous constitution of 320 repealing the Augustan penalties for celibacy and childlessness (*CTh* 8.16.1).

In order to encourage marriage and child-bearing among upper-class Romans, Augustus had deprived unmarried men between the ages of 25 and 60 and unmarried women between 20 and 50 of the ability to receive inheritances or legacies from those beyond the sixth degree of kinship. Those who were married but childless could take only half of what had been left them, and only a tenth of their spouse's property (unless they had been granted the *ius liberorum*, giving them the same privileges as those with children). When the recipient of a legacy could not take it, it could be claimed by eligible relatives of the deceased; failing that, it went to the public *aerarium*. After the Edict of Caracalla in 212, these restrictions would have applied to all imperial subjects, and by the time of Caracalla unclaimed legacies (*caduca*) were going directly to the imperial *fiscus*.[6]

The effects and extent of application of Augustus' laws have often

[5] Replies to reports or requests: *CTh* 6.4.1 (326); 11.27.2 (322); 16.10.1 (320); cf. *Sirm. Const.* 1 for complete example. Cases involving private citizens: 10.11.1 (317); 4.6.2 and 3 (336). Records of hearings: 7.20.2; 8.15.1. See A.H.M. Jones, *Later Roman Empire* (1964, rpt. 1986; hereafter *LRE*), 347-57; F. Millar, *The Emperor in the Roman World* (1977), 328-41.

[6] *Regulae Ulpiani* 15-18 (*FIRA*[2] 2, 278-80); Millar (cited above), 158-63; even before this the *fiscus* seems to have received at least part of *caduca* in the provinces.

been exaggerated. In fact, these restrictions affected only those whose wealth and social prominence made it likely that they would receive legacies beyond the sixth degree of kinship; they did not apply to most inheritances within families. They were originally aimed at those Romans whose moral and social behaviour was of the greatest importance to Augustus – that is, the Roman senatorial aristocracy, and the wealthier and more distinguished classes in general.[7] We know from Tacitus and others that the Augustan laws on marriage and adultery were long a source of irritation to the upper classes. Nor, apparently, were they ever particularly effective, at least in regard to increasing the population and improving the morality of well-born citizens. Ironically, the last we hear of the penalties for celibacy before they were repealed in 320 is in a panegyric of 307, where the marriage of Constantine and Fausta is extolled as the highest expression of obedience to the Augustan laws (Mynors 7.(6)2.3-4).

On 31 January 320, an edict addressed 'to the people', was issued from Serdica; on 1 April it was posted at Rome. Seven excerpts from this edict survive, scattered throughout the Theodosian and Justinian Codes. Three of these, preserved only in the Code of Justinian, relax what had been very strict rules regarding the proper wording and witnessing of wills, so that inheritance would no longer be forfeited because of the failure of the dying to use an exact formula and procedure (*CJust* 6.9.9; 6.23.15; 6.37.21). Two of the excerpts found in the Theodosian Code mitigate what had been very harsh treatment of delinquent debtors (*CTh* 3.2.1; 11.7.3).[8]

But the most famous decision of this edict was the repeal of the Augustan inheritance restrictions (*CTh* 8.161.1). Constantine proclaimed that those who had formerly been penalised are now freed from the 'imminent terrors of the laws'. The childless will no longer be at a disadvantage, and women are released from the 'demands of the law placed on their necks like yokes'. But Constantine did not relax the restrictions on inheritance between childless spouses, 'whose false flatteries are usually scarcely restrained by the opposing rigour of the law'. This disapproval of legacies between spouses is very much in keeping with earlier Roman law, and there continued to be restrictions on inheritance between childless spouses for almost another century.[9]

[7] P. Brunt, *Italian Manpower* (1971), 558-66; A. Wallace-Hadrill, 'Family and Inheritance in the Augustan Marriage Laws', *PCPhS* 207 (1981), 58-80.

[8] There are problems with the dates of some of these extracts, esp. the ones in *CJust*, but most scholars agree in joining them: see vol. 1.1, 214-15 of Mommsen's text; Seeck, *Regesten*, 59. But M. Sargenti, 'Il diritto privato nella legislazione di Costantino', *Accademia Romanistica Costantiniana: Atti I Convegno* (1975), 229-332, at 296-7, disagrees.

[9] Until rescinded in 410 (8.17.2 & 3) in the East, but evidently in the West not until the publication of *CTh*. Under intestate succession agnatic relatives were always preferred to spouses: cf. 4.21.1 (395) and esp. 5.1.9 (428). Gifts between living spouses were

Discussions of Constantine's repeal of the Augustan penalties usually ignore the original context and imply that it was a separate law in and of itself, whose sole purpose was the lifting of the financial penalties on celibates. But it was in fact only part of a wide-ranging law designed to facilitate inheritance procedures in general and to prevent the mistreatment of debtors. The surviving extracts indicate that in enacting it Constantine claimed to be liberating his subjects from a number of arcane and oppressive regulations which had inhibited their property rights.

A panegyric by the Gallic rhetor Nazarius, delivered at Rome in 321, can help us understand how Constantine's law was presented to and understood by his subjects at Rome. In his peroration, the orator thanks Constantine for the benefits he has conferred on Rome since the defeat of Maxentius in 312. 'New laws have been laid down for governing morals (*mores*) and subduing vices ... Modesty (*pudor*) is safe; marriages have been strengthened ... Nor is there any fear of having as much as possible, but in such an abundance of good things (*bona*) there is great shame in not having' (Mynors 4.(10)38.4-5). Elsewhere Nazarius praises the emperor's chastity and commitment to the old family values (4.(10) 35.3).

Like the panegyricist who celebrated the marriage of Constantine and Fausta in 307, Nazarius saw Constantine as a defender of marriage and traditional Roman morality. Indeed, there is no reason to think that Constantine was ever hostile to the old Roman view of legitimate marriage and procreation – on the contrary, as we will see, his hostility was aimed at unions which were not in accordance with Roman law and at attempts by one partner to break up an already established union. What also angered him, to judge from the laws he enacted on the subject, were the exploitation of ordinary citizens by imperial officials and the pernicious activities of informers, 'the single greatest evil to human life' (*CTh* 10.2).[10] According to Tacitus, the Augustan legislation on marriage and adultery had been primarily responsible for the rise of the notorious *delatores* whose activities bred fear and suspicion among the senate (*Annales* 3.25). Repeal of the inheritance restrictions would thus have removed one of the opportunities for informers to terrorise wealthy citizens.

By abolishing what had always been an unpopular law, whose effectiveness must have seriously deteriorated by the fourth century, Constantine was conferring a favour on the wealthier classes who were

---

forbidden: *Dig* 24.1.3; *FV* 273 of Constantine (315: in *FIRA*² 2, 523).

[10] Abuses by imperial officials: see C. Dupont, *Le droit criminel dans les constitutions de Constantin: les infractions* (1953), 87-109. Informers: *CTh* 10.10.1 (313); 10.10.2 (prob. 312); 10.10.3 (335); 9.5.1 is prob. a law of Licinius: Barnes, *NE* (cited n. 3), 127-8; exceptions to Constantine's discouragements of informers in 9.16.1 (319); 9.9.1 and 9.24.1 (both 326). Informers and the fiscus: Jones, *LRE* (cited n. 5), 422.

the only ones really affected by the Augustan laws. Foremost among these beneficiaries was the senatorial aristocracy of Rome. Much of Constantine's legislation in the first decade of his reign was aimed specifically at Rome (including two other important inheritance laws, *CTh* 5.1.1. and 8.18.1), to demonstrate his good will and his desire to eradicate the abuses of Maxentius.[11] It is in this context that we should see the law of 320.

The usual explanation for Constantine's repeal of the penalties for celibacy and childlessness attributes its enactment to Christian motives. Proponents of this interpretation point to a passage in Eusebius' *Life of Constantine* discussing the repeal of the Augustan penalties along with other laws that Eusebius explicitly attributes to Christian motives (*VC* 4.26). The implication is that Constantine was showing his support for Christian asceticism by repealing the unfair penalties such practices entailed.[12]

Certainly, Constantine's repeal of the Augustan penalties would have benefited those Christian celibates who were wealthy enough to be affected by the law. But how many wealthy ascetics were there in the Roman West in 320? At that time most Christians, wealthy or not, lived in the eastern half of the Empire, still ruled by Licinius, and Constantine's laws would not have applied to them until after Licinius' defeat in 324. This law was directed at Rome, especially the senatorial aristocracy of Rome, where Christians were still very much a minority.[13] The well-known enthusiasm for Christian asceticism among some senatorial families is a post-Constantinian phenomenon, no doubt encouraged by Constantine's removal of the old inheritance restrictions.

It is possible that Constantine's abolition of the Augustan penalties was supported by farsighted Christian leaders, who realised that the emperor's acceptance of Christianity would encourage the conversion of many more members of the upper classes. In that case, Constantine's edict of 320 was a master-stroke of political strategy, a law that could be applauded by pagans and Christian alike. At the expense of some loss to the imperial treasury, easily made up by other measures,[14] Constantine removed a thorn from the side of the

---

[11] See Gaudemet 1983 (cited n. 1), 142-5. The *populus* of constitutions addressed '*ad populum*' (like 8.16.1) is usually the people of Rome.

[12] Cf. also Sozomen, *HE* I.9. Arguments for and against Christian inspiration for *CTh* 8.16.1 are summarised and discussed by M. Humbert, *Le remariage a Rome* (1972), 360-73. J. Gaudemet has consistently doubted the 'Christian' content of this law; see 'Tendances nouvelles de la legislation familiale au IVe siecle', *Transformation et conflits au IVe siècle ap. J.C.* (1978), 187-206, at 194-5.

[13] A.H.M. Jones, 'The Social Background of the Struggle between Paganism and Christianity', *The Conflict between Paganism and Christianity in the Fourth Century*, ed. A. Momigliano (1963), 17-37, at 17-21.

[14] Like the confiscated treasures of pagan temples (Eusebius *VC* 3.54.6); and the *collatio lustralis* (Jones, *LRE* 110). How much revenue the fiscus took from *caduca* is

wealthier classes, particularly the senatorial aristocracy. At the same time, he could be seen as promoting Christian ascetic ideals, and his action could be interpreted by contemporary and future Christians (and by modern historians) as a fundamentally 'Christian' law.

B. Betrothal and divorce

Another group of laws sets out the circumstances in which a betrothal or marriage may be dissolved by one partner. Two laws concern the return of gifts given by one party to the other before the marriage.

The exchange of gifts by betrothed couples was an old Roman tradition, but problems could arise about the ownership of the gifts if the marriage did not actually take place. In classical Roman law, a distinction had been made between gifts, often of substantial value, which had been given by the prospective husband specifically for the purpose of cementing the marriage alliance, and gifts which were made by either fiancé(e) simply out of affection. The latter type, usually of less value, could not be reclaimed by the giver if the marriage did not take place, but gifts given 'for the sake of contracting an alliance' could be (unless the giver had been responsible for breaking the betrothal). Though logical from the legal point of view, such a distinction could lead to confusion in actual practice, and there are many third-century imperial rescripts responding to requests for advice on broken betrothals and the status of pre-nuptial gifts.[15]

Constantine simplified matters by doing away with the distinction between the two types of gifts. In a law of 319 (*CTh* 3.5.2), he declared that, since the 'opinion of the ancients is displeasing', henceforth if a betrothal is broken off unilaterally, the partner responsible for the break-off must forfeit to the other any gifts either given or received. If a man had given presents to his fiancée and then rejected her, he could not reclaim them, whatever their value, but if she had been the one to break off the alliance she had to return them. The law also regulated the return of gifts in the event that one fiancé(e) died before the marriage took place. It was modified by a law of 336 (3.5.6), giving special status to betrothals in which a kiss had been exchanged between the betrothed. In those cases, if either partner died, half of any pre-nuptial gifts given by the man were to be returned, but half were to be kept by his fiancée, or if she had died, by her heirs. The nature of the 'kiss' referred to in the law has been much discussed.[16]

---

unknown, so the impact of *CTh* 8.16.1 is unclear.

[15] The classical rule is given at *Dig* 39.5.1.1 and *FV* 262 (*FIRA*² 2, p. 519); Corbett (cited n. 2), 18. Rescripts: *CJust* 5.3.1-14; cf. *Epitome Cod. Greg. et Herm. Wisigothica* 2.1 (*FIRA*² 2, 657-7).

[16] See L. Anne, *Les Rites des Fiançailles et la donation pour cause de mariage sous le Bas-Empire* (1941), 299-306; M.B. Pharr, 'The Kiss in Roman Law', *CJ* 42 (1947), 393-7.

This legislation has been seen as the first appearance in Roman law of the concept of *arrhae sponsaliciae*, the contractual exchange of betrothal gifts. The origin of *arrhae sponsaliciae* is still debated; some scholars think that it came into Roman law from eastern sources, perhaps Greek, perhaps Semitic; others think it was an internal development in Roman law.[17] The term *arrhae sponsaliciae* is not found in extant Roman law until 380, by which time a penalty had been added: the party breaking the betrothal without justification had to return four times the value of the gifts that he or she had received (3.5.10-11; 3.6.1; 3.11.1). Neither the four-fold penalty nor the term arrhae appears in Constantine's laws as we have them.

In 332 another law, subsequently cut in two by the Theodosian compilers, set a statute of limitations of two years on betrothals (3.5.4 and 5). If a man had made a betrothal agreement with a girl, but had not married her after two years or more, she could marry someone else. But if she had been engaged to a *soldier*, and married someone else before two years elapsed, her father or guardian was to be relegated to an island.

Constantine's legislation indicates that he considered betrothal a serious undertaking not to be entered into lightly. It diverges significantly from classical Roman law in making betrothal a binding legal contract and enacting sanctions against those who break it. The role of possible Christian or Near Eastern influences on these laws is debatable: betrothal pacts were always considered serious matters by upper-class Romans before and after Constantine, and in very early Roman law they had been legally actionable. And most of the evidence for the importance of betrothal among Christians is post-Constantinian.[18]

There is more reason to look for Christian motives behind the divorce law, enacted in 331 and addressed to the praetorian prefect Ablabius, in which Constantine drastically restricted the legal possibilities for initiating an unilateral divorce (3.16.1). In classical law, either partner could end a marriage by notifying the other of his or her intentions. A husband who repudiated his wife would have to return her dowry, though he might retain part of it if there were any children or if her behaviour had been open to question. Under Augustus' law on adultery, husbands were required to divorce adulterous wives; if they did not, they were themselves liable to charges of *lenocinium* (pimping).[19]

---

[17] For eastern influence, see C. Dupont, *Les constitutions de Constantin et le droit privé au début du IVᵉ siècle* (1937), 88-92; cf. 120-2; cf. Anne, esp. 87-135, who sees Constantine himself as having introduced the concept of *arrhae* into Roman law.

[18] See further J. Evans Grubbs, 'Abduction Marriage in Antiquity: a law of Constantine and its Social Context', *JRS* 79 (1989), 59-83, at 79-81; Anne, 476-86; Gaudemet 1978 (n. 12), 195-7.

[19] On the classical law on divorce, see Gardner (n. 2), 81-95.

Under the new law of Constantine, a woman could repudiate her husband for only three reasons: if he were a murderer, an employer of magic, or a destroyer of tombs. In those cases she would receive praise and recover her entire dowry. But if she repudiated him for any other reason, because he was a drunkard or a gambler or ran around with other women, she would be deported to an island, and her husband would get everything she owned, 'down to a hairpin'. A husband could only legally divorce his wife if she were an adulteress, a poisoner, or a procuress. Otherwise, he had to return her entire dowry (which he would probably have had to do anyway under earlier law). He was also not supposed to remarry, but if he did, his former wife had the right to enter his home and seize the second wife's dowry (however, the second marriage was evidently still valid).

In effect, a spouse could initiate a unilateral divorce with impunity only if the other partner were guilty of a serious crime. Murder, magic, destruction of tombs, and adultery by or with a married woman were all capital crimes in the Late Empire, for which there could be neither appeal nor pardon, and which would probably have resulted in the guilty person's execution.[20] Furthermore, unlike earlier imperial legislation, Constantine's law was much harder on a woman who wanted divorce than on a man. However, it applied only to cases where one partner wanted a divorce and the other refused. Divorce by mutual consent, which was probably more common than unilateral repudiation, was still unpenalised. In any case, the law of 331 was repealed less than 35 years later by the emperor Julian (whose law is no longer extant). And although restrictions on unilateral divorce were reintroduced by fifth-century emperors, divorce by mutual consent continued to be legal until it was prohibited in 542 by Justinian (and *his* law was soon repealed by his successor Justin).[21]

Constantine's divorce law is notable for its unusual vocabulary. Eight words in this law appear nowhere else in the Theodosian Code, including *muliercularius*, to describe a womanising husband; *moechus* and *moecha* rather than the classical legal terms *adulter* and *adultera*; *medicamentarius* instead of the classical *veneficus*, to describe a poisoner or user of magic, *conciliatrix*, which apparently means a procuress or go-between, and *acucula*, hairpin. The odd vocabulary, and the distinctly non-classical idea that an unjustly divorced wife could invade her ex-husband's home and seize his new wife's dowry, led Edoardo Volterra to suggest that this law was written by someone

[20] Cf. *CTh* 9.40.1 and 11.36.1 (314); 11.36.7 (344 or 348); 9.38.1 (322); 9.38.3 (369); 4 (368 or 370); 6 (381); 7 (384); 8 (385). Presumably violation of tombs here means interfering with the corpses (sc. for magical purposes), not despoiling architectural elements as in 9.17.1-5.

[21] Julian's law is known from Ambrosiaster, *Liber quaestionum veteris et nov. testamenti* 115.12 (*CSEL* 50, p.322); *CTh* 3.13.2 (363) may be part of the same law. Justinian's law: *Nov.* 117.10 (542), overturned by *Nov.* 140 (566) of Justin.

outside the imperial chancellery, who was unfamiliar with classical Roman law, in fact a Christian cleric.[22]

Ecclesiastical authorship of Constantine's divorce law is unlikely, but Volterra was not alone in attributing it to Christian influence. Until recently scholars generally agreed in seeing Christian inspiration behind *CTh* 3.16.1, since condemnation of divorce goes back to the New Testament and was echoed by many ante-Nicene writers. But recently this interpretation has been questioned.[23] For the law (as we have it) gives no indication of Christian motivation, and in fact conflicts with Christian teachings in several respects. Constantine allowed divorce for reasons other than adultery, whereas Christian writers stressed that adultery by the wife was the only possible justification. And whereas (at least in theory) Christian writers believed that both men and women should be held to the same standard of sexual conduct, Constantine upheld a double standard. And although Christians felt that a marriage could not be dissolved even if both partners wished it, Constantine's law did not ban divorce by mutual consent.

However, Constantine's law could still have been inspired by Christian teachings as they were understood by Constantine and his advisers. Christian doctrine in the early fourth century was *not* a monolithic body of beliefs agreed upon by Christians throughout the Empire. One need only look at the canons of the Council of Elvira, held in central Spain in the first decade of the fourth century, to see that not all church leaders felt that men and women should adhere to the same rules of sexual morality. And in fact, the majority of ante-Nicene writers (following Matthew 19:9) believed that divorce was justified, indeed necessary, if the wife had committed adultery (one of the few causes for divorce allowed by Constantine).[24] Despite the high-minded insistence of some Christians that husbands were held to the same marital fidelity as wives, it is clear that in practice the old double standard continued, sanctioned by earlier law and custom. Most Christians would probably not have thought Constantine's law differed significantly from their own beliefs.

Nor, as Antti Arjawa has suggested, would most pagans.[25] Contrary

[22] E. Volterra, 'Intorno ad alcune costituzioni di Costantino', *Rendiconti dell' Accademia Nazionale dei Lincei* (1958), 61-89, at 75-80; and 'Quelques remarques sur le style des constitutions de Constantin', *Melanges Levy-Bruhl* (1959), 325-34, at 330-4.

[23] Carlo Castello, 'Assenza d'ispirazione cristiana in *CTh* 3.16.1' in *Religion, société et politique. Mélanges en hommage à Jacques Ellul* (1983), 203-212; R. Bagnall, 'Church, State and Divorce in Late Roman Egypt' in *Florilegium Columbianum: Essays in Honor of Paul Oskar Kristeller*, ed. R.E. Somerville and L.-L. Selig (1987), 41-61.

[24] Council of Elvira, canons 8-11, in J. Vives, *Concilios visigoticos e hispano-romanos* (1963), pp. 1-15. See M. Sargenti, 'Matrimonio cristiano e società pagana', *SDHI* (1985), 367-91, at 376-8.

[25] A. Arjawa, 'Divorce in Later Roman Law', *Arctos* 22 (1988), 5-21.

to the once popular view of pagan Roman society as a hotbed of immorality where multiple marriages and divorces were common, divorce seems to have been rare outside the senatorial aristocracy, and not very common even there.[26] Most Romans, and Greeks too, did not approve of divorce, and especially disliked the idea of the wife initiating a divorce. Thus although Christians were certainly the most outspoken opponents of divorce, they may have been expressing in extreme form what many others felt.

As with the repeal of the inheritance penalties for celibacy, then, *CTh* 3.16.1 responded to concerns that were not exclusively Christian. But in the end, we have to ask why this constitution, so harsh and so opposed to classical law, was enacted in 331. It is possible that there had been an increase in the number of unilateral divorces, especially those initiated by women, and that some particularly sordid divorce cases had made their way through the judicial system to the last court of appeal, the emperor or his representative the praetorian prefect. From 329 to 337 Ablabius, a Christian, was praetorian prefect, in 331 he was also consul; the divorce law is addressed to him. Perhaps Ablabius had been disgusted at the freedom with which one partner was able to break up a marriage, and had suggested to Constantine that it was time to put a stop to this, particularly in view of the emperor's professed Christian beliefs.[27]

This is all hypothetical. We do not know, nor have we any way of knowing, whether there had been any increase in the divorce rate in the years before 331. But we may recall that eleven years earlier, Constantine had repealed the Augustan legislation penalising the unmarried and childless (8.16.1, above). Thereafter those who had married in order to escape the Augustan penalties might have decided not to continue in unsatisfactory unions. Whatever Constantine's reasons for repealing the Augustan laws, he surely did not intend to encourage the dissolution of already existing unions. How ironic if, after nullifying Augustus' attempts to promote marriage and childbearing, he was later forced to replace them with measures of his own.

C. Prohibited unions

In contrast to the divorce law, which sought to prevent the dissolution of marriages, other laws forbid and penalise unions between those of different social status, particularly between freeborn people and slaves.

[26] I. Kajanto, 'On Divorce among the Common People of Rome', *Mélanges Marcel Durry (REL* 47 bis, 1969), 99-113; M.-T. Raepsaet-Charlier, 'Ordre sénatorial et divorce sous le Haut Empire: un chapitre de l'histoire des Mentalités', *Acta Classica Univ. Scient. Debrecen.* 17-18 (1981-2), 161-73.

[27] That Ablabius was behind *CTh* 3.16.1 was suggested by Sargenti 1975 (cited n. 8), 280-1.

Roman law had never recognised as legal marriages the sexual relationships of slaves, nor those of free people with slaves. Before Constantine, however, unions of free men and slave women, though deprived of the privileges of legitimate marriage, were not prohibited or punished. A free woman who cohabited with someone else's slave fell under the provisions of the *s.c. Claudianum* of AD 52. If the owner of the woman's partner condoned the union, she was reduced to the status of his freedwoman; if not, she became his slave, and children of the union were also slaves. Under the marriage legislation of Augustus, senators and their descendants could not contract legal marriages with former slaves or with actors, and freeborn people could not marry prostitutes, pimps, or others branded with legal infamy. If a man of senatorial rank had wanted to live in a monogamous relationship with his freedwoman, she could have been his concubine – a perfectly acceptable relationship, though not accorded the privileges of legitimate marriage. Their children would be illegitimate, but could still have received legacies from their father if he included them in his will.[28]

Constantine extended the Augustan prohibition on marriage between senators and freedwomen to apply also to the marriages of local and provincial dignitaries with former slaves, the daughters of slaves, and other women of low birth or occupation. Such unions would no longer be legal marriages, and children born from them would be illegitimate. Furthermore, he threatened with severe sanctions men who attempted to give financial benefits, either during their lifetime or in their wills, to any children they had by such women or to the women themselves (*CTh* 4.6.2 and 3).[29]

Even harsher was the punishment ordained for a decurion who forsook his municipal responsibilities to take refuge on another landholder's estate and cohabited with one of the landholder's slaves. The decurion was to be deported, his property was to be handed over to his town council, and the slave woman was to be sent to the mines (12.1.6). Four laws modifying the provisions of the first-century law on the unions of free women with someone else's slave, were promulgated under Constantine (4.12.1-4).[30] And if a free woman was cohabiting with her own slave, they were both to be exiled and their children deprived of all inheritance rights. If any such unions were discovered

[28] *S.c. Claudianum:* P.R.C. Weaver, *Familia Caesaris* (1972), 162-9; Gardner (cited n. 2), 141-2. Augustan legislation: Gardner 32-3; 57-8.

[29] *CTh* 4.6.1 is missing (as is most of 4.6.2); it may have been the law revived by Zeno in 477 (*CJust* 5.27.5). It is not likely that the 'son of Licinianus' mentioned at the end of 4.6.2 and 3 is an (otherwise unattested) illegitimate son of Constantine's erstwhile fellow emperor Licinius: see Sargenti 1975, 267, and above p.117.

[30] *CTh* 4.12.1 (314) is attributed to Licinius by some scholars, but for insufficient reasons; see Barnes 1982 (cited n. 3), 127.

in the future, the woman would be executed and the slave burned alive (9.9.1).

The unions that Constantine sought to suppress were not promiscuous or extramarital affairs symptomatic of some sort of general moral decline, as has sometimes been supposed, nor is there any reason to see Christian influence in these laws.[31] It is quite clear from the wording of this legislation that it is aimed at long-term quasi-marital relationships, and virtually every one of these laws mentions children whom the parents had wished to make legitimate heirs. What Constantine seems to have found so alarming, in fact, was the possibility that children of slaves or others of low social status would inherit the rights and property of freeborn and socially respectable people. He was particularly anxious to preserve the distinction between slave and free birth. Another law, known only from its revival by the fifth-century emperor Zeno, decreed that if a man married his freeborn concubine, children she had previously borne to him would be legitimated, provided he was not already married and had no legitimate children from a previous marriage (*CJust* 5.27.5). The key word here is *ingenua* – freeborn. The law did not apply to concubines of slave origin, even if their children had been born after they were freed. On the other hand, Constantine's attitude was quite different when it was a question of unions between slaves rather than between slave and free, as we see in his law forbidding the break-up of slave families on imperially owned estates when the estates were leased out to new proprietors (*CTh* 2.25.1).

The explanation for these laws lies in the social and economic confusion of the third century. The social and legal distinctions between slaves and the lower-class free were becoming increasingly blurred. And although after 212, Roman law was supposed to replace the local legal systems of the various provinces, many people, particularly among the lower, less educated classes, remained ignorant of Roman law. Third-century legal sources provide abundant evidence for this confusion of status boundaries. Slaves or former slaves could live for years 'as if freeborn'. Free people might contract what they believed to be valid marriages with slaves, unaware either of their partner's true status or that unions with slaves were not recognised under Roman law. Questions would then arise about the status of children of such unions or validity of dowry.[32]

The social mobility of the third century, which continued under Constantine, had brought about a sort of status dissonance: people's status under the law did not necessarily correspond to their actual

[31] See Sargenti 1975, 261-72.
[32] Slaves or freedmen living 'as if freeborn': *CJust* 7.20.1; 7.21.6 and 7; free woman inadvertently marries slave: *CJust* 5.18.3; *Dig* 24.3.22.13; confusion about status of children: *CJust* 7.16.17; cf. 4.19.10; 4.19.17; 7.16.28.

position in society or to their perceptions of what was socially acceptable. Constantine's legislation sought to arrest this intermingling of social classes, and to re-establish traditional status distinctions. Later legislation on such unions by his successors indicates that, not surprisingly, he failed to do so.[33]

D. The sale and abandonment of children

Quite a few Constantinian laws are devoted to the legal protection of fatherless minors (those under twenty-five) and the duties of their guardians. In general, this legislation reinforces or supplements earlier imperial laws. More interesting and innovative are a few laws concerning the abandonment or sale of children by their parents.

In classical Roman law, the sale or pledging of freeborn children was illegal, and the child's claim to free birth was not impaired by the sale. However, some parents did sell or pledge their own children, usually because of poverty or food shortage. As for infants who had been abandoned at birth, pre-Constantinian Roman law maintained that they also retained their original status. Thus if a freeborn child who had been exposed was brought up by someone else as a slave, he was still legally free and could be reclaimed years later by the parents who had abandoned him. Clearly this could result in conflicts between a child's natural parents, who had exposed it at birth, and the legally invalid but often compelling claims of those who had rescued the infant and perhaps even brought it up as their own child.[34]

Before the Edict of Caracalla the legal status of exposed children varied from province to province. After 212, the Roman rule that freeborn children kept their *ingenuitas* (right of free birth), and that fathers who exposed their children still retained legal power (*patria potestas*) over them would in theory have held for the whole Empire. But in all probability local customs still prevailed, and confusion about the status of *expositi* prompted a number of third-century imperial rescripts. Emperors continued to expound the Roman law that such children retained the status they had had when born and could be reclaimed by their natural parents, or, if they were slaveborn, by their mother's master. Frequently, however, they added those who picked up an infant ought to be repaid the price of the child's rearing.[35]

The legal collection known as the *Vatican Fragments* preserves two

---

[33] E.g. *CTh* 4.12.5 (362); 4.12.6 (366); 7 (398); 4.6.4 (371); 5 (397); 6 (405); 7 (426-7); 8 (428); *NTh* 22.1 (442); *NVal* 31 (451); *NMarc* 4 (454); *NMaj* 7 (458); *NAnth* 1 (468) etc.

[34] Parents selling or pledging children: *CJust* 7.16.1; 8.16.1; 8.16.6; 2.4.26; 4.43.1; 7.16.37; cf. *Dig* 20.3.5; 21.2.39.3. Infant exposure: *Dig* 40.2.29; *CJust* 5.4.16; cf. 8.51.1.

[35] Cf. Pliny, *Ep.* 10.65-6, on which see A.N. Sherwin-White, *The Letters of Pliny* (1966), 650-66.

private rescripts from early in Constantine's reign, both addressed to women, concerning free people who had been sold. One of these, posted at Rome in 315, repeated the classical rule that *ingenuitas* is not changed by an illegal sale (*FV* 33). But two years earlier, another rescript had informed its recipient that her purchase of a newborn infant was valid and that if the child's parents wished to get it back, they must give her another slave or the equivalent payment (*FV* 34).[36] The wording of this rescript is unclear and the circumstances in which the child had been bought are not stated; its parents may have been slaves or even barbarians. But later laws of Constantine on the status of children sold or abandoned by their parents give the same decision.

A law dated 18 August 329 is found in both the Theodosian Code and the Code of Justinian, although the addressees and texts are different (*CTh* 5.10.1; *CJust* 4.43.2).[37] Both contain essentially the same ruling: parents, under the pressure of extreme poverty, may sell their children, and the buyer of a newborn infant has the right to use the child as a slave and can even sell it to pay his debts. If those who sold the child later with to reclaim it, they must pay the market price or provide another slave in its place. It has been suggested that this was not a real sale into slavery, but more of a long-term 'hiring-out' (*locatio*) of the child's services, perhaps to pay off a parent's debt. Clearly such a distinction was rather vague and was probably frequently ignored: no doubt children often fell into permanent servitude, especially if their parents died before redeeming them.[38]

Constantine went even further in a law of 331 on the status of children who had been abandoned by their parents or masters and rescued and brought up by someone else (5.9.1). In this law, addressed to the praetorian prefect Ablabius, the emperor declares that the child's rescuer has all rights over it and can bring it up as a slave or as his own child, and any attempt by the natural parent or original owner to reclaim the child is forbidden. Once a father has rejected a child, his *patria potestas* over it ceases. This law is indeed innovative, because although earlier emperors had felt that those who brought up abandoned children ought to be compensated for their trouble, they had

[36] *FV* 33 and 34 are found in *FIRA*[2] 2, pp. 468-9 (where 33 is incorrectly dated 313). Sargenti 1975, 238-42, suggested that 34 was the product of the eastern chancellery of Licinius, but it is in line with Constantine's later legislation, and there is no reason to assume (as Sargenti and others do) that 33 concerns the illegal sale of a freeborn *infant*; it probably refers to an adult, perhaps the recipient herself.

[37] I believe that the *CJust* text was also part of the original Constantinian law, though it is often assumed to be a Justinianic reworking. Note that *CTh* 5.10.1 addresses issue from the viewpoint of the buyer, while *CJust* 4.43.2 is from the seller's (parent's) viewpoint.

[38] For this interpretation, see M. Humbert, 'Enfants à ouer ou à vendre: Augustin et l'autorité paternale (*Ep.* 10* et 24*)', *Les lettres de Saint Augustin découvertes par Johannes Divjak* (1983), 189-203, at 193-6.

always respected the claims of paternal power.[39]

Two other laws should be considered along with these rulings. In 322 Constantine learned that impoverished parents were selling or pledging their children and ordered that officials all over Africa immediately provide such families with assistance from imperial grain storehouses (11.27.2). Another constitution, again addressed to Ablabius, begins by declaring, 'Let a law, written on bronze or wax tablets or linen cloth, be posted through all the cities of Italy to turn parents' hands from parricide and change their desire for the better' (11.27.1).[40] Ablabius is then instructed to see that parents too poor to raise their children be provided with food and clothing at once, 'since the raising of a newborn infant cannot suffer delays'.

Unlike the alimentary scheme begun by Trajan two centuries earlier, these enactments apparently did not set up a long-term programme of aid to needy families, but were temporary measures meant for Africa and Italy. They were reactions to emergency situations, perhaps regional food shortages.[41] Constantine's rulings that those who bought a newborn baby or rescued an exposed infant had full power over the child were probably also responding to contemporary social conditions. This does not mean that the exposure and sale of infants had increased in Late Antiquity, for there is plenty of testimony to both phenomena in earlier times. But there had always been confusion about the status of such children, and Constantine's laws, though out of line with earlier imperial policy, attempted to settle the question.

There is reason to see Christian influence behind the alimentary laws and the law of 331 on *expositi* (5.9.1). Christian writers had long denounced the abandonment of infants, and one of the most impassioned condemnations of exposure was made by Lactantius in his *Divine Institutes*. Lactantius, who served as tutor to Constantine's son Crispus, dedicated the *Divine Institutes* to Constantine, and we may reasonably assume that the emperor was familiar with the work.[42] Both *CTh* 5.9.1 and 11.27.1, the law directing that aid be given to impoverished families in Italy, were addressed to Ablabius, a known Christian. But, like Constantine's law on divorce (also enacted in 331 and addressed to Ablabius), the ruling on exposed infants is not entirely in line with Christian thought. A completely 'Christian' law

[39] Volterra 1958 (cited n. 22) 83-5, thought *CTh* 5.9.1 (like 3.16.1) was composed by an ecclesiastic. Sargenti 1975, 246, saw it as the product of the eastern chancellery at Constantinople, now under Constantine (cf. n. 36).

[40] The MS date is 315, but Ablabius (an easterner) is not known to have held office under Constantine that early; Seeck redated to 329.

[41] On which see P. Garnsey, *Famine and Food Supply in the Greco-Roman World* (1988).

[42] Lactantius, *Div. Inst.* 6.20; cf. 5.9. See T.D. Barnes, 'Lactantius and Constantine', *JRS* 63 (1973), 29-46.

would have banned the exposure of infants altogether (which was not done until 374: *CJust* 8.51) and would not have allowed the person who picked up an exposed child to use it as a slave. For what most distressed the Christian writers who spoke out against the exposure of infants was precisely the possibility of their enslavement, and worst of all, of their use as slave prostitutes.[43] Constantine's law probably discouraged parents from exposing their newborn children, and encouraged others to rescue abandoned infants, but it did not by any means guarantee that *expositi* would have a decent life.

E. The behaviour of women

A number of laws stress the need to preserve female *pudor* (modesty, chaste behaviour) and to prevent women, both married and unmarried, from being insulted by others or bringing shame upon themselves. A law of 316 warns that any official who 'drags into public' a matron owing tax debts 'is to be put to death with exquisite tortures' for having exposed to public view a woman who 'keeps herself within her home out of consideration for her sex' (1.22.1). According to a law of 326 against abduction marriage, even girls who were abducted against their will are to be penalised by loss of inheritance rights since 'they could have preserved themselves at home until their marriage day' (9.24.1).[44] Another law, enacted only a few days after the law on abduction, commands that when a fatherless girl has reached marriageable age, her guardian must prove that her virginity has been preserved intact. If she is discovered to be no longer a virgin, suspicion then falls on the guardian himself, and if he cannot prove his innocence, he is to be deported and his property confiscated (9.8.1).

In a law (2.17.1) allowing males over 20 and females over 18 to request official release from the need for a guardian, Constantine specified that this permission was to be given only to girls with a good reputation. He hastened to add that 'because of [their] modesty and sense of shame We do not force them to be pointed out by witnesses in a public assembly'; they could send legal representatives with documents and witnesses. Indeed, Constantine felt that public exhibitions by women were to be avoided at any time. In 315, he decreed (*CJust* 2.12.21) that husbands were fully authorised to represent their wives in court, 'lest, on the pretext of pursuing a lawsuit, women rush disrespectfully into abuse of their matronly modesty or be compelled to attend the gatherings of men or trials'. In 322 (*CTh* 9.1.3), advocates are warned not to take up the cause of women who 'perhaps rush forth into illegal action, relying on their sex

---

[43] E.g. Justin Martyr, *Apology* 1.27; Lactantius, op. cit.
[44] On this law, see J. Evans Grubbs (cited n. 18).

for security'. And the divorce law of 331 (3.16.1) castigated women who repudiate their husbands 'on account of their own depraved desires' and threatened them with exile for their audacity.

However, in keeping with Constantine's status consciousness, this concern with female behaviour only extends to women above a certain social level. Thus women tavernkeepers are considered high up enough on the social scale to be liable for prosecution if they commit adultery, 'since from these women a standard of modesty (*pudicitia*) is required'. But those who are merely employed in such taverns are because of the 'vileness' of their origins beneath the consideration of the law (9.7.1).

Classical Roman law had also placed restrictions on women's legal independence, most notably by means of the *tutela mulierum*, which consigned women to legal guardianship throughout their lives. By Constantine's day, *tutela mulierum* seems to have become largely obsolete.[45] This would explain in part the presence of new laws restricting the appearance of respectable women in court, since in the classical period such women would have been represented by their guardians. It might be tempting to see in this attention to female behaviour a reflection also of Constantine's new Christian ideals, but though a concern with female chastity can certainly be found in early Christian writers (most notably Tertullian), it was by no means unique to Christians. Already in the rescripts of Alexander Severus, there is increased concern for women's modesty, and the emphasis on *pudor* is particularly marked in the legislation of the Tetrarchy, both in rescripts and in the edict against incestuous marriage mentioned above.[46] And respect for female *sophrosyne* also appears in Late Antique pagan writers like Menander Rhetor and Libanius.[47]

The attitude toward women expressed in Constantine's laws are essentially those of the Mediterranean male, from Hesiod to the villagers and shepherds studied by twentieth-century ethnographers.[48] Women are light-minded and lack self-control, and the protection of their virtue requires constant supervision. But, when they behave in a suitably chaste and modest manner, they are to be treated with respect and consideration. Christian teachings on the importance of sexual chastity and female modesty merely reinforced age-old attitudes.

[45] See S. Dixon, '*Infirmitas Sexus*: Womanly Weakness in Roman Law', *Tidjshrift voor Rechtsgeschiedenis* 52 (1984), 343-71

[46] J. Beaucamp, 'Le vocabulaire de la faiblesse feminine dans les textes juridiques romains du IIIᵉ au IVᵉ siècle', *RHDFE* 54 (1976), 485-508.

[47] Libanius, *Oration* 1.4 and 7: cf. Menander Rhetor 2.6 (on *epithalamia*): 'As for the girl, be cautious in describing her beauty because of the scandal that may be caused, unless you are a relation ...', quoted from p. 145 of the edition and translation by D.A. Russell and N.G. Wilson (1981).

[48] E.g. J. Campbell, *Honour, Family and Patronage* (1964), esp. pp. 31, 169, 199ff.; 270-1 and 277-8 (Sarakatsani shepherds in Epirus); J.A. Pitt-Rivers, *The People of the*

What conclusions can be drawn about Constantine's legislation on the family? As already mentioned, the emperor was often not the instigator of imperial legislation, which might evolve from the suggestion of a particular official or as a solution to a legal dispute between private citizens. But although many of Constantine's laws may have been promulgated in response to situations not of his own making, we can still see some patterns in his decisions. For instance, the preservation of status distinctions was clearly important to Constantine: a distinct dichotomy between the freeborn, privileged classes and those of slave or 'base' birth appears in many of his laws, not just those on marriage. Of course, concern with status distinctions in Roman law was hardly new with Constantine.[49] But the number of laws attacking marriages between those of different statuses tells us two things: Constantine himself, unlike his Christian God, was very much a respecter of persons; and imperial attempts to keep social boundaries fixed were simply not working. Ironically, Constantine also *encouraged* social mobility by his promotion of relatively humble families to high status, particularly in the East.[50]

In much of his legislation, Constantine was simply giving a solution to problems that individuals had been bringing to the emperor for at least two centuries, on issues like the status of abandoned infants or the fate of betrothal gifts in a broken engagement. After the decline in use of the rescript system in the later years of Diocletian's reign, there would have been a need for general rulings on such issues.[51] Constantine was replacing the individual responses given by earlier emperors, composed by the secretary *a libellis*, with edicts composed by the quaestor. Unfortunately, the result of instituting general policies to cover situations previously dealt with on a case-by-case basis is that instead of the generally straightforward replies of the rescripts, we get heavy-handed and sometimes clumsily worded decrees imposing a uniform policy, accompanied by the threat of fines, exile or worse for those who dare to disobey.

It has been said that Christian influence on Constantine's legislation is most apparent in his laws on the family.[52] But this raises an often-ignored question: was there, in the early fourth century, a

Sierra (1954), esp. chapter 8 (central Spain). Cf. Evans Grubbs 1989, esp. 61-5.

[49] P. Garnsey, *Social Status and Legal Privilege in the Roman Empire* (1970).

[50] *See* Jones, *LRE* 106-7; A. Chastagnol, 'Les modes de recrutement du sénat au IVe siècle apres J.C.', *Recherches sur les structures sociales dans l'Antiquité classique* (1970), 187-211, at 188-90. Although Chastagnol's assumption that Constantine founded the Senate at Constantinople is debatable (cf. Jones, *LRE* 527), the promotion of such men as Ablabius (see n. 55) and Optatus (co. 334 and patrician, see Libanius *Or* 42.26 and Barnes *NE*, 107) must have alarmed traditionalists; cf. *VC* 4.1.

[51] On the rescript system see Millar 1977, 240-72 and 537-49; and T. Honoré, *Emperors and Lawyers* (1981), who sees a deliberate change from rescripts to edicts under Diocletian.

[52] C. Dupont (cited n. 17), p. 77.

recognisably 'Christian' ethos of marriage and family relationships to which Constantine could look if he had wanted to incorporate Christian teachings in his legislation? In fact, it is quite anachronistic to attribute a developed set of ideas on the marital bond to ante-Nicene writers; not until Augustine was any real attempt made to define marriage in Christian terms, and even then Augustine certainly did not speak for all Christians. Indeed, as Constantine discovered to his dismay, fourth-century Christians were not inclined to agree about many issues of doctrine or discipline.[53]

Ante-Nicene writers who do discuss Christian marriage and family life only mention those aspects in which they claim Christians differ significantly from pagans (or in which mainstream Christians differ from the radical fringe who rejected marriage and sexuality altogether). Briefly summarised, these are: rejection of divorce and of the practice of infant exposure, and preference of celibacy over marriage, particularly chaste widowhood over remarriage. None of these attitudes were alien to the non-Christian Roman world, but Christians claimed to put into practice ideals to which pagans gave only lip service.[54]

When only those aspects of Christian marriage ideology that can be found among Christians of the first three centuries are considered, it appears that in only a handful of cases can any argument be made for Christian influence on Constantine's legislation on marriage and the family, perhaps half a dozen out of the more than eighty extant laws relevant to the family. Even in those cases, Constantine offers a solution only partly in keeping with contemporary Christian principles (as with the laws on divorce and infant exposure), in responding to concerns held by non-Christians as well as Christians (as with the repeal of the Augustan penalties for celibacy). Therefore I am inclined to see only four laws as being primarily 'Christian' in intent: the divorce law (3.16.1), the law concerning infants exposed by their parents (5.9.1), and the laws directing that aid be given to parents whose poverty may drive them to sell or kill their children (11.27.1 and 2).

Three of these laws (3.16.1; 5.9.1; 11.27.1) have the same addressee,

[53] See M. Sargenti 1985 (cited n. 24), 368-71.

[54] The famous encomium of 'Christian marriage' by Tertullian, *Ad Uxorem* 2.8.6-9, is meant to point up the horrors of marriage to a pagan by contrast; otherwise, Tertullian's views on marriage are quite negative. The third book of Clement of Alexandria's *Stromata*, the fullest ante-Nicene exposition of sex and marriage from a Christian point of view, was a response to the 'radical fringe' of Gnostics and encratites who denied the validity of marriage altogether. Other Christian views on sex and the family before Constantine (in addition to Paul, I Corinthians 7) are found in the apologists, e.g. Justin, *Apol.* 1.15, 27 and 29; Tertullian *Apologet.* 6-9; Minucius Felix, *Octavius* 31. The canons of the Council of Elvira (see n. 24) contain many prescriptions regarding marriage, betrothal, celibacy and the behaviour of women. For Lactantius on sex and marriage, see *Div. Inst.* 3.21-2; 6.23; and n. 42.

Ablabius, Constantine's right-hand man during the last eight years of his reign, and they are the only extant laws concerning the family that are addressed to Ablabius. This may only be an accident of the preservation of our sources, but it is worth considering the possibility that Ablabius himself was responsible for the enactment of these 'Christian' laws. As praetorian prefect from at least 329 to 337, he was the second most powerful man in the Empire (and therefore was killed after Constantine's death along with all other possible rivals to Constantine's sons). Originally from Crete and of allegedly humble origins, Ablabius was said by Eunapius to have treated Constantine as though the emperor were 'a disorderly *demos*'. It is clear that he was a Christian, but his understanding of both Roman law and Christian theology may have been quite tenuous.[55]

In general, Constantine, rather than applying 'Christian' principles to imperial law, preferred to grant to Christians (those whose brand of Christianity he recognised) powers and privileges that enabled the Church to take over new functions and to amass more wealth and influence. Granting bishops judicial authority in civil cases was simpler and more efficient (though not without problems) than trying to make secular officials employ 'Christian' doctrine in their decisions (*CTh* 1.27.1, *Sirm. Const.* 1 to Ablabius). We know from church historians that Constantine not only lavishly endowed church buildings but also provided local churches with funds for supporting the needy. According to another law sent to Ablabius, the emperor felt that 'the rich ought to take upon themselves the needs of the saeculum, and the poor ought to be sustained by the wealth of the churches' (16.2.6).[56]

There is no doubt that much of Constantine's family legislation pursues policies quite different from what we know of the classical law of his predecessors. But our knowledge of pre-Constantinian law is very incomplete, being for the most part dependent on the Justinianic corpus. Unlike Theodosius, Justinian did not instruct his compilers to include legislation which had since been superseded. If the same criterion had been used in assembling the Theodosian Code, much less of Constantine's legislation would have been preserved, since it was often considerably modified by later emperors.[57] Constantinian policies that appear innovative may have had precedents in earlier

[55] Eunapius, *Vitae Phil.* 463-4 (Loeb ed.). On Ablabius, see Barnes 1982, 104; A. Chastagnol, 'L'inscription constantinienne d'Orcistus', *MEFRA* 93 (1981), 381-416, esp. 393-7. For his Christianity and apparent lack of legal knowledge, cf. *Sirm. Const.* 1; cf. n. 27 above for suggestion that he was behind the divorce law.

[56] Eusebius, *VC* 4.28; Theodoret *HE* 1.11 and 4.4; Jones, *LRE* 898-9. On problems with *CTh* 1.27.1 and *Sirm. Const.* 1, see Sargenti 1975, 280-1, n. 82.

[57] E.g. changes in the divorce law (besides Julian's repeal): *CTh* 3.16.2 (421); *NTh* 12 (439); *NVal* 35.11 (452); *CJust* 5.17.8 (449), etc. Changes in the laws on mixed-status unions: see n. 33.

imperial decisions that were not preserved because they were not in line with the law of Justinian's day.

Interestingly, several of Constantine's laws, while imposing policies that differ markedly from classical Roman law, appear to hark back to a much earlier period. In the early Republic, betrothals were considered contractual agreements and a broken betrothal was legally actionable. Divorce on insubstantial or unfair grounds was subject to penalties (mainly financial), and for legal and social reasons, wives did not initiate divorces. Fathers could sell their children, but their right of recovery was restricted.[58]

One example of this apparent return to pre-imperial Roman law is the policy on adultery accusations (9.7.2, 326). In the Republic, a woman's adultery had been a private matter to be dealt with by her husband and her family. But Augustus had made adultery a public crime and had allowed third parties who were not related to the woman to bring charges against her if neither her husband or father chose to prosecute. Constantine abolished the right of anyone but the woman's husband or male relatives to bring charges and thus effectively returned control over a married woman's chastity to her family (although adultery remained a capital crime).[59]

The attitudes found both in Constantine's legislation and in early Roman law had probably always existed, but were usually not expressed in classical legal writings because classical law was aimed primarily at the urban, wealthier, more sophisticated classes. Indeed, classical law did not always reflect the attitudes of even the upper classes: recent research on the Roman family has shown that frequently law lagged behind popular expectations and practices, particularly in regard to inheritance.[60] Constantine's legislation reflects (though it does not always endorse) what had long been the *de facto* situation among many of his subjects – those in the Greek East, but also many in the Roman West.

And, unlike the classical jurists, Constantine also addressed issues of concern to those outside the urban upper classes. Perhaps as a result of the changeover from private *subscriptiones* to public edicts as the main vehicle for imperial decisions, issues like abduction marriage or infant exposure, more relevant to the rural lower classes than to the urban elite, are now appropriate subjects for general laws. Thus Constantine's legislation may provide some clues to the private lives of ordinary people, who are otherwise so invisible in the ancient sources.[61]

[58] For early Roman law, see A. Watson, *The Law of Persons in the Later Roman Republic* (1967) and *Roman Private Law around 200 BC* (1971).

[59] The version of this law in *CJust* (9.9.29) contains phrases not in the text of *CTh* 9.7.2: cf. *CJust* 9.9.19.2 and 4 (this last taken from *CTh* 9.36.4 of 339).

[60] E.g. S. Dixon, *The Roman Mother* (1988), ch. 3.

[61] See Evans Grubbs 1989, esp. 81-2.

Constantine was not trying to introduce a new morality; rather, he was recognising a very ancient moral code which had persisted in many areas of the Mediterranean, east and west, and which still exists in more isolated regions today. To return to Julian's accusation, I would agree that Constantine was an overturner of law, but not necessarily of custom.

6. Christianising the Roman Empire: the evidence of the Code

David Hunt

Papers and books about Christianising the Roman Empire ought not to be encouraged. The concept is certainly a snare, and very probably a delusion as well. It is so big an aspect of Late Antiquity as to be all but beyond the control of the historian, and admits of so many layers of meaning and varieties of interpretation that it is in danger of becoming meaning*less*. If and when we have arrived at some understanding of the term, and of what factors may have led people to change to being Christians from having been something else, it is still hard to know what it would mean to any individual to shift religious allegiance in the generations after Constantine.[1] Perhaps we are the inevitable prisoners of an inheritance which has itself indelibly 'Christianised' the way we look at the religious transformation of the late Roman world. It is always salutary to recall that Ammianus Marcellinus could write a history of his times without hang-ups about Christianisation or changes in religious allegiance, a record of events in which Christian leaders and Christian institutions come and go as natural components of the contemporary scene, with an 'unforced occurrence and sense of normality'.[2]

Roman emperors from Constantine onwards issued very many laws which condemned all forms of religious allegiance other than officially sanctioned Christianity. But laws, of course, 'do not a Christian make'. The relationship between official discrimination and actual religious commitment is inevitably complex, but Christianisation, whatever it

---

[1] Ramsay Macmullen, *Christianizing the Roman Empire (AD 100-400)* (1984), recognised the 'problems of approach' (e.g. p. 5: 'the boundaries around my subject are in danger of dissolving completely'); his efforts were pronounced a failure by R.P.C. Hanson, in *CR* 35 (1985), 335ff. Macmullen pursued his minimalist view of Christianisation in 'What Difference Did Christianity Make?', *Historia* 35 (1986), 322-43. For more positive perceptions, see now Robert Markus' introduction to his *The End of Ancient Christianity* (1990).

[2] John Matthews, *The Roman Empire of Ammianus* (1989), 439. Others find Ammianus less detached, notably R.L. Rike, *Apex Omnium: Religion in the Res Gestae of Ammianus* (1987), and T.D. Barnes, in Graeme Clarke (ed.), *Reading the Past in Late Antiquity* (1990), 59-92.

may be, was not to be achieved simply by making paganism and heresy *illegal*.[3] Questions about the nature and purpose of laws, and degrees of enforcement, lie outside the remit of this Chapter: suffice it to say – obviously – that there is a great gulf set between the emperor's issuing a law banning pagan sacrifices and what actually happens 'on the ground' in the local setting.[4] In the eyes of Eusebius the laws themselves became more Christian: Constantine had remodelled ancient legislation to make it 'more holy' (*hosioteron*), exemplified in Eusebius' view by his removal of the long-standing testamentary restrictions on the childless.[5] Yet the reasons Eusebius furnishes for the relaxation of the law are not, it has to be said, especially Christian, and seem more concerned with *phusis* and *philosophia* (despite his reference to women 'consecrated to God's service' who have adopted a life of virginity). To look more widely at Constantine's laws, however, is to be unconvinced by these claims for their greater 'holiness'. Certain individual instances, such as the famous prohibition on marking the face of condemned criminals (*CTh* 9.40.2), may advertise the stamp of the emperor's Christianity (even if in this law of 316 consignment to gladiators was still an accepted penalty), but any general Christian input is remarkably elusive.[6] I would not be the first to note that both the social structure reflected in the laws and the nature of the penalties which they admit appear impervious to the demands of Christianity. Indeed in the savage rhetoric of late Roman legislation there is precious little of the religion which even a pagan observer like Ammianus – albeit ironically – could acknowledge as 'preaching only justice and mercy'.[7]

Yet it would be perverse to deny that the laws in the Code do at least reflect changes in the public life of the Empire directly connected with the new standing of Christianity: the restructuring of the calendar, for example, to accommodate the observance of Sunday and the insertion of Easter into the round of public festivals – marked by an amnesty for lesser offenders;[8] and the forty days of Lent, the days 'when the absolution of souls is awaited', to be signalled, according to a law of 389 (9.35.5), by an absence of torture. Such provisions are the voice of a

[3] As recognised by Macmullen, *Christianizing*, 95. On the relationship between laws and religious change, see further P. Brown, 'Religious Coercion in the Later Roman Empire: the case of north Africa', in his *Religion and Society in the Age of Saint Augustine* (1972), 301-31.

[4] The debate over the existence and extent of a Constantinian law banning sacrifices tends to obscure the point: law or no law, sacrifices did not stop.

[5] *VC* 4.26 (for the surviving edict, see *CTh* 8.16.1). On Christian influence in the law, see T.D. Barnes, *Constantine and Eusebius* (1981), 52.

[6] On another famous Constantinian law now shown to be less subject to Christian influence, see J. Evans Grubbs, *JRS* 79 (1989), at pp. 75-6.

[7] Amm. Marc. 22.11.5. Cf. R. Macmullen, 'Judicial Savagery in the Roman Empire', *Chiron* 16 (1986), 147-66.

[8] For Sunday and Easter, see esp. *CTh* 2.8.19 (389); and for Easter amnesty, 9.38.3ff.

government reordering public religion into a Christian framework.

It is primarily as evidence for this redrawing of the boundaries of legitimate religion that I propose to approach the laws. Their religious terminology can prove an illuminating starting point, as demonstrated in a recent article by Professor Salzman, who has drawn attention to the Code's deployment of the focal distinction between *religio* and *superstitio*.[9] By the last years of the fourth century, and the Theodosian enforcement of Catholic Christianity, 'superstitio' has come to denote in the laws not only outlawed *pagan* rites, but (more commonly, in fact) heretical groups and Jews: its antithesis, 'vera religio', is reserved for the pure milk of the Catholic faith. In the year of Alaric's sack of Rome, for example, the emperor Honorius (16.11.3) orders that 'what was ordained by antiquity or established by the religious authority of our fathers or confirmed by our Serenity in regard to the Catholic law shall be preserved unimpaired and inviolate, the new superstition being abolished' (in this case, a reference to Donatism). The 'Catholic law' is here accorded the sanction of tradition, a leading credential of approved *religio*, while the schismatic group are excluded as the purveyors of novelty and illicit religion (in the pre-Constantinian Empire it had of course been the Christians themselves who represented the novel superstition which had offended against the true religion of traditional adherence to the old gods). A law (16.5.63) issued to the proconsul of Africa from Aquileia in the summer of 425, after the suppression of Johannes' usurpation, opens with a sentence which could well stand for much of the legislation in book 16 of the Code: 'we prosecute all heresies and perfidies, all schisms and superstitions of the pagans, all false doctrines inimical to the Catholic faith.'[10] The religious stance, specifically here that of the new western government in 425, could hardly be more definitive.

Yet, as Salzman observes, the use of 'superstitio' in connexion with *pagan* rites has emerged from a period of ambiguity before the era of Theodosius, when the boundary of legitimacy between Christianity and paganism had been blurred by the concessions extended to harmless versions of divination, so-called 'white' magic. Constantinian laws had permitted at least the public practice of 'superstitio' in this form;[11] and the tolerant Valentinian I in 371 had even strikingly sanctified the tradition of benevolent *haruspicina* with the label of

[9] Michele R. Salzman, 'Superstitio in the Codex Theodosianus and the persecution of Pagans', *Vig. Christ.* 41 (1987), 172-88; for the history of the term, see D. Grodzynski, 'Superstitio', *REA* 76 (1974), 36-60.

[10] This was one of several sections of a large law issued at this time, cf. further extract cited on p. 154 and Matthews' discussion above, p. 41.

[11] 9.16.1-3, 16.10.1. On the persistence of divination, see A.A. Barb, 'The survival of magic arts', in A.D. Momigliano (ed.), *The Conflict between Paganism and Christianity* (1963), 100-25.

'religio' (16.10.9). Yet for Valentinian, as for Constantine and his successors, the distinction at issue in the matter of divination was not strictly the 'religious' one of isolating outside the law rituals which offended against legitimate cult – 'superstitio' in that sense was roundly condemned – but rather the long-standing secular boundary between white and black magic: in the wording of Valentinian's law, between *haruspicina* and *maleficium*.[12] Not until a law of Honorius in 409 do religious grounds explicitly enter the condemnation of magic arts in the Code: specifically in this case it is the *mathematici*, astrologers, whose is a 'false doctrine' ('error') from which they are to be recalled to the 'worship of the Catholic religion', and their books are to be 'consumed in flames before the eyes of the bishops' (9.16.12). They have thus joined the roll-call of condemned groups whose existence challenges authorised religion (and no longer just the safety of the state).

Salzman summed up the use of the term 'superstitio' in the Code as 'to separate normative from non-normative religious practices'. From the Theodosian age onwards it was Catholic Christianity which was to enshrine normative – and hence traditional, non-'superstitious' – religion. Theodosius' edict to the people of Constantinople issued from Thessalonica in February 380 (16.1.2) specified this lawful 'religio' as that transmitted to the Romans by the 'divine apostle Peter', and currently upheld by bishops Damasus of Rome and Peter of Alexandria, 'that we shall believe in the single deity of Father, Son and Holy Spirit, in equal majesty and in holy trinity'. Such was the 'religio' sanctioned by tradition, now defined as the apostolic tradition from Peter, and defined so specifically as to bring the language of Christian doctrine into the realms of Roman law.[13] Eleven months later, when Theodosius had established his court at Constantinople, and entered the lists of the ecclesiastical politics of the East, the yardstick of traditional religion had been modified to become the faith of Nicaea 'transmitted long ago by our ancestors and confirmed by the testimony and declaration of divine religion' (16.5.6). This law of January 381 defines 'the upholder of the Nicene faith and the true adherent of Catholic religion' by reference to a credal statement included in the text, even down to the detail of the equivalence of the Latin *substantia* and the Greek *ousia* in the definition of the indivisible Trinity. Any who do not subscribe to such doctrine usurp the name of 'true religion'. I forbear to comment, even if I were competent to, on the theology of

---

[12] That the issue was not primarily religious is argued by H. Funke, 'Majestäts- und Magieprozesse bei Ammianus Marcellinus', *Jb. Ant. Chr.* 10 (1967), 145-75. It was an accusation of *maleficium* which was the downfall of Priscillian: Sulp. Sev. *Chron.* 2.50.8.

[13] For discussion of *Cunctos populos*, see, e.g., W. Ensslin, *Die Religionspolitik des Kaisers Theodosius d. Gr.* (1953), 15ff.; A.M. Ritter, *Das Konzil von Konstantinopel und sein Symbol* (1965), 28ff., 221ff.; A. Lippold, *RE Suppl.* 13 (1973), 846ff.

the creed set out in this law;[14] but it is surely a matter of note that the substance of right doctrine, the true religion of Catholic Christianity, should now be ensconced in the legal pronouncements of the Roman emperor. Traditional 'religio' is no longer merely normative *practice*: it has become a defined set of *beliefs* authorised by descent from the apostles and from Nicaea, and now issuing out of the mouth of the Roman ruler.

Moreover, the punishment with which the emperor threatens the defiant is exercised in tune with nothing less than the will of God. 'They shall be smitten first by divine vengeance,' thunders Theodosius' 380 edict, 'and afterwards by the retribution of our punishment, which we shall assume in accordance with the judgment of heaven ("ex caelesti arbitrio")'. A few months earlier (3 August 379) Gratian had proclaimed from Milan, 'all heresies forbidden by the laws of God and the emperor shall cease forever' (16.5.5).[15] Later, in 388, Theodosius held out to all who belonged to 'diverse and perfidious sects' the threat that they would pay the penalty 'both to God and to the laws' (16.5.15); while in November 395 Arcadius, in claiming his father's precedent for banning heretics from the *militia* of imperial service, denounced the offence as leading to the 'destruction of our laws and of religion' (16.5.29).[16]

This propensity to equate the laws of the emperor with those of God introduces another element in the Code's religious terminology, the offence of *sacrilege*. Where the emperor's orders are 'divine', as they are in the world of the Code, to disobey them is to risk committing sacrilege. To usurp a rank not accorded by the emperor, for example, renders one liable to an accusation of sacrilege (6.5.2); to erect unauthorised public buildings in Rome is 'sacrilegious audacity' (15.1.27); to disregard the tax exemptions with which Valentinian favoured teachers of painting incurs the penalty of sacrilege (13.4.4) – and so on. In most instances in the Code the threat reads like a standard formula, and is issued in cases which have nothing to do with religion as such. Yet this fundamental association of the term is not entirely absent. Prohibiting tampering with tombs, Julian at Antioch in 363 affirmed that 'our ancestors regarded it as tantamount to sacrilege ("proximum sacrilegio") even to move a stone, disturb the earth or tear up the turf ...' (9.17.5).[17] For Christian rulers, on the other hand, it was for instance the observance of Sunday which it was sacrilegious to

[14] In the words of R.P.C. Hanson, *The Search for the Christian Doctrine of God* (1988), p. 805, 'the correct Nicene faith was described (we can hardly call it defined)'.

[15] The substance of the law is more limited in scope, and not a wholesale renunciation of the toleration Gratian inherited from his father: K.L. Noethlichs, *Die gesetzgeberischen Massnahmen der christlichen Kaiser des vierten Jhdts. gegen Heretiker, Heiden und Juden* (1971), 104ff.

[16] No such Theodosian prohibition survives in the Code.

[17] For Julian's more extended reasoning on the subject, see his *Ep.* 136b (ed. Bidez).

contravene, to 'turn aside from the inspiration and ritual of holy religion' (in a law which occurs three times in the Code);[18] or again, to attempt to seize fugitives seeking sanctuary in church precincts was to lay 'sacrilegious hands' upon them (9.45.4, 431). In these instances the notion of sacrilege retains something of its import as the desecration of the observance of true religion. In a context which sees the emperor's laws as the source of that true religion, and his punishments as tantamount to God's punishments, the two aspects of sacrilege come together: the genuinely 'religious' dimension coincides with, and reinforces, the language of late Roman bureaucracy. We might conclude that 16.2.25 ('qui divinae legis sanctitatem aut nesciendo confundunt aut neglegendo violant et offendunt, sacrilegium committunt') was merely a formulaic denunciation of defiance of the emperor's law, were it not in fact a detached fragment of the edict of February 380 setting out Theodosius' standard for true Catholic 'religio':[19] the heretic commits sacrilege not merely in the bureaucratic sense of refusing imperial orders, but also in the religious sense of challenging the true faith which issues from the emperor. A law of Honorius of 407 (16.5.41), for example, sees earlier laws against heretics as aimed at the 'destruction of sacrilegious minds': men's 'profane desires' are to be punished, while the protection of the laws is for the benefit of 'right worship' ('rectum cultum'). A later text from 415 (16.5.56) sees all heretics as 'desecrating by their contagion true and divine worship ("vera divinaque reverentia")'. Such language implies an understanding of sacrilege in which it has become impossible to disentangle disobedience to the Roman emperor from defiance of the law of God.[20]

We have arrived, it would appear, at a picture of a Roman emperor whose laws prescribe true religion, dictate the beliefs required by that religion, and set the bounds of what is, and what is not, the proper worship of God. But so far we only have the foreground of the picture: further observation of the landscape reveals that in practice such declarations of true religion were not mere imperial whim.[21] As with all the legislation in the Code, we have before us the end product of the processes through which representations were channelled and legal decisions arrived at.[22] In the case of the laws on Christian orthodoxy, the background is a network of episcopal politics and church councils,

---

[18] 2.8.18, 8.8.3, 11.7.13.

[19] It was Gothofredus who first put the two texts together: Ensslin, op. cit., p. 17; Noethlichs, op. cit., p. 132.

[20] Thus some have tried to equate sacrilege and *maiestas*, e.g. *RE* 2.1 (1920), 1680-1, although this is dismissed as a 'facile assumption' by R. Bauman in *ANRW* 2.13 (1980), 203ff., esp. n. 271.

[21] Despite hostile allegations like the notorious 'Let my will be a canon' charge against Constantius II: Athanasius, *Hist. Arian.* 33.

[22] Cf. A.M. Honoré, 'The Making of the Theodosian Code', *ZSS RA* (1986) at 136ff., with J.D. Harries, in *JRS* 78 (1988), 164ff.

aided and abetted by the emperor and his officials. Such had been the pattern established by Constantine, who always professed a somewhat ostentatious deference to the authority of bishops in matters of faith: the emperor merely prescribed what bishops had decided.[23] In presenting true religion as a matter of imperial fiat, and the emperor as the conduit of right belief, the texts in the Code represent the voice of the emperor's majesty disembodied from its full context. There is a glimpse of this context, paradoxically, in Valentinian II's law of January 386 (16.1.4, cf. 16.4.1) granting right of worship to Arian congregations (an interesting survival amid all the laws denouncing heretics and denying them possession of churches).[24] Valentinian here aims to benefit those who 'believe according to the doctrines which in the times of Constantius of blessed memory were decreed as those that would endure for ever, when the priests had been called together from all the Roman world and the faith was set forth at the council of Ariminum ... and confirmed at Constantinople', an allusion to the complex episcopal deliberations which lay behind Constantius II's endorsement of his Arian creed in 359-60. In the Theodosian legislation of 380-1, while there is no explicit reference to the conciliar background, there are a number of indications that it is close at hand, and that the emperor is making his own what the bishops had decided.[25] References in the laws to the *fides Nicaena* perhaps need be no more than a routine formula, but it should be noted that the canons of the council of bishops which Theodosius assembled in Constantinople in 381 open with an affirmation of the 'faith of the 318 fathers gathered at Nicaea in Bithynia'.[26] The imperial order on the rightful possession of churches sent to the proconsul of Asia on 31 July 381 (16.1.3) sets out a summary of belief in an undivided Trinity which flows from, even if it fails to mention, the Constantinople council. Among the documents of the council is a letter in which the bishops requested the emperor to 'ratify' the decisions of the council, and the text to the proconsul of Asia in the Code appears to be a copy of Theodosius' response to this request.[27] We catch sight here of something of the substructure of the Code's seemingly Olympian pronouncements of right belief.

[23] E.g. after Nicaea, 'everything that is done in the holy councils of bishops is an expression of the divine will' (Euseb. *VC* 3.20), or again 'what has pleased the three hundred bishops together is nothing other than the judgment of God' (Athan. *De Decretis*, 38).

[24] On this law, see Noethlichs, op. cit., 122ff., and (for its political setting) John Matthews, *Western Aristocracies and Imperial Court AD 364-425* (1975), 188-9.

[25] See Ritter, op. cit., 221ff. (countering Ensslin's emphasis on Theodosian initiative).

[26] Canon 1 (Ritter, 121ff.).

[27] Ritter, 124ff., 236ff. Sozom. 7.9.5ff. interpreted the text of 16.1.3 as the *nomos* giving authority to the decisions of the council (correcting Socrates' misunderstanding of it as a list of 'patriarchates').

This same law of July 381 proceeds to a list of eleven named bishops who are officially authorised as setting the standard of correct doctrine. Again this can be closely related to decisions of the council of Constantinople, for Theodosius' list conforms to the organisation of the ecclesiastical hierarchy which the bishops had just approved:[28] the bishop of Constantinople heads the list, according to the 'primacy of honour' newly granted him by Canon 3 of the council, followed by representative bishops from each of the (secular) eastern dioceses: Egypt (where the traditional prerogatives of the bishop of Alexandria make him the only match for Constantinople), Oriens, Asiana, Pontica and Thrace. Canon 2 of the council had recognised just such an episcopal organisation reflecting the secular dioceses, and the law departs from it only in failing to include for Oriens the bishop of Antioch (who ranked with Alexandria in terms of special status), a silence explicable – as many have observed – in the light of the disputed claims to that see in the wake of bishop Meletius' death during the council.[29] That the structure of Theodosius' list of 'authoritative' bishops is derived from the eastern church council is further apparent from the absence of the bishop of Rome, who had only the previous year (as we have seen) been upheld by the emperor as a purveyor of right doctrine.

The imperial pronouncements which make the true faith of Christianity into a matter of official legislation and the endorsement of legitimate 'religio' thus have behind them mechanisms of ecclesiastical authority and decision-making which have been evolving since Constantine. These mechanisms are further visible in an eastern law of 421 addressed to the praetorian prefect of Illyricum, which orders that 'all innovation shall cease, and the ancient ecclesiastical canons which have been in force up till now shall be observed through all the provinces of Illyricum' (16.2.45). Aside from implying the now familiar association of approved religion and the traditional, this law openly endorses the authority of the church's own procedures; and there is explicit legal echo of church canons in this text's identification of the special ecclesiastical standing of the bishop of Constantinople, 'that most reverend man of the sacred law', whose see 'enjoys the prerogatives of old Rome'.[30] That the conclusions of church councils should be incorporated in this way into the legal responses of the

[28] Ritter, 85ff.

[29] E.g. Ensslin, op. cit., p. 37; N.Q. King, *The Emperor Theodosius and the Establishment of Christianity* (1961), 45; Matthews, *Western Aristocracies*, p. 126.

[30] Constantinople Canon 3 had described Constantinople as 'new Rome': for this designation, see further G. Dagron, *Naissance d'une capitale: Constantinople et ses institutions de 330 à 451* (1974), 43ff. The episcopal authority of 'new Rome' was being challenged in Illyricum by the bishop of Thessalonica's 'vicariate' on behalf of the pope of old Rome: on this political context of 16.2.45, see Ch. Pietri, *Roma Christiana* (1976), 1112-19.

emperor is a development implicit since Constantine, and a measure of the *institutional* standing which Christianity has come to enjoy in the Roman Empire during the fourth century.[31]

It is to the laws as illustration of this institutional position that I now wish to turn: not so much the 'background landscape' of rarely mentioned church councils, as the explicit recognition of the church's privileged place in the eyes of the state. The 421 law cited above includes the insistence that matters of ecclesiastical dispute are to be reserved for the judgment of bishops, and it can serve to introduce the pervasive theme of episcopal authority and privilege.[32] Bishops have some claim to be counted among the Code's leading characters. We have already encountered them summoned up as exemplars for the official definition of the true faith, but once such matters have become the concern of the law it is not so surprising that the bishops as creed-makers should find themselves deferred to in a legal context. More striking, perhaps, that the law should concern itself with the death-bed salvation of people of the stage, and their fitness to receive the last rites: only after the approval of bishops, ordains this 371 law of Valentinian I (15.7.1), is such a favour to be granted. In a law of Honorius from 409 (9.3.7) it is the 'laudable care of the bishops of the Christian religion' which is to press judges into the humane treatment of prisoners (one area, incidentally, where the Code does appear to reflect the influence of Christian principles);[33] and in the group of laws concerned with the provision of sanctuary in churches and their precincts, it is the bishops who share with the secular power the authority for enforcing the procedures: it is from them that the penalty may be exacted if debtors are unlawfully harboured (9.45.1, 392); and if fugitives in sanctuary refuse to surrender arms then emperor and bishops together share responsibility for their forcible exclusion (9.45.4, 431). In 407 Honorius allows the role of bishops in prohibiting the practice of pagan funeral rites, in the same breath as acknowledging the authority of *agentes in rebus* in enforcing the laws against heretics and pagans (*Const. Sirm.* 12 = 16.10.19). In these and similar contexts bishops are being invoked as the allies and instruments of a Christian government.

Few laws, though, are directly addressed to bishops.[34] Bishops after

---

[31] See generally, J. Gaudemet, *L'église dans l'empire romain* (1958); A.H.M. Jones, *The Later Roman Empire 284-602* (1964) ch. 22. According to Eusebius, *VC* 4.27 (and accepted by Barnes, *Constantine and Eusebius,* p. 244), Constantine had given legal authority to the conclusions of church councils.

[32] For full documentation on bishops in the legal sources, see K.L. Noethlichs, 'Materialen zum Bischofsbild aus den spätantiken Rechtsquellen', *Jb. Ant. Chr.* 16 (1973), 28-59.

[33] Cf. *Const. Sirm.* 13 (419) on bishops making compassionate visits to prison, as well as the famous Constantinian law on the condition of prisoners at 9.3.1.

[34] 4.7.1 (to Ossius); 16.2.8 (to 'clergy'); 16.2.10 (edict to 'all bishops'); 16.2.14 (to Felix);

all had no official standing in the imperial pecking-order. 'Friends of Caesar' they certainly were, and endowed with privileged access to the emperor's ear; yet as Ambrose discovered, they remained outside the government and vulnerable to the resentments of those within it.[35] Bishops were not part of the secular hierarchy: there are none of them in the *Notitia Dignitatum*. The few occasions when they appear as recipients of laws may indicate circumstances when the bishops themselves through their informal association with the court succeeded in eliciting the responses which have found their way into the Code. Elsewhere such episcopal intervention is actually alluded to: the sparing, for example, of those accused of betraying previously unknown skills of shipbuilding to the barbarians 'because of the petition of the most reverent Asclepiades bishop of the city of Chersonesus' (9.40.24, 419); and we might justifiably suspect a successful personal intervention behind the exemption from certain tax arrangements of 'Cyrus the most reverend bishop of the city of Aphrodisias, whose merits are so great that even contrary to the provisions of a general sanction of this kind he shall not be prohibited from enjoying a special benefit ...' (11.1.37, 436).[36] Here are glimpses of that episcopal lobbying which must have been ever present at the late Roman court.[37]

As a testament to the institutional recognition of the church in the Empire, where bishops are concerned the Code is naturally preoccupied with their powers of jurisdiction. A bishop's judgment, according to the first surviving text on the subject of *episcopalis audientia* (318), is nothing less than 'sacred'; once resorted to, it is final (1.27.1 'pro sanctis habeatur quidquid ab his fuerit iudicatum'). Many years later, in 408, the judicial decisions of bishops are reaffirmed, as given by 'those whom we (*sc.* the emperors) necessarily venerate', and accorded the same respect as the authority of praetorian prefects, 'from which there is no appeal' (1.27.2). It is a lofty comparison, since it was only because they represented the emperor himself that praetorian prefects could not be appealed against.[38] Constantine's extension of judicial authority to bishops needs to be seen in conjunction with his professed view of episcopal synods: on more than one occasion he

---

16.2.20 (to Damasus); 16.2.23 (to four named bishops 'and the rest').

[35] See, e.g., the diplomatic caution of the opening paragraphs of Ambrose's approach to Theodosius (*Ep.* 74 (ed. Zelzer, *CSEL* 82.3, p. 54)) on the subject of the Callinicum synagogue; after this episode Ambrose was actually barred from the court (*Ep. extra coll.* 11.2 (ibid. p. 212)).

[36] Cyrus' favourable treatment may not be unconnected with his support of anti-Nestorian policy at Ephesus: Ch. Roueché, *Aphrodisias in Late Antiquity* (1989), 60-1.

[37] I have touched on this theme in 'Did Constantius II have Court Bishops?', *Stud. Patristica* 19 (1989), 86-90.

[38] 'Qui soli *vice sacra* cognoscere vere dicendi sunt' (11.30.16).

likened the verdict of bishops to nothing less than the judgment of God.[39] Small wonder that laws use terms like 'sacred' and 'sacrosanct' of bishops' judicial decisions. The *locus classicus* is Constantine's famous reply to the prefect Ablabius' enquiry on the status of the 'sententiae episcoporum' (*Const. Sirm.* 1: 5 May 333). Good Christian that Ablabius was, as praetorian prefect he may well none the less have been aghast at the extravagant rhetoric of the emperor's unqualified endorsement of bishops assuming the role of judges: 'the authority of holy religion searches out and reveals many things which the ensnaring bonds of legal technicality do not allow to be produced in court.' In both criminal and civil cases the judgment of bishops is to last for ever, without the possibility of a review; a bishop's word is necessarily true and incorruptible, issuing as it does from a holy man 'in the consciousness of an undefiled mind'. The verdicts bishops hand down are thus for ever inviolable and sacrosanct.

Such a universal commendation of the superiority of episcopal judgments is a remarkable pronouncement to come from a Roman emperor. Hardly surprising, then, that later laws aimed to refine the scope of the bishops' role.[40] By 408, for example, it was being envisaged that the consent of both parties was required for a case to be brought before a bishop, on the analogy of the appointment of a private arbitrator (whereas Constantine [1.27.2] had allowed the unilateral choice of either defendant or plaintiff to have the case transferred). More pervasively in the Code, laws reflect efforts in the years after Constantine to enforce separate spheres of secular and ecclesiastical jurisdiction, and to circumscribe the judicial functions of bishops. Succinctly put, as in a law of 399 (16.11.1), 'in cases involving religion it is appropriate to trouble ("agitare") bishops; other matters to do with ordinary judges and the public law should be heard in accordance with the laws'.[41] On the same general principle, we encounter laws prohibiting clerical interventions in the secular judicial process, and, conversely, denouncing those bishops condemned by their peers who then attempt recourse to the secular courts and the emperor.[42] These latter laws in fact have to do with the operation of church councils, and derive from the long-standing Constantinian emphasis on the autonomy of councils and their independence from the Roman state: they thereby introduce a confusion into the view of episcopal

[39] Above, n. 23, for his remarks after Nicaea; cf. after the council of Arles in 314, 'sacerdotum iudicium ita debet haberi ac si ipse dominus residens iudicet' (Optatus (ed. Ziswa, *CSEL* 26) App. 5).

[40] For more discussion of the development of *episcopalis audientia*, see Gaudemet, op. cit., 230ff., and W. Selb, 'Episcopalis audientia von der Zeit Konstantins bis zur Nov. XXXV Valentinians III', *ZSS RA* 84 (1967) 162-217.

[41] Cf. 16.2.23 (376).

[42] 11.36.31, 9.40.16 (against clergy intervention); 11.36.20, *Const. Sirm.* 2 = 16.2.35 (no recourse to secular court).

jurisdiction to be found in the Code, by blurring the distinction between bishops gathered in synods and addressing questions of church doctrine or discipline, and bishops presiding as judges in their own courts.[43] The difficulty is compounded by redrawing the separation between ecclesiastical and secular jurisdiction not only in terms of the nature of the alleged offence ('to do with religion'), but in terms of personnel: the state's jurisdiction is thus not meant for the Christian clergy, who have their own judges in their bishops. So as early as 355 Constantius II was forbidding bishops to be accused in secular courts, ostensibly for their own protection, and ordering their cases to go before other bishops (16.2.12); and in 384 Theodosius reiterated the same injunction to the prefect of Egypt (*Const. Sirm.* 3), again with the implication that it was unjust to bishops to drag them through the normal courts: 'they have their own judges and have nothing in common with the public laws, as far as ecclesiastical cases are concerned, which are properly decided by the authority of bishops.' Theodosius' law ends with specific commendation of bishop Timothy of Alexandria, who is to have charge of all clerical proceedings in the prefect's domain.

Whatever kind of episcopal jurisdiction, whether of synods or of individual bishops' courts, is envisaged in such laws, it is evident that the reservation of cases involving church business and church personnel for the judgment of bishops was seen in the official view of the Code as an aspect of the privileged status of the church in the Empire: bishops were not to be 'troubled' by litigation which was not their concern, and it was as the leaders of a favoured institution that they were authorised to escape from the shackles of the secular courts.[44] When church privileges were reasserted after the overthrow of Johannes in 425, it was specified once more (*Const. Sirm.* 6 = 16.2.47) that clerical cases were not to come before secular judges, but were the preserve of *episcopalis audientia*: 'for it is not right', the law continues, 'that ministers of God's service should be subject to the judgment of the powers of this world ("temporalium potestatum")'.

Nor was it right, in the Christian Roman Empire, that they should be diverted from God's service by having to undertake civic responsibilities and serve on local *curiae*. The point had been put by Constantine in a letter to the proconsul of Africa in the months immediately following the Milvian Bridge, and in a law addressed to the governor of Lucania in October 313 (the earliest on the subject of clerical exemptions preserved in the Code) which insists on the same justification for the privilege: clergy are not to be turned aside from the

---

[43] A distinction at least noted by K.M. Girardet, *Kaisergericht und Bischofsgericht* (1975), 64-5.

[44] Contrast the realities as experienced by Augustine at Hippo: P. Brown, *Augustine of Hippo* (1967), 193ff.

'divina obsequia' which it was their task to uphold (16.2.2).[45] Alongside
the juridical position of bishops, the enforcement of clergy immunities
and tax exemptions is the Code's most obvious and insistent assertion
of Christianity's new standing in the Roman Empire. More restricted
and selective definitions of the entitlement follow in the wake of the
first blanket pronouncements, even within Constantine's own era, in
the interests of maintaining local councils;[46] but still there is the same
rhetoric of justification for freeing the clergy from public burdens.
Constantius, for example, at Antioch in 361 (16.2.16) singled out for
privileges those of particular Christian probity: 'since we know that
our state is sustained more by religious observances ("religionibus")
than by official duties and the labour and sweat of the body' (even
though a few months later (12.1.49) he sought to protect councils and
their finances from illicit clergy evasion). It is the Christian clergy who
are now seen to maintain the state's essential religious services. Many
years later (412) Honorius demanded that the churches be free to
devote 'every moment of every hour' to preaching and prayer: 'let them
rejoice for ever protected by our generosity, as we rejoice in their
devotion to the worship of eternal piety' (*Const. Sirm.* 11 = 16.2.40).
This religious sustenance of the Empire kept company with the more
material sustenance of the poor, which the laws recognise as an
obligation demanded of the clergy. Thus in the competing
requirements of church and curia, the former was not to be denied the
resources necessary for its work of charity. A law which exempts clergy
from the tradesmen's tax (the *collatio lustralis*) for example, justifies
the privilege on the grounds that the profits incurred were expended
on the benefit of the poor.[47]

The technicalities of the immunities and exemptions granted to the
clergy are beyond the scope of this paper:[48] sufficient to observe that in
the sight of the laws they are the necessary adjunct for a privileged
caste charged with the conduct of approved *religio*. We are back to the
drawing of religious boundaries. For it is of the essence of clerical
privileges that they should be confined to the proponents of authorised
orthodoxy: when first encountered, as we saw, they are being accorded
to the Catholics in Africa to the exclusion of the Donatists. One of the

[45] Constantine's letter to the proconsul Anullinus is preserved by Eusebius, *HE* 10.7.

[46] As 16.2.3, with reference to an earlier law (not extant) restricting access to the
clergy to those not of curial means; cf. 16.2.6. Seeck assigns both these laws to 329.

[47] 16.2.10 (346 Seeck); cf. 16.2.14, and, for the principle, 16.2.6 'opulentos enim saeculi
subire necessitates oportet, pauperes ecclesiarum divitiis sustentari'. The same point is
made by Basil, *Ep* 104, appealing for tax exemptions for clergy.

[48] For discussion, see C. Dupont, 'Les privilèges des clercs sous Constantin', *RHE* 62
(1967), 729-52; K.L. Noethlichs, 'Zur Einflussnahme des Staates auf die Entwicklung
eines christlichen Klerikerstandes', *Jb. Ant. Christ.* 15 (1972), 136-53; T.G. Elliott, 'The
Tax Exemptions Granted to Clerics by Constantine and Constantius II', *Phoenix* 32
(1978), 326-36.

most regular features of the litany of laws denouncing heretics is not only that the offenders should be denied possession of churches and places of assembly, but that their bishops and priests are not clergy at all – they are false practitioners of false religion, who have placed themselves outside the limits of the Empire's legitimate worship (and of any accompanying benefits): 'their bishops shall not dare to infiltrate ("insinuare") the faith which they do not have, nor to create clergy, which is what they are not' (16.5.24, 394). To read through this relentless section of the Code is to be struck by the regularity of the language of separation and segregation used against condemned groups. From first to last the Manichees, for example, 'have nothing which they share with the rest of mankind', and their gatherings are to be banished from city and countryside; their presence is a contagion, which leaves no place for them on earth.[49] The Manichees, admittedly, are the ultimate offenders;[50] but the rest, too, are the object of similar demands for their isolation. In 381 the newly condemned Eunomians and Arians are to be allowed no opportunity to build churches 'in the city or in the country' (16.5.8); in 388 the praetorian prefect Cynegius is instructed to exclude Apollinarians and others from everywhere, 'from the walls of cities, from gatherings of honourable men, from the communion of saints'. They are to be denied clergy and right of assembly: 'let them go to the places which will best separate them, as though with a rampart, from association with mankind' (16.5.14).[51] The newest heretics in the Code, the Nestorians, are to have a similar fate visited on them, to be deprived of all meeting-places of every description (16.5.66, of 435). Even more specific deprivations levelled at heretics, such as testamentary restrictions and confiscation of property, are also presented in terms of this wholesale exclusion from the rest of society – finances, wills etc. are part of the normal dealings between human beings which they are to be denied.[52] The drawing of the boundary around legitimate religion has almost ceased to be metaphorical: the laws envisage a Roman world the borders of which are coextensive with Christian orthodoxy, and which harbours no corner of refuge for the dissenting.

In projecting this image of an exclusively Christian state the Code reflects the era of its compilation. It is surely no mere coincidence that the latest text denouncing heretics should explicitly uphold the decisions of the council of Ephesus of 431; while the whole section *de haereticis* is by and large a dossier of the religious policy of the dynasty

---

[49] 16.5.18 (389) 'nihil ad summum his sit commune cum mundo'; for similar language, see 16.5.3, 16.5.40 ('nihil ex moribus, nihil ex legibus sit commune cum ceteris').

[50] 16.5.65 'qui ad imam usque scelerum nequitiam pervenerunt'.

[51] Cf. Gratian's rescript against Priscillian and his supporters, 'quo universi haeretici excedere non ecclesiis tantum aut urbibus, sed extra omnes terras propelli iubebantur' (Sulp. Sev. *Chron.* 2.47).

[52] E.g. 16.5.17, 16.5.40.

of Theodosius. The 'renowned Constantine' may have been the starting-point for the compilers of the Code, but for the purpose of asserting normative religion for the Empire Theodosius was the real place to begin. Conspicuously they did not include any pronouncements of Constantius or Valens on the subject of right doctrine, which would have accorded ill with the aspirations to universal Catholic orthodoxy to which book 16 of the Code testifies.[53]

But the laws' presentation of an empire of Catholic unanimity remains, of course, a very partial view of the Roman world of the Theodosian age. Despite the penalties and denunciations, and despite the threats of confiscation against those who allowed their houses and estates to be used for illicit worship, heretical churches and congregations did not disappear. To look no further than Constantinople itself, beneath the eyes of the imperial court, Arians and others continued to assemble in and around the capital and to appoint their clergy – even a succession of bishops.[54] In the case of paganism, even the laws themselves are less than wholehearted when it comes to specific regulations. Theodosius' anti-pagan legislation of the early 390s (16.10.10-12), despite the apparent comprehensiveness of its prohibitions, is in fact directed at the behaviour of public figures, and not at the population at large;[55] and later laws (399) continue to assert the protection of temple buildings and local festive gatherings (16.10.15, 17-18). We have to wait until November 435, and one of the latest texts in the Code (16.10.25), for a clear-cut pronouncement from Constantinople which orders magistrates to destroy all remaining pagan shrines and replace them with the 'sign of the venerable Christian religion'.[56] This law contains a revealing phrase, 'if any shrines still remain intact' ('si qua etiam nunc restant integra'): by now the menace from paganism is evidently deemed to be minimal, and hence the concentration of the outrage of the laws against the more present threat of heresy. But that little phrase also sharply exposes the limitations of law as a vehicle of 'Christianisation'. For it reflects a contemporary world in which the destruction of paganism has been advancing apace (at least since the last quarter of the fourth century) at the hands of missionary bishops, fanatical monks and pious individuals, a process which laws have been powerless to control: they can only close the stable door on a horse which has irretrievably bolted. Similarly, a succession of laws in the early fifth century vainly proclaims the protection of Jewish synagogues from Christian

[53] *Pace* Honoré, op. cit. (n. 22), p. 182 on the Code's neutrality.

[54] See, e.g., J.H.W.G. Liebeschuetz, *Barbarians and Bishops: Army, Church, and State in the Age of Arcadius and Chrysostom* (1990), 152-3.

[55] Thus 16.10.10 speaks of 'iudices' and provincial governors and their *officia*; 16.10.12 has 'nullus ... vel in potestate positus vel honore perfunctus ...'.

[56] Although the destruction of statues and altars had already been sanctioned in a law of 407: 16.10.19 (= *Const. Sirm.* 12).

violence: their repetition of the prohibition on burning down synagogues is a telling indication of where the real front line now lay in Christianising the Roman Empire.[57] To borrow an analogy from Peter Brown, the laws, like the Duke of Plaza Toro, led the regiment of Christianisers from the rear.

---

[57] 16.8.21, 25, 26. For one incident, see my 'St. Stephen in Minorca: an episode in Jewish-Christian relations in the early 5th century AD', *JTS* 33 (1982), 106-23.

Part III

Nachleben: the Code in the Middle Ages

Introductory Note

Ian Wood

The Theodosian Code was promulgated in AD 438. Within a century much had happened to undermine its significance. In the eastern Empire, the birthplace of the Code, the emperor Justinian's legal reforms had rendered it obsolete. In the West the collapse of imperial rule and the establishment of the successor states might equally well have invalidated its status as a repository of law. Perhaps surprisingly, this was not to be the case. In 506 the Visigothic king Alaric II authorised the promulgation of the *Lex Romana Visigothorum*, which was largely based on the Code, and forbad the use of any other Roman law.

The *Lex Romana Visigothorum*, or Breviary of Alaric as it was often known, was to prove significant in the transmission of the contents of the Theodosian Code to the medieval world and beyond. Yet it was not the Visigoths who ensured the ultimate survival of either the Code or the *Lex Romana Visigothorum*. Later Visigothic codes, although heavily influenced by Roman law, banned the use of previous legal compilations, among them the Breviary of Alaric and the Code of Euric. It is, in fact, largely in the Frankish kingdom, whose own legislation is usually seen as being among the least Romanised of the laws of the successor states, that both the Code and the *Lex Romana Visiogothorum* survived. Merovingian legislation was directly influenced by Roman law. Moreover, narrative sources reveal that members of the administrative classes learned the Code, or perhaps the Breviary, as part of their schooling. To the narrative sources may be added the evidence of the manuscripts, which show that the Theodosian Code was at least as important as the Breviary in the sixth, seventh and eighth centuries.

In addition to the manuscript evidence for the Code itself, there is

159

that for the Sirmondian Constitutions, which have often been seen as a satellite collection. Here the evidence suggests ecclesiastical involvement. Mark Vessey's analysis of the manuscript tradition of the Sirmondian Constitutions shows that the earliest context in which they are known to have been preserved is ecclesiastical, and that the collection may well be associated with the growing power of the bishops of Lyons in the sixth century. Again, the narrative sources are compatible showing that Merovingian ecclesiastics, like their secular counterparts, were educated in Roman law.

Indeed the church, and especially the Frankish church, played a role alongside, and greater than, that of the Merovingian kings in transmitting Roman law, and especially the Code, to posterity. As Dafydd Walters shows, western churchmen cited the Code frequently from the sixth to the eleventh century, and it is likely that the Theodosian Code, or the breviary of Alaric, provided some, if not the majority of the *lex Romana* envisaged in the phrase *ecclesia vivit lege Romana*. It was not until the Investiture dispute that the legal compilations of Justinian came to take precedence in the West over their Theodosian counterpart.

Between the sixth and eleventh centuries the Code, or the Breviary, was transcribed and cited. As a result, while the *Codex Theodosianus* was ignored in the Byzantine Empire, it was preserved in the early medieval West, and it is to the lawyers and churchmen of the western Dark Ages that we owe much of our knowledge of Theodosius' legal achievement.

7. The Code in Merovingian Gaul

Ian Wood

The Franks and their neighbours were well aware of the importance of the emperor Theodosius as a law-giver. Writing in the mid-seventh century, Fredegar attributed to Theodosius I the emendation of laws.[1] In all probability he meant to refer to Theodosius II. A century later the compiler of the Bavarian law-code, the *Lex Baiwariorum*, included within his preface a list, derived from Isidore, of great legislators of the past, Roman as well as Frankish; among them Theodosius.[2] Knowledge of the Theodosian Code in Francia and its satellites is not surprising. Theoretically, the Roman population of the Visigothic and Burgundian kingdoms had been subject to Roman law,[3] and to judge by Agobard's complaints of legal pluralism in the ninth century this continued to be the case.[4] Further, in the *Lex Ribvaria*, the seventh-century code of the Ripuarian Franks, the church is said to have been subject to Roman law.[5] Nevertheless, it is not always easy to be specific about the use and influence of Roman law, and in particular of the Theodosian Code, in the Merovingian kingdom.

The history of the transmission and influence of the Code in Merovingian Gaul is complicated for the historian by a number of crucial factors relating both to Roman and barbarian law. To take the issue of Roman law first: the Code was never intended as a complete collection of the law of the Roman Empire. It was a compilation of imperial laws which had been addressed to officials responsible for the great courts. Even so it did not contain all imperial legislation. Nor did it contain the customary law which was current in provincial courts. As a result, when Burgundian and Frankish sources talk of *leges Romanae* they may not always have the law of the Code in mind; they

[1] Fredegar II 50.

[2] *Lex Baiwariorum* praef.

[3] *Lib. Const., prima constitutio* 8.

[4] Ag., *Lib. Adv. leg. Gund.* 4: I.N. Wood, 'Ethnicity and the Ethnogenesis of the Burgundians', in H. Wolfram and W. Pohl, *Typen der Ethnogenese und besonderer Berücksichtigung der Bayern* (1990), 53.

[5] *Lex Rib.* 61, 1. For an example of the dependence on Roman law of legislation relating to clerics, compare *Lex Baiw.* I 12 with *CTh* 16.2.24.

may instead be refering to provincial law, which was Roman if not imperial. Thus in the Angers Formulary, which contains some apparently sixth-century *formulae*, although the collection was probably compiled in the seventh century, the phrase *lex Romana* occurs in four instances,[6] but none of them seem to refer to the Theodosian Code. Further, in one instance *lex Romana* is linked to *antiqua consuetudo*.[7] Nor does the one direct reference made to Roman legal practice by Gregory of Tours, concerning the period of time which should elapse between a man's death and the reading of his will,[8] relate to the Code.

Moreover, even when there is a directly stated appeal to the Code, it is possible that the appeal is not, strictly speaking, to the Code itself, but rather to the *Lex Romana Visigothorum*, or Breviary of Alaric, the Visigothic version of the Theodosian Code, produced around the year 506. Thus, in his edition of the Merovingian *formulae*, Zeumer identified references to the *Theodosiani Libri* as being to the Breviary rather than the Code. For instance, in the mid-eighth-century Tours Formulary the so-called *epistola collectionis* quotes *ex corpore Theodosiani libri quinti*, but the sentence in question is contained in an *interpretatio* of the Breviary of Alaric.[9] And in the *donatio in sponsa facta* to be found in one ninth-century manuscript of the same Formulary, the reference to the clause *in Theodosiano codice 'de sponsalibus et ante nuptias donationibus'* appears to relate to another *interpretatio* in the *Lex Romana Visigothorum*.[10] Indeed, rightly or wrongly, Zeumer consistently identified the Roman sources of the Merovingian *formulae* as being the *Lex Romana Visigothorum* and the *Sententiae* of Paul, rather than the Code itself.[11] Citations of the Theodosian Code, therefore, are not necessarily citations of the original compilation; they could as well refer to the *Lex Romana Visigothorum*.

Nor was the Breviary of Alaric the only compilation of Roman law from sixth-century Gaul which might have been cited in place of the Theodosian Code. The *Lex Romana Burgundionum* is a difficult text. It is not clear whether it was an official compilation or not. Certainly it is closely related to the *Liber Constitutionum* of the Burgundians,[12] a work which is popularly, though misleadingly, known as the

---

[6] *Form. And.* 40, 46, 54, 58.

[7] *Form. And.* 46.

[8] Greg., *VP* VIII 5, ed. B. Krusch, *MGH SRM* I, 2 (1885).

[9] *Form. Tur.* 11.

[10] *Form. Tur.*, appendix 2.

[11] *Form. Arv.* 3; Marculf, II 17; *Form. Tur.* 11, 16, 17, 22, 24, 25, 29, 32, app. 2, 4; *Form. Bit.* 9. The classic study of use of the *LRV* in the successor states is A. de Wretschko, 'De usu Breviarii Alariciani forensi et scholastico per Hispaniam, Galliam, Italiam regionesque vicinas', in Mommsen, *CTh*, pp. cccvii-ccclx.

[12] *Leges Burgundionum* (ed. de Salis), 164-7.

Burgundian Code.[13] Certainly, also, the Romans within the Burgundian kingdom were bound by Roman law: the *prima constitutio* of the *Liber Constitutionum*, issued by Sigismund on 29 March 517, states explicitly: 'We order that cases between Romans ... should be judged by Roman laws, as decreed by our *parentes*; and let them know that they must accept the written form and exposition of the law, when judgment is made, so that no one may excuse themselves out of ignorance.'[14] This suggests that there must have been an officially recognised law-book, but whether this was the *Lex Romana Burgundionum*, the Theodosian Code or even the Breviary of Alaric, it is impossible to say.

In his edition of the *Lex Romana Burgundionum*, which consists of a mere 47 clauses, de Salis noted 64 references to the Theodosian Code, three to the novels of Theodosius II, seven to those of Valentinian III, one each to the novels of Majorian, Marcian and Leo and Severus, in addition to a reference to an unidentified novel, and two to laws preserved only in the Justinianic Codex. Further, there are seven references to Gaius, 22 to Paul, four to the *Codex Gregorianus* and six to the *Codex Hermogenianus*.[15] Not all the passages which the *Lex Romana Burgundionum* claims to have used have been identified, even when the title of the relevant law is provided. It may be that the compiler had access to fuller texts of the Theodosian Code and to the works of Gaius than now survive.[16]

Whatever the nature of the text, the *Lex Romana Burgundionum* is a remarkable compilation, made from a number of Roman legal sources: these it often specifies, citing the number of the book of the Theodosian Code, the emperor who issued the edict, and its recipient, or the title.[17] From the point of view of the historian studying the transmission and use of the Theodosian Code, however, this clarity of citation may be a hindrance. Because the *Lex Romana Burgundionum* cites the Code so clearly and fully, it is possible that some later texts which claim to cite the Code were actually drawing on the *Lex Romana Burgundionum*, even when chapter and verse is quoted.

Barbarian law presents rather more intractable problems. First, it is by no means clear that this law is Germanic. Even if some clauses of the codes of the barbarian kingdoms can reasonably be seen as reflecting Germanic custom, many of them have a very good claim to

---

[13] I.N. Wood, 'Disputes in Late Fifth- and Sixth-century Gaul: Some Problems', in W. Davies and P. Fouracre, *The Settlement of Disputes in Early Medieval Europe* (1986), 10; idem, 'Ethnicity and the Ethnogenesis of the Burgundians' (cited above in n. 4), 54.

[14] *Lib. Const., prima constitutio* 8.

[15] *Leges Burgundionum* (ed. de Salis), 168-70.

[16] *Lex Rom. Burg.* V 1; VI 2; XII 2; XVII 6; XXXI 4; XXXVII 4.

[17] *Lex Rom. Burg.* I 1; II 1, 2; III 1, 2; IV 1; V 1; VI 2; VII 1, 5; VIII 2; IX 3, 4; X 1, 2, 5; XII 2; XIV 6; XVI 2; XVII 6; XIX 4; XXII 2, 4, 9; XXV; XXVI 1; XXXI 4, 5; XXXII 2; XXXV 3, 4; XXXVI 4, 9; XXXVII 4, 6; XXXVIII 1, 3, 4; XXXIX 3; XLII; XLIV 3; XLV 2.

represent the provincial law of the Roman Empire.[18] For instance, the direct parallels between the Latin codes of the Germanic kingdoms and the Byzantine Farmer's Law can more reasonably be seen as reflecting provincial law than as indicating the existence of an otherwise unknown Gothic community in a particular district of Asia Minor.[19] Some barbarian groups may have received Roman law considerably before the fifth century; in a panegyric on Constantius Chlorus Maximian is said to have restored the *laetus* to his position, leaving the Frank, *receptus in leges*, cultivating the fields of Trier.[20] One might wonder whether the four obscure lawmen of the preface to the *Pactus Legis Salicae*, Wisogast, Arogast, Salegast and Widogast,[21] had their origins in some transmission of Roman provincial law to the Franks. Provincial law does not, of course, bear witness to the transmission of the Theodosian Code. Nevertheless, it is likely that barbarian law is to be seen as being very much more Roman than was once thought.

Both Roman and barbarian law, therefore, present considerable problems to the historian of Merovingian Gaul. It is possible, however, to shed a little more light on the issue of the influence of the Theodosian Code and its derivative, the Breviary of Alaric, by considering the evidence of the manuscripts of the Code and the Breviary, and also by assessing the rare comments on the acquisition of legal knowledge in the Merovingian kingdom. This may shed light on the processes of legislation in post-Roman Gaul and Francia.

In *Codices Latinae Antiquiores* Lowe listed nine manuscripts of the Theodosian Code, or rather parts of it,[22] one manuscript of a breviary of the Code,[23] as well as a manuscript of the Novels.[24] Of these he assigned four manuscripts of the Code and the manuscript of the Novels to France;[25] one of the Code to Italy,[26] and two, of which one was the breviary, to Egypt.[27] The two remaining manuscripts could either have been written in Italy or France, and both seem to have been within Frankish territory at a later date.[28] By any estimate, Gaul and Francia played a significant role in the preservation and transmission of early manuscripts of the Code, accounting for half of the total surviving at least. Further, the geographical spread of these manuscripts within the Frankish kingdom is of interest. Two of them,

---

[18] R. Collins, *Early Medieval Spain* (1983), 28; Wood, 'Disputes in Late Fifth- and Sixth-century Gaul: Some Problems' (cited above in n. 13), 20.

[19] Collins, *Early Medieval Spain* (1983), 28.

[20] *Pan. Lat.* (ed. Mynors), 8.21.1.

[21] *Pact. Leg. Sal.*, praef. 2.

[22] *CLA* I/IV 46; I 110; II 211; IV 440; V 591; VII 1016; VIII 1049, 1212; X 1529.

[23] *CLA* V 625.

[24] *CLA* VIII 1199.

[25] *CLA* I/IV 46; I 110; V 591; VIII 1049, 1199.

[26] *CLA* VIII 1212.

[27] *CLA* II 211; X 1529.

[28] *CLA* V 625; VII 1016.

both from the sixth century, Lowe assigned to Lyons, giving that city a considerable reputation in legal studies.[29] That of the Novels, from the second half of the eighth century, he assigned to the Loire region; later it was to be at Regensburg.[30] Other manuscripts were to reach Northern France,[31] Switzerland[32] and the Italian monastery of Bobbio,[33] which had close links with Francia, in particular with the monastery of Luxeuil in Burgundy. Knowledge of the Code does not, therefore, seem to have been confined to one or two centres; nor was interest in the text confined in time. Of the seven manuscripts which he thought might have been written in Gaul or Francia, Lowe dated one, which he assigned to Gaul or Italy, to the fifth or sixth century,[34] and in addition to the two said to have come from Lyons he placed another, which he thought had come from Southern France or Italy, in the sixth century.[35] Of the remaining three, he dated one to the seventh,[36] one to the second half of the eighth,[37] and one to the eighth or ninth century.[38]

Ten manuscripts may not seem to be a very significant number. The only other legal text, however, to have survived in similar numbers of Latin manuscripts from before the ninth century is the Breviary of Alaric.[39] Of course most of the barbarian codes were compiled considerably later than the Code, so the comparison is not strictly equal. As for manuscripts of the *Lex Romana Visigothorum*, since it was clearly cited as containing the law of Theodosius, they can reasonably be used to further our consideration of the impact of the Code on Merovingian Gaul. Here we are dealing with fourteen manuscripts, all of which, bar one,[40] appear to be of Frankish provenance. This Frankish near-monopoly of manuscripts of the Breviary of Alaric should not surprise us. The evidence for the Visigoths suppressing law-codes which they regarded as outmoded is considerable; the survival of only one Spanish manuscript of the *Lex Romana Visigothorum* is simply a tribute to Gothic legal efficiency.[41] Nevertheless, the distribution of the Frankish

---

[29] *CLA* I 110; V 591.
[30] *CLA* VIII 1199.
[31] *CLA* V 625.
[32] *CLA* VII 1016.
[33] *CLA* I/IV 46.
[34] *CLA* VII 1016.
[35] *CLA* I 110; V 591, 625.
[36] *CLA* I/IV 46.
[37] *CLA* VIII 1199.
[38] *CLA* VIII 1049.
[39] For instance, Lowe only lists two MSS of the Lombard Code, *CLA* IV 471; VII 949: one of the *Lex Visigothorum*, *CLA* I 111: one of the *Codex Euricianus*, *CLA* V 626: two of the *Lex Alamanorum*, *CLA* VII 950; IX 1382: and two of *Lex Salica*, *CLA* VII 950; IX 1395. There are, of course, some difficulties in determining whether some MSS belong in the eighth or ninth century: Rosamond McKitterick has a rather fuller list of MSS of *Lex Salica* than does Lowe, *The Carolingians and the Written Word* (1989), 48-55.
[40] *CLA* XI 1637.
[41] R.J. Collins, *Early Medieval Spain* (1983), 25-6, 123-5.

manuscripts is interesting. Despite the Aquitainian origin of the text, there are only two manuscripts which may have come from Southern France;[42] a further one possibly originated in the Loire region,[43] and another from Lyons.[44] Two more seem to have been written in Burgundy,[45] a third in Autun or the nearby monastery of St Georges at Couches[46] and a fourth in Western Switzerland.[47] Lowe assigned one manuscript to Rheims,[48] and three more to Northern France,[49] one of them to the monastery of Corbie.[50] The remaining manuscript appears to have been of Rhaetian provenance.[51] The distribution of these manuscripts of the Breviary thus covers much of the Frankish kingdom.

The date of the manuscripts, again, suggests that an interest in the text existed throughout the Merovingian period. Lowe dated one manuscript of the Breviary to the second half of the sixth century,[52] and another to the sixth or seventh.[53] One he placed in the seventh,[54] and another in the seventh or eighth century.[55] Seven he saw as being eighth-century manuscripts,[56] and two as either being eighth- or ninth-century.[57] Most of these later manuscripts are likely to have been Carolingian rather than Merovingian, and it is possible that they reflect an escalation of interest in the Breviary in the Carolingian period. Indeed the general chronology of the manuscripts of the Code and the Breviary may suggest that it was the Code which was marginally the more common text in the Merovingian period; a point which may indicate that Zeumer was over-hasty in identifying all citations of material from the Code in the *formulae* as being taken from the Breviary. Nevertheless, there is enough manuscript evidence to show that Frankish interest in the Breviary began before the eighth century. More generally the evidence of the distribution and chronology of the manuscripts of the Theodosian Code and the Breviary of Alaric is in absolute accord with the stated subordination of Romans and of the church to *lex Romana*.

---

[42] *CLA* V 705a; IX 1324.
[43] *CLA* VIII 1199.
[44] *CLA* VIII 1064.
[45] *CLA* VIII 1059, 1395.
[46] *CLA* VI 793.
[47] *CLA* VII 950.
[48] *CLA* X 1596.
[49] *CLA* V 556, 617; S 1752.
[50] *CLA* S 1752.
[51] *CLA* IX 1362.
[52] *CLA* VIII 1064.
[53] *CLA* V 703a.
[54] *CLA* IX 1324.
[55] *CLA* V 617.
[56] *CLA* V 556; VI 793; VII 950; VIII 1199; IX 1395; X 1596; S 1752.
[57] *CLA* VIII 1059; IX 1362.

Outside the evidence of the manuscripts, and that of other legal texts, such as the Frankish and Burgundian laws and the Formularies, there is pitifully little evidence for the use of the Code. There are, however, a handful of interesting pieces of information relating to legal education in the Merovingian kingdom. The earliest comes in the account of the slave Andarchius, given by Gregory of Tours in his *Histories*.[58] Here, Andarchius is said to have been learned in the works of Virgil and in *legis Theodosianae libri*. It is possible that it was the Breviary of Alaric that he knew, rather than the Code, since he seems to have spent his early, servile, career in the Marseilles district; that is in territory which had once been in the hands of the Visigoths. But, as we have seen, no clear distinction was made between the two texts. Andarchius used his cultural and legal skills to rise up the social hierarchy, attempting to make a good marriage and then to dispossess his intended father-in-law of one of his estates, before the latter's slaves killed him.

In the seventh century, there is some further evidence of the knowledge of the Theodosian Code. The most detailed references relate to Praeiectus, bishop of Clermont. He became involved in a lawsuit at the court of Childeric II (662-75) during the Easter festivities in 675. Accused of taking the land of a lady named Claudia, he refused to face his accusers on the grounds that Roman and canon law forbad the hearing of cases òn Easter Saturday.[59] The reference here is to a law contained in both the Theodosian Code[60] and also the Breviary of Alaric.[61] As an Auvergnat,[62] Praeiectus is likely to have been classified as a Roman, and, in any case, since the *Lex Ribvaria* explicitly states that the church was subject to Roman law,[63] as a churchman he would have fallen under its aegis. What is important about his case is the clear evidence that Roman law was specifically invoked. In 675 the legal prescriptions relating to the church were being observed, and Praeiectus' hagiographer thought fit to record the exact procedure followed by the bishop. The Theodosian Code, or perhaps the Breviary of Alaric, was thus of distinct importance at Childeric II's court in the 670s.

Another Auvergnat, Bonitus, a younger contemporary of Praeiectus, who later held the see of Clermont, is also said to have known the Theodosian Code. In his *vita* he is described as *grammaticorum inbutus iniciis necnon Theodosii edoctus decretis*.[64] Other seventh-century bishops are also said to have been learned in Roman law. For instance, Desiderius, later bishop of Cahors, was educated first in *litterarum*

[58] Greg., *DLH* IV 46.
[59] *Pass. Praeiecti* 24.
[60] *CTh* 2.8.19.
[61] *LRV* 2.8.2.
[62] *Pass. Praeiecti* 1.
[63] *Lex Rib.* 61, 1.
[64] *Vit. Bon.* 1; see P. Wormald, 'The Decline of the Roman Empire and the Survival of its Aristocracy', *JRS* 66 (1976), 224.

studia, and then, at the royal court, in *legum Romanorum ... studium,*
'so that Roman *gravitas* might temper the richness of Gallic eloquence
and the brightness of its speech'.[65] A more important figure was
Praeiectus' exact contemporary, Leodegar, who was also involved in
the lawsuit at Childeric's court. Before becoming bishop of Autun, he
was said to have learned *doctrinae legum,*[66] and to have been a
terribilis iudex, knowing *mundanae legis censura.*[67] That his legal
knowledge really was considerable is suggested by a record of his
revising the laws of previous kings; 'having taken on the government of
the kingdom, whatever he found to be useless, and in contradiction to
the laws of ancient kings and the greater nobility, he restored to its
former state'.[68] What this might have entailed is indicated by the
statement that 'all sought king Childeric, so that he might command
throughout the three kingdoms which he had obtained, that judges
should preserve the law and custom of each *patria,* as used to be the
case'.[69] The three kingdoms were Neustria, Austrasia and Burgundy:
the standard units of the Merovingian *regnum.*

It may be that some evidence for these legal revisions survives in the
earliest frankish law code, the *Pactus Legis Salicae.* The epilogue to
what some manuscripts identify as book three of the *Pactus* contains a
famous account of Merovingian legislation from the time of an
unnamed first king, down to Chlothar I, who died in 561. This account
is followed by an equally famous list of kings, which begins with
Theuderic III, who succeeded his brother Childeric II in 675. Childeric
was the king under whom Leodegar is said to have carried out his legal
reforms; that the king-list of the *Pactus* should start after his reign
suggests that it marked a caesura of some kind. The king-list may, in
fact, have originally been a list of royal authenticators of Leodegar's
version of the *Pactus.* If this is the case, it may be possible to ascribe
some of the variants within the texts of the *Pactus Legis Salicae* to a
Leodegarian recension. For instance it may be that those manuscripts
of the text which contain the epilogue stem ultimately from Leodegar's
reforms of the 670s. Further, since one clause of the *Pactus* seems to be
applicable only to Neustria,[70] it may be that the manuscripts in
question descend ultimately from Leodegar's recension of the law of
the Neustrian kingdom. If this interpretation is correct, it may be that
Leodegar also revised the *Lex Ribvaria* for the Austrasians, and the
Liber Constitutionum for the Burgundians.

Leodegar's legal knowledge would not have been confined to the

[65] *Vit. Des.* 1.
[66] *Pass. Leudegarii* II 2.
[67] *Pass. Leudegarii* I 1.
[68] *Pass. Leudegarii* II 5.
[69] *Pass. Leudegarii* I 7.
[70] *Pact. Leg. Sal.* 47, 1, 3. For a full statement of this case see the chapter on law in my
forthcoming book on *The Merovingian Kingdoms, 450-751.*

barbarian codes. Roman law would still have been applicable to those who were defined as Romans;[71] being brought up in Poitiers in Aquitaine, Leodegar would have been well acquainted with a region dominated by a legally Roman population.[72] Moreover, as a churchman, Leodegar himself would, like Praeiectus, have been subject to Roman law. It has been suggested that he was associated with the compilation of the great canon collection of the Merovingian period, the *Vetus Gallica*.[73] This would tend to strengthen the case for his being interested in the law to which the church was subject, and, as we have seen, this, according to the *Lex Ribvaria*, was Roman.[74]

There is some reason, therefore, for seeing the 670s not only as a period when the law of the Theodosian Code, or perhaps the Breviary of Alaric, was used in lawsuits, and but also for interpreting the decade as one of considerable legal activity, with Leodegar involved in the revision of a variety of legal texts, including the *Pactus Legis Salicae*: he may even have been responsible for compilation of a version of the *Pactus*, containing its first 93 chapters. There is nothing, however, to suggest that Leodegar was an initiator of new legislation. For the sixth century, on the other hand, there is considerable evidence for the creation of new law. Bearing in mind the range of legal knowledge which Leodegar appears to have possessed, it is worth looking at the work of earlier legislators, and considering whether the Theodosian Code may have influenced that too.

The notion of compiling a law-code may, in itself, reflect admiration for the Theodosian Code, and a desire to emulate it. But a further observation is perhaps significant. Despite the format of many of the clauses of the barbarian codes, a proportion of the laws preserved within the codes are in fact edicts. This is readily apparent in the case of the *Liber Constitutionum* of the Burgundians, where a number of edicts are preserved in their entirety.[75] It is also apparent in the major additions to the *Pactus Legis Salicae*, in the *Pactus pro tenore pacis* of Childebert I and Chlothar I, in the *edictus* of Chilperic I and in the *decretus* of Childebert II, apparently issued between 594 and 596.[76] It is less apparent in the *Lex Ribvaria*, where only the phraseology of individual clauses indicates their origins in royal edicts.[77] Nevertheless, it is clear that Burgundian and Frankish kings did issue edicts,

---

[71] *Lib. Const., prima constitutio* 8; see also *Cap. Merow.* 8, *Chlotharii Praeceptio* 4.

[72] *Pass. Leodegarii* I 1; II 1.

[73] H. Mordek, *Kirchenrecht und Reform im Frankenreich* (Berlin 1975), 82-5.

[74] *Lex Rib.* 61, 1.

[75] P. Wormald, '*Lex Scripta* and *Verbum Regis*: Legislation and Germanic Kingship from Euric to Cnut', in P.H. Sawyer and I.N. Wood, *Early Medieval Kingship* (1977), 112.

[76] *Pact. Leg. Sal.* 79-91 (*capitulare* 2); 106-16 (*capitulare* 4); *capitulare* 6.

[77] *Lex Rib.* (ed. Beyerle and Buchner), 108-9; I.N. Wood, 'Administration, Law and Culture in Merovingian Gaul', in R. McKitterick, *The Uses of Literacy in Early Medieval Europe* (1990), 66.

and it is therefore worth wondering to what extent this practice was influenced by the Theodosian Code itself.

It is as well to begin with the *Liber Constitutionum* of the Burgundians, for here we have the clearest evidence for law-making in action in one of the barbarian successor states of what had been Roman Gaul. Although much of the legislation in the Book of Constitutions can be assumed to be the result of royal legislation simply from the tone of individual chapters, in seven cases the law itself is dated, and the place of issue given;[78] one of these laws, which is specifically called an *edictum*, is also prefaced with the name of the king, *Sigismundus rex Burgundionum*.[79] One additional law is prefaced with the title, *Gundobadus rex Burgundionum omnibus comitibus*,[80] while the last law of all has the unfortunately unspecific heading *incipit capitulus, quem domnus noster gloriosissimus Ambariaco in conventu Burgundionum instituit*.[81]

Among these laws are some of the best known of the *Liber Constitutionum*, including the notorious one in which Gundobad instituted trial by battle as an alternative to oath-taking, because the Burgundians were taking perjury rather too lightly.[82] More interesting for understanding one context in which law was issued is the chapter concerned with the breach of promise committed by the widow Aunegild, who enjoyed a *consuetum flagitium* with Balthamod, although she was betrothed to the king's *spatarius*, Fredegiscl.[83] Here, a description of the case and the royal judgment is set out in full in order to stand in perpetuity. A specific sentence given by a king could thus become enshrined as law.

Two other observations can be made about the context of the Aunegild case. The royal judgment was given on 29 March 517, which also happens to be the date of the *prima constitutio*, which prefaces the *Liber Constitutionum*, and thus dates the original promulgation of the compilation.[84] The case was, therefore, brought to the very gathering which was to issue the law-book of the Burgundian kingdom. The law which arose from the royal sentence cannot, as a result, have been in the original *Liber Constitutionum*, but it was delivered to an audience ready to hear legislation. Second, the gathering of 29 March 517 was the king's Easter court; for this reason Sigismund did not enforce the

[78] *Lib. Const.* 42, 45, 52, 62, 76, 79, *constitutio extravagans* 20.

[79] *Lib. Const.*, *constitutio extravagans* 20.

[80] *Lib. Const.*, *constitutio extravagans* 19.

[81] *Lib. Const.*, *constitutio extravagans* 21.

[82] *Lib. Const.* 45; Wood, 'Disputes in Late Fifth- and Sixth-century Gaul: Some Problems' (cited above in n. 13), 16-17, with the correction in idem, 'Ethnicity and the Ethnogenesis of the Burgundians' (cited above in n. 4), 54.

[83] *Lib. Const.* 52.

[84] Wood, 'Disputes in Late Fifth- and Sixth-century Gaul: Some Problems' (cited above in n. 13), 10.

death penalty, putting reverence for the time of year before public punishment. In so doing, he may well have had the chapter of the Theodosian Code *de indulgentiis criminum* in mind.[85]

That the Theodosian Code was not far from the mind of the legislators of the Burgundian court can be seen in other instances,[86] not least in matters of rape,[87] marriage,[88] slaves,[89] manumission,[90] and *postliminium*.[91] But the clearest example of the way in which the Theodosian Code weighed on the court of Sigismund is to be found in another edict, the first of his reign, issued on 8 March 516.[92] Here bishop Gimellus of Vaison is said to have drawn to attention the problem of foundlings who were not being cared for, because the finders feared that the true parents of the children would claim them in due course. Sigismund ordered that the *legis Romanorum ordo* should be followed, and he announced that in cases involving Romans and Burgundians the king's decree should hold good. There can be no question that the *legis Romanorum ordo* is the title of the Theodosian Code, *de expositis*.[93] Since the legislation on foundlings was inspired by a bishop, it is possible that the requisite knowledge of Roman law was supplied by the clergy; on the other hand, it is worth calling to mind Syagrius, whom Sidonius had described a generation earlier as a new Solon of the Burgundians,[94] and his contemporary, Leo of Narbonne, whom some have seen as having a hand in the creation of the *Codex Euricianus*.[95] Whether it was Gimellus and his fellow bishops, or secular officials at court, who drew the relevant law to Sigismund's attention is of no consequence – in 516 we see a Burgundian king legislating not just for the Romans, but also for his own people, with the Theodosian Code in mind.

Burgundian law is remarkably imperial in many ways; this is not surprising. As Ricimer's nephew,[96] and as the man who raised Glycerius to the imperial throne,[97] Gundobad came as close to the heart of Empire as any barbarian leader in the fifth century. And he

---

[85] *CTh* 9.38.

[86] cf. the parallels cited by de Salis in *Leges Burgundionum*, 164-7.

[87] *Lib. Const.* 12, 5.

[88] *Lib. Const.* 24.

[89] *Lib. Const.*, *constitutio extravagans* 21, 9.

[90] *Lib. Const.* 40.

[91] *Lib. Const.*, *constitutio extravagans* 21, 2.

[92] *Lib. Const.*, *constitutio extravagans* 20.

[93] *CTh* 5.9.

[94] Sid. Ap., *Ep.* V 5.

[95] Sid. Ap., *Carm.* xxiii; Wormald, 'The Decline of the Roman Empire and the Survival of its Aristocracy', *JRS* 66 (1976), 222.

[96] Wood, 'Ethnicity and the Ethnogenesis of the Burgundians' (cited above in n. 4), 60.

[97] Priscus, fr. 65 (John of Antioch, fr. 209, 2), ed. R. Blockley, *The Fragmentary Classicising Historians of the Late Roman Empire: Eunapius, Olympiodorus, Priscus, Malchus* (1981).

was later to receive the title of *magister militum* which his son, Sigismund, held after him.[98] No Merovingian could quite match Gundobad's imperial pedigree, but Clovis was the recipient of some major honour from the emperor Anastasius in 508,[99] and his successors certainly had an eye on the Roman past.[100] Merovingian legislation, however, is not usually thought of within the same context as the Theodosian Code.

As with the legislation of the Burgundian Gibichungs, the best starting point for understanding the laws of the Merovingians is their royal edicts. Of these there are a significant number, beginning with that issued by Clovis I (481-511) as he invaded the kingdom of the Visigoths in 507.[101] Offering protection to widows, orphans and those whom the church wished to defend, it was clearly a sop to the Catholic episcopate, and it may mark Clovis's first move in favour of Catholicism, rather than Arianism, which was also present at his court.[102] Another piece of secular legislation, the Treaty of Andelot agreed between Guntram (561-93) and Childebert II (575-96) in 587, is preserved in the Histories of Gregory of Tours.[103] But the majority of the surviving Merovingian edicts are incorporated into the *Pactus Legis Salicae*. There are six so-called *capitularia* attached to the *Pactus*. The first[104] and fifth[105] are unattributed, the second and third, the decrees of Childebert I (511-58) and Chlothar I (511-61) make up the *Pactus pro tenore pacis*,[106] the fourth is the edict of Chilperic I (561-84) of the same title,[107] and the sixth, the decree of Childebert II, is made up of legislation issued on three occasions, at Andernach, Maastricht and Cologne.[108]

The legislation of Childebert, Chlothar and Chilperic *pro tenore pacis* is of major importance for an understanding of Frankish law. The preface to Childebert's decree, delivered *apud nos maioresque natus Francorum palacii procerum*, allows a slight insight into the context of the legislation.[109] At the same time the dependence of the *pactus* of Childebert and Chlothar on the Roman *centena* provides an important clue to the imperial origins of the Frankish system of enforcing the

[98] Avit. of Vienne, *Epp.* 83-4.

[99] Greg., *DLH* II 37; M. McCormick, *Eternal Victory* (1986), 335-7.

[100] M. Reydellet, *La royauté dans la littérature latine de Sidoine Apollinaire à Isidore de Seville* (1981), 320-3.

[101] *Cap. Merow.* 1.

[102] I.N. Wood, 'Gregory of Tours and Clovis', *Revue Belge de Philologie et d'Histoire* 63 (1985), 270.

[103] Greg., *DLH* IX 20; for the context of the treaty IX 9-10.

[104] *Pact. Leg. Sal.* 66.

[105] *Pact. Leg. Sal.* 117-33.

[106] *Pact. Leg. Sal.* 79-93.

[107] *Pact. Leg. Sal.* 106-16.

[108] *Pact. Leg. Sal.*, *capitulare* 6.

[109] *Pact. Leg. Sal.* 79.

law.[110] Chlothar's contribution, moreover, shows unquestionable ecclesiastical influence.[111] Chilperic's edict of the same title constitutes by far the richest account of the process of Merovingian law in local courts.[112] Nevertheless, it is the so-called *decretus* of Childebert II which is most revealing of the circumstances of Frankish legislation, and the sources on which it could draw. The three meetings at which the decrees were issued were held at Andernach, Maastricht and Cologne between 594 and 596. In the first and last cases the day of the meeting was 1 March; the context in which this legislation was issued was probably the Frankish *campus Martius* or Marchfeld, the royal court at the beginning of the campaigning season.[113] The legislation itself, however, particularly that issued at Maastricht looks away from Frankish tradition. It draws clearly on the *Liber Constitutionum* of the Burgundians over the thirty-year rule,[114] homicide[115] and the question of witnesses.[116]

In considering the influences on this legislation it is necessary to consider the role of Asclepiodotus, whose name appears at the end of the Cologne decree, in the phrase *Aslepiode recognovit*. He was the referendary of Childebert,[117] but he is known previously to have served Childebert's uncle, Guntram (561-93), attending the ecclesiastical council of Valence summoned by that king in 585.[118] In addition he has been associated with Guntram's edict of the same year, and the Treaty of Andelot two years later.[119] Like Leodegar, he has been identified as a possible author of a recension of the *Pactus Legis Salicae*,[120] although there are difficulties in this identification.[121] As a servant of

[110] A.C. Murray, 'From Roman to Frankish Gaul: "centenarii" and "centenae" in the administration of the Merovingian kingdom', *Traditio* 44 (1988), 76.

[111] *Pact. Leg. Sal.* 90.

[112] *Pact. Leg. Sal.* 106-16: P. Fouracre, ' "Placita" and the Settlement of Disputes in Later Merovingian Francia', in W. Davies and P. Fouracre, *The Settlement of Disputes in Early Medieval Europe* (1986), 39-41.

[113] But for the origin of the term see J.M. Wallace-Hadrill, *The Long-Haired Kings* (1962), 103.

[114] *Decretus Childeberti* 2, 1: *Lib. Const.* 79, 5; *Lex Rom. Burg.* 31, 1.

[115] *Decretus Childeberti* 2, 3: *Lib. Const. 2, 1; Lex Rom. Burg.* 2.

[116] *Decretus Childeberti* 2, 5: *Lib. Const.* 43, 1; 99, 1.

[117] K.F. Stroheker, *Der senatorische Adel im spätantiken Gallien* (1948), n. 38; Wormald, 'The Decline of the Roman Empire and the Survival of its Aristocracy', *JRS* 66 (1976), 224.

[118] *Concilium Valentinum* A.583-5, ed. C. de Clercq in *Conc. Gall. A.511-695, Corpus Christianorum Series Latinorum* 148A (1963); for the date O. Pontal *Die Synoden im Merowingerreich* (1986), 143-4;

[119] *Cap. Merow.* 5; Greg., *DLH* IX 20; Stroheker, *Der senatorische Adel im spätantiken Gallien* (1948), n. 48.

[120] Wormald, 'The Decline of the Roman Empire and the Survival of its Aristocracy', *JRS* 66 (1976), 224.

[121] The objections arise from the fact that the *Pactus Legis Salicae* appears to be a Neustrian text, while all Asclepiodotus' identifiable work was in Burgundy and Austrasia: see the chapter on law in my forthcoming book on *The Merovingian*

Guntram, whose kingdom included territory which had been ruled by the Burgundian Gibichungs at the beginning of the century,[122] he may well have been an expert in Burgundian law. On the other hand, at Valence he appears as a *vir illustris*, which should mean that he was a Roman, subject to Roman law. It is not impossible that he knew the Theodosian Code, or the Visigothic recension of it, every bit as well as the slave Andarchius before him, and bishop Praeiectus after him.

Thus, even though much of the *Decretus Childeberti* can be seen as a continuation of Burgundian law, it is important to recognise its earlier, Roman, origins. In the case of the thirty-year rule Burgundian legislation looked back to Roman law,[123] and with regard to the number of witnesses required the *Liber Constitutionum* itself was following the Theodosian Code, without necessarily understanding why five or seven witnesses might be needed.[124] On rape, Childebert followed the *Lex Romana Burgundionum*,[125] which again was dependent on the Theodosian Code.[126] Finally, on matters of possession the *Decretus Childeberti* seems to have been following the *Lex Romana Visigothorum*.[127] Childebert may not have had the Theodosian Code itself at hand, but he had all the alternatives. His is sophisticated legislation in a sub-Roman tradition.

Childebert II's legislation can, therefore, be set within a context which looks back ultimately to the Theodosian Code. The same is true of the legislation of his cousin, Chlothar II (584-629). This is a point most clearly made in the *Praeceptio Chlotharii*,[128] which is preserved independent of the *Pactus Legis Salicae*. The preamble and four other clauses of the *Praeceptio* have been seen as having parallels with the *Lex Romana Visigothorum*.[129] One concerned with rescripts which are contrary to law[130] and another dealing with royal authorisation of marriage[131] are particularly close to imperial legislation.[132] From these clauses it is clear enough that Chlothar's legal advisers included someone versed in Roman law. Chronology and politics suggest that the man in question is unlikely to have been Asclepiodotus himself. Nevertheless whoever drafted the *Praeceptio* may, like Asclepiodotus,

---

Kingdoms, 450-751.
    [122] E. Ewig, 'Die fränkischen Teilungen und Teilreiche (511-613)', in idem, *Spätantikes und fränkisches Gallien* I (1976), 135-8.
    [123] *NVal* 26; 34.
    [124] Wood, 'Disputes in Late Fifth- and Sixth-century Gaul: Some Problems' (cited above in n. 13), 19.
    [125] *Decretus Childeberti* 2, 2: *Lex Rom. Burg.* 9.
    [126] *CTh* 9.24.
    [127] *Decretus Childeberti* 2, 1: *Paul. Sent.* 5, 2, 3-4.
    [128] *Cap. Merow.* 8.
    [129] *Chlotharii Praeceptio* 1; 2; 5; 7; 13.
    [130] *Chlotharii Praeceptio* 2.
    [131] *Chlotharii Praeceptio* 7.
    [132] *CTh* 1.2.1; 3.10.1.

have had Burgundian connections, for another clause reaffirms the authority of *romanae leges* in suits between Romans,[133] something which had been proclaimed in similar terms at the beginning of the Burgundian *Liber Constitutionum*.[134] Regardless of such specifics, the legislation from late sixth- and early seventh-century Francia reveals the influence of men learned in the Theodosian Code, or one of its derivatives.

The main body of the *Pactus Legis Salicae* does not belong to the same legal tradition as the edicts of Childebert II and Chlothar II; much of it concerns the legal procedures appropriate to small communities,[135] and if they have antecedents in Roman law, those antecedents are likely to have been drawn from the laws in force in the provincial courts of the Empire.[136] Yet it may be wrong to make a complete distinction between the legislation of the Theodosian Code and that of the main body of the *Pactus Legis Salicae*. Even in the first sixty-five chapters of the *Pactus*, that is, before the so-called *Capitula Legi Salicae addita*, there are laws which are likely to have been edicts in origin.[137] Royal edicts also underlie much of the other major Merovingian code, the *Lex Ribuaria*, even though the only indication of the original nature of individual laws is to be found in their phraseology.[138]

Of the clauses in *Lex Ribuaria* which unquestionably had their origin in edicts, those dealing with church freedmen[139] are the most immediately instructive. The use of the verb *iubere* at the start of the section indicates clearly that we are dealing with an edict. This is borne out by what follows, since it is here that the subordination of the church to Roman law is emphasised. In addition, Roman influence is apparent in individual clauses; none more so than in those dedicated to the offspring of slaves. Thus the descendants of a church freedman and a Ripuarian servant are to be servile, as are those of a church or king's freedwoman and a Ripuarian slave, but the freed parent does not lose status;[140] similarly if a Ripuarian man marries a royal ecclesiastical or freedman's maidservant, he keeps his status, but his offspring are to be slaves;[141] the equivalent situation and legislation appears in two laws of Con-

---

[133] *Chlotharii Praeceptio* 4.

[134] *Lib. Const., prima constitutio* 3.

[135] e.g. Fouracre, ' "Placita" and the Settlement of Disputes in Later Merovingian Francia' (cited above in n. 112), 39-41.

[136] Wood, 'Disputes in Late Fifth- and Sixth-century Gaul: Some Problems' (cited above in n. 13), 22.

[137] e.g. *Pact. Leg. Sal.* 39, 2: Wood, 'Disputes in Late Fifth- and Sixth-century Gaul: Some Problems', 21-2. The issue of actions *trans mare in Pactus Legis Salicae* 39, 2 may have its origins in legislation similar to *NVal* 33, 1.

[138] Wood, 'Administration, Law and Culture in Merovingian Gaul' (cited above in n. 77), 66.

[139] *Lex Rib.* 61.

[140] *Lex Rib.* 61, 10.

[141] *Lex Rib.* 61, 14.

stantine preserved in the Theodosian Code.[142] On the other hand, in the *Lex Ribvaria*, if a free Ripuarian marries an unfree Ripuarian, then the two of them and their issue are to be slaves;[143] as regards free women marrying servile men, once again there is an imperial equivalent in a law of Constantine preserved in the Code.[144] Whoever was responsible for chapter 61 of the *Lex Ribvaria* was probably a churchman, and he certainly had access to Roman law in some shape or form.

There is, therefore, in Frankish legislation itself, as in the *Liber Constitutionum* of the Burgundians, an indication that the laws which were being composed in the sixth and seventh centuries were drawn up with some awareness of Roman precedent. Whether or not the precedent was to be found directly in the Theodosian Code or in the Breviary of Alaric, or even the *Lex Romana Burgundionum* is impossible to say. Nevertheless, a little can be said about the legislators. Sidonius' correspondents, Syagrius and Leo, clearly knew their Roman law;[145] they may not have known much about barbarian custom; Asclepiodotus was equally at home in a church council as at the king's court; Gimellus and Leodegar were bishops; as such they ought to have known something about Roman law. Leodegar, however, could also be entrusted with revising the laws of Neustria, Austrasia and Burgundy. In the light of this, Roman influence on the laws of the Merovingians is scarcely surprising.

For a man like Leodegar Roman and barbarian law certainly applied in different instances, but a knowledge of both was required. Some of the earliest manuscripts of the *Pactus Legis Salicae*, *Lex Alamanorum* and the Formularies seem to make the same point, since they also include texts of Roman law. In one eighth-century manuscript the *Pactus* is to be found together with the *Lex Alamanorum* and the *Lex Romana Visigothorum*,[146] in another it is preserved with a *Summa* of the Breviary of Alaric.[147] Similarly, the Angers Formulary is accompanied by the Breviary, and by the Novels of the Theodosian Code,[148] while the earliest copy of Marculf is contained in a manuscript which includes the *Epitome Aegidiana* of the *Lex Romana Visigothorum*.[149] Roman law and barbarian law go together.[150]

[142] *CTh* 4.12.3, 5; see also 4.6.7.
[143] *Lex Rib.* 61, 15, 16.
[144] *CTh* 9, 9; compare *NAnth* 1, 1.
[145] Sid. Ap., *Ep.* V 5; *Carm.* xxiii.
[146] *CLA* VII 950. On this MS (St Gall 731) see McKitterick, *The Carolingians and the Written Word* (1989), 46.
[147] *CLA* IX 1395. On this MS (Wolfenbüttel, Weissemburg 97) see McKitterick, *The Carolingians and the Written Word*, 44.
[148] *CLA* VIII 1199.
[149] *CLA* X 1576.
[150] For a list of Carolingian legal MSS, and their contents, see McKitterick, *The Carolingians and the Written Word*, 48-55.

There is perhaps a final twist to all this; the student of early medieval law has no option but to look back to the Theodosian Code in order to understand the history of Burgundian and Frankish law. At the same time, the history of the reception, preservation and transmission of the Code necessarily runs through post-Roman Gaul. Although Late Roman scholars may feel unhappy about venturing into the apparently alien world of the *Liber Constitutionum* and the *Pactus Legis Salicae*, those texts are relevant to the history of Theodosius' great legal compilation.

8. The Origins of the *Collectio Sirmondiana*: a new look at the evidence

Mark Vessey

I. Introduction

The Theodosian Code was meant to replace all other collections of 'general laws' from the period which it covered, and largely succeeded in doing so. Historians might wish that its success had been less complete. We should like to know what materials were available to the compilers of the Code, what they did with them, and how faithfully they carried out the emperor's instructions. The survival of a substantial body of fourth- and early fifth-century imperial legislation transmitted independently of the Code would have enabled us to answer these questions. But because the actual and potential sources for the composition of the Code were also the immediate victims of its imposition we are, for the most part, left to infer the process from its product. This unfavourable state of affairs is not without significant parallel in other areas of late antique literature. The literary historian of this period is constantly confronted with the results of a number of more or less successful attempts to canonise one text or version of a text at the expense of others. We have only to think of the honour given to Virgil in Macrobius' *Saturnalia* or the privilege accorded certain 'approved' writers in the *Commonitorium* of Vincent of Lérins (both works closely contemporary with the Theodosian Code) to be reminded that the early fifth century was a time of critical importance in the formation of more than one kind of literary canon. Yet the grammarians and the authors of Christian orthodoxy seem, if anything, to have been more sparing of the extra-canonical than Theodosius and his legal commissioners, at least to judge from the quantities of classical and patristic 'apocrypha' that were allowed to slip through their nets, compared with which the body of *leges extra collectionem* that we are able to set beside the Theodosian Code is small indeed. Within this category of *extravagantes*, a special place is held by the group of imperial constitutions first published in 1631 by the Jesuit scholar Jacques Sirmond under the suggestive, if potentially misleading, title of *Appendix Codicis Theodosiani*.[1]

The 'Sirmondian Constitutions', as they are usually called, are a series of sixteen (or properly eighteen) laws issued between AD 333 and 425, dealing mainly with ecclesiastical issues. As an ensemble, they have three obvious claims to consideration by students of the Theodosian Code. They include matter which, not being reproduced in the Code, may be the kind of thing that Theodosius' commissioners either missed or purposely disregarded.[2] They contain laws that are reproduced in the Code in an abbreviated form or according to different original copies, and so shed light on the editorial practice of the Code's compilers and the nature of their sources.[3] Finally, their existence as a collection may be the result of a private initiative in legal codification as early as, or even earlier than, the making of the Code itself. In other words, the Sirmondian Constitutions may be seen (1) as a *supplement* to the Code, (2) as a control on the Code, and (3) as a minor *analogue* of the Code. While all these aspects of the Sirmondians have been recognised by students of the Theodosian, the third could bear more attention than it has yet received.

If the Sirmondian Constitutions represent a late antique legal *collection*, as is commonly supposed, they raise a number of questions similar to those which we are accustomed to ask of the Theodosian Code itself. What kind of a collection was it? When, where, and how did it take shape? What purpose was it meant to serve? How much of the original collection has survived? Of course it is one thing to ask such questions of a text as well presented and attested as the Theodosian Code, quite another to ask them of an anonymous untitled compilation containing no identifiable editorial matter and transmitted 'entire' (if that is the right word) in only two manuscripts, one of which was copied from the other. Given the intrinsic difficulty of the problem posed by the origins of the *Collectio Sirmondiana*, we might expect to find an interesting diversity of modern solutions to it. In fact we find an almost perfect consensus. The handbooks tell us that the collection was formed between 425 (the date of its latest law) and 438 (the date of the Theodosian Code) in Gaul or North Africa.[4] The unanimity of their

[1] *Appendix Codicis Theodosiani novis constitutionibus cumulatior. Cum epistolis aliquot veterum conciliorum et pontificum Romanorum nunc primum editis. Opera et studio Iacobi Sirmondi presbytero Societatis Iesu* (Paris 1631).

[2] *Const. Sirm.* 1, 3, 5, 7, 8 and 13.

[3] *Const. Sirm.* 2, 4, 6, 9, 10-12, 14-16. The parallels with *CTh* are signalled ad loc. in Mommsen's edition (cited n. 5 below). Note that *Const. Sirm.* 17-18 in Sirmond's *Appendix* are excerpted from *CTh*: see n. 11 below.

[4] Thus, *inter alios*, P. Krüger, *Geschichte der Quellen und Literatur des römischen Rechts* (2nd ed., Munich and Leipzig, 1912), 333-4; L. Wenger, *Die Quellen des Römischen Rechts* (Vienna 1953), 542; H.F. Jolowicz and B. Nicholas, *Historical Introduction to the Study of Roman Law* (3rd ed. Cambridge, 1972), 465; J. Gaudemet, *Institutions de l'Antiquité* (2nd ed. Paris 1982), 739 n.3, summarising the author's detailed presentation of the Sirmondians in the *Dictionnaire de Droit Canonique* 7

notices is due to their being derived from a common source: the prolegemona to Mommsen's 1905 edition of the Sirmondian Constitutions, published as a complement to his edition of the Code.[5] Now Mommsen's opinion, like Papinian's (*CTh* 1.4.3), must be allowed to carry a certain weight in such matters. But in this case he is scarcely an independent witness. In most major respects his preface resumes the findings of his countryman Gustav Haenel, which had first appeared in print in 1840.[6] Conceived partly as a rejoinder to Godefroy's denial of the authenticity of the first three constitutions, Haenel's essay remains to this day the only extended treatment of the transmission and provenance of the *Collectio Sirmondiana*. One hundred and fifty years later, it is perhaps not too soon to reopen the discussion.

*

Broadly speaking, we may distinguish three kinds of evidence for the origins of the Sirmondian collection: the *external* evidence of manuscripts and attestations, the *internal* evidence of the contents and their arrangement, and the *circumstantial* evidence of relevant compilatory activity in places and periods in which such a collection might have been put together. Any satisfactory solution to the problem will presumably depend upon the tracing of these three lines of evidence to a point of convergence. Following Haenel's example, I have chosen to begin with the external evidence. For practical reasons, I base my observations mainly on the published findings of other scholars; insofar as their work appeared after 1905, or too late to influence Mommsen, it may conduce to a view of the *Collectio Sirmondiana* significantly different from the current *communis opinio*. Needless to say, I have no wish to preempt further study of the manuscript tradition of the collection and the various texts associated with it. Such study may, in due course, provide data to replace the guesswork to which I have at times resorted. Nevertheless, without undertaking any new palaeographical or codicological research, I hope to be able indicate the limits within which a set of answers to the questions posed above can reasonably be sought.

(1962), cols. 1229-30, s.v. 'Théodosien (Code). Compléments'. For a different view, long since out of favour, see L. Duchesne, *Fastes épiscopaux de l'ancienne Gaule* I (2nd ed. Paris 1907), 147, with P. Fournier and G. Le Bras, *Histoire des collections canoniques en Occident* I (Paris 1931), 28.

[5] T. Mommsen and P.M. Meyer, *Theodosiani libri XVI cum constitutionibus Sirmondianis et leges novellae ad Theodosianam pertinentes* (1905), i, cccxxviii-ccclxxx. The constitutions follow at 907-21.

[6] G. Haenel, *De constitutionibus quas Iacobus Sirmondus Parisiis a. 1631 edidit dissertatio* (Leipzig, 1840), substantially reproduced in his *Novellae constitutiones imperatorum Theodosii II, Valentiniani III, Maximi, Maioriani, Severi, Anthemii. XVIII constitutiones, quas Iacobus Sirmondus divulgavit* (Bonn, 1844), cols. 409-39.

II. External evidence

First we must determine the extent of our 'collection'. That is, we must decide whether we are dealing with a single collection of legal texts or with two (or more) separate, contiguous or overlapping series. Haenel divided the manuscripts of the Sirmondians into three classes according to their contents.[7] His first class consisted of manuscripts containing *Const.* 1-18, the second of those containing *Const.* 1-7 or odd items from within that series, the third of those containing *Const.* 1-3 only. Since it is now known that one of the two manuscripts in his third class was copied on the other, and as we may suspect that the earlier of those manuscripts represents a truncated variant of his second class, I shall limit my discussion to the first two classes.[8] These I shall distinguish as (1) manuscripts representing a long recension of the *Collectio Sirmondiana* and (2) manuscripts representing a short recension of the collection.

Manuscripts representing the long recension

Berlin, Deutsche Staatsbibliothek lat. 83 (Phillipps 1745) + Leningrad, Saltykov Schedrin Public Library F.v.II.3 [= Mommsen's Z]
Paris, Bibliothèque Nationale lat. 1452

Sirmond's *Appendix* or *imperatoriarum aliquot legum collectio* consists of 21 laws, the last three of which, he states, were derived from sources other than those that supplied the first eighteen.[9] These three laws are of considerable interest, since two of them (dated 417 and 430) are not in the Theodosian Code while the third, though in the Code, appears to have been transmitted separately from it.[10] However, the history of their transmission does not directly concern us here and I shall have no more to say about them. For the present purpose, the *Collectio Sirmondiana* in its long recension consists of the first eighteen constitutions printed by Sirmond. His sources for these were a Lyons canon-law manuscript (now divided between Leningrad and Berlin) and its apograph, a *Codex Anitiensis* (i.e. from Le Puy, now in Paris). These manuscripts present the constitutions in a single sequence numbered I-XVIII. *Const.* 17 and 18 are both introduced as *de Teodosiano sub titulo XXVII, de episcopali definitione*, or as taken from the twenty-seventh section of Book 1 of the Theodosian Code, where

---

[7] *Novellae constitutiones*, cols. 411f.

[8] The MSS in question are Ivrea, Biblioteca Capitolare 35 and its apograph, Paris, Bibliothèque Nationale lat. 4406 (Mommsen's E and *E). See also n. 13 below.

[9] *Appendix Codicis Theodosiani*, 56.

[10] Haenel, *Novellae constitutiones*, cols. 475-6 (note g); Gaudemet in *Dict. de Droit Canonique* 7, col. 1229.

indeed they may be found.[11] This is usually assumed to imply that they were added as an afterthought to a collection assembled without reference to the Theodosian. Mommsen prints only *Const.* 1-16 in his edition of the Sirmondians and modern scholars are at one in regarding that as the primitive form of the collection. Plausible as the reconstruction may appear, it is based on a circular argument. Only if we know when and how such a 'primitive' collection was formed can we say for certain what could or could not have belonged to it. Granted, if Sirmond's collection was in existence before 438 it could not then have contained items *de Teodosiano*. Yet we have as yet no evidence that it was in existence by that date. *Const.* 1-18 all appear in the same hand in the Lyons manuscript, which is not likely to have been written much before 700.[12] Study of the codicological context may enable us to push back the *terminus ante quem* for this state of the collection by a few decades, but it will hardly take us into the fifth century. I shall come to the codicological evidence in a moment. First it will be convenient to glance briefly at the manuscripts of the shorter recension of the *Collectio Sirmondiana*.

Principal manuscripts representing the short recension[13]

Ivrea, Biblioteca Capitolare 35 [E]
Berlin, Deutsche Staatsbibliothek lat. 82 (Phillipps 1741) + Vatican City, Biblioteca Apostolica reg. lat. 1283 [Y]
Paris, Bibliothèque Nationale lat. 12445 [D]
Oxford, Bodleian Library Selden B.16 [O]

These manuscripts all present *Const.* 1-7 as complements to Book 16 of the Theodosian Code in the form transmitted by the Breviary of Alaric.[14] Interestingly enough, no manuscript of the Breviary is known to contain any of *Const.* 8-16. Owing to the relatively late date (ninth century onwards) of EYDO and associated manuscripts, the significance of their contents for the textual history of the Sirmondian collection(s) is unclear. If we could assume that the archetype of such manuscripts belonged to a first generation of expanded forms of the Breviary, we should have a strong reason for postulating the existence of the short recension of the Sirmondians as early as the beginning of the sixth century. A question would then arise as to the relation

---

[11] *Const. Sirm.* 17-18 = *CTh* 1.27.1-2. The text of the Berlin MS breaks off before the end of *Const. Sirm.* 18; since a final leaf is missing it is possible that the collection originally contained an additional law, albeit a relatively short one.

[12] See below.

[13] Described in detail by Mommsen, 'Prolegomena in Theodosianum', viff.

[14] Ibid., lxxxii-xcii.

between this short recension and the longer recension attested by the Lyons manuscript. *A priori*, there would seem to be only two possibilities: either the long recension grew out of the shorter, or the short recension is a truncated form of the longer. Since the 'break' between the short and long forms occurs between *Const.* 7 and 8, both of which refer to the release of petty criminals at Easter, we should have to suppose either that the continuator of the short recension began his work with a law on the same topic as the one which he found at the end of the existing collection, or that the two parts of the original long recension were accidentally separated at that point. Neither alternative seems to me inherently more probable than the other and I therefore submit that the evidence of the Breviary manuscripts containing Sirmondian constitutions does not – as presently understood – help us determine which of the two recensions, long or short, is the earlier.

Having registered this negative point, we may return to our primary source for the long recension of the *Collectio Sirmondiana*: the Lyons canon-law manuscript.

The Codex Lugdunensis from Sirmond to the present day

In the preface to his *Appendix Codicis Theodosiani*, Sirmond informs us that he had first transcribed the 'new' constitutions from a Lyons manuscript (*Codex Lugdunensis ecclesiae*), then collated his transcription against a manuscript of Le Puy (*Anitiensis alter*). He further specifies that neither of these manuscripts contained the Theodosian Code itself (i.e. neither contained an interpolated text of the Breviary of Alaric). Both, instead, were canon-law manuscripts containing, among other material, the acts of African and Gallic councils: *non Theodosianas leges, sed synodos partim Africanas, partim Gallicanas continebant.*[15] It is evident that the two manuscripts in question were those to which Sirmond frequently refers in the apparatus to his edition of the Gallic councils, published in 1629, and whose general agreement he there observes.[16] The Le Puy manuscript, as already mentioned, was copied on the one from Lyons; though useful to editors as a source of readings for parts of the text now illegible in, or missing from, the Lyons manuscript, it is of no independent value for a study of its contents. We may therefore confine ourselves to the Lyons manuscript.

In Sirmond's preface to the *Concilia Antiqua Galliae*, this manuscript is described more precisely as having belonged to the the chapter library of Lyons cathedral (*Lugdunensis ... Ecclesiae*

---

[15] *Appendix Codicis Theodosiani*, sig. a2ᵛ.

[16] *Concilia antiqua Galliae ... cum epistolis pontificum, principum constitutionibus, et aliis Gallicanae rei ecclesiasticae monumentis*, 3 vols. (Paris 1629).

Metropolitanae codice) and as containing the *Collectio Dionysiana* (i.e. one of the canon-law collections compiled by Dionysius Exiguus) followed by the acts of nineteen Gallic councils from Arles I (314) through Mâcon I (581/3).[17] Thanks to work done by C.H. Turner at the beginning of this century it is now possible to trace an almost complete history of the *Codex Lugdunensis* from the moment it entered Jacques Sirmond's hands to its current resting-places in Leningrad and Berlin. That history is chiefly important as confirmation that the portion of the manuscript now in Berlin is our sole independent witness to the long recension of the *Collectio Sirmondiana*. It also shows how the fortunes of a manuscript even in recent times can affect – and occasionally reflect – the course of historical scholarship.

Some time after Sirmond had used it, the Lyons manuscript made its way into the library of the Jesuit Collège de Clermont in Paris. How it got there is not known, though we may surmise with Turner 'that Sirmond, in his wanderings round France, found the monks or canons more willing to lend him the manuscripts he pressed them for than to take the trouble to ask for them back'.[18] In any case, a large number of other manuscripts used by the great editor also ended up at the Collège de Clermont (where Sirmond lived from 1608 until his death in 1651). By the time the Jesuit house was suppressed and its library put up for sale in 1764, the *Codex Lugdunensis* had apparently been divided into three parts.[19] The first and second parts, numbered 563 and 564 in the Clermont catalogue, subsequently fell into the hands of the Russian bibliophile Peter Dubrovsky who, as secretary to the Russian ambassador in Paris at the time of the French Revolution, managed to obtain a considerable quantity of manuscripts belonging to the Benedictine Abbey of St Germain des Prés, which he later gave to the Imperial Library in St Petersburg. (It is possible, therefore, that Clermont 563-564 had gone to St Germain des Prés in 1764.)

---

[17] Ibid., sig. e3ʳ: 'In Lugdunensi ... Ecclesiae Metropolitanae codice, post Dionysianam collectionem, quem primo habet loco, Synodi Gallicanae subiiciuntur XVIII, Arelatensis I, Valentina, Regensis, Arausicana I, Vasensis I, Arelatensis II, Agathensis, Aurelianensis I, Epaonensis, Arelatensis sub Caesario, Carpentoratensis, Arausicana II, Arvernensis, Aurelianensis III, Aurelianensis V, Arelatensis sub Ravennio, Vasensis II, Arelatensis sub Sapaudo, & alia manu post adiecta Matisconensis I.'

[18] C.H. Turner, 'Chapters in the History of Latin MSS.', *JTS* 1 (1900), 435-41 at 436. For information on the life and scholarly career of J. Sirmond (1559-1651) one may begin with the *Oratio in obitum Iacobi Sirmondi S.I.* by Henri de Valois (Valesius), published separately in 1651 and later prefixed to Sirmond's *Opera varia*, 5 vols. (Paris 1696; repr. Venice 1728). There is a bibliography of his works in C. Sommervogel, S.J., *Bibliothèque de la Compagnie de Jésus* VII (Brussels and Paris, 1896), cols. 1237-61. The fullest modern notice is by P. Galtier, S.J., in the *Dictionnaire de Théologie Catholique*, 14.2 (1941), cols. 2186-93.

[19] The sale of the College's library was advertised in a *Catalogue des livres de la Bibliothèque des ci-devant soi-disant Jésuites du Collège de Clermont, dont la vente commencera le 19 mars, etc.* (Paris 1764). A 'Catalogue des manuscrits' was to have been issued separately; I have not been able to ascertain whether it appeared.

Meanwhile, the third part of the Lyons manuscript (Clermont 569), containing among other things the text of the *Collectio Sirmondiana*, was sold in 1764 to the Dutch collector Gerard Meerman, in whose library it bore the number 578.[20] When the Bibliotheca Meermanniana went to sale in 1824, the English bidders at the auction included Dr Thomas Gaisford, Regius Professor of Greek at Oxford and later Dean of Christ Church, acting for the Bodleian Library, and Sir Thomas Phillipps, a wealthy private collector whose library at Middlehill in Worcestershire (transferred in 1863 to Thirlestaine House, near Cheltenham) was for many years one of the most important repositories of Greek and Latin manuscripts anywhere in the world.[21] Gaisford acquired 58 volumes for the Bodleian, including the oldest surviving copy of Jerome's *Chronicle*.[22] Canon-law manuscripts were evidently not high on his shopping-list (a Greek manuscript numbered 20594 in Madan's catalogue and said by him to contain 'Canons, etc.' appears to have been the only purchase of this kind). Sir Thomas Phillipps, we are told, was unwilling to bid against the Bodleian's representative. It may therefore be assumed that the latter showed no interest in the many canon-law manuscripts, including a portion of Sirmond's *Codex Lugdunensis* (Clermont 569 = Meerman 578 = Phillipps 1745), that passed at that moment into the Middlehill collection.

While it was in England, Sirmond's manuscript was inspected by Gustav Haenel, who gave a full description of it in the prolegomena to

[20] See the entry in the sale-catalogue of the Meerman Library, *Bibliotheca Meermanniana; sive catalogus librorum et codicum manuscriptorum, quos maximam partem collegerunt viri nobilissimi Gerardus et Joannes Meerman ... Quorum publica fiet auctio die VIII sqq. Junii, anni MDCCCXXIV Hagae Comitum in aedibus defuncti, Tomus IV: Catalogus codicum manuscriptorum*, no. 578: 'Collectio canonum Galliae. – Notitia provinciarum et urbium Gallicanarum. – Encyclica Leonis Papae adversus Hilarium, Arelatensem Episcopum. – Rescripta varia Imper. Constantini, Valentiniani, Theodosii et Honorii [i.e. the Sirmondian Constitutions]. In membr., saec. VIII. fol. 116., charactere rustico majori, forma quadratus, initio mutilus, summis foliorum valde exesis ...' In the Bodleian Library's copy of the catalogue (Mus. Bibl. III. 8°. 108) this item and others bought by Phillipps are marked with a handwritten 'P'. A marginal note on p. 1: 'P = bought by Sir Thomas Phillipps' is in C.H. Turner's hand, though the 'P' notations are not his.

[21] On Sir Thomas Phillipps see the anonymous article in the *Dictionary of National Biography*, 15 (1909), 1078-8 (first published as vol. 45 [1896], 192-5), and S. de Ricci, *English Collectors of Books and Manuscripts (1530-1930) and Their Marks of Ownership* (Sandars Lectures, 1929-30; Cambridge 1930), 119-30. The history of his library has been copiously documented by A.N.L. Munby in his *Phillipps Studies*, 5 vols. (1951-60) and summarised by N. Barker in *Portrait of an Obsession, the Life of Sir T. Phillipps the World's Greatest Book Collector* (London 1967). The circumstances of the Meerman sale are recounted in *Phillipps Studies* I, 19 (Phillipps' preface to his own catalogue of 1828) and III, 25-8.

[22] F. Madan, *A Summary Catalogue of Western Manuscripts in the Bodleian Library at Oxford* IV (Oxford 1897), 433-42. The sixth-century Jerome MS, now Bodleian Library Auct T. 2. 26, was described by Mommsen in *Hermes* 24 (1889), 393-401.

his edition of the Constitutions, and by Georg Pertz, who in the summer of 1844 spent a fortnight at Middlehill making a list of manuscripts relevant to the programme of the recently launched *Monumenta Germaniae Historica*.[23] In 1887, following the death of Sir Thomas Phillipps, the Sirmondian manuscript was one of a large number of former Meerman (i.e. ultimately Clermont) manuscripts bought en bloc by the Royal Library in Berlin, where they would henceforth be at the disposal of Theodor Mommsen and other scholars working on the *MGH*.[24]

A full descriptive catalogue of the Meerman manuscripts in Berlin was published in 1892.[25] Among the first to use the new Berlin, Königliche Bibliothek lat. 83 (formerly Phillipps 1745) was Friedrich Maassen, whose long-awaited edition of the Merovingian church councils for the *MGH* finally appeared in 1893.[26] A little less than three decades earlier, Maassen had been told by informed persons in Oxford that he would not be allowed access to Sir Thomas Phillipps' library, and had therefore relied on Haenel's account of Phillipps 1745 for the description which he gave of it in his catalogue of Latin

---

[23] G. Haenel, *Catalogi Librorum manuscriptorum qui in bibliothecis Galliae, Helvetiae, Belgii, Britanniae M., Hispaniae, Lusitaniae asservantur* (Leipzig 1830), cols. 803-96, covering Phillipps 1-2986, largely copied from Sir Thomas Phillipps' own published catalogue; *Novellae constitutiones*, cols. 413-16, on Phillipps 1745. G.H. Pertz, 'Reise nach London und Middlehill, Juli bis September 1844', *Archiv der Gesellschaft für ältere deutsche Geschichtskunde* 9 (1847), 486-504 at 499. Munby, *Phillipps Studies* III, 40-1. Letters from both men to Phillipps are quoted by Barker, *Portrait* (cited n. 21 above; see under their names in the index).

[24] Munby, *Phillipps Studies* V, 22-6 provides details of the sale. The possibility that the Prussian government might acquire the Phillipps-Meerman MSS was apparently first raised by Mommsen himself after a visit to Thirlestaine House in 1885. A letter from Sir Edward Maunde Thompson recommending him to the administrator of the library casts interesting light on the German scholar's contemporary reputation: 'Professor Mommsen who is here in London tells me that he is to go down to Cheltenham. I shall be very much obliged to you if you will do everything you can for him. You will find him a very pleasant man – and he speaks English very well. He is one of the most tremendous swells that they have in Germany – and at his name every German student shakes in his thick boots and knocks his shock head on the pavement in adoration. I believe he has never been known to make a mistake in his life, and he has the power of dictating ten books at a time to as many scribes. But as you are an Englishman you need not tremble [!] – only be kind to him' (*Phillipps Studies* V, 19-20). The autograph of this letter is in the Bodleian Library.

[25] *Verzeichniss der von der Königlichen Bibliothek zu Berlin erworbenen Meerman-Handschriften des Sir Thomas Phillipps* (1892), including V. Rose, *Die lateinischen Meerman-Handschriften des Sir Thomas Phillipps in der Königlichen Bibliothek zu Berlin*, republished as Bd. 1 of Rose's *Die Handschriften-Verzeichnisse der Königlichen Bibliothek zu Berlin* (Berlin 1893; same pagination). The description of Phillipps 1745 (no. 83 in the new catalogue) is at 167-71. For details of Phillipps MSS subsequently acquired by the Royal Library see E. Jacobs, 'Die von der königlichen Bibliothek zu Berlin aus der Sammlung Phillipps erworbenen Handschriften', *Zentralblatt für Bibliothekswesen* 28 (1911), 23-9.

[26] F. Maassen, *Concilia aevi Merovingici, MGH Leges* III, *Concilia*, I (Hannover 1893), with a brief description of Phillipps 1745 at XIII.

canon-law manuscripts.[27] Contrary to Haenel, Maassen correctly identified the Phillipps manuscript as Sirmond's *Codex Lugdunensis* minus the first 22 quires. However, he had no idea where to look for the missing portion. The reconstruction of the *Codex Lugdunensis* as a whole only become possible in 1879 when another collaborator on the *MGH*, Karl Gillert, published an inventory of Latin manuscripts in the Imperial Library of St. Petersburg. His list included the former Clermont 563-564, since reunited as Petersburg F.v.II.3.[28] Even then, the connection between the two halves of the original codex would only have been apparent to an exceptionally sharp-sighted connoisseur of canonical manuscripts. Such a man was Cuthbert Hamilton Turner of Magdalen College, Oxford, who in 1890 had embarked on an ambitious project to edit the earliest Latin documents of canon law.[29] Turner narrowly missed the opportunity to collate Phillipps 1745 while it was still in England.[30] Even so, he was able to set Gillert's description of the St. Petersburg manuscript against the description of its other half in the Berlin catalogue and reconstruct a unity corresponding to Sirmond's *Codex Lugdunensis*. His article reporting the discovery appeared in the first volume of the *Journal of Theological Studies* in 1900,[31] too late for

[27] 'Bibliotheca Latina juris canonici manuscripta', *Sitzungsberichte der Kaiserlichen Akademie der Wissenschaften zu Wien, Phil.-Hist. Cl.* 56 (1867), 157-212 at 169-80; *Geschichte der Quellen und der Literatur des canonischen Rechts im Abendlande bis zum Ausgange des Mittelalters* I (Graz 1870), 775-7.

[28] K. Gillert, 'Lateinische Handschriften in St. Petersburg', *Neues Archiv* 5 (1879), 597-617 at 616-17. On p. 617 the author writes: 'wo der Codex [F. v. II. 3], bevor er in die Hände Dubrowsky's gelangte, aufbewahrt worden sei, habe ich nicht feststellen können.'

[29] This lifetime's labour issued in the two great volumes of Turner's *Ecclesiae Occidentalis Monumenta Iuris Antiquissima*, published in parts between 1899 and 1939 (the final fascicle appearing posthumously). It is clear that Turner intended from the first to edit the Gallic councils of the fourth and fifth centuries, for which Sirmond's Lyons codex would have been a capital source. Among other miscellaneous papers of his now at Pusey House, Oxford, is a copy (dated 22.9.92) of the following letter from Mommsen, apparently written in response to an inquiry by Turner: 'Dear Sir, The synods included in our collection [i.e. the *MGH*] begin with Orléans 517, and include the 6th and 7th century: the previous of the 4th and 5th have been excluded, as also the *statuta eccl[esiae] ant[iqua]*. They do not belong to the part under my direction, and I cannot approve the decision; but it has been taken by our council, and so you are at liberty regarding the earlier Gallic councils. Yours truly, Mommsen.' In the event, Turner was only able to publish the acts of the councils of Arles I and II and of Vaison, and the *Statuta ecclesiae antiqua*. There is a notice on C.H. Turner by H.N. Bate in the *Dictionary of National Biography, 1922-1930* (Oxford 1937), 861-4, based on a longer memoir prefixed to Turner's posthumously collected papers, *Catholic and Apostolic* (London and Oxford, 1931).

[30] *Ecclesiae Occidentalis Monumenta Iuris Antiquissima*, II.i: *Concilia Ancyritanum et Neocaesariense* (Oxford, 1907), praef., vii: 'Codicem [sc. Berlin, Phillipps lat. 83] ipse non vidi, quippe qui iter longinquum Berolinense suscipere non valuerim (non enim *cuivis homini contingit adire Corinthum*) neque ut in Angliam per spatium temporis exiguum commodaretur impetrari potui. Utinam adhuc apud nos constitutum contulissem!' Turner had the relevant parts of the MS collated for him by a member of Magdalen College and by his friend Alexander Souter.

[31] Cited n. 18 above.

Mommsen to take account of it in his edition of the Theodosian Code. It was followed three years later by another containing a detailed study of the St Petersburg part of the manuscript, which Turner had arranged to consult on loan in the Bodleian.[32] After Dr Gaisford's failure to raise an eyebrow at the Meerman sale of 1824, this was the closest Oxford ever came to housing Sirmond's Lyons codex.

The Codex Lugdunensis: contents and successive states

The *Codex Lugdunensis* originally contained 306 folios made up 38 quaternions and a single bifolium.[33] The first and last folios having been lost, those that remain are now numbered 1 through 185 in the Leningrad part and 1 through 119 in the Berlin part. The manuscript begins with the preface of Dionysius Exiguus to the second edition of his collection of canons, followed by capitula or summary lists of contents for the councils in the Dionysian collection, the Council of Ancyra, and twelve Gallic councils of the fourth, fifth, and early sixth centuries. Next comes the full text of the councils, in the order given by the capitula down to the Council of Epaon (517). Thereafter the relation between capitula and text becomes somewhat confused. It is clear that the collection announced in the initial summary of contents was progressively augmented with new matter. There are acts from an further seven Gallic councils, together with a variety of other ecclesiastical texts. The *Collectio Sirmondiana* is the final item among these additions. How did it get there? Unless its inclusion was a scribal accident, we must assume that someone judged this a fitting place for such material, and that the character – and perhaps even the origins – of the collection may therefore be illuminated by its codicological context. Before we can understand that context, it is necessary to reconstruct the stages by which the 'Lyons' collection (as I shall call it) acquired the form presented by the *Codex Lugdunensis*. We shall look first at the main sequence of councils down to Arles V (554), then at the final supplements to the collection including the Sirmondian Constitutions.

---

[32] 'Chapters in the History of Latin MSS. III. The Lyons-Petersburg MS of Councils', *JTS 4* (1903), 426-34.

[33] See the descriptions by Turner (article cited in previous note), Rose (cited n. 25 above) and, for the Leningrad portion of the MS, A. Staerk, O.S.B., *Les manuscrits latins du Ve au XIIIe siècle conservés dans la bibliothèque impériale de Saint-Pétersbourg* I (St Petersburg 1910), 13-15.

1. The main conciliar sequence: Gallic councils to Arles V (554)

As already indicated, the full text of the councils in the Lyons codex follows the order given in the initial summary of contents as far as the Council of Epaon (517). The discrepancies between the capitula and the main text after that point may be seen from the following table:

Table 1: Contents of the *Codex Lugdunensis*

Capitula	*Text*
XXII Epaon (517)	XXIII Epaon (517)
XXIIII Arles 'secunda'*	XXIIII Arles IV (524)
[Vaison II (529)]**	XXV Carpentras (527)
[End of capitula]	Capitula s. Augustini
	XXVI Orange II (529)
	Clermont (535)
	Orléans III (538)
	Orléans V (549)

* Capitula relate to Orange II (529)
** Number and title missing

At the end of the acts of the Fifth Council of Orléans (549) the copyist wrote EXPLICIT FELICITER AMEN (fo. 80), then continued with three more councils, namely:

> Arles III (449/461)
> Vaison II (529)
> Arles V (554),

before concluding a second time with the prayer DEUS ADIUVA ME. Up to this point the task of copying seems to have been performed mainly by two scribes (with occasional assistance from a third and possibly a fourth). Scribe A wrote Leningrad fo. 1-15^v, 63^v, 154-185^v and Berlin fo. 187^v (i.e. as far as the prayer DEUS ADIUVA ME) in a predominantly uncial hand, while Scribe B wrote Leningrad fo. 16-63^r and 64-153^v in semi-uncial. Thus:

Mark Vessey

Table 2: Scribes of the *Codex Lugdunensis*

	Scribe A fo.	*Scribe B* fo.
Leningrad F.v.II.3	1-15^v	
		16-63^r
	63^v	
		64-153^v
	154-185^v	
Berlin lat.83	1-87^v	

[Fo. 88-119 unassigned; see below]

As Turner points out, irregularities in the quiring of the Leningrad portion of the manuscript suggest that, at least for some of the time, the two men worked simultaneously from detached parts of a single exemplar.[34]

Various explanations have been advanced for the inconsistencies between capitula and text, and for the disorderly arrangement of the councils between Arles IV (524) and Arles V (554). Despite the objections recently raised by Hubert Mordek,[35] I see no reason to dissent from Turner's view that the capitula represent a primitive collection to which additions were subsequently made. The collection in its *first state* would have contained:

(1) The Dionysiana in its second edition.
(2) The Council of Ancyra.
(3) Twelve Gallic councils numbered XIII-XXV, in strict chronological order, beginning with Arles I (314) and going down to Vaison II (529), with Orange II (also 529) in next-to-last place.

(On this view, the reading *Arelatensis secunda* in the capitula [no. XXIIII] must be explained as an error resulting either from confusion of *Ar[elatensis]* and *Ar[ausicana]* or from the prominence of Caesarius of Arles at Orange II.) Such a collection could have been made in or shortly after 529. It had evidently not been in existence long before someone noticed that it lacked both Arles IV (524) and Carpentras

[34] 'Chapters in the History of Latin MSS. III.', 427-8.
[35] *Kirchenrecht und Reform im Frankenreich. Die Collectio Vetus Gallica, die älteste systematische Kanonessammlung des fränkischen Galliens* (Berlin 1975), 45 n. 34.

(527) and had these inserted in their proper place in the text, though without attempting to revise the capitula. The anti-Manichaean *Capitula s. Augustini* were presumably added at the same time.[36] Exactly what happened to Vaison II at this juncture is hard to say, but as a natural complement to Orange II it would, both before and after the addition of new material, have been the last item in the corpus and so the one most likely to be lost through damage or accidental separation.

If this reconstruction is substantially correct, the 'Lyons' collection in its *second state* would have contained a chronological series of Gallic councils numbered XIIII-XXVI (or XIIII-XXVII as long as the acts of Vaison II were still present). At least one, and probably as many as three, further supplements were added before the collection attained the form in which it appeared to the copyists of the present manuscript.

First, three more councils – Clermont in the Auvergne (535), Orléans III (538) and Orléans V (549) – were added in correct chronological order but (apparently) without ordinal numbers. The terminal clause EXPLICIT FELICITER AMEN that occurs after Orléans V marks the end of the collection in its *third state*.

The next set of additions – consisting of Arles III (449/461), Vaison II (529) and Arles V (554) – is rather a mixed bag. Only the last council, which provides a *terminus post quem* for the collection in its *fourth state*, is chronologically posterior to what comes before. The other two councils, including Vaison II (which, I have suggested, may have fallen out of the collection at an earlier stage) are manifestly gap-fillers. Either these items were already present in the exemplar of our Lyons manuscript, or they were added by the Lyons scribe from another source. Given the early date (554) of the last addition relative to the probable (late seventh-century) date of the Lyons manuscript itself (see below), the former alternative is the more likely. In this case, the ejaculatory DEUS ADIUVA ME that follows the acts of Arles V would derive, like the previous EXPLICIT FELICITER AMEN, from the exemplar, and we can conclude, with Turner, that the whole of the Leningrad and Berlin manuscript down to and including the Fifth Council of Arles 'represents a collection made, or rather completed, soon after the middle of the sixth century'.[37]

The attempt to distinguish successive stages in the development of the canonical collection contained in the first 273 folios of the original

---

[36] See E. Dekkers, O.S.B. and A. Gaar (ed.), *Clavis Patrum Latinorum* (2nd ed., Steenbrugge, 1961), no. 534: *'Prosperi' anathematismata seu capitula s. Augustini*, 'Anno 526, vel 515'. Text in J.P. Migne (ed.), *PL* LXV, cols. 23-6, repr. from Sirmond's *Concilia Antiqua Galliae*.

[37] 'Chapters in the History of Latin MSS. III.', 434. See also J. Gaudemet, *Les sources du droit de l'Eglise en Occident* (Paris 1985), 143.

Codex Lugdunensis (i.e. Leningrad, fo. [0]-185 + Berlin, fo. 1-87) is a necessary preliminary to study of its remaining contents, which include the *Collectio Sirmondiana* in its long recension. There, as in what precedes, we are confronted with a semblance of disorder resulting, in all probability, from a series of rational but imperfectly coordinated initiatives. Unfortunately, Turner's interest in the Lyons codex did not extend this far and no student of the Sirmondians has (to my knowledge) yet attempted to replace the collection in the codicological context which he so successfully reconstructed. Not having had an opportunity to inspect either part of the codex, I shall not pretend to solve all the problems that remain. The following remarks may at least help set an agenda for future research.

2. *Final supplements; the Collectio Sirmondiana*

So far as we can now tell, the last 33 folios of the Lyons codex (i.e. Berlin, fo. 88-[120]) contained the following four items:

(1) An *Adnotacio provinciarum adque urbium Gallicanarum*, i.e. the *Notitia Galliarum*.[38]
(2) The letter *Divinae cultum* of Pope Leo the Great to the bishops of Viennensis concerning metropolitan authority in that province at a time when it was being wantonly usurped by Hilary of Arles.[39]
(3) The acts of the First Council of Mâcon (581/583).
(4) The *Collectio Sirmondiana* in its long recension (*Const.* 1-18).

Maassen, following Haenel's description, observes that these pages of the manuscript are written in a different hand from the one which had copied the preceding items and concludes that they represent a later addition.[40] Turner, relying on Rose's description in the Berlin catalogue, mentions the appearance of a new hand at this point but wisely abstains from making any inference. Having detected the work of more than one scribe in the Leningrad portion of the codex, he naturally wished to know 'which, if any, of these hands continue to write in the Berlin portion' but (since the Berlin Library would not part with the manuscript) never had a chance to find out.[41] E.A. Lowe saw and described both parts of the Lyons codex in separate volumes of his *Codices Latini Antiquiores* but made no attempt to sort out the relation of the scripts.[42] With the help of Lowe's descriptions and facsimiles it is nevertheless possible to give a partial answer to Turner's question.[43]

---

[38] Text ed. Mommsen in *MGH AA*. IX (1892), 552-612. See also n. 56 below.
[39] Text in *PL* LIV, 628-36. See also n. 57 below.
[40] *Geschichte der Quellen*, 777. Compare Mordek, *Kirchenrecht*, 45-6.
[41] 'Chapters in the History of Latin MSS. III.', 428.
[42] *CLA* VIII (Oxford 1959), no. 1061; XI (1966), no.**1061.
[43] In addition to the facsimiles published in *CLA*, I have used those in Lowe's earlier

As we would expect, the first hand in the Berlin part of the manuscript is the same as that on the last folio of the Leningrad part (see Table 2), described by Lowe in one place as 'a curious narrow uncial' and in another as 'a heavy uncial with long ascenders and descenders and short uprights knob-like or wedge-shaped at the head-line'. This is our Scribe A, responsible for some 45 of the Leningrad folios and all of the Berlin manuscript down to DEUS ADIUVA ME (fo. 87^v), the end of the conciliar collection in what we have taken to be its *fourth state*. According to Lowe, the rest of the Berlin manuscript, including the *Collectio Sirmondiana*, was written in half-uncial by two different scribes, one of whom produced ascenders that are 'long and club-shaped', while those of his collaborator were 'often wedge-shaped'. Comparison of facsimiles published in *CLA* and elsewhere reveals that the semi-uncial hand with the long and club-shaped ascenders is the same as that found in the Leningrad manuscript and that the copyist whom I have called Scribe B was at work in the latter part of the Berlin manuscript. More particularly, it shows that this scribe copied (all or at least part of) the *Notitia Galliarum* and (all or at least some of) the acts of the First Council of Mâcon.

Did he also copy the Sirmondian Constitutions? It seems he did. A lithographic print included by Haenel in his 1840 Dissertatio reveals that the lines introducing *Const.* 1 (*exemplum legis de confirmando etiam inter minores aetates iudicio episcoporum et testimonium unius epi accepto ferri*) are in the same hand as the immediately preceding text of Mâcon I, that of Scribe B.[44] Without access to the manuscript, that is as much as one can say with confidence. The part assigned to Lowe's other copyist (Scribe C) remains obscure. There is, however, no indication in the apparatus of Haenel's or Mommsen's edition, or in Rose's description of Phillipps 1745, of a change of scribal hand in the text of the Sirmondians. We may therefore assume that the whole series of constitutions was copied at the same time as the other final supplements to the 'Lyons' collection, and that it formed part of a putative *fifth state* of the collection whose *terminus post quem* is fixed by the First Council of Mâcon. A *terminus ante quem* for that state is provided by the date of production of the manuscript. Consequently, if we can fix the latter with reasonable precision we shall have established chronological limits within which to look for a *Sitz im Leben* for the *Collectio Sirmondiana*.

3. Date and place of production of the codex

Palaeographers who have studied the *Codex Lugdunensis* – Turner,

---

monograph on the Lyons scriptorium, cited n. 46 below.

[44] I owe my photocopy of this page of Haenel's *Dissertatio* to the kindness of Professor T.D. Barnes.

Ludwig Traube, and Lowe – agree in dating it to the seventh century, with a preference for the period *c.* 650-700.[45] In his epoch-making monograph on the *Codices Lugdunenses Antiquissimi*, published in 1924, Lowe went so far as to claim that the manuscript 'showed every sign of being a product of the Lyons [calligraphic] school'.[46] As Rosamond McKitterick has recently reminded us, however, Lowe was inclined to be over-enthusiastic in his detection of such signs.[47] With respect to this particular manuscript, he himself came in time to take a more cautious view, giving as his opinion in *CLA* that it was 'written in a Burgundian centre under Insular influence, to judge from the script'.[48]

Certainly the codex was at Lyons by the ninth century when it was used and annotated by the deacon Florus, and for that reason it deserves the epithet *Lugdunensis* applied by Sirmond and retained (partly for the sake of convenience) in this chapter. But the presence of a book at Lyons in the ninth century is not by itself an argument for its production there two centuries earlier. As McKitterick points out, it 'may simply represent the zeal with which Florus ... and his predecessors collected books from the surrounding region'.[49] Apart from these general grounds for scepticism, it is unlikely that a canon-law collection copied in Lyons in the second half of the seventh century would stop short at the First Council of Mâcon of 581/583. Thanks to Mordek's masterly study of the systematic canon-law collection renamed by him the *Vetus Gallica*, we now know that the last years of the sixth and first part of the seventh century were a period of intense conciliar and canonical activity in the church of Lyons. Already by *c.* 600, this activity had issued in the production of the *Vetus Gallica*, a work largely based (for the Gallic councils) on the 'Lyons' collection in what we have taken to be its fourth state but also drawing on other sources for the acts of the First, Second and Third Councils of Lyons and those of the First and Second Councils of Mâcon.[50] Even allowing for a decline in the intellectual vigour of Lyons canonists in the second half of the seventh century, one can hardly imagine that the same collection would be reproduced there at that time with so few complements. Rather than admit such an improbability, I prefer to suppose that the so-called *Codex Lugdunensis* was copied somewhere else in the period *c.* 650-700.

[45] Traube's notice is in his *Vorlesungen und Abhandlungen* I (Munich 1909), no. 238.

[46] *Codices Lugdunenses Antiquissimi* (Lyons, 1924), 45.

[47] 'The Scriptoria of Merovingian Gaul: A Survey of the Evidence', in H.B. Clarke and M. Brennan (ed.), *Columbanus and Merovingian Monasticism* (1981), 178. See also her article on 'Knowledge of Canon Law in the Frankish Kingdoms before 789', *JTS*, n.s. 36 (1985), 105.

[48] *CLA* VIII, 12.

[49] 'The Scriptoria of Merovingian Gaul', 182.

[50] *Kirchenrecht*, 45-6.

Whoever copied it presumably either had access to an exemplar containing everything that we now find in the manuscript or else found the collection in its fourth state (i.e. including everything down to DEUS ADIUVA ME at the end of Arles V) and added four further items, perhaps but not necessarily drawn from a single manuscript source.

That the manuscript was produced in a Burgundian centre, as the palaeographers suggest, is borne out both by the fact that the main core of the text derives from a collection also known to have been at Lyons by *c.* 600 (when it was used for the *Vetus Gallica*) and by the presence of the acts of the First Council of Mâcon.

4. Historical development of the 'Lyons' collection: from Arles to Lyons

Having obtained a clear idea of the contents and likely successive states of the 'Lyons' collection, we must now try to place its evolution in a historical context. In doing so, we may hope to recreate the circumstances in which the Sirmondian Constitutions came to jostle with the other texts listed above.

Mordek has shown how, in the course of the half-century following the death of bishop Caesarius of Arles in 542, the responsibility for major initiatives in the conciliar life of the church of south-eastern Gaul passed gradually from Arles to Lyons.[51] The process of accretion of specifically Gallic conciliar and other materials in the 'Lyons' collection ought, I believe, to be viewed against the background of this *translatio sacerdotii*.

In its earliest recoverable state, as indicated by the original sequence of capitula, the collection may be said to present an Arles-centred corpus of Gallic councils, perhaps completed by a person or persons operating outside the immediate sphere of Caesarian influence (and thus capable of missing two of the less obvious councils from the period 517-529). Those missing councils, as we have seen, were duly inserted in the *second state* of the collection. The *third state* discloses a definite 'northern' bias: omitting the Caesarian council of Marseille (533), it includes both the Third and Fifth Councils of Orléans, both of which were presided by the bishop of Lyons, but passes over an intervening council in the same city presided by the metropolitan of Bordeaux and attended by only two bishops from Lugdunensis. The *fourth state* is attained with the addition of an important supplement of Arlesian material – most of which, however, reached the compiler too late to find its proper chronological place.

The collection ending DEUS ADIUVA ME (Berlin, fo. 87ᵛ) should thus

[51] Ibid., 16, 74-5; see already P. Fournier and G. Le Bras, *Histoire des collections canoniques* I, 44. J. Gaudemet, *Les sources du droit de l'Eglise* (Paris, 1985), ch. IX is a good summary of current knowledge about Gallic canon-law collections of the sixth and seventh centuries.

have taken shape somewhere in the ecclesiastical provinces of Viennensis and Lugdunensis, probably closer to Lyons than to Arles, in the years following the Fifth Council of Arles of 554. In c. 570 a council attended by fourteen bishops or their representatives from sees within the Burgundian realm of King Guntram met at Lyons under the joint presidency of bishops Philippus of Vienne and Nicetius of Lyons. As was by then customary, the council invoked the authority of existing canon law in enacting its own canons, of which there were just six.[52] One or more *codices canonum* would presumably have been available to members of the council during its sittings. But there is nothing in the *acta* that requires us to suppose that the bishops at Lyons in c. 570 had at their disposal a text of canon law as extensive as the *Collectio Lugdunensis* in its fourth state.

A decade or so later the situation had changed significantly. The sixteen Burgundian bishops who assembled at Mâcon (near Lyons) at the command of King Guntram in 581/583 and who there enacted twenty canons on a wide variety of disciplinary issues were evidently subscribing a legislative programme drawn up on the basis of a careful collation of texts. Besides the usual prefatory reference to the *patrum statuta*, the acts of the First Council of Mâcon contain verbatim extracts from the canons of Epaon (517) and of Clermont (535) and a possible allusion to a canon of Orléans III (538).[53] All three of these councils are included in the 'Lyons' collection in its fourth state, a copy of which is known to have been at Lyons by c. 600. The presiding bishop at Mâcon I, as at Mâcon II a few years later, was Priscus of Lyons, a prelate much maligned by Gregory of Tours but who nevertheless appears, on the evidence of these councils, to have been a zealous reformer somewhat after the manner of Caesarius of Arles. Although Mordek is inclined to deny him a role in the confection of the *Vetus Gallica*, Priscus' conciliar activity may not be wholly unrelated to the renewed interest in canon law that animated the church of Lyons at this time.[54]

[52] Maassen (cited n. 26 above), 139: 'Cum in nomine Domini in Lugdunensi urbe ad synodale concilium venissemus *tam pro renovandis sanctorum patrum institutis, quae praesentis temporis necessario fecit opportunitas iterari*, quam his, etc.' There is another edition of the Merovingian councils by C. de Clercq, *Concilia Galliae A.511-A.695* (Corpus Christianorum, Series Latina, 148A; Turnhout, 1963). See also now J. Gaudemet and B. Basdevant (ed.), *Les Canons des conciles merovingiens*, 2 vols. (Paris, 1989) and O. Pontal, *Die Synoden im Merowingerreich* (Paderborn, 1986).

[53] Maassen, 155: 'Cum ad iniunctionem gloriosissimi domni Guntramni regis tam pro causis publicis quam pro necessitatibus pauperum in urbe Matiscenis nostra mediocritas convenisset, primo in loco visum nobis est, ut in nomine Domini *non tam nova quam prisca patrum statuta sancientes* id ipsum, quod constituimus, titulis praesentibus in canonibus legeretur insertum.' The parallels with canons of earlier councils are noted in the apparatus of Maassen and de Clercq; Pontal, *Die Synoden* 157 n. 11 provides a useful conspectus.

[54] *Libri Historiarum* IV, 36 (Priscus' evil conduct); VIII, 20 (Priscus at Mâcon II, an

And not only in canon law. The acts of Mâcon I and II contain a number of references to *canones et leges*, to *civil* as well as well as ecclesiastical law.[55] The implications of this usage, which marks a new departure in both the style and substance of Gallic conciliar pronouncements, are beyond the scope of the present paper. We should note, however, that the two councils refer explicitly to *leges* in connection (a) with the privileges of ecclesiastical courts and (b) with relations between Christians and Jews, both topics treated in Sirmondian Constitutions (*Const.* 1, 3, 6; 4). The conjunction is a significant one, for it points to a time and milieu in which special efforts were being made to coordinate Roman law with the law of the church and to produce (or at least invoke) the textual warrant for both. When the authors of conciliar *acta* were so concerned to cite the *lex Romana*, a series of imperial edicts on matters affecting the church might easily be appended to a collection of conciliar texts.

The appearance of the *Collectio Sirmondiana* as the coda to a mainly canonical collection, and as the immediate sequel to the canons of Mâcon I, may thus be interpreted as a symptom of developing attitudes towards law and legal texts in late sixth-century Gaul. What else can we deduce from the evidence of the *Codex Lugdunensis*? Of the supplements that characterise the 'Lyons' collection in what we have taken be its fifth and final state, two have yet to be discussed: the *Notitia Galliarum* and the letter *Divinae cultum* of Pope Leo the Great. Both texts, I suggest, are items of propaganda designed to assist a restructuring of Gallic ecclesiastical politics in the time of King Guntram. As Jill Harries has shown, the *Notitia Galliarum* in the form in which we have it is an ecclesiastical document, probably 'compiled or published in response to a specific crisis concerning the status of metropolitan cities' in Gaul.[56] In the context of the 'Lyons' collection, it may be seen as an endorsement of the metropolitan claims of Lyons and Vienne at the expense of those of Arles, there presented merely as a *civitas* in the *provincia Viennensis*. This interpretation is corroborated by the inclusion with the *Notitia* of Pope Leo's famous letter to the bishops of Viennensis, in which he

---

interesting addition to the canonical record). Mordek, *Kirchenrecht*, 75ff. places the compilation of the *Vetus Gallica* at Lyons in the pontificate of Priscus' immediate successor, bishop Eutherius (*c.* 586-602).

[55] Mâcon I, c.16 (Maassen): 'Et licet, quid de Christianis, qui aut captivitatis incursu aut quibuscumque fraudibus Iudaeorum servitio inplicantur, debeat observari, *non solum cannonecis statutis, sed et legum beneficio iam pridem fuerit constitutum*; sed quia nunc, etc.' Mâcon II, c.11: 'Licet *reverentissime canones et sacratissime legis* de episcopali audientia in ipso pene Christianitatis principio sententiam protulerint, etc.'; c.14: 'Ex interpellatione quorundam cognovimus calcatis *canonibus et legibus* ..., secundum *canonum atque legum* tenore, etc.' Cf. c.13: '... tractatis omnibus, *quae divine vel humane iuris fuerunt*.'

[56] 'Church and State in the *Notitia Galliarum*', *JRS* 68 (1978), 28.

rejected the jurisdictional claims of the most ambitious and turbulent fifth-century bishop of Arles.[57]

III. Conclusions

As was stated at the outset, solving the problem of the origins of the *Collectio Sirmondiana* requires recourse to at least three kinds of evidence: external, internal, and circumstantial. Since this paper only addresses the external evidence of the manuscript tradition, it cannot provide any final solution. That said, however, our review of the tradition has enabled us to reach a number of tentative conclusions which, while they may not fix the ultimate origin of the collection, at least suggest a plausible *Sitz im Leben* for its emergence.

1. There is is no evidence at present for the existence of a Sirmondian 'collection' before the last quarter of the sixth century. It is possible that further study of the tradition of the short recension (i.e. *Const.* 1-7, transmitted with Book 16 of the Theodosian Code in the form of the Breviary of Alaric) will cause this conclusion to be revised. Meanwhile, since we have no reason to suppose the short recension earlier than the long one, discussion of the origins of the collection must focus on the long recension, represented by Sirmond's *Codex Lugdunensis*.

2. On palaeographical grounds, the *Codex Lugdunensis* should probably not be dated earlier than *c*. 650. The collection which it contains (including the Sirmondians) could, however, have come into existence at any time after the First Council of Mâcon (581/583). Indeed, since it does not contain the canons of the Second Council of Mâcon (585), there is a strong *prima facie* case for dating this state of the 'Lyons' collection to the period between 581 and 585.[58]

3. As one of four documents together distinctive of the final state of the 'Lyons' collection, the *Collectio Sirmondiana* belongs to a milieu in which (a) new attention was being paid to the relation between civil

---

[57] On the events that called forth Leo's letter see now R.W. Mathisen, *Ecclesiastical Factionalism and Religious Controversy in Fifth-Century Gaul* (Washington, 1989), ch. VII. The text is known to have been included in a Gallic conciliar collection at a relatively early date: H. Wurm, *Studien und Texte zur Dekretalensammlung des Dionysius Exiguus* (Kanonistische Studien und Texte, 16; Bonn, 1939), 101 n. 42.

[58] The fourteenth Sirmondian Constitution, mistakenly numbered 43 (XLIII for XIIII), is independently attested in an early seventh-century addition to the important Corbie MS of canon law, now Paris, Bibliothèque Nationale lat. 12097. From this evidence Maassen, *Geschichte der Quellen*, 795, concluded that the *Collectio Sirmondiana* 'müsste ... zu Ende des 6. oder doch spätestens zu Anfang des 7. Jahrhunderts schon existirt haben'.

and canon law, (b) special care was being taken to collect and present texts recording law of both kinds, and (c) legal documents were being used to support the metropolitan claims of one major Gallic see at the expense of those of another. The milieu in question is that defined by the conciliar and political activity of bishop Priscus of Lyons in the early 580s. In order to be more precise than this we should have to make a full study of the relation between the historical circumstances just adumbrated and the specific contents of the *Collectio Sirmondiana*.

*

The position outlined above is very similar to that taken by Haenel in the 1840s.[59] As was mentioned earlier, Mommsen's prolegomena to the Sirmondian Constitutions are largely indebted to Haenel's research. Only in the matter of dating the collection did Mommsen differ significantly from his predecessor, believing that such a collection could not have come into existence after the promulgation of the Theodosian Code. In fact, Haenel's view of the emergence of the collection is perfectly compatible with Mommsen's assumption concerning its ultimate origins. If Mommsen is right, the compiler who added the final supplement to the 'Lyons' collection in *c*. 580-585 (as I have argued) would have found all or most of his imperial constitutions in a single document more or less contemporary with the papal letter *Divinae cultum*.

The collection we know as the Sirmondian Constitutions may have begun its existence as a minor anticipatory analogue of the Theodosian Code, the work of some unknown Gallic (?) compiler of the early fifth century. But it owes its survival to a currency achieved at a later date. This chapter may help to reinstate the *Collectio Sirmondiana* as a document of Merovingian as well as late Roman history and literary culture – like the Theodosian Code itself.

---

[59] *Novellae constitutiones*, cols. 421-4, locating the compilation of the Sirmondians at Lyons between *c*. 580 and *c*. 700.

9. From Benedict to Gratian: the Code in medieval ecclesiastical authors

Dafydd Walters

The enigmatic phrase in the Ripuarian Frankish law, *ecclesia vivit lege Romana*[1] is amply illustrated in ecclesiastical and secular legislation, in canonical collections and in Christian authors generally in western Europe from the fifth century onwards. In both eastern and western Europe, secular imperial law and canon law bolstered one another, for example under Theodosius II or Justinian, and under Charlemagne. Canon law in the West enjoyed vigorous and ultimately independent growth, but it continued to acknowledge the authority of Roman law, and not only in matters explicitly ecclesiastical. After the apparatus of Byzantine imperial government failed in the western lands beyond the exarchate, *lex Romana* continued to be regarded by the Church as authoritative even when it was subtly edited. The *lex Romana* in question was, in the main, the Theodosian Code together with the *novellae constitutiones* of Theodosius II's successors and their anonymous *interpretatio* (possibly a clerical addition). The formal source for most of the citations in this paper is the composite version of the *CTh* and its satellites known as the *Lex Romana Visigothorum* (*LRV*) or Breviary of Alaric II (506), the manuscripts of which also include an epitome of Gaius' Institutes and other fragments of classical law. Just why the canonists acknowledged the authority of this source deserves more attention than can be given here, where the purpose is rather to see to what extent and for how long the *CTh* or *LRV* remained the *lex Romana* the canonists so unquestioningly accepted.

Gratian's *Decretum* or *Decreta* (more properly his *Concordia Discordantium Canonum* (*c*. 1140) not only marks the transition from the *ius antiquum* of the canonists to the *ius novum*, it also brings to an end the practice of citing the Theodosian Code. Gratian, or his earliest redactors, followed Ivo of Chartres in substituting texts from the *Corpus Iuris Civilis* (*CIC*) of Justinian for those from *LRV* which earlier western compilers of canon law collections had used: evidence

[1] *Lex Rib.*, 61(58).1, ed. F. Beyerle and R. Buchner, *MGH Leges* III.2 (Hannover, 1954).

for one consequence of the reception of Justinian's law in northern Italy at the end of the eleventh century.

The texts in this chapter have been chosen to illustrate the use made of both these sources, Theodosian and Justinianic. They comprise the *Rule* of St Benedict (died *c.* 520): the *Etymologiae* of Isidore of Seville (*c.* 560-636); Merovingian *formulae* of the sixth and seventh centuries; genuine and spurious decretals and capitularies of the Carolingian era; and the works of three eminent compilers of canon law collections before Gratian: the *de synodalibus causis* of Regino of Prüm (*c.* 906), the *Decreta* of Burchard of Worms (*c.* 1012), and the *Panormia* (*c.* 1095) of Ivo of Chartres, together with the *Decretum* attributed to him.

1. The Rule of St Benedict. St Benedict drew on many sources for his monastic or coenobitic Rule, and showed familiarity with St Basil and John Cassian. In his 59th chapter he specified the legal forms to be used when young children were offered[2] to a monastery by their parents (*de filiis nobilium aut pauperum qui offeruntur*, where *nobiles* is equivalent to *divites*). A rich parent who chose to endow the monastery at the same time as giving it his son might reserve to himself a usufruct (life interest) in the property given, but the son was not to enjoy the remainder at the father's death because, contrary to the normal rule *de familiae herciscundae*, such a son, if a monk, had no share in family property. The word used for what the son was *not* to have is *possessio*, not *dominium*, so it appears to follow that such a son would have been debarred from invoking the possessory interdicts (*CTh* 4.21-23) and would also have been excluded from the rights of succession set out in *CTh* 5.1 (*de legitimis hereditatibus*). Something akin to the oblate's 'civil death' is to be found in this text.

2. Isidore of Seville. The popularity of Isidore's *Etymologies*[3] as the pocket encyclopaedia of the earlier middle ages is well-known. Gratian himself was still enthusiastically citing them some 500 years after they were written. In Books II and V, Isidore twice set out a list of 27 legal categories[4] among which is the following:

> Erit autem lex honesta,[(a)] justa, possibilis, secundum naturam, secundum patriae consuetudinem,[(b)] loco temporique conveniens, necessaria,[(c)] utilis,[(d)] manifesta quoque, ne aliquid per obscuritatem in

[2] i.e. as *oblati* in the sense of those intended to be brought up in the monastery, in contrast with adult *conversi*. Later canon law gave such children the same right to reject the decision made by the parents on their behalf as was given to *impubes* who were betrothed by their parents.

[3] ed. W.M. Lindsay (Oxford, 1911). The sources are discussed by B. Kübler, 'Isidorusstudien', *Hermes* 25 (1890), 496; R.W. Carlyle and A.J. Carlyle, *History of Mediaeval Political Thought in the West* (Edinburgh, 1903-36), vol. 2, part 2, 96-101.

[4] See Appendix 1. The first list is preceded at the end of II.10.5 by *Legis enim praemio aut poena vita moderatur humana.* [6" *Erit autem*, etc.

captionem contineat,[(e)] nullo privato commodo sed pro communi civium utilitate conscripta.[(f)] (II.10.6; V.21)

This passage suggests the following possible Theodosian sources: (a) *CTh* 8.12.1, *Ep[itome] G[aii]* 2.9.18 (*contra bonos mores*); (b) *CTh* 5.12.1 and *int*; (c) *CTh* 2.29.2.pr and *int* (where the *interpretatio* has *necessitates* for *desideria* in the text); (d) *Ep.G* 2.9.5 et s; (e) *CTh* 1.1.2 and *int*; (f) *CTh* 1.1.4 and *int*.[5] In its turn, the Isidorian passage is copied in Ivo of Chartres, *Decretum* 4.168 and *Panormia* 2.142, in the *Collectio in III partibus* 3.6.10 and by Gratian, *Distinctio* 4.2.

Evidence of Isidore's more direct familiarity with *CTh* is found in c.2 of the canons of the 2nd Council of Seville (619) concerning a claim to certain disputed parishes between Fulgentius, bishop of Ecija and Honorius, bishop of Cordova, where the Roman thirty-year prescription rule is invoked. The canon ends with a verbatim extract from *CTh* 2.26.4 (385): *sed tam longi temporis reprobatur obiecta praescribtio ... repetentis iura sine mora restituetur.*[6]

3. Merovingian formulae. The *formulae* (protocol collections, styles or precedents) from the Merovingian Frankish epoch were drawn up by clerks acquainted with vulgar Roman notarial practice, to record gifts to churches and other juristic acts in which the church had an interest, like divorce agreements. A selection is provided below. The sources are *LRV*, and texts other than *CTh* and the novels are cited (e.g. the epitome of Gaius and fragment of Ulpian). Justinian's law is also occasionally quoted.[7]

(i)   *Formulae Andecavenses* (Anjou) (3rd quarter of 7th cent.?)
         no. 41 (p. 18) n. 1: *NVal* III 4, *int*.
                  Isid. Etym. 5.24 < *CTh* 8.17.2.2.
                  [Ulp. *Frag.* 16.1][8]

(ii)   *Arvernenses* (Clarus Mons, i.e. Clermont in the Auvergne).
         (mid-sixth cent.?)
         no. 3 (p. 30) conferment of freedom *secundum legem Romanam* (line 14): [*LRV. Lib. Gaii* 1.]

---

[5] These possible sources are suggested by reading M. Conrat (Cohn), *Breviarium Alaricianum* (Leipzig, 1903), an attempt to reconstruct the contents of the *Lex Romana Visigothorum* systematically.

[6] J. Vives, *Concilios Hispano-Visigoticos* (Barcelona, 1963); but *CTh* is not acknowledged as the source.

[7] The examples are quoted from *MGH Leges, Formulae Merowingici et Karolini Aevi*, ed. K. Zeumer (Hannover, 1886). (Texts from sources other than *CTh* are noted in square brackets.)

[8] p. 190 n. 1: *Paul. Sent.* 2.24.6 (and *Dig.* 39.6.1, *Inst.* 2.7.1.).

(iii)   Marculfian Formulary (early 2nd half 7th cent.)
          Bk. II no. 17, testament (in single instrument, not testament
          and codicil):[9]
          p. 86 line 14, *ut Romane legis decrevit*: [*LRV, Paul. Sent.* 6.6]
          p. 88 line 5, *Dig.* 28.4.1.1.
                 no. 18,[10] taking security in homicide cases where
                 parties compose:
          p. 88 n. 3 = p. 89, *LRV, Paul. Sent.* 2.18.10 *int.*
          p. 89 no. 19, sale of land, *LRV, Paul. Sent.* 2.17.1 *int.*

(iv)   *Turonenses* (Tours) (end of 6th cent.)
          Note the frequency of the phrase *lex Romana declarat*, etc.
          no. 4, p. 137 [paraphrase of *J. Inst.* 2.7.2 (*cessio*)].

Some explicit citations:
          no. 11, p. 141, *epistola collectionis* (declaration of 'adoption' of
an abandoned child following fruitless enquiry as to its family of
origin). This *formula* describes, in common form, the finding of a
new-born child wrapped in cloth and left at the church door, being in
danger of death, three days' inquiry as to its origins having been made
without success, etc; and concludes: *decrevimus* (the *matricularius* of
St Martin's of Tours] ... *quae data est ex corpore Theodosiani libri
quinti dicens*: 'si quis infantem a sanguine emerit aut nutrierit ... etc.'
i.e. *interpretatio* to *CTh* 5.10.1 (*LRV* 5.8.1).[11]
          no. 14, p. 142, gifts between future spouses, begins with *CTh*
and *LRV* 3.5.2, *int.* (most of first sentence, in slightly modified form.
CTh int. has: *Quotiens inter sponses et sponsas de futuris nubtiis ...
firmaverit* (rest of *int.* not in formula). The formula has: *Quicquid inter
sponsum et sponsam etc ... firmetur* (the 'quotation' ending there).
          Further examples in summary form are listed in Appendix 2.

*4. Decretals and capitularies of the Carolingian era, genuine and
spurious.*[12] Time has not permitted a thorough examination of the lists
of Frankish capitularies for traces of Theodosian law, though many are
to be found. Some are discussed below in connection with the *Decretum*

---

[9] A. de Wretschko, 'De usu Breviarii Alariciani forensi et scholastico per Hispaniam,
Galliam, Italiam regionesque vicinas', in *CTh*, ed. Mommsen, I.1, cccvii-ccclxix, omits no.
17.
[10] de Wretschko says no. 19.
[11] Also Regino of Prüm, *de synodalibus causis*, I.22 and II.71. A recent discussion of
this text is John Boswell, *The Kindness of Strangers* (London, 1989), 217.
[12] The use of secular Roman legal texts by the pseudonymous 'Benedict Levita' and
other forgers, pious of intention or otherwise, received attention at the congress held by
the editors of *Monumenta Germaniae Historica* at Munich in September 1986
(*Fälschungen im Mittelalter*), the proceedings of which have now been published. This
extensive material was not available to me at the time of writing, but the essential
biographical references are given in Appendix 3.

attributed to Ivo of Chartres, Book 16. Mommsen, in his edition of the Theodosian Code (I, p. ccclxi), noted an example in the Capitulary of Herard of Tours (died 870).[13]

5. *Regino of Prüm.* Regino was abbot of the Benedictine abbey of Prüm, on the river of that name, a tributary of the Moselle above Trier, from 892 until 899 when he left for St Martin's at Tours, it is said to escape from intrigue. He died there in 915. *De synodalibus causis*[14] is primarily a manual for prelates exercising visitatorial functions, and contains much secular law in its second part, having been compiled when bishops, filling a vacuum in the administration of lay justice, often judged secular as well as ecclesiastical causes.

Book I begins with *notitia* (*inquisitiones*) 'quid episcopus vel ejus ministri in suo synodo diligenter inquirere debeant vicos publicos sive villas atque parochiae propriae diocesis', i.e. 96 visitation articles on the care and furnishing of churches, clerical conduct etc. There follow 455 cc. illustrating these matters, but only two cite *CTh*:

c.22 *CTh* 5.10.1, cf. *LRV* 5.8.1, *int.*, cited from the *Epitome Aegidii*: 'si quis infantem a sanguine emerit et nutrierit, habendi eum et possidendi habeat potestatem', etc., though whether *in potestate* like a *filiusfamilias*, or in servitude as the *CTh* text says, is unclear (*CTh*, AD 329 which says '... *obtinendi eius servitii habeat potestatam* ...' Cf. Regino II c.71, below).

c.418 *CTh* and *LRV* 4.7.1 (a rescript of 321, repeated in *CJust* 1.13.2, Constantine to [H]osius of Cordoba), *int.*, that slaves manumitted in church in the presence of the higher clergy (*sacerdotes*), or the slaves of clergy whenever manumitted, gain their freedom and *cives esse Romanos*.

[c.429 is a quotation from *LRV*, *liber Gaii* 4.8: Haenel, 318 (cf. Gaius 1.64).]

Book II comprises 454 cc. chiefly on secular law, including crimes and other wrongs. Cc. 4 & 5 set out 89 visitation articles inquiring into secular conduct (and cf. cc. 419, 420). Leaving aside 11 citations from Paul's *Sententiae*, there are 24 texts based on *CTh*, one from the novels of Majorian and one from the Sirmondian Constitutions:

c.57 *de parricido*: *int.* to *CTh* 9.15 (*de parricidis*). 1 > *LRV* 9.12.1.

c.59 *si servus occiditur a domino* ...: *int.* to *CTh* 9.12.2, *si servus, dum culpam dominus vindicat, mortuus fuerit*, etc. > *LRV* 9.9.1.

c.69 *de expositis infantibus*: *int.* to *CTh* 5.9.1. > *LRV* 5.7.1.

c.70 (*de eadem*) *int.* to *CTh* 5.9.2 > *LRV* 5.7.2.

c.71 (*de eadem*) *int.* to *CTh* 5.10.1 > *LRV* 5.8.1 (identical with Bk I

---

[13] The starting-point for a full investigation is F.L. Ganshof, *Recherches sur les capitulaires* (Paris, 1958) (see Appendix 3).

[14] ed. F.G.A. Wasserschleben (Leipzig, 1940; repr. Graz, 1964) in preference to Migne, *PL* 132.

c.22 above)

[c.85 *de eo, qui aliquem interficit*: *LRV*, *Paul. Sent.* 5.25.3.]

[cc. 86-90 also from *Paul. Sent.*, collated by Haenel with Regino's work: see Haenel, *LRV* p.436.]

c.116 *ne episcopi sententia retractetur*. The text reads: *Constantinus Imp. dicit*: [a] 'Pro sanctis et venerabilibus habeatur, quidquid episcoporum fuerit sententia terminatio, [b] nec liceat ulterius retractari negotium, quod episcoporum sententia deciderit.' Fragment [a] is from the third sentence of the first Sirmondian Constitution (Constantine to the Praetorian Prefect Ablatius, in 333: Mommsen, *CTh* 1:2, 907 lines 7-9) which has the rubric (omitted by Mommsen) *de confirmando etiam inter minores aetates judicio episcoporum*, etc. Fragment [b] is from the seventh sentence (Mommsen, 908 lines 1 and 22). The First Sirmondian Constitution is of course one of six (out of 16 published by Sirmond, 1631) not represented elsewhere in *CTh*.[15]

c.121-2: c.121 is a quotation from the Synod of Worms, (753) dealing with what is to happen to slaves who cohabit as husband and wife, and who risk being separated when the land to which they are *adscripti* is sold, and ends with the words: *sed lex Romana longe melius de hac duntaxat causa praecipere videtur*: passing then to c.122, *CTh* (and *LRV*) 2.25. (*de communi dividundo*), 1, *int.*, i.e. that since the separation of children from parents, or wives from husbands, is unjust, care is to be taken when imperial or public estates are divided to substitute other slaves so that slave families remain together, *quod sollicitudo ordinatium debet specialiter custodire, ut separatio fieri omnino non possit*.[16]

[cc. 128, 129: from *Paul. Sent.*]

cc. 142-146 deal with marriage, etc:

c.142 *CTh* 9.7.5 (AD 388) (*LRV* 9.4.4) *int.*: no intermarriage between Jews and Christians, and any such unions to be treated as adultery.

c.143 *CTh* 9.7.2 (AD 326) (*LRV* 9.4.2) *int.* : only specified close kinsmen can accuse a woman of adultery (the penultimate sentence, forbidding outsiders to accuse, is omitted by Regino).

c.144 ibid., final sentence of *int.*, allowing a husband the right to accuse his wife on suspicion of adultery.

c.145 *CTh* 9.7.4 (AD 385) (*LRV* 9.4.3), *int.*: household slaves (*familiae*) of either spouse can be tortured for evidence of wife's adultery, subject to certain conditions etc.

c.146 *CTh* 9.9.1 (AD 326) (*LRV* 9.6.1), int.: death sentence for free woman who takes her own slave as sexual partner, etc.

[15] See de Wretschko in Mommsen, *CTh* 1:1 at p. ccclii n. 6; the identification was noted by M. Conrat, *Geschichte der Quellen und Literatur des römischen Rechts im früheren Mittelalter* I (Leipzig, 1891), 147 n. 6 and 259 n. 5.

[16] Regino II c.122 continues with a further statement emphasising this rule, which may be his own addition.

[cc. 147-9: from *Paul. Sent.*]

c.173 *NMaj* 6.5. (*de sanctimonialibus vel viduis*) (AD 458) (Mommsen 2, p. 164, lines 53-61 and p. 165 lines 64-67), with some slight variation.[17] Widows who neither re-marry or take religious vows within five years of their husbands' death are to lose their property to those who would be their heirs; whom failing, to the fisc.

c.174, cites *CTh* by name (2.12.5, *LRV* also; AD 393), *int.*: women are reminded that they are barred from prosecuting or otherwise conducting lawsuits other than their own. In c.174 this rule is used to reinforce a canon from a synod at Nantes, that as women are bidden to be silent in church by St Paul, so too they must not argue in court or in public assemblies nor dispute openly with men. It concludes by forbidding nuns from acting as advocates in the legal business of their Houses, unless the bishop give them licence.

c.262 *CTh* 9.7.6 (AD 390) (*LRV* 9.4.5). Here Regino gives the Theodosian text, which lacks an *interpretatio* (public death by burning for male homosexuals who act the female role).

c.307 *CTh* 4.16.2 (AD 379) (*LRV* 4.14.1), *int.*: in private cases, a litigant is not bound save by the decision of his own judge.

c.308 *CTh* 2.18.3 (AD 325) (*LRV* 2.18.2), *int.*, first half of last sentence: cases are not to be heard partly by one judge and partly by another.

c.313 *CTh* 2.18.1 (AD 321) (and *LRV*), *int.*, omitting second half of last sentence, from *quia si apud ipsum*, etc: duties of judge when hearing a case.

c.352 *CTh* 9.18.1 (AD 315) (*LRV* 9.14.1), *int.*: death penalty for kidnappers.[18]

c.360-362 Death penalty for magicians, fortune-tellers, *mathematici* etc.

c.360 *CTh* 9.16.3 (AD 321/4?) (*LRV* 9.13.1), *int.*

c.361 *CTh* 9.16. 4 (AD 357) (*LRV* 9.13. 2), *int.*

c.362 *CTh* 9.16. 7 (AD 364) (*LRV* 9.13.3), *int.*[19] The *interpretationes* to these (and comparable) provisions of *CTh* omit reference to some of the harsher fourth- and fifth-century Roman punishments, e.g. forfeiture of property and exile, *CTh* 9.16.1, cf. 9.16.12; execution by sword, 9.16.4; the rack (*eculeus*) etc., 9.16.6. Where death is the penalty, the *interpretatio* usually says merely *capite puniatur*. This may partly be the reason for the preference shown in canonical collections for citing the *interpretatio* rather than the Theodosian texts themselves and suggests an ecclesiastical origin of the *interpretatio*.

---

[17] e.g. *in fine*, where the *NMaj* has *cum fisco patrimonium partiatur*, Regino has ... *dividat*.

[18] The rubric to c.353, proposing the same source for c.352, is incorrect.

[19] c.363, from a penitential, adds 'raisers of storms', *immissores tempestatum*, to the list.

From Appendix I to Regino:

c.23 *CTh* 9.1.9 (AD 366?) (*LRV* 9.1.4) *int.*: a written complaint by the accuser must precede any trial, civil or criminal.

c.24 *CTh* 9.1.14 (AD 383) (*LRV* 9.1.8), *int.*: those who accuse others of homicide must acknowledge in writing that they will suffer the same fate (if a false accuser). The rest of the *interpretatio* is omitted in c.24.

c.25 *CTh* 9.1.15 (AD 385) (*LRV* 9.1.9), *int.*: criminal accusations are not to be made by the accuser's agent, even if an imperial rescript is held permitting it; etc.

c.26 *CTh* 9.1.19 (AD 423) (*LRV* 9.1.11), *int.* (c.26 repeats the first sentence of the *interpretatio* as far as *tradendus*): 'criminal' means when so decided by the judge, and not before that.

From Appendix III to Regino:

c.74 Wasserschleben (p. 495, n.) notes the influence *inter alia* of *CTh* 9.1.15, *int.* (see Regino, Appendix I c.25, above), but the change in procedure is interesting: c.74 says accusations are to be made orally, not in writing; and no absent person may be either accuser or accused. The primacy of written accusation in the Code has given way to the primacy of oral, public accusation of early medieval secular law, and perhaps not only because accusers were commonly illiterate.[20]

6. Burchard of Worms.[21] Burchard's *Decreta* was compiled some time between 1012 and 1028.[22] He was born *c.* 965, became bishop of Worms in 1000 and died in 1025, having been at the court of the emperor Otto III before his consecration. Although it owes something to the arrangement of Regino's *notitia*, and to the organisation of the subject-matter found in the *Collectio Anselmo Dedicata* (the work of Anselm II, Archbishop of Milan, died 896), Burchard's work has been called the first thematic, as opposed to mainly chronological, collection of canon law.[23] He is also the author of the oldest surviving collection of Germanic manorial customs.[24] It is unfortunate that the edition published by the abbé Migne is a random example of the available manuscripts: 'worthless' according to Stefan Kuttner.[25] A proposed new edition by Otto Meyer was abandoned when his papers were destroyed, but he recorded that Burchard's work was known in Italy by *c.* 1035, on the evidence of Peter Damian and the catalogue of the

[20] Text: Wasserschleben, not Migne *PL* vol. 132.
[21] See in general G. Duby, *La femme, le chevalier et le prêtre* (Paris, 1981): English translation: *The Knight, the Lady and the Priest* (New York, 1983).
[22] Colin Morris, *The Papal Monarchy* (Oxford 1989), 30.
[23] W. Ullmann, *Law and Politics in the Middle Ages* (London, 1975), 131. The *Collectio Anselmo Dedicata* has not been printed in full, but for the first of its twelve books see J.C. Besse, *Revue de droit canonique* 9 (1959), 207ff., at 214. See also id., *Histoire des textes du droit de l'Eglise au moyen âge de Denis à Gratien. Collectio Anselmo Dedicata* (Paris, 1960).
[24] U.R. Blumental, *The Investiture Controversy* (Philadelphia, 1988).
[25] A judgment based *inter alia* on his examination of Vatican MS 16.

Library of the Abbey of Nonantola, near Modena.

The *Decreta* consists of 20 books and a form for opening a synod. The Roman legal texts are of the kind seen in Regino and which are to be found again in Ivo, but the absence of any trustworthy text makes detailed examination almost useless. However, here is one example of an indirect citation from the Codex suggested by some references in E.A. Friedberg's *Canonessammlungen zwischen Gratianus und Bernardus von Pavia*.[26] The passage in question is the *interpretatio* to *CTh* 9.7.2 > *LRV* 9.4.2 given above.[27] Burchard repeats this passage at XVI.57 and it reappears fifty years after Gratian in Bernard of Pavia's *Compilatio prima* (c. 1190), V 13.5,[28] in a title on adultery and rape (*stuprum*) from which it was copied in 1234 in the *Liber Extra*, 5.16.4.[29] Regino's text is also found in two other works, the *Collectio Parisiensis secundo* 84.4 and in the Leipzig collection, 42.7.[30]

7. Ivo of Chartres (c. 1040-1116). This canonist had been a pupil of Lanfranc at the abbey of Bec and, although a supporter of Gregory VII, was a moderate in the Investiture contest.[31] He became bishop of Chartres in 1090 and his *Panormia* is dated c. 1095. The *Decretum* is usually attributed to him, though less certainly than the *Panormia*.[32] In Ivo we find clear evidence that the *Corpus Iuris Civilis* was available to canonists.[33] The contents of the *Panormia*[34] are given in Appendix 4, the following being examples of its use of Roman legal authority:

Book 2, cc.64-71, prescription and possession: No Roman text is cited (*CTh* 4.14.1 > *LRV* 4.12.1 would have been appropriate), but c.67 applies the 30-year prescription rule to a bishop claiming rightful possession of his diocese.

Book 2, cc.138-168, *de legibus*, the contents being largely repeated by Gratian in *Dist.* 10: e.g. c.145, *de legibus Justiniani* is a reference to *Dig.* 1.2, *de origine juris* etc. and naming the Codex, Digest, Institutes

[26] Leipzig, 1887; repr. Graz, 1958.

[27] Regino, *De synodalibus causis* II.143, 144: the denunciation of a wife', adultery.

[28] *Quinque Compilationes Antiquae*, ed. E.A. Friedberg (Leipzig, 1882), 58.

[29] See vol. 2 of E.A. Friedberg's edition of *Corpus Iuris Canonici* (Leipzig, 1879-81), col. 806.

[30] At pp. 44 and 124 respectively of Friedberg's *Canonessammlungen*.

[31] See F. Barlow, *The English Church 1066-1154* (London, 1979), 146, 299 and n. 106; C. Morris, *The Papal Monarchy*, 400-403 (though the statement about the *Tripartita* repeats doubtful learning).

[32] On the authenticity of the *Decretum* see P. Fournier, 'Les collections canoniques attribuées à Yves de Chartres', *Bulletin de l'Ecole des Chartes* 57 (1896), 645-98; 58 (1897), 26-77, 410-44 and 624-76; P. Fournier and G. Le Bras, *Histoire des collections canoniques en occident*, 2, 55-114.

[33] For *CJC* in the works of Ivo and Gratian see J. Gaudemet, 'Le droit romain dans le pratique et chez les docteurs aux XIe et XIIe siècles', *Cahiers de Civilisation Médiévale* 8 (1965), 374.

[34] *Panormia Ivonis Carnotensis episcopi libri VIII*, ed. S. Brant (Basle, 1499): repr. in Migne, *PL* 161.

and Novels; c.147, citing *J.Inst.* 1.2 and *Dig.* (Ulpian) 1.4.1.1 on royal statute law; and cf. cc.160, 162, 163 quoting the Institutes and *CJust* (1.8.1 and 8.2) respectively.

Book 3, cc.167-173, *de vita clericorum*: e.g. c.169: a bishop or presbyter who consults a prophet or the auspices is to be deposed,[35] which Gratian repeats in *can.* 26 q.5 c. *si quis episcopus*. This is in fact contrary to a provision in *CTh* 16.10.1 *pr* (AD 320) in which Constantine had ordered such consultations to take place; although the next *lex* of the same title (AD 341) says 'superstition shall cease'.

Book 5, *de causis et negotiis laicorum*, cc.23-76: e.g. c.23 (repeated by Gratian, *can.* 11 q.1 c. *omnes*) apparently citing *CTh* (... *omnes itaque comprimente*, and see c.24 *et seq*).

Book 6, *de nuptiis et matrimoniis* etc., cc.129 (& cf. Book 7): e.g. c.1, which is *CICiv. Dig.* 1.9.1 (repeated by Gratian, *causa* 29 q.1, *dict. ante*).

The *Decretum*[36] attributed to Ivo (see n. 32 above) consists of a prologue and seventeen books. The Roman texts are chiefly imperial laws described by the author as *novellae constitutiones* but taken from the *Epitome Iuliani*, as the examples from Book 8 show (see Appendix 5). In Book 4, cc.168-177, there is a list of legal sources, here shown in brackets, which the author treats as authoritative:

c.168 *quid sit lex honesta* (< Isid. *Etym* V c.21).

c.169 *quod leges temporales postquam institutae sunt, servandae sint* (< St Augustine, *de vera relig.* 31).

The text of cc.170-172 illustrates the transition to citations from Justinian's *Corpus Iuris Civilis*:

(c.170 *de libro constitutionum Theodosii* [< Isid. *Etym.* V.1]).[37]

(c.171 *de libro quam appellant codicam Justiniani et de libro Pandectarum et de eoquem appellant codicam Novellarum* [< Paul the Deacon's *Historia Langobardorum* 1.25; not V.25 as in Migne]).[38]

---

[35] From the 4th Council of Toledo (633) c.30; c.29 (ed. Vives), 203. There is earlier canonical prohibition of such practices: 2nd Council of Braga (572) cc. 72-4 (Vives, 103), condemning astrology, the observing of secular seasons, incantation when collecting medicinal herbs, etc., and 3rd Council of Toledo (589) c.23 (Vives, 133), against the custom of dancing and secular singing during liturgical services.

[36] *Ivonis Carnotensis episcopi Decretum in partes XVII*, ed. J. Molin (Louvain, 1561): carelessly reprinted in Migne, *PL* 161.

[37] c.170: *De libro constitutionum Theodosii*. Isidorus, *Etymologiarum libro v, cap. i.* (*Dist.* 7, c. *Fuerunt autem hi*) Theodosius minor Augustus ad similitudinem Gregoriani et Hermogeniani, codicem factum institutionum, a Constantini temporibus sub proprio cujusque imperatoris titulo disposuit, quem a suo nomine Theodosianum vocavit.

[38] c.171: *De libro quem appellant codicem Justiniani, et de libro Pandectarum, et de eoquem appellant codicem Novellarum. Ex historia Longobardorum* [i.e. of Paul the Deacon] *libro*, v. [*recte* i] cap. 25. Justinianus Augustus leges Romanorum, quarum prolixitas nimia erat et inutilis dissonantia, mirabili brevitate correxit. Nam omnes constitutiones principum, quae utique multis in voluminibus habebantur, intra duodecim libros coarctavit, idemque volumen codicem Justiniani appellari praecepit.

(c.172 *item de libro Justiniani quam vocant Novellas consti-tutiones*.)[39]

c.173 *quod constet esse legam quidquid imperator per epistolam constituit ..., Inst.* 1.2. (6, *in medio*).

c.174 *de capitulis a Carolo (Magno) legibus insertis.*

c.175 *de lege Anglorum ab Ebelberto rege edita Beda ...*

c.176 *de capitulis a Lothario Augusto legibus additis.*

c.177 *leges christianorum regum ab ecclesiis recipiendis* (and cf. cc.178-188).

Book 16, *de officiis laicorum et causis eorundem*, in 362 chapters, contains Theodosian material which de Wretschko identified.[40] Ivo's chief proximate sources are the False Capitularies of 'Benedict Levita'.[41] Citations of *CJust* as well as *CTh* and the other materials in *LRV* are included. The first Theodosian text listed by de Wretschko is c.61:

(Rubric from c.59) '*Servi testimonio adversus dominum minime standum*. Cod. [i.e. *CJust*] 9.1.20'. This is a constitution of 397; it corresponds with *CTh* 9.6.3 > *LRV* 9.3.2:

'Si quis ex familiaribus vel ex servis cujuslibet domus, cujuscunque criminis delator atque accusator emerserit, ejus existimationem, caput, vel fortunas periturus, cujus familiaritati vel dominio inhaeserit, ante examinationem judicii in ipsa expositione criminum, atque accusationis exordio, ultore gladio feriatur ...' Thus far Ivo; *CJust* and *LRV* complete the constitution: 'vocem enim funestam intercidi oportet potius quam audiri, maiestatis crimen excipimus.' Ivo does not give the *interpretatio: Si servus*, etc; though a version of it appears in the epitome of Aegidius which he frequently cites elsewhere.[42]

Rursus singulorum magistatuum sive judicum leges, quae usque ad duo millia pene libros erant extensae, intra quinquaginta librorum numerum redegit, eumque codicem Digestorum sive Pandectarum vocabulo nuncupavit. Quatuor etiam Institutionum libros in quibus breviter universarum legum textus comprehenditur noviter composuit. Novas quoque leges quas ipse statuerat in unum volumen redactas, codicem Novellarum appellari sancivit.

[39] c.172: *Item de libro Justiniani, quem vocant Novellas constitutiones. Ex historia Anastasii bibliothecarii Romanae Ecclesiae*. Removit Justinianus Augustus contrarias leges, faciens singularem codicem, et vocans eum Novellas constitutiones, in quibus non permittit principem, in quibus praeest, tenere possessionem, aut aedificare domum, aut haereditari extraneam personam, nisi quis sibi cognitus cognatus existat. (J. Molin's text in Migne, *PL* 161, col. 304).

[40] In *CTh*, ed. Mommsen 1:1 p.cccvii et seq., at pp. cccxv-vi: 53 texts are listed which are derived from *LRV* (15 from *CTh* and 36 from *Paul. Sent.*), and see p. cccxvii for a further nine texts derived from *Aegidii epitome* (seven from *CTh* and two from *Paul. Sent.*), plus one from the Sirmondian Constitutions (Ivo, 16.312).

[41] *MGH Leges in folio* 2:2, *Capitularia spuria*, 17-158, ed. G.H. Pertz (Hannover, 1837): the ed. cited by de Wretschko, q.v. at pp. cccxxxiv-vi: see section 4 above, and Appendix 2. Not all Benedict's texts are false, of course, and de Wretschko lists the genuine ones, chiefly Theodosian, at pp. cccxxxv-vi. (For citation of *CTh* and *N.* in the *capitula Angilramni* see ibid., cccxxxvii: text in P. Hinschius, *Decretales Pseudo-Isidorianae et capituli Angilramni* (Leipzig, 1863; repr. Aalen, 1963), 755-69 & cf. cxi-xvi & cxlii-clxxxii.)

[42] G. Haenel, *Iuliani epitome latina novellarum Iustiniani* (Leipzig, 1873), 174-6.

The immediately preceding c.60 in Ivo, Bk 16, under the same rubric, is however an almost exact reproduction of *CJust* 4.20.8, a constitution of 294, nine years earlier than the first constitution of *CTh*. This pattern of indirect citation from *CTh*, chiefly via Benedict Levita, and directly from *CJust*, is repeated throughout Ivo's *Decretum*.[43]

8. Gratian's Decretum, c. 1140, in the earliest redactions that have survived, shows an almost total acceptance of Justinian's *Corpus Iuris Civilis*. The abandonment of citation from *CTh* is not quite complete, however, although this may be due to oversight, or to an unwillingness to change the text of proximate sources which themselves included Theodosian matter. In the introduction to his edition of Gratian, Friedberg lists some of the surviving citations from vulgar Roman law, less than 20 in all, in contrast with about 150 citations from *CICiv*.[44] The citations given by Friedberg are from Haenel's edition of *CTh*:[45]

CTh 11.39.8, cited by Gratian in *causa* 11, q.1, c.9.

CTh 16.2.16, in *causa* 23, q.8, c.23.

CTh 16.2.29, in *causa* 25, q.2, c.20.

From Haenel's edition of *Lex Romana Visigothorum*, Friedberg lists 10 citations from Paulus' *Sententiae* (e.g. *Paul. Sent.* 2.20.4 in *causa* 32, q. 7 c.26). There are two further citations from *CTh*: 9.3.2 or the *interpretatio* in *causa* 2, q.7 c.53 and *interpretatio* 9.37.1 in *causa* 2, q.3 c.8, together with eleven citations of imperial constitutions from the *epitome Iuliani*, seven of them from Novel 115 in the *Ep. Iul.* numbering.

The canon lawyers owned no loyalty to the authors of the laws they cited and incorporated. Evidently they still admired the *lex Romana*, but they came to prefer that version of it which was recovered in the course of the controversies between the western empire and the papacy which are disguised under the name of the quarrel over Investitures: Justinian's *Corpus Iuris Civilis*. Probably no single reason can explain the reception of this law, but it provided the better text (though not the fuller one: not all of *CTh* is reproduced in *CJust*), and, in the wake of the Reception, Theodosius had to make way for Justinian.

Appendix 1

Isidore of Seville (*c.* 560-636), *Etymologiae* Bk V (cols. 197-228 in Migne, *PL* 82: *Sancti Isidori Hispaliensis episcopi Etymologiarum libri XX*; also ed. W.M. Lindsay [Oxford, 1911]).

---

[43] Though the task of identifying the former is not assisted by Migne's editor's habit of supplying *CJust* references whenever they incorporate constitutions from *CTh*.

[44] *CICan*, vol. 1, at col. xl. I have not yet checked these references against T. Reuter's *Concordance* to Gratian, which was not available to me when writing this chapter.

[45] Bonn, 1842.

De legibus [cc.1-27; omitting *de temporibus*, cc.28-39].
 1. de auctoribus legum (ss 1-7)
 2. de legibus divinis et humanis (1,2)
 3. quid different inter se jus, leges et mores (1-4)
 4. quid sit jus naturale (1,2)
 5. quid sit jus civile
 6. quid sit jus gentium
 7. quid sit jus militare (1,2)
 8. quid sit jus publicum
 9. quid sit jus Quiritium (1,2)
10. quid lex
11. quid scita plebium
12. quid senatusconsultum
13. quid constitutio et edictum
14. quid responsa prudentium
15. de legibus consularibus et tribunitiis (1,2)
16. de lege satyra
17. de legibus Rhodiis
18. de privilegiis
19. quid possit lex
20. quare facta sit lex
21. qualis debeat fieri lex
22. de causis
23. de testibus (1,2)
24. de instrumentis legalibus (1-31)
25. de rebus (1-37) (e.g. hereditas, jura, peculium etc.)
26. de criminibus in lege conscriptis (1-27)
27. de poenis in legibus constitutis (1-38).

Appendix 2

Further examples of the influence of Roman Law in the *Formulae Turonenses*, given in summary form (wording mostly modified as illustrated above):
    no. 15, p. 143, lines 18, 19, *CTh* 8.12.1, *LRV* 8.5.1, *int.* (bride's antenuptial *traditio* of movables) (not noted by Zeumer).
    [no. 16, p. 143, first sentence, *LRV, Paul. Sent.* 2.20.2, *int.* (*Ep. Aeg.*) (father endows daughter following marriage to which he did not consent).]
    [no. 17, p. 144, line 20, *LRV, Paul. Sent.* 2.24.5, *int.* (gift between spouses to take effect at death of donor).]
    no. 19, p. 145, line 24, *CTh* and *LRV* 3.16.1, *int.* first twelve words (divorce in the form of *repudium* by either spouse of the other).
    no. 20, p. 146, lines 10-12, *CTh* and *LRV* 2.12.4, *int.* (husband who sues for his wife is bound by her mandate).
    no. 21, p. 146, lines 23-5, *CTh* and *LRV* 2.24.1, *int.*; first half of first sentence: (*de familiae herciscundae*: respect for testament, even if imperfect, when property divided among certain descendants).
    no. 22, p. 147, first two lines, ref. to previous example, and line 15, where *CTh* and *LRV* 5.1.4 is applied, but not cited (nephews instituted as heirs).
    no. 23 at pp. 147-8, 2nd sentence: cf. *CTh* and *LRV* 5.1.2, *int.* (adoption) [p. 147, 1st line: cf. *LRV, Lib. Gaii* 5.1: adoption].
    no. 24 p. 148, line 15, cf. *CTh* and *LRV* 3.18.1, *int.*; line 16, cf. *CTh* and *LRV* 3.17.3, *int.*; line 20, cf. *CTh* 3.30.6, *LRV* 3.19.4, *int*; Zeumer adds *Lex Raetica*

Curiensis 3.19.4 (contract of pupillage/wardship).

no. 25 p. 149, lines 8, 9: '*Romanamque legem ordinantem*' cf. *CTh* 2.9.3, *LRV* 2.9.1 (breach by adult of pact or compromise freely made).

[no. 29, p. 152: '*Lex Romana pro utilitate humani generis exposcit, ut*' followed by (cf.) *LRV, Paul. Sent.* 5.39. *int. (Ep. Aeg.)*].

ibid: second para: *CTh* 9.1.14, *LRV* 9.1.8, *int.* (whoever prosecutes for homicide must, in writing, agree that he accepts the same fate if proved false as would the one he falsely accuses: also cited by Regino, Appendix I to edition cited, c.24). In this case, the *int.* is reproduced verbatim, not in paraphrase.

no. 30 at p. 153, first word: *CTh* 9.14.2, *LRV* 9.1.8, *int.* (self-defence in cases of highway robbery etc at night).

no. 32, p. 154, lines 25-6: cp *CTh* 9.24.1, *LRV* 9.19.1, *int.* (punishment in cases of marriage and abduction).

ibid., p. 155, last two lines: cf. *CTh* 9.24.3, *LRV* 4.12.1, *int.* (accusations of ravishment: prescription after five years).

no. 39, p. 157, line 7, cf. *CTh* 4.14.1, *LRV* 4.12.1, *int.* (thirty-year prescription period for certain actions).

Additamenta no. 1, p. 159, line 22: *CTh* 8.12.1, *LRV* 8.5.1, *int.* (on requirement of publicity for gifts to be valid).

Appendix no. 2, p. 163, line 29: cf. *CTh* and *LRV* 3.5.1, *int.* (antenuptial gifts '*sicut in Theodosiano codice "de sponsalibus et ante nuptias donationibus" narrat auctoritas*': lines 26-7: line 29 refers to gifts or promises made in a series of documents).

Appendix no. 3, p. 164, line 23: '*Rerum omnium scripturarum traditio subsequatur*' (an oft-repeated quotation in such texts): cf. *CTh* and *LRV* 3.5.2, *int.* (antenuptial gift from H to W '*omni eam scripturarum sollemnitate firmaverit*', Mommsen 1.2, p. 134, line 2; cf. above, *Turonenses*, no. 14).

Appendix no. 4, p. 165, '*Mos antiqua et lex Romana declarat auctoritas ut:*' followed by *CTh* and *LRV* 2.12.4, *int.* (see above, *Turonenses* no. 20).

(Text of the above: *Formulae Merowingici et Karolini aevi*, ed. K. Zeumer, from which the *LRV* refs. have been taken. The dates of the collection are suggested by Zeumer: (i) p. 2, (ii) p. 27, (iii) pp. 32-4 and (iv) pp. 128-9.)

Appendix 3

Basic bibliography to establish citation of the *Codex Theodosianus* etc. in *Benedict Levita*, False Capitularies and *Pseudo-Isidore*, False Decretals; and the question of medieval forgeries.

1. Capitularies

Texts: *MGH Leges in folio* 1 & 2:1 and 1 and 2:2 (2:2 includes Benedict Levita's *spuria*); *Leges in 4to, Capitularia Regum Francorum* 1 (inc. *Collectio Ansegis*) and 2:1-3, ed. G.H. Pertz.

Commentaries:
P. Hinschius, see 2, below, tabula fontium at cxii-cxvi and comm., cxliii-clxiii; clxxxiii-clxxxvi.
E. Seckel, 'Studien zu Benedictus Levita', *Neues Archiv* 26 (1901); 29 (1904); 31 (1906); 34 (1909); 35 (1910); 39 (1914) 39 NA; 40 (1916); 41 (1917): and see

Zeitschrift der Savigny-Stiftung/kanonistisches Abteilung 22 (1934) and 25 (1935).

F.L. Ganshof, *Recherches sur les capitulaires* (Paris, 1958) (with tables and indices: without them in *Revue de l'histoire de Droit français et étranger* 35 (1957).

2. Decretals

Text: *Decretales Pseudo-Isidorianae et capitula Angilramni*, ed. P. Hinschius (Leipzig 1863; repr. Aalen l963).

Commentaries:
P. Hinschius, op. cit. above 1863, [Intro.] Pt II, lxxvii-cix; and *LRV* < *Paul. Sent.* and *C.Greg.*, loc. cit. cxxxiii.
S. Williams, 'The pseudo-Isidorian problem today', *Speculum* 19 (1954), 704.
ibid., [Proceedings of the] *Congrès de droit canonique médiévale* (Louvain and Brussels, 1959), 92-3 for evidence of the defects in Hinschius' edition, based on the collation of 79 mss.
H. Fuhrmann, *Einfluss und Verbreitung der pseudoisidorischen Fälschungen*, 3 vols (1972-4), *MGH Schriften* Bd. 24.

3. Recent commentaries etc. on these and other medieval forgeries

J.M. Wallace-Hadrill, 'Archbishop Hincmar and the authorship of *Lex Salica*', *Tijdschrift voor Rechtsgeschiedenis* 21 (1952): repr. as chapter 5 of *The Long-Haired Kings* (London, 1962; repr. Toronto 1982). (The demolition of the views of S. Stein, 'Lex Salica', *Speculum* 22 (1947), 113-34 & 395-418 are in pt. III of Wallace-Hadrill's paper, 106 et seq. in the 1962 reprint.)
Fälschungen im Mittelalter (5 vols + Index vol.), *MGH Schriften*, Bd. 33 (proceedings of *MGH* congress, Munich, Sept. 1986): esp. vol. 2, *Gefälsche Rechtstexte*: Peter Landau, 'Gefälschtes Recht in den Rechtssammlungen bis Gratian', 11-50; G. Schmitz, 'Die Waffe der Fälschung zum Schutz der Bedrängten? Bemerkungen zu gefälschten Konzils- und Kapitularientexten', 79-110; W. Hartmann, 'Fälschungsverdacht und Fälschungsnachweis im früheren Mittelalter', 111-27; H. Schneider, 'Ademar von Chabannes und Pseudoisidor – der "Mythomane" und der Erzfälscher', 129-50.

Appendix 4

Ivo of Chartres, *Panormia (Panormia Ivonis Carnotensis episcopi libri VIII)*
Prologus: de multimoda distinctione Scripturarum sub una cartorum eloquiorum contentarum.
    1. *de fide, de diversis haeresibus, de baptismate ... consecrandorum ...* etc: cc. 1-112 on baptism; 113-122 on confirmation; 123-162 on the Eucharist.
    2. *de constitutione ecclesiarum et oblatione fidelium* etc.: the church and

church buildings etc., 1-24; burial, 25-27; presbyters and their churches, 28-56; tithes, 58-63; prescription & possession, 64-71; seekers of sanctuary, 72-78; sacrilege, 79-81; tutelage of children, 82, 83; alienation and exchanges of church property, 85-88; canon of scripture, councils and approved authors, 89-137; *de legibus*, 138-168; Sunday observance, etc., 169-173; fasting, 174-189; almsgiving, 190-195.

3. *de summi pontificis electione* etc.: consecration of bishops and ordination of other clergy etc., 1-215, inc. clerical continence, 84-115; murderers etc. who are clergy, 153-155; usury, 156-162; *de vita clericorum*, 167-173; *de religiosis*, etc., 174-215.

4. *de primatu Romanae ecclesiae* etc.: councils, rights of metropolitans and other bishops, 1-136, inc. *de restitutione spoliatorum*, 42-52; *de accusationibus*, 53-82; *de testibus*, etc. 83-104; *de judicibus*, etc. 108-119; *de appellationibus*, 120-136.

5. *de clericis sola infamia absque testibus accusatis*, 1-22; *de causis et negotiis laicorum*, 23-76; *de ... excommunicatione*, etc., 77-136.

6. *de nuptiis et matrimoniis*, etc. (inc. concubinage, and separation on the grounds of fornication), 1-129.

7. *de separatione conjugii carnalis*, etc. 1-13; *de interfectoribus suarum conjugum*, 14-17; *de adulterio*, 18-26; *de fornicatione spirituali*, 27-34; *de reconciliatione conjugum*, 35-38; *de ... juramento reconciliationis*, 38-51; *quare ... non fit conjugium*, 52-67; *de consanguinitate et affinitate*, 68-75; *... legitima fieri connubia ...* 76-84; *qui accusare matrimonium possunt, etc.*, 85-89; de gradibus cognationum, 90.

8. *De homicidio*, etc., 1-60; *de divinationibus et incantationibus* etc., 61-82; *de juramento licito et illicito*, 83-123; *de mendacio*, 124-134; *de electione pontificis*, 135, 136; *... libri ... legendi in ecclesia* (and consorting with excommunicates, clerical continence, tithes not to be in possession of laity, qualification for ecclesiastical orders and offices, Truce of God (c.147) and misc. offences, 137-154 (of which 138-154 are also listed as 14 *capitula*).

Appendix 5

From the *Decretum* attributed to Ivo of Chartres:
Book 8. *de legitimis conjugiis, de virginibus et viduis non velatis. de raptoribus ... et de eorum separatione, de concubinis* etc. (cc.1-334).

c.1 *quid sit matrimonium ... [J.Inst.]* 1.9.[1].

c.20 *quod in sponsalibus, sicut in nuptiis, consensus requirendus est ... [Dig.]* 23.1 [7.1; *Paul. Sent.*].

c.21 *quod alii viro mulier legitime nubere possit, si invita et repugnans alteri a patre tradita fuerit [Dig.* 23.1.11, Julian; 23.1.12, Ulpian and 23.1.13, Paul].

c.22 *(de eodem) [Dig.* 23.1.14, Modestinus].

c.31 *si concubina usque ad mortem cum aliquo nobili permanserit, ut ab haeredibus ejus cum filiis suis liberetur, CJust* 7.15.3 (AD 531) (and cf. c.32).

c.34 *de eo qui cum muliere quam ducere potuit consuetudinem habuerit*: 'Const. *Nov.* 32.3' (i.e. *Epitome Juliani* 32.112.3).

c.35 *ne legitima repudiatur*. 'Constitutio 37.7' (? *Ep. Jul.* 108.380.3).

c.36 *quod si concubina potest legitima fieri*. 'Constitutio 64.14'.

c.37 *quod liceat meretricibus honestam vitam eligere*. 'Const. *Nov.* 46.1'.

c.44 *quod legitima sit*, etc. 'Const. *Nov.* 65.1' (i.e. *Ep. Jul.* 67.244.4; the rubric reading *Si quis divinis tactis scripturis*, not *actis* as in Migne c.44): a source for

Gratian, *Decretum causa* 30 q.5 c.9.

c.56 *si quis per errorem duxerit ancillam uxorem, liberam eam putans, vel si qua servum duxerit maritum, non subsistere tales nuptias.* Const. *Nov.* 37 (*Ep. Jul.* 36.133.3).

c.62 *quod in librae mulieris consuetudine nuptiae intellegendae sint* [*Dig.*] 23.2 [24, Modestinus].

c.68 *quod de legitimis nuptiis procreati patrem, vulgo quaesiti matrem sequantur.* [*Dig.*] 1.5. [19, Celsus].

c.69 *quis sit vulgo, quaesitus.* [*Dig.* 1.5.23, Modestinus, omitting final sentence].

c.70 *quod matrem potius quam patrem sequuntur de non legitimo conjugio nati.* [*Dig.* 1.5.24, Ulpian, omitting the *int. nisi lex specialis aliud inducit*; *Dig.* 1.5.26: *tamquam furtivum usu non capitur*; Julian].

c.71 *quod liberorum status dependeat a conditione matris, non patris* [*Inst*] 1.4 [*pr.*, in full; c.71 continues with quotations from Isidore, *Etym.* IX].

c.79 *de repudio mariti si debitum uxori reddere non poterit* [*CJust* 5.17.10, AD 528].

c.81 (*de eadem re*) 'Const. *Nov.* 37' (*Ep. Jul.* 36.163.33).

c.109 *quomodo repudianda sit adultera* 'Nov. Const. 5.7' cc.110-112, ibid., 'cc.8, 14, 15'.

c.123 *quomodo accusandus sit servus de adulterio dominae suae infamatus* [*Dig.*] 1.12. [5, Ulpian].

c.246 *ut donec certum est virum in captivitate vivere, nunquam uxor alium ducat* [*Dig.*] 24.2 [6, *in medio*; Julian].

c.266 *de abjicienda adultera. CJust* 9.9.2.

c.272 *de poena nubendis viduae intra annum luctus.* 'Nov. Const. 37.11' (*Ep. Jul.* 36.141.11).

c.273 *ut mulier si ad secundas nuptias migraverit, prioris maritii privilegio non utatur.* ibid. 'c.23'.

c.274 de eodem 'Const. 84.1' (*Ep. Jul.* 87. 366.1).

c.304 *quod lenocinium facit, qui quaestuaria mancipia habuerit.* [*Dig.*] '4.2', recte 3.2.4 (Ulp.) 2, omitting last eight words.

c.307 *quod turpitudo dantis est non accipientis, in hoc quod mererici datur* [*Dig.*] '12.4' recte 12.5.4 (Ulp.) 3.

c.312 *de poena ejus quae defuncto marito clanculo concepit* 'Nov. Const. 38.2' (?*Ep. Jul.* 37.165.2).

EPILOGUE

Mommsen's Encounter with the Code

Brian Croke

Theodor Mommsen (1817-1903) was over eighty when he was invited by the Berlin Academy in December 1898 to embark on a new edition of the Theodosian Code. When death overtook him almost five years later he was in the process of revising the proofs of the prolegomena to the completed edition. By any editorial standards the Code is a large and complex job – not the normal task set for octogenarians, and not the sort of project to be completed virtually single-handedly in so few years. Indeed, the English translation of the Code took a whole cohort of scholars twenty years,[1] while his distinguished predecessor J.G. Godefroy (1587-1652), or Gothofredus, had taken thirty years to produce his pioneering edition. The year after taking on this new assignment Mommsen was in Paris where many of the necessary manuscripts were. For the first, and last, time he met the eminent Roman historian Jérôme Carcopino. As Carcopino explained it:

> Mommsen was always the last in bed and the first up – a habit that stayed with him all his life. The only time I met him was by chance, in 1901 or 1902 [actually June 1899], in the rue de Richelieu between midnight and one o'clock in the morning. He was on his way back, arm in arm with one of his daughters [Adelheid], to the Hôtel Louvois. That is where he always stopped in Paris because he only had to cross a small square, without climbing a stair or waiting a minute, to reach the manuscripts he assiduously worked on in the French National Library.[2]

---

[1] C. Pharr et al. *The Theodosian Code and Novels and the Sirmondian Constitutions* (New York, 1952), vii-viii (acknowledging the unavoidable difficulties and setbacks). This comparison is slightly, but only slightly, unfair because Mommsen did not himself edit the Novels although he worked closely with his collaborator Paul Meyer (1866-1926) who was entrusted with them.

[2] J. Carcopino, 'The Life and Works of Theodor Mommsen' in *Nobel Prize Library* (New York, 1971), 377. For this, Mommsen's final Parisian sojourn, see L. Wickert, *Theodor Mommsen. Eine Biographie*, vol, IV (Frankfurt, 1980), 169-70 and A. Mommsen, *Theodor Mommsen in Kreise der Seinen* (Berlin, 1936), 62.

What this episode illustrates is one of the secrets of Mommsen's productivity: by sleeping very little he was able to compress two working lifetimes into one. As the Director of the German Archaeological Institute in Rome, Wilhelm Henzen (1816-1887), put it, when you had Mommsen coming as a guest the best way of coping with him and his exhausting schedule was to get to bed three or four days beforehand.

Mommsen may have been far from young in 1898, but the Berlin Academy knew their man. When he was commissioned to undertake the edition of the Code, Mommsen had just successfully concluded another enormous and complex project: The *Auctores Antiquissimi* section (1875-1898) of the *Monumenta Germaniae Historica* (*MGH*) to which he contributed directly the texts of Jordanes, the *Chronica Minora* (3 vols) and Cassiodorus' *Variae* as well as having played a significant role in most of the other volumes.[3] The *MGH* had brought out his innate organisational capacity and scholarly perseverance which had also been exemplified by the *Corpus Inscriptionum Latinarum* (*CIL*). Both projects, particularly his editions of the chronicles, had demonstrated his ability to master the most complicated of textual and philological problems and traditions, based on a commitment to research exhaustively every single aspect of a document and its transmission. These works also bore witness to his scholarly method, namely to inspire and organise others to contribute to a necessarily collaborative enterprise. Mommsen was always encouraging and depended on his colleagues to assist in his own work, just as he was unstinting in assisting theirs.

The Academy knew that Mommsen could be counted on and that all it would be required to provide would be his expenses. He would do the rest in his usual way: by indefatigable effort and by prevailing upon the good services of every available collaborator. In the case of the Code in particular Mommsen possessed a unique advantage, namely an intimate knowledge of it derived from long use. The aim of this chapter is to outline Mommsen's encounter with the Code over nearly seventy years, the making of his edition late in life (drawing on unpublished correspondence) and the aftermath of his edition including the unresolved personal anguish it generated for two of his long-time friends and collaborators, Otto Seeck (1850-1921) and Paul Krüger (1840-1926). In particular I want to suggest that the reason for the relatively speedy completion of his edition was not simply long hours, but more because he had already spent decades in studying the sources of the Code and had already grasped its essential philological problems and the way to solve them. In addition he was able to utilise

---

[3] For details see B. Croke, 'Theodor Mommsen and the Later Roman Empire', *Chiron* 20 (1990), 163-93.

the considerable preparatory labours of Krüger. Mommsen's edition of the Code was in a real sense the culmination of a life's work, not just another new project to be dutifully mastered and completed.

I

Born in 1817, the eldest son of a resourceful Schleswig pastor, Mommsen entered the University of Kiel in 1838 already possessed of a prodigious talent, especially for languages and literature. Yet he did not enrol in the philosophical faculty in order to study languages and literature. Instead he opted for the faculty of law which attracted the majority of students in those days. As a graduate in law he would be trained to take part in the apparatus of government (of either the Danish king or one of the German states) for which law was a prerequisite, or perhaps as an advocate. At this stage, however, especially in Germany, law meant substantially Roman law and Roman law meant the Digest and Codes. Moreover professors of Roman law enjoyed great prestige and exerted considerable influence in contemporary discussions concerning the development of a common law code for the various German states.[4] Over successive semesters from Summer 1838 to Winter 1842/3 Mommsen took courses in a range of subjects which included Mathematics and Byron's 'Childe Harold's Pilgrimage'. Still, most of his courses were in law: German private, public and criminal law plus Roman private and public law including the great Roman legal texts (Pandects). The end-of-course comments he received were invariably 'very industrious', 'extraordinarily industrious' 'remarkable' and so on.[5] This period of instruction at Kiel decidedly shaped his lifelong scholarly interests and approaches. Of all his teachers Mommsen seems to have owed most to Privatdozent Eduard Osenbrüggen (1809-1879) with whom he studied *Römische Privatsaltertümer* and *Römische Staatsaltertümer* as well as Institutions and *Römisches Gerichtswesen*.[6] While Osenbrüggen was not the sort of person with whom Mommsen was likely to form a close relationship, he did learn from his teacher how historically correct philology could be combined with the study of Roman antiquities and institutions. Osenbrüggen had originally graduated in philology but had moved into Roman law when he returned to Kiel in 1835. He worked in the border region between philology and history which bore

[4] J.Q. Whitman, *The Legacy of Roman Law in the German Romantic Era* (Princeton, 1990), 105ff.; F. Wieacker, *Römische Rechtsgeschichte* (Munich, 1988), 37ff.

[5] This document from the family archive is published in L. Wickert, *Theodor Mommsen. Eine Biographie*, vol. I (Frankfurt, 1959), 448-9.

[6] Left aside here are two of his other teachers, Otto Jahn (1813-1869) who steered Mommsen in an epigraphical direction, and Johann Friedrich Kierulff (1807-1894) whose lectures on the nature and spirit of the *Digest* provided a different perspective to that of the historical school of Savigny.

fruit in his edition of the Novels of Justinian (1840). From Kiel he moved to Russian Dorpat from where he was eventually expelled because of his pro-German sentiment. Subsequently he devoted himself to German law.[7] The other teacher whom Mommsen claims to have learnt most from at Kiel was Georg Burchardi (1795-1882) who lectured on Institutions, *Erbrecht* and *Rechtsfälle*. More importantly, it was through Burchardi that Mommsen discovered the work of Savigny.[8]

Friedrich Carl von Savigny (1779-1861) was by this stage the founder of a school of historical jurisprudence and the master of medieval legal history whose work on Roman law in the Middle Ages traced the development of legal systems in the barbarian kingdoms which became established within the old Empire. In particular he traced the fortunes of Roman legal procedures and jurisprudence which in turn throws light on the tradition of the Code of Theodosius, the basis of most of the later barbarian Codes. The other special feature of Savigny's work was the way he used inscriptions, that is epigraphical copies of Roman laws and edicts. He was therefore one of the few who realised the important potential of Mommsen's epigraphical researches in the 1840s and 1850s and his influence was decisive in the eventual involvement of Mommsen in the Academy's *CIL*.[9] In general terms, however, Savigny himself was the heir to a hallowed tradition of philology which originated in sixteenth-century France. In fact it was the growth of studies in Roman law at that time which revolutionised the theory of history by shifting attention to institutional, cultural and social history. Philology and classical learning formed the basis of Roman law.

This revolution in the study of Roman law was initiated by Guillaume Budé (1468-1540) with his Annotations on the Pandects (1508-57) and extended into the epigraphical area by Andreas Alciato (1492-1550), the pioneering editor of the *Notitia Dignitatum*. Of special interest to the French students of Roman law and institutions was the Theodosian Code. The first significant edition of the Code was by Jacques Cujas (1522-1590) in 1566. Cujas' main strength was in detecting errors and interpolations in the Code, and providing conjectural emendations of difficult passages. His edition was supplemented by François Pithou (1543-1621) and his elder brother Pierre Pithou (1539-1596), who modelled his work on that of Cujas. Pithou's edition of the Novels, dedicated to Cujas, appeared in 1571

[7] *Allgemeine Deutsche Biographie* 24 (1887), 463-8.

[8] Wickert, *Theodor Mommsen*, vol. I, 163-71.

[9] See the documents published in I. Stahlmann, 'Friedrich Carl von Savigny und Theodor Mommsen. Ihr Briefwechsel zwischen 1844 und 1856' in P. Kneissl and V. Losemann (edd.), *Alte Geschichte und Wissenschaftsgeschichte* (Darmstadt, 1989), 465-501.

and he then went on to publish in 1574 the first edition of the *Comparison of the Mosaic and Roman Laws* from a manuscript at St Denis. Pithou was also interested in collecting inscriptions, especially legal ones, and concentrated on those to be found in Switzerland, a feat later emulated by Mommsen while a professor at Zurich in the early 1850s.[10]

A Jesuit scholar, Jacques Sirmond (1559-1651), first published the manuscript of the late Roman constitutions which still bear his name and which Mommsen included in his edition of the Theodosian Code. Occasionally Sirmond clashed with the Genevan lawyer Gothofredus whose annotated edition of the Code is one of the most remarkable products of seventeenth-century erudition. Soon after, the Code was exploited extensively by Le Nain de Tillemont (1637-1698) in his researches on Roman imperial and ecclesiastical history. The works of both Gothofredus and Tillemont were fundamental and of enduring value. In the final analysis Mommsen considered Tillemont superior in matters of history and prosopography but when it came to legal and administrative matters 'nemo adhuc Gothofredum nec superavit nec aequavit' (prol., cxvii). Indeed Paul Maas (1880-1964), in reviewing Mommsen's edition, thought that Gothofredus would never be surpassed.[11]

During Mommsen's student days, however, there appeared a new edition of the Theodosian Code which was to remain the standard until his own, sixty years later. The edition was by Gustav Haenel (1792-1878) who had originally been inspired by the first two volumes of Savigny's *Roman Law in the Middle Ages* to devote his life to researching and editing the pre-Justinianic legal sources and their Germanic successors. For seven long years (from 1821) Haenel travelled extensively throughout Europe and Britain working in all the available archives and laying the foundation for a half-century of detailed work on the sources of law and their transmission.[12] What resulted was an edition of the Gregorian and Hermogenian Codes (1837) followed by the *Codex Theodosianus* (1837-42), then the *Novels* and *Sirmondian Constitutions* (1844) and the *Lex Romana Visigothorum* (1849), that is the Breviary of Alaric. In addition Haenel produced in 1857 what he called a *Corpus Legum* which was simply a combined edition of Roman imperial laws from all non-legal sources, literary and non-literary, but in chronological order. This was a project he had been working on for a long time. It proved to be (and remains) a very useful

[10] Details of these scholarly developments are to be found in D.R. Kelley, *Foundations of Modern Historical Scholarship* (New York, 1970), especially 113ff. (Cujas) and 249ff. (Pithou).

[11] *Göttingische gelehrte Anzeigen* (1906), no. 8, 649 (= *Kleine Schriften*, ed. W. Buchwald [Munich, 1973], 616).

[12] On Haenel see *Allgemeine Deutsche Biographie* 49 (1904), 751-5.

work and it is a pity that there is not a modern version of it.[13]

Meanwhile at Kiel Mommsen gradually became impelled to undertake the task of providing a critical edition of epigraphical copies of Roman legal documents, as his ambition turned from law to philology. It was also while a student at Kiel that Mommsen, so it appears, first formulated the idea of providing modern editions of Roman legal documents.[14] Certainly it was during this period that he developed the skilful mastery of legal philology which he applied to so many texts during his life, culminating in the Theodosian Code.[15] A few weeks before his death over six decades later he was able to remark to his friend and colleague Otto Hirschfeld (1843-1922) that 'The Roman legal sources I have fortunately brought under shelter; only for Paulus [= *Sententiae*] must something still be done after my death'.[16]

As a philological lawyer Mommsen always appreciated and sought to establish the human and administrative context of laws, that is to say who prepared them, how they were framed and how they were communicated and acted upon. Likewise he was always interested in how collections of laws arose and were transmitted. What was a codex? What was a digest? How did a collection get its title? What was a 'pragmatic sanction'? What exactly was a 'subscription' to a law? And what was meant by the 'edition' of a constitution? – these were the sorts of questions Mommsen was forever puzzling over.[17] At the same time his continuing researches exhibited his conviction in the underlying continuity of Roman history from the regal to the late imperial period, and even beyond. Indeed he was able to stress that the kingdom of the Ostrogoths in Italy, for example, was essentially Roman in terms of its legal and administrative structures and procedures.[18]

As a professor of Roman Law at Leipzig, Zurich and Breslau successively, Mommsen was constantly engaged in interpreting

---

[13] cf. J. Gaudemet, *La formation du droit séculier et du droit de l'église aux IVe et Ve siècles*, 2nd ed (Paris, 1979), 73 n. 4.

[14] At the same time he planned a treatise on Roman criminal law, i.e. *Römisches Strafrecht* (1899) as well as an edition of the Pandects, i.e. *Digest*, (1872), as stated in his letter to Gustav Freytag on 13 March 1877 cited in L. Wickert, *Theodor Mommsen. Eine Biographie*, vol. III (Frankfurt 1969), 655.

[15] W. Kunkel, 'Theodor Mommsen als Jurist', *Chiron* 14 (1984), 370-1.

[16] O. Hirschfeld, 'Theodor Mommsen', *Abhandlungen der königlichen Preussischen Akademie der Wissenschaften* (1904), 1025 = *Kleine Schriften* (Berlin, 1913; repr. New York, 1975), 959.

[17] 'Die Bedeutung des Wortes *digesta*' (1868) (= *GS* 2, 90-6); 'Die Benennungen der Constitutionssammlungen' (1889) (= *GS* 2, 359-65); 'Die Heimath des Gregorianus' (1901) (= *GS* 2, 366-70); 'Sanctio pragmatica' (1904) (= *GS* 2, 426-8); 'Uber die Subscription und Edition der Rechtsurkunden' (1851) (= *GS* 3, 275-85).

[18] 'Ostgotische Studien', *Neues Archiv* 14 (1889), 225-49, 453-544; 15 (1890), 180-6 (= *GS* 3, 362-484;) cf. 'Das römisch-germanische Herrscherjahr', ibid. 16 (1891), 51 (= *GS* 6, 343).

Roman legal texts in the light of their original context but also with an eye to their contemporary significance, at a time of great debate on the relationship between the Roman law taught in the universities and the practical legal demands of the German states. This was also the period during which the celebrated *Römische Geschichte* appeared. In 1858 Mommsen was called back to Berlin where he spent the remainder of his life. Initially he came to work on the *CIL* for the Berlin Academy but later became a Professor of Ancient History for the first time. Still, his historical technique and vision remained primarily anchored in the great juristic texts such as the Theodosian Code.

In 1859 Mommsen published an article on Frankish interpolations in the Theodosian Code. A law of Constantine to Euphrasius, *rationalis* of the three provinces (Sicily, Sardinia and Corsica) in AD 325, specified the correct weights for tax payments in gold (*CTh* 12.7.1). Mommsen observed that the stated rate of seven *solidi* for an ounce of gold reflected the situation in sixth-century Gaul rather than fourth-century Italy where the exchange was six *solidi* per ounce. In Mommsen's view this interpolation showed how Roman laws and the Code in particular were handled in Frankish Gaul.[19] Three years later he was forced to elaborate on his arguments in answering the criticism of the current editor of the Code, Haenel.[20] Meanwhile, in 1860 he produced an important study of the chronology of the laws of Diocletian and his tetrarchic colleagues[21] which remains fundamental as one can see from the way it has been used, for example, by T.D. Barnes in his *The New Empire of Diocletian and Constantine*.[22] In this article Mommsen pointed out that most of the subscriptions to the tetrarchic laws are in the *Codex Justinianus*, yet they have never been properly studied. He then proceeded by means of a collation of the main manuscripts, to determine critically the correct dates and places of each law. Previous attempts, according to Mommsen, had been too mechanical and had ignored essential philological and historical criticism.

The importance of this study was that for the first time it was demonstrated what improvements accurate criticism could bring to a text such as the *Codex Justinianus*. In addition it focused attention on the inscriptions and subscriptions to the laws. Traditionally the Codes had been the preserve of students of jurisprudence who were mainly interested in their legal content. As an historian, however, Mommsen's interest was just as much in establishing their procedural and contemporary context. Mommsen clearly possessed a masterful

[19] 'Fränkische Interpolation im Theodosischen Codex' (1859) (= *GS* 2, 408-9).
[20] 'Zu Cod. Theod. 12.7.1' (1862) (= *GS* 2, 410-11); cf. prol. xlvi.
[21] 'Über die Zeitfolge der Verordnungen Diocletians und seiner Mitregenten' (1860) (= *GS* 2, 195-291).
[22] Cambridge Mass., 1982.

knowledge of the Theodosian Code and this was shown once more in an 1863 article in which he was able to make sense of the background to two unidentified rescripts on papyrus,[23] just as he was able over a decade earlier to identify an inscription as being the record of a lost constitution dating to 386/7[24] and one decade later as being a certain constitution of Julian.[25]

Mommsen was not only concerned with the Theodosian Code. He was equally involved with the Digest. As early as 1844 on his first trip to Italy he spent time in Florence collating the famous Medicean manuscript of the Digest and by 1862 he addressed the implications of the then inadequate state of the text. In doing so he foreshadowed a new text free from later interpolations and corruptions. At this point he examined the manuscripts and divided the material into five categories. As Mommsen noted, Savigny had been the first to research carefully the tradition of the Digest and related texts; now he was asking that those philologically inclined jurists and those philologists who were not above working with jurists submit the Digest manuscripts to preliminary research and report the findings to him.[26]

Two years later Mommsen had commenced his edition, having found a diligent and competent collaborator in the person of Paul Krüger. The twelfth child of a Berlin dance instructor, Krüger had been a talented mathematician before turning to jurisprudence at the University of Berlin. He was already a very independent worker and after graduation began a career in the Prussian civil service. At the same time, however, he kept up his investigations into Roman civil law and in the summer of 1864 secured his *Habilitation* into the faculty of jurisprudence at Berlin. It was just at this time that he met Mommsen and was invited to join him to work on the Digest. By the time the Digest edition was completed Mommsen had already set Krüger to producing a critical edition of the Code of Justinian, which he completed in 1877.[27] Mommsen himself was not actively engaged in extensive research on the Code of Justinian but he did possess a profound knowledge of the text, as evidenced in an 1892 article discussing the implications of a new inscription [now *CIL* III S.12116 = *ILS* 1050] from Hierapolis dedicated to a certain imperial legate of Cilicia, Rutilianus, in AD 215. On the basis of the inscription he was able to correct the text of a certain rescript (*CJust* 9.43.1) which in turn enabled him to show that the text of Haloander was derived from a reliable tradition and should not have been so easily discarded as it had been by Krüger.[28]

[23] 'Fragmente zweier lateinischer Kaiserrescripte auf Papyrus' (1863) (= *GS* 2, 342-57).
[24] 'Halsring mit Inschrift' (1852) (= *GS* 2, 358).
[25] 'Ein Edict des Kaisers Julianus' (1875) (= *GS* 2, 341).
[26] 'Über die kritische Grundlage unseres Digestentextes' (1862) (= *GS* 2, 133).
[27] F. Schulz, 'Paul Krüger', *ZSS RA* 47 (1927), ix-xxxii.
[28] 'Zur Kritik des Codex Justinianus' (1892) (= *GS* 2, 422-5).

In the late 1860s, with the Digest behind him, Krüger was funded by the Savigny-Stiftung to travel extensively for the purpose of studying and collating Roman legal manuscripts, in particular those of Justinian's Code. By now too he had resolved, probably at Mommsen's prompting once again, to complete an edition of the Code of Theodosius. So he was able at that stage to examine most of the main manuscripts. In the same year in which his edition of the Code of Justinian appeared (1877) he contributed an article on the Theodosian Code to the *Festschrift* in honour of Mommsen's sixtieth birthday. Soon afterwards he published his apograph of the Turin fragments.[29] By about 1880 or so Krüger had collected most of the important material for an edition of the Code. Yet it showed no signs of appearing; in fact he seems to have lost the will to finish it altogether.[30] In 1888 Krüger was called to Bonn and for the next decade did not progress much further with the Code.

It was during the 1870s and 1880s that Mommsen was working on what he regarded as likely to be his most durable work, namely the *Römisches Staatsrecht*. The *Staatsrecht* was a large-scale analytic description of the system and procedures of Roman public law. Although concentrating on the period largely before the scope of the Code, Mommsen nevertheless made extensive use of it.[31] Likewise, in his other major systematic analysis of Roman law, the *Römisches Strafrecht*, he used the Theodosian Code extensively. All through these researches he was relying on the edition of Haenel, whose shortcomings had been itemised by Krüger in 1886.[32]

By the 1890s there was clearly a burning need for a new edition of the Theodosian Code. Haenel's Codex looked out of place alongside Mommsen's *Digest* and Krüger's *Codex Justinianus*. Its inaccurate and unscientific apparatus was a major flaw; but there had also been some significant textual discoveries too – most notably the Turin palimpsest, but also the Ambrosian manuscript containing the *gesta senatus*.[33] It was therefore no surprise when Mommsen agreed to prepare a new edition in 1898. Moreover he acknowledged that, although Haenel had been a great traveller and a tireless worker, his qualities deserted him when it came to textual criticism (prol., cxviii). Yet he had shown the

---

[29] P. Krüger, 'Über die Zeitbestimmung der Konstitutionen aus den Jahren 364 bis 373. Ein Beitrag zur Kritik des Codex Theodosianus' in *Commentationes philologae in honorem Th. Mommsen* (Berlin, 1877), 75ff.; 'Codicis Theodosiani fragmenta Taurinensia', *Abhandlungen der Berliner Akademie der Wissenschaften* 1879 (Berlin, 1880).

[30] Schulz, 'Paul Krüger', xix.

[31] Mommsen's use of the *CTh* in these works can be traced through J. Malitz, *Römisches Staatsrecht – Stellenregister* (Munich, 1979) and *Römisches Strafrecht – Stellenregister* (Munich, 1982).

[32] 'Die Vaticanischen Scholien zum Codex Theodosianus', *ZSS RA* 6 (1886) 138ff. cf. Maas, *Göttingische gelehrte Anzeigen* (1906), no. 8, 608.

[33] P. Jörs, *RE* 4 (1901), 1973.

way, and Mommsen believed that the wealth of information accumulated by Haenel for his edition made his own work all the easier. Mommsen knew that Krüger had long been engaged in preparations for an edition but must have finally decided he would never complete it. After all, Krüger had been sitting on the material for nearly thirty years. He was therefore rather stunned at Mommsen's announcement because he did plan to complete the task himself eventually. Indeed, initially Krüger was reluctant to co-operate with Mommsen's request to use his materials but was soon persuaded by Mommsen's persistence and generous spirit.[34] So it was that, having secured the necessary support of Krüger, Mommsen set about a task he had never previously contemplated.[35] He did so against a background of increasing expectation of the value of codes of law, just when the German nation was in the process of producing its own civil Code (*Bürgerliches Gesetzbuch*) which finally came into effect on 1 January 1900.

II

Reconstructing the Theodosian Code from what remains of it is no easy task, not least because there is no complete manuscript of all sixteen books. Apart from fragments such as that in Milan, there are only four manuscripts of the Code itself (at Paris, Rome and Turin) which between then only cover Books 1 and 6-16. Special importance is therefore attached to the early sixth-century *Lex Romana Visigothorum* or Breviary of Alaric which was so dependent on the Code and which survives in many versions; there are some complete versions, some incomplete ones, abbreviated versions and partially abbreviated ones. However, the most important of the manuscripts for the Breviarium is O – from the Selden collection in the Bodleian Library at Oxford.

In preparing his edition of the Theodosian Code and the Sirmondian Constitutions Mommsen proceeded in three main ways, just as he had always done. First he inspected manuscripts himself at first hand. This was why he was in Paris in 1899 when Carcopino spied him in the early hours of the morning.[36] It was evidently the only journey he made for the purpose of the Code. Secondly he arranged to have manuscripts transferred to Berlin where he could work on them

---

[34] See the interesting letters of Mommsen to Krüger published in Schulz, 'Paul Krüger', xxii-xxvii.

[35] Letter to Krüger, 12 February 1903 (ibid. xxii).

[36] This was when he collated the important Paris 9643 (prol. xliv) and the Breviary manuscript Paris nouv. acq. Lat. 1631 (lxxix). In the same year he was also in Milan to work on Ambrosianus c.29 (lxxiii), a manuscript only discovered after Haenel's edition, but which contained the hitherto unknown *Gesta senatus*.

there.[37] The third aspect of Mommsen's *modus operandi* was to press into service all his friends and colleagues in order to collate manuscripts and check details for him. He did not personally inspect the sixth-century Turin palimpsest but preferred to rely on Krüger's copy of it 'facta peritissime et diligentissime' (prol., xxix).[38] For the sixth-century Gallic manuscript, Vat. Reg. 886, he relied on the collation of Books 9 to 15 previously undertaken for the Berlin Academy by Rudolf Schoell (1844-1893) and that of Krüger who collated Book 16 (lvi), as well as Meyer who checked the manuscript when in Rome in 1901 (prol., xlvii, l); while for the Ivrea manuscript of the Breviary he had the manuscript photographed by his friend Giacosa in Turin (prol., lxviii). Other scholars cited for assistance in collating manuscripts include Zeumer, Goetz, Girard and Clark (through the intervention of Traube), while Mommsen credited the young Paul Maas with pointing out the correct meaning of 'post alia' and 'et cetera' in several laws (prol., ccix).[39] All these names were familiar at the time for they were all reputable students of Roman or medieval law and legal texts. Moreover they were nearly all well-known to Mommsen himself.

Increasingly threatened by blindness, Mommsen launched into the task with youthful enthusiasm (as observers remarked)[40] and accomplished most of the work for the edition during 1899 and 1900. The Academy provided research subventions on 9 February 1899 (1200 Marks) in order to get the venture under way, then a more substantial amount on 8 June (2,400 Marks),[41] presumably to cover Mommsen's trip to Paris, and 4,000 Marks on 21 June 1900.[42] By now Mommsen had a collaborator, Paul Meyer, who was responsible for editing the Novels. Originally Mommsen was working by himself but was casting about for an appropriate person to take on the Novels.[43] At the end of 1899 he actually called for volunteers.[44] Meyer was already a well-established scholar, having produced an acclaimed thesis on the Roman concubinate (1895), and more recently had worked his way into papyrology which was subsequently to become his main field of

[37] As with the *Breviarium* manuscripts Par. Lat. 4403, 4404 and 4405 (prol. lxxii, lxvii).

[38] Published by Krüger: 'Codicis Theodosiani fragmenta Taurinensia'. The manuscript was destroyed in 1904 in a fire at the library (Maas, *Göttingische gelehrte Anzeigen* [1906], 608 n. 1).

[39] Maas was particularly proud of the letter of thanks he received from Mommsen: E. Mensching, *Über einen verfolgten deutschen Altphilologen: Paul Maas (1880-1964)* (Berlin, 1987), 15.

[40] Maas, *Göttingische gelehrte Anzeigen* (1906), 628; Diels, *SBAW* (1904), 238.

[41] *SBAW* (1899), 109, 529.

[42] *SBAW* (1900), 656.

[43] On 8 October 1898 he was already on the lookout (letter to Krüger in Schultz, 'Paul Krüger', xxiii).

[44] *SBAW* (1900), 45.

interest. He was a particularly careful and painstaking scholar with just the right temperament for Mommsen's assignment.[45] They worked closely with each other, so it would appear, and each provided valuable support for the other's work.[46]

As noted, one of the more significant manuscripts which needed to be taken into account was one from the Selden collection in the Bodleian Library at Oxford. Furthermore, there is a set of documents relating to the collation of this manuscript which explain and bring to life the daily workings of Mommsen while preparing his edition of the Theodosian Code. The unpublished correspondence of Francis Haverfield (1860-1919), later Camden Professor at Oxford, and Mommsen provides a valuable illustration of precisely how Mommsen engaged others in his own work and how he relied on their expert assistance in contributing together to a common achievement.[47]

As an undergraduate at Oxford Haverfield developed an interest and aptitude for Roman epigraphy and in 1883 began a serious professional correspondence with Mommsen which soon developed into a strong personal friendship.[48] In response to a card from Haverfield on the occasion of his 81st birthday, Mommsen wrote:

> Your card for many happy returns (may they not be too many!) arrived just as I was about to demand you a service. It is an exceptional way of returning thanks, but you will not take it amiss.
>
> We have begun here a new edition of the Theodosian Code, that is to say our Academy has given orders to collect the materials. Among these probably it will be necessary to get collated your Seldenianus 32 (Bodlei – 3362).[49] For the moment I want only the fourth book (3 in the manuscript, where the first book is deficient), and I think you will be able to find some person able and willing to undertake this work at a reasonable contribution.
>
> I tried to get the book sent to Berlin, but Mr Nicholson answers that by the gift this is impossible for the Seldeniani; so either we must send some of our young men thither or turn [?] to our Oxonian friends ....
>
> I send with this letter a copy of the fourth book; his varia lectio may be written either on the margins or on blank leaves inserted. As by this

---

[45] W. Kunkel, 'Paul Martin Meyer', *ZSS RA* 56 (1936), 428-9.

[46] Meyer, *Novellae*, prol., cix.

[47] Mommsen's letters and cards to Haverfield, all in his nearly faultless English, are in the Ashmolean Library, Oxford; Haverfield's letters to Mommsen are in the Deutsche Staatsbibliothek, Berlin (Nachlass Mommsen).

[48] On Haverfield see G. Macdonald, 'F. Haverfield', *PBA* 9 (1919), 475-91 and H.H.E. Craster, 'Francis Haverfield', *EHR* 35 (1920), 63-70.

[49] The manuscript had been numbered 32 (originally 16) in the Selden library and became 3362 in the numeration of the Bodleian when it absorbed the Selden collection. Haenel had inspected the manuscript in Oxford in 1827 and described it fully in *Lex Romana Visigothorum* (Berlin, 1849), lv-lvii; c., Mommsen's description (prol. lxv-lxvii). The manuscript had been the specific object of attention in C. Witte, *de Guilelmi Malmesburiensis codice legis Romanae Wisigothorum* (Bratislava, 1831).

specimen I shall be able to determine what further measures will be necessary, I want very much to have this work done as soon as possible.[50]

Mommsen had evidently asked the Bodleian's librarian E.B. Nicholson if the manuscript could be forwarded to Berlin for collation but had been advised that 'all the Selden MSS were given under the condition that they should not be lent. There is no dispensing power and we should be obliged to give the same reply to the Queen.'[51] Mommsen therefore turned immediately to Haverfield who was convalescing in the Alps at the time but replied that he was writing to Oxford that night to ask if anyone could collate the manuscript; if not, he volunteered to undertake the task himself on his return.[52] Although there is a gap in the correspondence at this point it appears that a certain Anna Parker was identified and agreed to work on Mommsen's behalf. Within three weeks he had received her collation of the specimen and replied as follows:

Honoured Miss,
Please accept my best thanks for your scholar work, which is admirable well done. I reserve a further answer after having entered the very curious ms. in my apparatus. It will be indispensable to get it collated entirely.[53]

Back in Oxford soon after, apparently recovered, Haverfield wrote to Mommsen that he was pleased that Miss Parker's collation was satisfactory and advised that he had himself paid Miss Parker £1 2s 6d. He went on to say that the Academy owed him that amount or if it was preferred he was prepared to regard the amount as a personal contribution to the projected edition.[54]

Mommsen was apparently not impressed at Haverfield's absence from Oxford and advised him that 'Young men like you should not take a health-trip' before going on to say;

You have obliged me greatly by procuring me the collation of the Seldenianus. It is quite satisfactory and the charge moderate. I hope Miss Parker will continue and collate the whole Theodosianus.
I send to you for Miss Parker a copy of the Breviarium for the remaining part of the collation. Please tell her to send the collation as the work proceeds by instalments.
I send too to you a check for 8; you will pay her as far as it reaches and then give me notice. At the close of work I want a receipt for the sum total

[50] Mommsen to Haverfield, 29 December 1898.
[51] Nicholson to Mommsen, 26 December 1898 (Deutsche Staatsbiblioteck, Berlin: Nachlass Mommsen).
[52] Haverfield to Mommsen, 5 January 1899.
[53] Mommsen to Parker, 22 January 1899.
[54] Haverfield to Mommsen, 29 January 1899.

containing my name for our academical accounts.

The MS in itself is not first rate, but derived from an excellent copy. The text has been corrected arbitrarily by William of Malmesbury. Perhaps you may inform me, if the works of this curious author have been recently studied in your country and his materials discussed. His classic library was of unusual extension; as far as I know he is the only medieval writer in England who knew the Breviarium.[55]

Haverfield soon responded that he had banked the cheque and referred Mommsen to Stubbs's edition of William, offering to send a copy if it were not to be found in Berlin. Stubbs had concluded that the MS was an autograph original of William and not, as Haenel had thought, a copy of William's original.[56] Mommsen readily concurred in this view when he wrote to ask Haverfield to send the final bill since the collation would now be complete:

I am greatly satisfied by my lady collationer. She will have finished; please pay her some pounds that may be wanting and send me her receipt for the sum total; so we will adjust our accounts. The MS is certainly written by William of M. himself; it is very curious and interesting.[57]

In setting out the final cost details (with the Academy in debt to the tune of £1 14s), Haverfield later reported that according to Miss Parker 'there are also many pages of Libri Legum Theodosi [i.e. Novels of Theodosius II] which she thinks you do not require, but can do if you wish'.[58]

Mommsen duly arranged for the arrears to be paid and wrote to Haverfield:

I have just finished the entering of Miss Parker's collation in my notes, and am generally satisfied with her careful and intelligent work. The Novellae for the moment are not wanted; probably they will be requested later, but I have dispossessed myself of this part of the future edition.[59]

Seven months later Mommsen again wrote to Haverfield, this time to ask Miss Parker to verify certain readings in the Selden manuscript. By now too he had come to consider that the manuscript is of 'the highest value'.[60] It appears that Haverfield himself did the verification and reported back to Mommsen on 17 November.

By the end of the following year (1900), that is just two years after

---

[55] Mommsen to Haverfield, 29 January 1899.
[56] Haverfield to Mommsen, 4 February 1899.
[57] Mommsen to Haverfield, 12 March 1899.
[58] Haverfield to Mommsen, 15 March 1899.
[59] Mommsen to Haverfield, 12 April 1899.
[60] Mommsen to Haverfield, 13 November 1899.

being entrusted with the task, the text of the edition was already complete as well as much of the preface, while by now Meyer had started work on the Novels.[61] At this stage Mommsen wrote once more to Oxford, this time to say that he now wanted the Selden Manuscript collated for the Novels.[62] It was Christmas time; Haverfield was away from Oxford for ten days but he agreed to have the collation done.[63] For once Mommsen was not in a rush. 'As the next century is not far off,' he wrote, 'take your time without any hurry. The collation may very well wait, we want it in two or three months. I send the book. Regarding the money I await your orders.'[64] Miss Parker completed the collation by April when Mommsen inquired about the amount due[65] which was eventually paid to Haverfield in July by his engineer son Hans Mommsen (1873-1941) who was visiting Oxford at that time.[66]

Typesetting of the edition was now proceeding and by the end of 1901 had reached the end of Book 9; while Meyer was advancing with his assignment, having spent the period from March to August 1901 collating manuscripts in Rome, Ivrea and Paris.[67] By the end of 1902 the edition was nearly finished and Mommsen fully expected it to appear in the course of 1903; at the same time Meyer too promised that his Novels would soon be ready.[68] What remained was to tidy up outstanding queries, and so in February 1902 Mommsen wrote with a query on one of his Theodosian novels[69] and over a year later it is clear that his work on the edition was drawing to a conclusion when he wrote to Haverfield:

> You remember the service rendered us by engaging Miss A. Parker to collate the Seldenianus. My collaborator Mr Paul Meyer has finished now the manuscript of the Novellae, but before sending it to the printer we want the answers to a questioning of some bulk, which will arrive to you next week. Please get Miss Parker or, if she is not to be had (I was fully satisfied with her work), some other male or female with that collation. We are quite willing to pay as before.[70]

The collation was completed by Miss Parker, quicker than either she or Haverfield expected, and the results were soon on their way to Berlin.[71] In acknowledging receipt of the work Mommsen again asked

---

[61] *SBAW* (1901), 79.
[62] Mommsen to Haverfield, 21 December 1900.
[63] Haverfield to Mommsen, 23 December 1900.
[64] Mommsen to Haverfield, 26 December 1900.
[65] Mommsen to Haverfield, 13 April 1901.
[66] Haverfield to Mommsen, 11 July 1901.
[67] *SBAW* (1902), 53.
[68] *SBAW* (1903), 103.
[69] Mommsen to Haverfield, 4 February 1902.
[70] Mommsen to Haverfield, 12 March 1903.
[71] Haverfield to Mommsen, 25 March 1903.

Haverfield for a bill.[72] Mommsen and Haverfield continued to correspond in the ensuing months about their common interest in inscriptions and the exploration of the *limes* in both Britain and Germany. Haverfield actually planned to visit Mommsen in June but apologised for not being able to fit Berlin into his itinerary.[73] This letter, dated 20 September 1903, was evidently their last communication. A few weeks later (1 November 1903) Mommsen was dead, with his edition of the Code all but complete. Days later his son Wolfgang Mommsen (1857-1930), who had been a businessman in London and was married to an Englishwoman, wrote to Haverfield to say that 'only a few days before his death I heard him mention your name, and he was telling me to remind him in a few days to write to you'.[74] Mommsen never had the chance.

What this exchange between Mommsen and Haverfield provides is an insight into how the great Berlin professor worked on a day-to-day basis. In the first place he was meticulous in planning out a project such as the edition of the Code so that he was able to manage several strands of research simultaneously. More importantly his understanding of scholarship as a collaborative venture under firm direction is highlighted here; that is, we can see at close range precisely how he went about arranging for his friends and colleagues to assist him in his work and how, at least in this case, they were only too happy to oblige. Also of interest is the way he necessarily trusted in the quality of the work undertaken by remote collaborators such as Anna Parker and Haverfield. It was through connections such as these in all the main libraries and manuscript collections of his day, and the main academic institutions, that Mommsen was able to organise complex textual projects so effectively and expeditiously.

III

Some months after Mommsen's death his edition of the Theodosian Code appeared. The Novels were all but ready as well and were expected in the winter of 1904,[75] although they did not finally emerge from the publisher until November 1905 – 'thereby completing Mommsen's last work'.[76] Not only was the new edition of the Code an important step in a textual sense but its preface contained a good deal of new and fundamental research on Mommsen's part, as well as an appendix (commissioned by Mommsen but completed after his death)

[72] Mommsen to Haverfield, 6 April 1903.
[73] Haverfield to Mommsen, 20 September 1903.
[74] Letter W. Mommsen to Haverfield, 9 November 1903 (Ashmolean Library, Oxford – preserved with Th. Mommsen's letters to Haverfield.
[75] *SBAW* (1904), 238. Anna Parker's contribution was duly acknowledged (prol., xlviii).
[76] *SBAW* (1906), 91.

by Alfred von Wretschko of Innsbruck on the medieval use of the Code
and its contents. In the first place Mommsen treated the composition of
the Code and its transmission with full details of its complex
manuscript tradition, as well as the early editions. More important,
however, was his discussion of the authors and recipients of the laws
as well as their dates and places. Mommsen began this section
(chapter 10) by explaining the nature of the constitutions and the
processes for transmitting them (*datae, acceptae, lectae, propositae,
praelatae, regestae*) (prol., cliii-clviii). He then says that he actually
agonised long and hard over whether or not to go into the questions of
the addressee, date and place of issue of the laws (prol., clvii). It would
not be so difficult to do this, Mommsen suggests, if confined to the
archetype manuscripts. However extending it to the *Codex Justinianus* adds great complications. Yet, if not the editor's duty, then it is
at least useful for the edition, but there is a danger that there will be
too much extraneous matter which would encroach on that 'excellent
man' Gothofredus, that is to say commentaries will be substituted for
an edition (prol., clviii). So Mommsen rested content with three tables:
(1) of emperors; (2) of addressees, with year and day date; (3) the laws
ordered chronologically with dates and places. Behind these tables lay
a considerable amount of preparatory research and thought. In
particular he was able to take for granted here what he had argued
three years earlier in a substantial article on the Code.[77] Mommsen
had shown, on the basis of the sections of a single original law
preserved differently in a number of constitutions, that many of the
constitutions were incorrectly dated.

As we have seen, Mommsen had long since dealt with the chronology
of the laws of the tetrarchs (mainly not from the Theodosian Code) and
had been followed in 1889 by the ambitious attempt by Otto Seeck to
do the same for the laws of Constantine.[78] Now a further eleven years
on and with the challenge of producing a critical edition largely behind
him, Mommsen conceded that it was forever difficult to strike the right
balance between overestimating and underestimating the indications
of date contained in the Code. In his view, Gothofredus and Tillemont
had gone too far one way while Seeck had gone too far the other; so far
in fact that Mommsen pronounced his article as 'academically
unusable'.[79] Having then queried some of the dates proposed by Seeck
he went on to argue that one must acknowledge the errors in the Code
and try to correct them. Seeck, however, dated all the laws but changed
dates too arbitrarily in order to suit his arguments. All of which made
his article, according to Mommsen, a *wissenschaftliche Nullität*.[80] This

[77] 'Das Theodosische Gesetzbuch' (1900) (= *GS* 2, 371-405).
[78] O. Seeck, 'Die Zeitfolge der Gesetze Constantins', *ZSS RA* 9 (1889), 1-44, 177-251.
[79] 'Das Theodosische Gesetzbuch' (= *GS* 2, 397).
[80] ibid. (= *GS* 2, 401.

was a forthright denunciation from a forthright man but Seeck was not one to be easily wounded.

The relationship between Mommsen and Seeck is an interesting and volatile one, but a very profitable one for the modern study of the Code. As a young man Seeck's interests were more strictly in the *Naturwissenschaften* and so he matriculated at Dorpat in Chemistry. Through reading Roman law books to a blind friend, and being captivated by Mommsen's *Römische Geschichte*, Seeck discovered that his real vocation was to be a Roman scholar. He therefore transferred to Berlin where Mommsen was lecturing on Roman antiquities and the Roman Empire. Mommsen may have recognised some of himself in Seeck: he was a very fast worker and spent little time asleep, as well as enjoying a good time. In addition he was widely read in foreign literature, was a great traveller and walker and a noted authority on art history. Despite having to catch up with Latin and Greek, Seeck advanced quickly and in 1876 produced an edition of the *Notitia Dignitatum* which he dedicated to Mommsen. Soon after, Mommsen set him to work on the *MGH* edition of the letters and speeches of Symmachus which eventually led to that splendid edition. Although punctilious and accurate in all his work, Seeck was occasionally erratic in his judgment, which led to his work often being regarded with suspicion by many scholars, including Mommsen.[81]

In the prolegomena to the Code Mommsen repeated his harsh view of Seeck's 1889 article on the chronology of Constantine's laws (*fortius opinor quam prudentius*; prol., clix) saying that he himself would never dare to go so far. While Mommsen's continuing public denunciations of Seeck's researches on the Code clearly worried some, Seeck himself was apparently unperturbed. In fact in the wake of Mommsen's passing he pointed out that since all his own work fell in a field where Mommsen had trodden before him he was inevitably able to find Mommsen's mistakes and felt obliged to point them out. Yet this never worried Mommsen for, although a man of strong views, he readily accepted his mistakes as contributing to the cause of scholarly progress. Obviously their friendship never suffered. Indeed Seeck proudly quotes a letter he received from Mommsen (undated but probably mid-1903) in which the ailing maestro, fearful he would be prevented from seeing the Code completely through the Press, asked Seeck if he would help in the laborious task of checking the references in the prolegomena. 'I know that, when it ought to count, I can find no truer and more caring friend

---

[81] For details: O. Seeck, 'Zur Characteristik Mommsens', *Deutsche Rundschau* 118 (1904), 75-108; L. Radermacher, 'O. Seeck', *Biographische Jahrbuch für Altertumskunde* 46 (1926), 50-60; W. Weber, 'Otto Seeck', *Encyclopedia of the Social Sciences*, vol 13 (1934), 642, K. Christ, *Römische Geschichte und Deutsche Geschichtswissenschaft* (Munich, 1982), 69-70.

than you', said Mommsen, 'to correct the mistakes of a dying man.'[82]

Three years later, however, the situation was not so clear. Stung into action by a comment of Eduard Schwartz (1858-1940), Seeck explained that he did not gladly engage in polemic, least of all with Mommsen. Instead, so he says, he remained silent in the conviction that in due course truth would prevail. Yet now Mommsen's articles on the tetrarchic consuls and prefects[83] are portrayed (by Schwartz) as fundamental and his own proposals ignored it is his scholarly duty to set the record straight and defend himself.[84] Seeck attempts to do this by pointing out that determination of correct dates for laws in the Code is a notoriously difficult and frustrating problem. Despite the occasional moment of despair he decided to commit himself to proposing some solutions in 1889. It was this which Mommsen attacked in his 1900 article. Then follows what appears to be an extraordinary piece of special pleading, given that Mommsen was long dead. Seeck claims that Mommsen regretted the tone of his article but it was too late to change it, that he himself wrote a reply which the editor of *Hermes* refused to publish, that he was now glad of this rejection because he would not have wanted to hurt the feelings of the aged Mommsen, but that now he was dead his mistakes needed contradiction.[85] So Seeck proceeds.

Finally, in his prolegomena Mommsen refrained from determining the tenure of magistrates and promised that there would be a late Roman prosopography which would be the appropriate place for treating such questions. It is evident that close work on the Code in recent years had set Mommsen thinking about the need for such a prosopography to establish the careers of the addressees. In fact he was actively preparing prosopographical slips while working on his edition. Likewise it was work on the text of the Code which made him realise how valuable it would be to have a chronological list of officials and dates for the period from Diocletian to Justinian.[86] In 1900 he submitted to his colleagues on the *Kirchenväterkommission*, set up to produce a series of texts on the Greek church fathers of the first three centuries, plans for a continuation of the recently completed *Prosopographia Imperii Romani* down to the end of the sixth century – in effect a 'Prosopography of the Later Roman Empire' to include both secular and ecclesiastical strands, and a secular strand under the direction of Seeck.[87] Work commenced

[82] Seeck, 'Zur Charakteristik Mommsens', 81-3 (letter on 82). Seeck's assistance was duly acknowledged (prol., ccclx).

[83] T. Mommsen, 'Consularia', *Hermes* 32 (1897), 538-53 (= *GS* 6, 324-38); plus the 'Nachtrag' in *Hermes* 36 (1901), 602-5 (= *GS* 6, 338-42).

[84] O. Seeck, 'Neue und alte Daten zur Geschichte Diocletians und Constantins', *RM* n.f. 62 (1907), 501.

[85] ibid., 502-3.

[86] *Hermes* 32 (1897), 538 (= *GS* 6, 324).

[87] For details F. Winkelmann, 'Prosopographia Imperii Romani saec. IV, V, VI' in J. Irmscher (ed.), *Adolf Harnack und der Fortschritt in der Altertumswissenschaft; zu*

on the prosopography in the winter of 1901/2 with Mommsen
excerpting prosopographical notices from the Theodosian Code which
he was in the course of editing, as well as from the Code of Justinian
and the histories of Ammianus Marcellinus and Zosimus. As the
material accumulated it provided the basis for several preparatory
studies. For example, it was work on the prosopography which gave
rise to many biographical entries written by Seeck for the early
volumes of the Pauly/Wissowa *Realenzyclopädie der Klassischen
Altertumswissenschaft*, in addition to his *Die Briefe des Libanius
zeitlich geordnet*[88] and the planned imperial and papal *Regesten* up to
the time of Justinian (actually to 600).[89] Only the period to 476 was
covered in the one published volume.[90]

As Seeck explicitly recognised in the preface to his *Regesten*,[91] the
edition of the Theodosian Code and the production of the Late Roman
prosopography had gone together in Mommsen's mind, as indeed had
the idea of a work such as the *Regesten* itself. Moreover, most of the
errors and flaws in the edition could be attributed to the fact that the
prosopography had not been completed before the edition. In the
intervening fifteen years or so work had progressed steadily on the
prosopography with the result that, as Mommsen had anticipated,
many of the constitutions could now be more correctly dated because it
was now possible to identify certain errors in the inscriptions and
subscriptions. What was now required was a systematic presentation
of Late Roman chronology taking all this into account – hence Seeck's
Regesten. It was now thirty years since Seeck had published his
preliminary study of the laws of Constantine and nearly twenty years
since Mommsen's riposte. This was long enough, especially given the
enormous amount of work which had been done in the meantime, for
Seeck to recognise the shortcomings of his original work. He
acknowledged that in matters of detail Mommsen had been right but
insisted that despite his mistakes he himself had established the right
methods and directions which led to the solutions of so many
problems.[92] In addition, the research for his *Geschichte des Untergangs
der antiken Welt* had obliged Seeck to analyse the date of each law
independently.[93] Finally he explained that he and Mommsen had
largely agreed on the doubtful dates but that Mommsen had thought it

---

seinem 50. Todestag (Berlin, 1981), 29-34; and for the original prosopography: K.-P.
Johne, '100 Jahre Prosopographia Imperii Romani', *Klio* 56 (1974), 21-7.
  [88] (Leipzig, 1906; repr 1966), 1-2.
  [89] See especially Seeck's letters to Hans Lietzmann in K. Aland (ed.), *Glanz und
Niedergang der deutschen Universität: 50 Jahre deutscher Wissenschaftsgeschichte in
Briefen an und von Hans Lietzmann (1892-1942)*, (Berlin/New York, 1979), 414 and 428.
  [90] *Regesten der Kaiser und Päpste für die Jahre 311 bis 476 n. Chr.* (Stuttgart, 1919).
  [91] ibid., vii.
  [92] ibid., 1.
  [93] ibid., 2.

impossible to correct some of them, whereas he had been prepared to try and do so. For Seeck Mommsen's approach had been too limited.[94] Ultimately, however, it can be acknowledged that many of the inscriptions in the Code do require radical correction but that the process of correction can be quite frustrating. Seeck discovered this, and it was reinforced by the rapid exchange in the mid 1930s between Jean-Rémy Palanque (b. 1898) on the one side with Ernst Stein (1891-1945) and Higgins, his pupil at the Catholic University of America (Washington, DC), on the other.[95] As we come to understand better how the Code was put together, and from what sources, we have a more compelling rationale for solving specific problems of imperial and consular dating by drastic emendation.[96]

IV

In the final analysis it must be said that Mommsen's edition benefited immeasurably from Krüger's preparatory work which was acknowledged on the very title page (*adsumpto apparatu P. Kruegeri*) and at other appropriate points.[97] Nevertheless, rather than reflect on what he owed to Mommsen (who had taken him on as a collaborator in his early twenties and set him on the path of his life's work in philological jurisprudence), Krüger carried to his grave the bitter feeling that Mommsen had deprived him of his greatest achievement.[98] For the decade after the appearance of Mommsen's edition Krüger continued to leave aside his own work on the Code. Then he produced a series of critical essays on various aspects of the text without himself contemplating a new edition.[99] On his retirement at Bonn, however, he directed his attention towards finalising a completely fresh edition and on 15 September 1921 signed a contract with Weidmann (Berlin) for a work 'in the same Format and similar layout as the *Codex Theodosianus* likewise published by Weidmann'.[100] By now too he was the same age Mommsen had been when editing the Code (his early eighties) but he was not as organised and had no collaborator on which

[94] ibid., 155-7.

[95] E. Stein, 'A propos d'un livre récent sur la liste des préfets du prétoire', *Byzantion* 9 (1934), 327-53; M. Higgins, 'Reliability of Titles and Dates in Codex Theodosianus', *Byzantion* 10 (1935), 621-40; J.-R. Palanque, 'Sur la liste des préfets du prétoire du IVe siècle', *Byzantion* 9 (1934), 706-13 and *Byzantion* 10 (1935), 641-2.

[96] Some examples in R. Bagnall, A. Cameron, S. Schwartz, K. Worp, *Consuls of the Later Roman Empire* (Atlanta, 1987), 71ff.; others in Barnes, *The New Empire of Diocletian and Constantine*, 47ff., 140ff.

[97] prol. xxxix (*operis nostri socio*), lxv, lxviii, lxxii, lxxvii, lxxxiii, lxxxiv.

[98] Schulz, 'Paul Krüger', xxvii.

[99] 'Beiträge zur Codex Theodosianus', *ZSS RA* 34 (1913), 1-12; 37 (1916), 88-103; 38 (1917), 20ff.; 40 (1919), 98ff.; 41 (1920), 1ff.; 42 (1921), 58-67.

[100] 'Verlagsvertrag' (Krüger's copy) among his papers preserved in Bonn (see n. 101 below).

to draw. Further, he was plagued by increasing personal trauma and loss of memory but did manage to produce half of his edition in print: vol. 1 (Books 1-6) in 1923; vol. 2 (Books 7-8) in 1926.[101] In all, it did not supersede Mommsen's edition although it improved on it in some particulars.

In reviewing Mommsen's edition Paul Maas concluded that 'It was not granted the tireless ploughman to gaze on the crop. May it spring up soon and abundantly.'[102] In general, it would appear that Maas's expectation was not met. Now that we have a serviceable prosopography, however, things are on the move. Yet interest has shifted from textual and chronological problems to the individuality of jurists, the structure and compilation of the Code, as well as its ideology and socio-economic context.[103] By the 1890s the sort of fundamental philological work embodied in Mommsen's edition was urgently required for the Later Roman Empire. As he phrased it himself, 'The dark transition between antiquity and modern history must be illustrated from both sides and science stands before it as engineers before a mountain tunnel ... .'[104] By his own conception, therefore, within a few years Mommsen was busy advancing into the tunnel and soon extracted the lode of the Theodosian Code.

Unfortunately, he did not live to exploit this rich ore. He certainly would have liked to. In fact in his latter years he used to say that if he could have his time over again he would devote it entirely to the period from Diocletian to Justinian.[105] None the less, all his scholarly life Mommsen had been intimately involved with the Theodosian Code because he was always thinking about it and engaged in solving the

[101] ibid xxx-xxxi. It appears that Krüger's edition of the remaining books (9-16) was actually completed and was still with the publisher (Weidmann, Berlin) when the archive was destroyed during the allied bombing of Berlin during the Second World War. Among the papers of Krüger preserved in the University Library at Bonn are the notes to his text of Books 9 to 16 as well as some pages which were evidently intended to form part of his prolegomenon. Also preserved there is the publication contract and a curt letter from the publishers (15 July 1925) testifying to Krüger's failing memory. In addition there is the Mommsen/Krüger correspondence concerning Mommsen's edition of the Code (1899-1903) used by Schulz in his article on Krüger in *ZSS RA* 47. I am grateful to Boudewijn Sirks (Amsterdam) for information on this discovery and for providing copies of some of the documents.

[102] Maas, *Göttingische gelehrte Anzeigen* (1906), 628

[103] Wieacker, *Römische Rechtsgeschichte*, 53-5; cf. T. Honoré, 'The Making of the Theodosian Code', *ZSS RA* 103 (1986), 133-222 and the literature there cited.

[104] 'Die Bewirthschaftigung der Kirchengüter unter Papst Gregor I', *Zeitschrift für Sozial. und Wirtschaftsgeschichte*, 1 (1893), 43 (= *GS* 3, 177). Mommsen's pupil Ludo Hartmann had asked him to set out his views on the management of church property under Pope Gregory the Great in the first number of Hartmann's new journal. Mommsen was apparently reluctant to oblige and in doing so pointed out that he was venturing 'beyond the boundaries of my field of work'.

[105] W. Ramsay, *Pauline and other Studies in Early Christian History* (London, 1906), 393 and Diary of L. von Pastor, 20 March 1902, in W. Wühr, ed., *L. von Pastor, Tagebücher-Briefe-Erinnerungen* (Heidelberg, 1950), 385.

philological and historical questions it poses. He regarded his edition as simply the foundation on which future scholarship could build.[106] Mommsen's edition of the Code has been an invaluable contribution to late Roman studies and remains so.

---

[106] L. Hartmann, *Theodor Mommsen* (Gotha, 1908), 99.

Bibliography

Primary sources and abbreviations

ACO = *Acta Conciliorum Oecumenicorum*, ed. E. Schwartz.

AE = *Année Épigraphique*.

Ag. Lib. Adv. leg. Gund. = Agobard, *liber Adversus legem Gundorbadi* (in *PL* 104).

AJPh. = *American Journal of Philology*.

Amm. Marc. = Ammianus Marcellinus, *Res Gestae*.

ANRW = *Aufstieg und Niedergang der Römischen Welt*.

Avit. = Avitus of Vienne, ed. R. Peiper, *MGH AA* vi 2 (1883).

Barnes, *CE* = T.D. Barnes, *Constantine and Eusebius* (1981).

Barnes, *NE* = T.D. Barnes, *New Empire of Diocletian and Constantine* (1982).

Besse = J.C. Besse, *Histoire des texts du droit de l'Église au Moyen âge de Denis à Gratien. Collectio Anselmo Dedicata* (Paris, 1960).

Blockley = R. Blockley, *The fragmentary classicising historians of the late Roman Empire: Eutropius, Olympiodorus, Priscus, Malchus* (Liverpool, 1981).

Brev. Alar. = *Breviarum Alaricianum*, ed. M. Conrat (Cohn) (Leipzig, 1903).

Cap. Merow. = *Capitularia Merowingica*, ed. A. Boretius, *MGH Capitularia Regum Francorum* I (1883).

CC = *Corpus Christianorum*.

CICan = *Corpus Iuris Canonici*, ed. E.A. Friedberg (Leipzig, 1879-81).

CICiv = *Corpus Iuris Civilis*.

CIL = *Corpus Inscriptionum Latinarum*.

CJ = *Classical Journal*.

CJust = *Codex Justinianus*.

CLA = *Codices Latini Antiquiores*.

CLRE = *Consuls of the Later Roman Empire*, ed. R.S. Bagnall et al. (1987).

Collatio = *Collatio legum Mosaicarum et Romanarum*.

Conc. Aev. Merow. = *Concilia Aevi Merowingici*, ed. F. Maassen, *MGH* Leges III Concilia I (Hannover, 1893).

Conc. Gall. = *Concilia Galliae* A.511-695 ed. C. De Clercq, *CC Ser. Lat.* 148A (1963).

Const. Sirm. = *Constitutiones Sirmondiae*: see Sirmond, *Appendix*.

Consultatio = *Consultatio veteris cuiusdam iurisconsulti*.

C.q.c. = *Causa, quaestio, canonum* in part II of Gratian, *Decretum*.

CSEL = *Corpus Scriptorum Ecclesiasticorum Latinorum* (Vienna).

CTh = *Codex Theodosianus*, ed. Th. Mommsen, 1905; also ed. G. Haenel (Bonn, 1842); tr. C. Pharr et al., *The Theodosian Code and the Sirmondian Constitutions* (New York, 1952).

Dig. = Justinian, *Digest*.

Dist. = *Distinctio*, a division of part I of Gratian, *Decretum*.
EHR = *English Historial Review*.
Ep. Aeg. = *Epitome Aegidii*.
Ep. Iul. = *Epitome Iuliani*, ed. G. Haenel (Leipzig, 1873).
FHG = *Fragmenta Historicorum Graecorum*, ed. C. Mueller.
FIRA² = *Fontes Iuris Romani Anteiustiniani* (2nd ed. 1940).
Form. And. = *Formulae Andecavenses* (Formulae of Angers).
Form. Arv. = *Formulae Arvernenses* (Formulae of Arverni (Clermont)).
Form. Bit. = *Formulae Bituricenses* (Formulae of Bourges).
Form. Tur. = *Formulae Turonenses* (Formulae of Tours).
Formulae; edited by K. Zeumer as *Formulae Merowingici et Karolini aevi*, *MGH Leges* (Hannover, 1886).
Fredegar, ed. B Krusch, *MGH SRM* II (Hannover, 1888).
FV = *Fragmenta quae dicuntur Vaticana* (*FIRA²* II, 464-540).
Gaudemet, J. and Basdevant, B., ed., *Les Canons des conciles merovingiens*, 2 vols (Paris, 1989).
GRBS = *Greek, Roman and Byzantine Studies*.
Greg. Tur. *DLH* = Gregory of Tours, *Decem Libri Historiarum*, ed. B. Krusch and W. Levison, *MGH SRM* I:1. (1951).
Greg. Tur. *VP* = Gregory of Tours, *Liber Vitae Patrum*, ed. B. Krusch, *MGH SRM* I.2. (Hannover, 1885).
GS = Th. Mommsen, *Gesammelte Schriften* (Berlin, 1905-13).
HE = *Historia Ecclesiastica*.
Hinschius, *Decretales* = P. Hinschius, *Decretales Pseudo-Isidorianae et capituli Angilramni* (Leipzig, 1863; repr. Aalen 1963).
IG = *Inscriptiones Graecae*.
ILS = *Inscriptiones Latinae Selectae*, ed. H. Dessau (1892-1916).
Inst. = Justinian, *Institutes*.
Int. = *Interpretatio* to a text in *CTh*, *LRV*.
IRMAE = *Ius Romanum Medii Aevi* (Giuffré, Milan).
Isidore = *Sancti Isidori Hispalensis episcopi Etymologiarum libri XX* in *PL* 82 and W.M. Lindsay, 2 vols. (Oxford, 1911).
Iuliani epitome latina novellarum Iustiniani, ed. G Haenel (Leipzig, 1873).
Ivo, *Decretum* = *Ivonis Carnotensis episcopi Decretum in partes XVII*, ed. J. Molin (Louvain, 1561); repr. carelessly *PL* 161.
Ivo, *Panormia* = *Panormia Ivonis Carnotensis episcopi libri VIII*, ed. S. Brant (Basel, 1499); repr. *PL* 161.
Jb. Ant. Chr. = *Jahrbuch für Antike und Christentum*.
JEA = *Journal of Egyptian Archaeology*.
Jones, *LRE* = A.H.M. Jones, *The Later Roman Empire AD 284-602: A Social, Economic and Administrative Survey* (Oxford, 1964).
JRS = *Journal of Roman Studies*.
JTS = *Journal of Theological Studies*.
Lact., *De Mort. Pers.* = Lactantius, *De Mortibus Persecutorum (On the Deaths of the Persecutors)*.
Lex. Burg. and *Lex. Rom. Burg.* = *Leges Burgundionum* and *Lex Romana Burgundionum* ed. L.R. de Salis, *MGH Leges* II.1. (Hannover, 1892).
Lex Baiw. = *Lex Baiwariorum*, ed. E. Heymann, *MGH Leges* V.1 (Hannover, 1926).
Lex Rib. = *Lex Ribvaria*, ed. F. Beyerle and R. Buchner, *MGH Leges* III.2 (Hannover, 1954).

Lib. Const. = *Liber Constitutionum* ed. L.R. Salis, *MGH Leges* II.1 (Hannover, 1892).
Liber Extra (or *X*) = Decretals of Gregory IX, 1234.
LRV = *Lex Romana Visigothorum*, ed. G. Haenel (Berlin, 1849) (see also *Brev. Alar.* above).
Marculf = Marculf, *Formulary*, ed. K. Zeumer, *MGH Formulae*.
MEFRA = *Mélanges de l'École française à Rome: Antiquité*.
MGH = *Monumenta Germaniae Historica*.
MGH AA = *Monumenta Germaniae Historica: Auctores Antiquissimi*.
MGH SRM = *Monumenta Germaniae Historica: Scriptores Rerum Merovingicarum*.
Mommsen, see *CTh*.
Nov. = Novel, *Novella Constitutio*.
Novellae constitutiones imperatorum Theodosii II, Valentiniani III, Maximi, Maioriani, Severi, Anthemii. XVIII constitutiones, quas Iacobus Sirmondus divulgavit (Bonn, 1844).
NAnth = Novel of Anthemius (Augustus 467-72).
NMaj = Novel of Majorian (Augustus 457-61).
NTh = Novel of Theodosius II (Augustus 402-50).
NVal = Novel of Valentinian III (Augustus 425-55).
Pact. Leg. Sal. = *Pactus Legis Salicae*, ed. K.A. Eckhardt, *MGH Leges* IV.1 (1962).
Pan. Lat. = *Panegyrici Latini*, ed. R.A.B. Mynors (Oxford, 1964).
Pass. Praeiecti = *Passio Praeiecti*, ed. B. Krusch, *MGH SRM* V (1910).
Pass. Leudegarii = *Passiones Leudegarii*, ed. B. Krusch, ibid.
Paul. Sent. = *Pauli Sententiae*.
PBA = *Proceedings of the British Academy*.
PCPhS = *Proceedings of the Cambridge Philological Society*.
PL = Migne, *Patrologia Latina*.
PLRE = *Prosopography of the Later Roman Empire* I (1971), II (1980).
P.Oxy. = *Oxyrhynchus Papyri*, ed. B.P. Grenfell et al. (1898-).
PSI = *Papiri greci e latini*, edd. G. Vitelli et al. (1912-).
QCA = *Quinque Compilationes Antiquae*, ed. E.A. Friedberg (Leipzig, 1882).
RE = *Real Encyclopädie*.
REA = *Revue des Études Anciennes*.
Regino = *Reginonis abbatis Prumiensis libri II de synodalibus causis et disciplinis ecclesiasticis*, ed. F.G.A. Wasserschleben (Leipzig, 1840; repr. Gray, 1964): also *PL* 132.
REL = *Revue des Études Latines*.
RHDFE = *Revue Historique du droit français et étranger*.
RHE = *Revue d'Histoire Ecclésiastique*.
RIC = *Roman Imperial Coinage*.
RIDA = *Revue Internationale des droits de l'Antiquité*.
RM = *Rheinisches Museum für Philologie*.
SBAW = *Sitzungsberichte der königlichen Preussischen Akademie der Wissenschaften zu Berlin*.
SChr = *Sources chrétiennes*.
SDHI = *Studia e Documenta Historiae Iuris*.
Seeck, *Regesten* = O. Seeck, *Regesten der Kaiser und Päpste für die Jahre 311 bis 476 n.Chr. Vorarbeit zu einer Prosopographie der christlichen Kaiserzeit* (Stuttgart, 1919).

Sid. Ap. = Sidonius Apollinaris, *Opera*, ed. A. Loyen (Paris, 1960-70).
Sirmond, *Concilia* = J. Sirmond, *Concilia Antiqua Galliae cum epistolis pontificum, principum constitutionibus, et aliis Gallicanae rei ecclesiasticae monumentis*, 3 vols. (Paris, 1629).
Sirmond, *Appendix* = J. Sirmond, *Appendix Codicis Theodosiani novis Constitutionibus cumulatior. Cum epistolis aliquot veterum conciliorum et pontificum Romanorum nunc primum editis* (Paris, 1631).
Stud. Patr. = *Studia Patristica*.
Symm = Q. Aurelius Symmachus, *Opera*, ed. O. Seeck, *MGH AA* VI (1883).
VC = Eusebius, *Vita Constantini*.
Vig. Christ. = *Vigiliae Christianae*.
Vit. Bon. = *Vita Boniti*, ed. B. Krusch, *MGH SRM* VI (Hannover, 1913).
Vit. Des. = *Vita Desiderii*; ed. B. Krusch, *MGH SRM* IV (Hannover, 1902).
Vives = J. Vives, *Concilios Hispano-Visigoticos* (Latin and Spanish tr. Barcelona, 1963).
Zos. = Zosimus, *New History*.
ZPE = *Zeitschrift für Papyrologie und Epigraphik*.
ZSS RA = *Zeitschrift der Savigny-Stiftung, Romanistische Abteilung*.

Secondary sources

ALAND, K. (ed.), *Glanz und Niedergang der deutschen Universität: 50 Jahre deutscher Wissenschaftsgeschichte in Briefen an und von Hans Lietzmann (1892-1942)* (Berlin/New York, 1979).
ALBANESE, B., 'Sul programma legislativo esposto nel 429 da Teodosio II', *APal* 38 (1975) 251-69.
———— 'L'abolozione postclassical delle forme solenni nei negozi testamentari', in *Sodalitas: Scritti in Onore di Antonio Guarino* 2 (Naples, 1984) 777-92.
Allgemeine Deutsche Biographie (Munich, 1875-1912).
ANDREOTTI, R., 'L'imperatore Licinio nella tradizione storiografica latina', in *Hommages à Léon Herrmann* (Brussels, 1956) 105-23.
———— 'Licinius (Valerius Licinianus)', in E. de Ruggiero (ed.), *Dizionario Epigrafico di Antichità Romane* vol. 4 fasc. 32 (Rome, 1959) 979-1041.
ANNE, L., *Les Rites des Fiançailles et la donation pour cause de mariage sous le Bas-Empire* (Louvain, 1941).
ARCHI, G.G., *Teodosio II e la sua codificazione* (Napoli, 1976).
ARJAWA, A., 'Divorce in Later Roman Law', *Arctos* 22 (1988) 5-21
AX, W., 'Probleme des Sprachstils als Gegenstand des lateinischen Philologie', in C.J. Classen, A. Heuss, K. Nickaü, W. Richter and P. Zanker, *Beiträge zur Altertumswissenschaft* (Hildesheim, New York, 1976).
BAGNALL, R.S., 'Church, State and Divorce in Late Roman Egypt', in *Florilegium Columbanum: Essays in honour of Paul Oskar Kristeller*, ed. R.E. Somerville and L.-L. Selig (New York, 1987) 41-61.
BAGNALL, R.S., CAMERON, A., SCHWARTZ, S.R., & WORP, K.A., *Consuls of the Later Roman Empire* (Atlanta GA, 1987).
BARLOW, F., *The English Church 1066-1154* (London, 1979).
BARB, A.A., 'The Survival of Magic Arts', in A.D. Momigliano (ed.), *The Conflict between Paganism and Christianity* (Oxford, 1963) 100-25.
BARKER, N., *Portrait of an Obession, the Life of Sir T. Phillipps the World's Greatest Book Collector* (London, 1967).
BARNES, T.D., 'Lactantius and Constantine', *JRS* 63 (1973) 29-46.

———— 'Three Imperial Edicts', *ZPE* 21 (1976) 275-81.

———— 'A Correspondent of Iamblichus', *GRBS* 19 (1978) 99-106.

———— 'The Editions of Eusebius' *Ecclesiastical History*', *GRBS* 21 (1980) 191-201.

———— *Constantine and Eusebius* (Cambridge, MA and London, 1981).

———— *The New Empire of Diocletian and Constantine* (Cambridge, MA and London, 1982).

———— 'Literary Convention, Nostalgia and Reality in Ammianus Marcellinus', in Graeme Clarke (ed.), *Reading the Past in Late Antiquity* (Rushcutters Bay, 1990) 59-92.

BATE, H.N., 'C.H. Turner', *Dictionary of National Biography, 1922-30* (Oxford, 1937) 861-4.

BEAUCAMP, J., 'Le vocabulaire de la faiblesse feminine dans les textes juridiques romains du IIIᵉ au IVᵉ sièle', *RHDFE* 54 (1976) 485-508.

van BERCHEM, D., *L'Armée de Dioclétien et la Réforme Constantinienne* (Institut Français d'Archéologie de Beyrouth, Bibliothèque Archéologique et Historique 56, Paris, 1952).

BESSE, J.C., *Histoire des textes du droit de l'Église au moyen âge de Denis à Gratien. Collectio Anselmo Dedicata* (Paris, 1960).

BLUMENTAL, U.R., *The Investiture Controversy* (Philadelphia, 1988).

BOSWELL, J., *The Kindness of Strangers* (London, 1989).

BRESSLAU, H., 'Die Commentarii der romischen Kaiser und die Registerbücher der Päpste', *ZSS RA* 6 (1885) 242-60.

BRIZZI, G., 'La vittoria sarmatica di Costantino e la propaganda liciniana', *Alba Regia* 17 (1979) 59-63.

BROWN, P., *Augustine of Hippo* (London, 1967).

————, *Religion and Society in the Age of Saint Augustine* (London, 1972).

BRUUN, P., *Studies in Constantinian Chronology* (Numismatic Notes and Monographs 146; New York, 1961).

———— 'The Heraclean Coinage of Maximinus Daza. A Drastic Proposal', in *Studies in Ancient History and Numismatics presented to Rudi Thomsen* (Aarhus, 1988) 179-94.

BURY, J.B., *The Constitution of the Later Roman Empire* (Cambridge, 1910).

Cambridge Ancient History XII: The Imperial Crisis and Recovery A.D. 193-324 (Cambridge, 1939).

CAMPBELL, J., *Honour, Family and Patronage* (1964).

CARCOPINO, J., 'The Life and Works of Theodor Mommsen', in *Nobel Prize Library* (New York, 1971).

CARLYLE, R.W. & A.J., *History of Medieval Political Thought in the West* (Edinburgh, 1903-36).

CASTELLO, C., 'Rapporti legislativi tra Costantino e Licinio alla luce dell' *subscriptio* di *CTh*. 8, 18, 1', in *Accademia Romanistica Costantiniana, Atti: Il Convegno Internazionale 1975* (Perugia, 1976) 39-47.

———— 'Assenza d'ispirazione cristiana in *CTh* 3.16.1', in *Religion, Société et Politique. Melanges en hommage a Jacques Ellul* (1983) 203-12.

CHASTAGNOL, A., *Les Fastes de la Préfecture de Rome au Bas-Empire* (Paris, 1962).

———— 'L'inscription constantinienne d'Orcistus', *MEFRA* 93 (1981) 381-416.

———— Les modes de recrutement du senat au IVᵉ siècle après J.C.', in *Recherches sur les structures sociales dans l'Antiquite classique* (1970) 187-211.

CHRIST, K., *Römische Geschichte und Deutsche Geschichtswissenschaft* (Munich, 1982).

CHRISTOL, M. & DREW-BEAR, T., 'Documents latins de Phrygie', *Tyche* 1 (1986) 41-87.

COLLINS, R., *Early Medieval Spain* (London, 1983).

CONRAT, M., *Geschichte der Quellen und Literatur des römischen Rechts im früheren Mittelalter* I (Leipzig, 1891).

CORBETT, P.E., *The Roman Law of Marriage* (Oxford, 1930).

COSTA, E.A., 'The Office of the *Castrensis Sacri Palatii* in the IVth Century', *Byzantion* 42 (1972) 358-87.

CRASTER, H.H., 'Francis Haverfield', *EHR* 35 (1920) 63-70.

CRAWFORD, M.H. & REYNOLDS, J., 'The Publication of the Prices Edict: A New Inscription from Aezani', *JRS* 65 (1975) 160-3.

CROKE, B., 'Theodor Mommsen and the Later Roman Empire', *Chiron* 20 (1990) 163-93.

DAGRON, G., *Naissance d'une capitale: Constantinople et ses institutions de 330 à 451* (Paris, 1974).

de DECKER, D., 'La politique religieuse de Maxence', *Byzantion* 38 (1968) 472-562.

DEKKERS, E. & GAAR, A., (edd.), *Clavis Patrum Latinorum* (2nd ed., Steenbrugge, 1961).

DELMAIRE, R., *Largesses Sacrées et 'Res Privata'. L' 'Aerarium' Impérial et son Administration du IVe au VIe Siècle* (Collection de L'École Française de Rome 121; Rome, 1989).

DIXON, S., '*Infirmitas sexus*: Womanly Weakness in Roman Law', *Tidjshrift voor Rechtsgesiednis* 52 (1984) 343-71.

——— *The Roman Mother* (London, 1988).

DOWNEY, G., *A History of Antioch in Syria from Seleucus to the Arab Conquest* (Princeton, New Jersey, 1961).

DUCHESNE, L., *Fastes episcopaux de l'ancienne Gaule*, 3 vols (2nd ed. Paris 1907-15).

DUBY, G., *La femme, le chevalier et le prêtre* (Paris, 1981); trans *The Knight, the Lady and the Priest* (New York, 1983).

DUPONT, C., *Les Constitutions de Constantin et le droit privé au debut du IVe siècle* (Lille, 1937).

——— *Le droit criminel dans les constitutions de Constantin: les infractions* (1953).

——— 'Les privilèges des clercs sous Constantin', *RHE* 62 (1967) 729-52.

ELLIOTT, T.G., 'The tax exemptions granted to clerics by Constantine and Constantius II', *Phoenix* 32 (1978) 326-36.

ENSSLIN, W., *Die Religionspolitik des Kaisers Theodosius d. Gr.* (Munich, 1953).

EVANS GRUBBS, J., 'Abduction Marriage in Antiquity: A Law of Constantine (*CTh* ix.24.1) and its Social Context', *JRS* 79 (1989) 59-83.

EWIG, E., 'Die fränkischen Teilungen und Teilreiche (511-613)' in idem, *Spätantikes und fränkisches Gallien* I (Munich, 1976).

FOURACRE, P., ' "Placita" and the settlement of disputes in later Merovingian Francia', in W. Davies and P. Fouracre (edd.), *The Settlement of Disputes in Early Medieval Europe* (Cambridge, 1986).

FOURNIER, P., 'Les collections canoniques attribuées à Yves de Chartres', *Bulletin de l'École des Chartes* 57 (1896) 645-98; 58 (1897) 26-77, 410-44, 624-76.

FOURNIER, P., & LE BRAS, G., *Histoire des collections canoniques en occident depuis les Fausses Décrétales jusqu'au Décret de Gratien*, 2 vols (Paris, 1931-2).

FRIDH, Å.J., *Terminologie et formules dans les Variae de Cassiodore: Étude sur le développement du style administratif aux derniers siècles de l'antiquité* (Stockholm 1956).

FRIEDBERG, E.A., *Canonessammlungen zwischen Gratianus und Bernardus von Pavia* (Leipzig, 1887; repr. Graz, 1958).

FUNKE, H., 'Majestäts- und Magieprozesse bei Ammianus Marcellinus', *Jb. Ant. Chr.* 10 (1967) 145-75.

FUSCO, S.-A., '*Constitutiones principum* und Kodifikation in der Spätantike', *Chiron* 4 (1974) 609-28.

GALTIER, P., 'Sirmond', *Dictionnaire de Théologie Catholique* 14, 2 (1941) cols. 2186-93.

GANSHOF, F.L., *Recherches sure les capitulaires* (Paris, 1958).

———— 'Le droit romain dans les capitulaires et collectio Ansegisis' (1969) *IRMAE* 1.2.b.cc.α>-6.

GARDNER, J., *Women in Roman Law and Society* (London, 1986).

GARNSEY, P., *Social Status and Legal Privilege in the Roman Empire* (Oxford, 1970).

———— *Famine and Food Supply in the Greco-Roman World* (1988).

GAUDEMET, J., *L'église dans l'empire romain* (Paris, 1958).

———— 'Théodosian (Code). Compléments', *Dictionnaire du Droit Canonique* 7 (1962) cols. 1229-30.

———— 'Le brévaire d'Alaric et ses epitome' (1965), *IRMAE* 1.2.b.c.c.6.

———— 'Le droit romain dans le pratique et chez les docteurs aux XIᵉ et XIIᵉ siècles', *Cahiers de Civilisation Médiévale* 8 (1965) 365-80.

———— 'Recherches sur la législation du Bas-Empire' in *Studi in Onore di Gaetano Scherillo* 2 (Milan, 1972) 693-715.

———— 'Tendances nouvelles de la legislation familiale au IVᵉ siècle', *Transformation et conflits au IVᵉ siècle ap. J.C., Antiquitas* 29 (Bonn, 1978) 187-206.

———— *La formation du droit séculier et du droit de l'église au IVe et Ve siècles* (Institut de Droit Romain de l'Université de Paris 15; Paris, 1979, 2nd edition).

———— 'Aspects politiques de la codification theodosienne', *Atti di un incontro tra storici e giuristi Firenze 2-4 maggio 1974* (Milano 1976), 261-79; repr. in J. Gaudemet, *Études de droit romain*, vol. I (Camerino 1979) 349-69.

———— *Institutions de l'Antiquité* (2nd ed., Paris, 1982).

———— 'Les constitutions Constantiniennes du Code Theodosien', *Accademia Romanistica Costantiniana: Atti V Convegno* (Padova, 1983) 136-55.

———— *Les sources du droit de l'Église en Occident du IIᵉ au VIIᵉ siècle* (Paris, 1985).

GERO, S., 'The True Image of Christ: Eusebius' Letter to Constantia Reconsidered', *JTS* 32 (1981) 460-70.

GIBBON, E., *Memoirs of My Life* (ed. G.A. Bonnard, 1966).

GILLERT, K., 'Lateinische Handschriften in St Petersburg', *Neues Archiv* 5 (1879) 241-65, 597-617; 6 (1880) 497-511.

GIRARDET, K.M., *Kaisergericht und Bischofsgericht* (Bonn, 1975).

GORCE, D., (ed. and transl.), *Vie de sainte Mélanie* (Greek version), *SChr* 90 (1962).

van GRONINGEN, A., *A Family-archive from Tebtunis* (Papyrologica Lugduno-Batava VI; Leyden, 1950).

GRODZYNSKI, D., 'Superstitio', *REA* 76 (1974) 36-60.

GWATKIN, H.M., *Studies of Arianism* (Cambridge, 1882).

HABICHT, C., 'Zur Geschichte des Kaisers Konstantin', *Hermes* 86 (1958) 360-78.

HABICHT, C. & KUSSMAUL, P., 'Ein neues Fragment des Edictum de Accusationibus', *Museum Helveticum* 43 (1986) 135-44.

HAENEL, G., *Catalogi Librorum manuscriptorum qui in bibliothecis Galliae, Helvetiae, Belgii, Britanniae M., Hispaniae, Lusitaniae asservantur* (Leipzig, 1830).

—— *De constitutionibus quas Iacobus Sirmondus a. 1631 edidit dissertatio* (Leipzig, 1840).

HANSON, R.P.C., *The Search for the Christian Doctrine of God* (Edinburgh, 1988).

HARRIES, J.D., 'Church and State in the *Notitia Galliarum*', *JRS* 68 (1978) 26-43.

—— 'The Roman Imperial Quaestor from Constantine to Theodosius II', *JRS* 78 (1988) 148-72.

HARTMANN, L., *Theodor Mommsen* (Gotha, 1908).

HEATHER, P. & MATTHEWS, J., *The Goths in the Fourth Century* (Liverpool, 1991).

HEICHELHEIM, F.M., 'The text of the *Constitutio Antoniniana* and the three other decrees of the Emperor Caracalla contained in Papyrus Gissensis 40', *Journal of Egyptian Archaeology* 26 (1940) 10-22.

HIGGINS, M., 'Reliability of Titles and Dates in *Codex Theodosianus*', *Byzantion* 10 (1935) 621-40.

HIRSCHFELD, O., 'Theodor Mommsen', *Abhandlungen der königlichen Preussischen Akademie der Wissenschaften* (1904) 1025.

HOLUM, J., *Theodosian Empresses* (Berkeley 1982).

HONIG, R.M., *Humanitas und Rhetorik in spätrömischen Kaisergesetzen. Studien zur Gesinnungsgrundlage des Dominats* (Göttingen 1960).

HONORÉ, T., 'Some Constitutions composed by Justinian', *JRS* 65 (1975) 107-23.

—— *Emperors and Lawyers* (London, 1981).

—— 'Ausonius and Vulgar Law', *IVRA* 35 (1984/1987) 75-85.

—— 'The Making of the Theodosian Code', *ZSS RA* 103 (1986) 133-222.

—— *Virius Nicomachus Flavianus* (Xenia Heft 23: Konstanz 1989, mit einem Beitrag von John F. Matthews).

HOPKINS, K., *Conquerors and Slaves: Sociological Studies in Roman History*, vol. 1 (Cambridge, 1978).

HUMBERT, M., *Le remariage à Rome* (1972).

HUNT, E.D., 'St. Stephen in Minorca: An Episode in Jewish-Christian Relations in the Early 5th Century AD', *JTS* 33 (1982) 106-23.

—— 'Did Constantius II have Court Bishops?', *Stud. Patr.* 19 (1989) 86-90.

JACOBS, E., 'Die von der königlichen Bibliothek zu Berlin aus der Sammlung Phillipps erworbenen Handschriften', *Zentralblatt für Bibliothekswesen* 28 (1911) 23-9.

JOHNE, K.-P., '100 Jahre Prosopographia Imperii Romani' *Klio* 56 (1974) 21-7.

JOLOWICZ, H.F. & NICHOLAS, B., *Historical Introduction to the Study of Roman Law* (Cambridge, 3rd ed. 1972).

JONES, A.H.M., 'The Roman Civil Service (clerical and sub-clerical grades)', *JRS* 38 (1948) 38-55: reprinted in *Studies in Roman Government and Law* (Oxford, 1960) 151-75.

—— 'The Social Background of the Struggle between Paganism and Christianity' in A.D. Momigliano (ed.), *The Conflict between Paganism and*

Christianity in the Fourth Century (Oxford, 1963) 17-37.

—— 'Collegiate Prefectures', *JRS* 54 (1964) 78-89.

—— *The Later Roman Empire 284-602: A Social, Economic, and Administrative Survey* (Oxford, 1964).

JONES, A.H.M., MARTINDALE, J.R. & MORRIS (edd.), *The Prosopography of the Later Roman Empire: Volume I, AD 260-395* (Cambridge, 1971), *Volume II, A.D. 395-527* (Cambridge, 1980).

KAJANTO, I., 'On Divorce among the Common People of Rome', *Mélanges Marcel Dury (REL* 66 1969) 99-113.

KASER, M., *Römische Rechtsquellen und angewandte Juristenmethode* (Wien/Köln/Graz, 1986).

KELLEY, D.R., *Foundations of Modern Historical Scholarship* (New York, 1970).

KING, N.Q., *The Emperor Theodosius and the Establishment of Christianity* (London, 1961).

KRÜGER, P., 'Über die Zeitbestimmung der Constitutionen aus den Jahren 364-373, ein Beitrag zur Kritik des Codex Theodosianus', in *Commentationes philologae in honorem Th. Mommsen* (Berlin, 1877) 75-83.

—— 'Codicis Theodosiani fragmenta Taurinensia', *Abhandlungen der Berliner Akademie der Wissenschaften* 1879 (1880).

—— 'Die Vaticanischen Scholien zum Codex Theodosianus', *ZSS RA* 16 (1886) 138-40.

—— 'Über Mommsens Ausgabe des Codex Theodosianus', *ZSS* 26 (1905) 316-31.

—— *Geschichte der Quellen und Literatur des Römischen Rechts* (2nd ed., Munich and Leipzig, 1912).

—— 'Beiträge zur Codex Theodosianus', *ZSS RA* 34 (1913) 1-12; 37 (1916), 88-103; 38 (1917) 20-34; 41 (1920) 1-14; 42 (1921) 58-67.

KÜBLER, B., 'Isidorusstudien', *Hermes* 50 (1890), 496-526.

KUHNER, R./HOLZWEISSIG, F., *Ausfuhrliche Grammatik der Lateinischen Sprache* (Hannover, 1912).

KUNKEL, W., 'Paul Martin Meyer', *ZSS RA* 56 (1936) 428-9.

—— An Introduction to Roman Legal and Constitutional History, tr. J.M. Kelly (2nd edition, Oxford, 1973).

—— 'Theodor Mommsen als Jurist', *Chiron* 14 (1984) 369-80.

LIEBESCHUETZ, J.H.W.G., *Barbarians and Bishops: Army, Church, and State in the Age of Arcadius and Chrysostom* (Oxford, 1990).

LIEBS, D., 'OM 13,1 und das Reskriptenwesen in der Historia Augusta', in *Historia-Augusta-Colloquium Bonn 1982/3, Antiquitas* 4.17 (Bonn, 1985) 221-37.

—— *Die Jurisprudenz im spätantiken Italien (260-640 n. Chr.)* (Berlin, 1987).

LINDER, A., *The Jews in Roman Imperial Legislation* (Detroit, Michigan, 1987); English translation from the Hebrew of *ha-Yehudim veha-Yahadut be-huke ha-kesarut ha Romit* (Jerusalem, 1983).

LOWE, E.A., *Codices Lugdunenses Antiquissimi. Le scriptorium de Lyon, la plus ancienne école calligraphique de France*, Bibliothèque de la Ville de Lyon, Documents paléographiques, tupographiques, icongraphiques, fasc. III-IV (Lyon, 1924).

—— *Codices Latini Antiquiores*, 11 vols and suppl. (Oxford, 1934-71).

MAAS, P., 'Besprechung Theodosianus cum const. Sirmondianis et leges novellae, edd. Th. Mommsen – P.M. Meyer', *147te Göttingische gelehrten Anzeigen* (1906) 641-62; repr. in P. Maas, *Kleine Schriften*, ed. W. Buchwald (Munich, 1973) 608-28.

MAASSEN, E., 'Bibliotheca Latina juris canonici manuscripta [III-VI]', *Sitzungsberichte der Kaiserlichen Akademie der Wissenschaften zu Wien, Phil.-Hist. Cl.* 56 (1867) 157-212.

—— *Geschichte der Quellen und der Literatur des canonischen Rechts im Abendlande bis zum Ausgange des Mittelalters* I (Graz, 1870).

McCORMICK, M., *Eternal Victory* (Cambridge, 1986).

MACDONALD, G., 'F. Haverfield', *PBA* 9 (1919) 475-91.

McKITTERICK, R., 'Some Carolingian Law-books and their Function', in *Authority and Power, Festschrift for Walter Ullmann*, ed. B. Tierney and P. Lineham (Cambridge, 1980), 13-27.

—— 'The Scriptoria of Merovingian Gaul: A Survey of the Evidence', in H.B. Clarke and M. Brennan (edd.), *Columbanus and Merovingian Monasticism*, BAR International Series, 113 (Oxford, 1981) 173-207.

—— 'Knowledge of Canon Law in the Frankish Kingdoms Before 789: The Manuscript Evidence', *JTS* n.s. 36 (1985) 97-117.

—— *The Carolingians and the Written Word* (Cambridge, 1989).

MACMULLEN, R., *Christianizing the Roman Empire (AD 100-400)* (New Haven, 1984).

—— 'What Difference Did Christianity Make?', *Historia* 35 (1986) 322-43.

—— 'Judicial Savagery in the Roman Empire', *Chiron* 16 (1986) 147-66; reprinted in *Changes in the Roman Empire: Essays in the Ordinary* (Princeton, 1990) 204-17.

MADAN, F., *A Summary Catalogue of Western Manuscripts in the Bodleian Library at Oxford*, IV (Oxford, 1897).

MALITZ, J., *Römisches Staatsrecht – Stellenregister* (Munich, 1979).

—— *Römisches Strafrecht – Stellenregister* (Munich, 1982).

MANFREDINI, A.D., 'Osservazioni sulla compilazione teodosiana (*CTh.* 1,1,5.6 e *Nov. Theod.* 1), in margine a *CTh.* 9,3,4 (*de famosis libellis*)', *Atti Accademia Costantiniana* 4 (1981) 385-428.

MARKUS, R., *The End of Ancient Christianity* (Cambridge, 1990).

MATHISEN, R.W., *Ecclesiastical Factionalism and Religious Controversy in Fifth-century Gaul* (Washington, 1989).

MATTHEWS, J., *Western Aristocracies and Imperial Court AD 364-425* (Oxford, 1975, repr. 1990).

—— 'Symmachus and his enemies', in *Colloque Genevois sur Symmaque, à l'occasion du mille six centième anniversaire du conflit de l'autel de la Victoire* (Paris, 1986).

—— *The Roman Empire of Ammianus* (London, 1989).

MENSCHING, E., *Über einem verfolgten deutschen Altphilogen: Paul Maas (1880-1964)* (Berlin, 1987).

MILLAR, F.G.B., *The Emperor in the Roman World (31 BC-AD 337)* (London, 1977)

MITCHELL, S., 'Maximinus and the Christians in AD 312: a new Latin inscription', *JRS* 78 (1988) 105-24.

MOMMSEN, A., *Theodor Mommsen in Kreise der Seinen* (Berlin, 1936).

—— *Römisches Staatrecht* (Leipzig, 19876-88).

—— *Römisches Strafrecht* (Leipzig, 1899).

—— 'Das theodosische Gesetzbuch', *ZSS RA* 21 (1900), 179-90.

—— *Prolegomena*, in *Theodosiani Libri XVI cum constitutionibus sirmondianis, edidit adsumpto apparatu P. Kruegeri Th. Mommsen* (Berolini, 1905), I,1: Prolegomena; repr. (Dublin/Zurich, 1970/1971).

——— *Gesammelte Schriften* (Berlin, 1905-13).

MORDEK, H., *Kirchenrecht und Reform im Frankenreich. Die Collectio Vetus Gallica, die älteste systematische Kanonessammlung des fränkischen Galliens*, Beiträge zur Geschichte und Quellenkunde des Mittelalters, I (Berlin, 1975).

MORRIS, C., *The Papal Monarchy* (Oxford, 1989).

MUNBY, A.N.L., *Phillipps Studies*, 5 vols. (Cambridge, 1951-60).

MURRAY, A.C., 'From Roman to Frankish Gaul: "centenarii" and "centenae" in the administration of the Merovingian kingdom', *Traditio* 44 (1988) 59-100.

NARDI, D., 'Ancora sul *ius vendendi* de *pater familias* nelle legislazione di Costantino', in *Sodalitas: Scritti in Onore di Antonio Guarino* 5 (Naples, 1984) 2287-2308.

NOAILLES. P., *Les collections de Novelles de l'empereur Justinien: Origine et formation sous Justinien* (Paris 1912).

NOETHLICHS, K.L., *Die gesetzgeberischen Massnahmen der christlichen Kaiser des vierten Jhdts. gegen Heretiker, Heiden und Juden* (Cologne, 1971).

——— 'Zur Einflussnahme des Staates auf die Entwicklung eines christlichen Klerikerstandes', *Jb. Ant. Chr.* 15 (1972) 136-53.

——— 'Materialen zum Bischofsbild aus den spätantiken Rechtsquellen', *Jb. Ant. Chr.* 16 (1973) 28-59.

OLIVER, J.H., 'The Governor's Edict at Aezani after the Edict of Prices', *AJPh* 97 (1976) 174-5.

PALANQUE, J.-R., 'Sur la liste des préfets du prétoire du IVe siècle', *Byzantion* 9 (1934) 703-13; 10 (1935) 641-2.

von PASTOR, L., *Tagebücher-Briefe-Erinnerungen*, ed. W. Wühr (Heidelberg, 1950).

PAULOVICS, I., 'Una legge di Costantino e Licinio in una tavola di bronzo recentemente scoperta in Ungheria', in *Atti del Congresso Internazionale di Diritto Romano 1933, Rome* vol. I (Pavia, 1934) 545-54.

——— *A Sz nyi Törvénytábla: La Table de Privilèges de Brigetio* (Archaeologia Hungarica 20; Budapest, 1936).

PERTZ, G.H., 'Reise nach London und Middlehill, Juli bis September 1844', *Archiv der Gesellschaft für ältere deutsche Geschichtskunde* 9 (1847) 486-504.

PHARR, M., 'The Kiss in Roman Law', *CJ* 42 (1947) 393-7.

PIETRI, Ch., *Roma Christiana* (Rome, 1976).

PONTAL, O., *Die Synoden im Merowingerreich*, Konziliengeschichte, hrsgb. von W. Brandmüller, Reihe A: Darstellungen (Paderborn, 1986).

POSNER, E., *Archives in the Ancient World* (Cambridge, MA, 1972).

RADERMACHER, L., 'O. Seeck', *Biographisches Jahrbuch für Altertumskunde* 46 (1926) 50-60.

RAEPPAEY-CHARLIER, M.-T., 'Ordre sénatorial et Divorce sous le Haut-Empire: un chapitre de l'histoire des Mentalités', *Acta Classica Univ. Scient. Debrecen.* 17-18 (1981-2) 161-73.

RAMSAY, W., *Pauline and Other Studies in Early Christian History* (London, 1906).

REYDELLET, M., *La royauté dans la littérature latine de Sidoine Apollinaire à Isidore de Seville* (Rome, 1981).

de RICCI, S., *English Collectors of Books and Manuscripts (1530-1930) and Their Marks of Ownership* (Cambridge, 1930).

RIES, G., *Prolog und Epilog in Gesetzen des Altertums* (Münchener Beiträge zur

Papyrusforschung und Antiken Rechtsgeschichte 76; Munich 1983).

RIKE, R.L., *Apex Omnium: Religion in the Res Gestae of Ammianus* (Berkeley, 1987).

RITTER, A.M., *Das Konzil von Konstantinopel und sein Symbol* (Göttingen, 1965).

ROSE, V., *Die lateinishen Meerman-Handschriften des Sir Thomas Phillipps in der Königlichen Bibliothek zu Berlin* (Berlin, 1892/3).

ROTONDI, G., 'Studi sulle fonti del codice giustinianeo', in *Scritti Giuridici I* (Milan, 1922) 110-283.

ROUECHÉ, C., *Aphrodisias in Late Antiquity* (London, 1989).

SALZMAN, M.R., '*Superstitio* in the Codex Theodosianus and the Persecution of Pagans', *Vig. Christ.* 41 (1987) 172-88.

SARGENTI, M., 'Il diritto privato nella legislazione di Costantino', *Accademia Romanistica Costantiniana: Atti I Convegno* (Padova, 1975) 229-332.

——— 'Contributi ai problemi della palingenesi delle costituzioni tardo-imperiali (*Vat. Fr.* 35 e *CTh.* 3. 1. 2)', in *Accademia Romanistica Costantiniana, Atti: V Convegno Internazionale 1981* (Perugia, 1983) 311-28.

——— 'Matrimonio cristiano e società pagana', *Studia et Documenta Historiae Iuris* (1985) 367-91.

SAUTEL, G., 'Usurpations du pouvoir impérial dans le monde romain et *rescissio actorum*', in *Studi in Onore di Pietro de Francisci* 3 (Milan, 1956) 461-91.

SCHULZ, F., 'Paul Krüger', *ZSS RA* 47 (1927) ix-xxxii.

SEECK, O., 'Zur Characteristik Mommsens', *Deutsche Rundschau* 118 (1904) 75-108.

——— *Die Briefe des Libanius* (Leipzig, 1906).

——— 'Neue und alte Daten zur Geschichte Diocletians und Constantins', *RM* n.f. 62 (1907) 489-535.

——— *Regesten der Kaiser und Päpste für die Jahre 311 bis 476 n. Chr. Vorarbeit zu einer Prosopographie der christlichen Kaiserzeit* (Stuttgart, 1919).

——— 'Die Zeitfolge der Gesetze Constantins', *ZSS RA* 10 (1889), 1-44, 177-251; reprinted with additional concordance as M. Sargenti (ed.), *Materali per una Palingenesia delle Costituzioni Tardo-Imperiali* 2 (Milan, 1983).

SELB, W., 'Episcopalis audientia von der Zeit Konstantins bis zur Nov. XXXV Valentinians III', *ZSS RA* 84 (1967) 162-217.

SESTON, W., 'Recherches sur la chronologie du règne de Constantin le grand', *REA* 39 (1937) 197-218.

SIMON, D.V., *Konstantinisches Kaiserrecht. Studien anhand der Reskriptenpraxis und der Schenkungsrecht* (Forschung zur Byzantinische Rechtsgeschichte 2; Frankfurt-am-Main, 1977).

SIRKS, A.J.B., 'From the Theodosian to the Justinian Code', *Atti dell'Accademia Romanistica Costantiniana: VI Convegno Internazionale* 6 (1983 [1986]) 265-302.

——— 'Observations sur le Code Theodosien', *Subseciva Groningana* 2 (1985), 21-34.

——— *Food for Rome* (Amsterdam, 1991).

SOMMERVOGEL, C., *Bibliothèque de la Compagnie de Jésus*, VII (Brussels and Paris, 1896).

STAERK, A., *Les manuscrits latins du v au xiii siècle conservés dans la bibliothèque impériale de Saint-Pétersbourg*, I (Saint Petersburg, 1910).

STAHLMANN, I., 'Friedrick Carl von Savigny und Theodor Mommsen. Ihr Briefwechsel zwischen 1844 und 1856', in P. Kneissl and V. Losemann (edd.), *Alte Geschichte und Wissenschaftsgeschichte* (Darmstadt, 1989) 465-501.

STEIN, E., 'A propos d'un livre récent sur la liste de préfets du prétoire', *Byzantion* 9 (1934) 327-53.

STROHEKER, K.F., *Der senatorische Adel im spätantiken Gallien* (Tübingen, 1948).

TRAUBE, L., *Vorlesungen und Abhandlungen*, I (Munich, 1909).

TURNER, C.H., 'Chapters in the History of Latin MSS.', *JTS* 1 (1900) 435-41.

———— 'Chapters in the History of Latin MSS.III. The Lyons-Petersburg MS of Councils', *JTS* 4 (1903) 426-34.

———— *Catholic and Apostolic* (London and Oxford, 1931).

———— *Ecclesiae Occidentalis Monumenta Iuris Antiquissima*, 2 vols. (Oxford, 1899-1939).

TURPIN, W., 'The Purpose of the Roman Law Codes', *ZSS RA* 104 (1987) 620-30.

———— '*Adnotatio* and Imperial Rescript in Roman Legal Procedure', *RIDA* 3rd series 35 (1988) 285-307.

ULLMANN, W., *Law and Politics in the Middle Ages* (London, 1975).

de VALOIS, H., *Oratio in obitum Jacobi Sirmondi* (Paris, 1651).

VAN DER WAL, N., 'Die Textfassung der spätrömischen Kaisergesetze in den Codices', *BIDR* (1986) 1-27.

———— '*Edictum und lex edictalis*. Form und Inhalt der Kaisergesetze im spätrömischen Reich', *RIDA* 3e s. 28 (1981) 277-313.

VERNAY, G., *Note sur le changement de style dans les constitutions impériales de Dioclétien à Constantin*, Études d'histoire juridiques offerts à P.F. Girard II (Paris, 1913) 263-74.

VIDEN, G., *The Roman Chancery Tradition. Studies in the Language of Codex Theodosianus and Cassiodorus' Variae* (Gothenburg, 1984).

VOCI, P., 'Il diritto ereditario romano nell'età del tardo impero, 1: Le costituzioni del IV secolo', *Iura* 29 (1978) 17-113 (reprinted in *Studi di Diritto Romano* 2 (Padua, 1985) 79-176).

VOLTERRA, E., 'Intorno ad alcune costituzioni di Costantino', *Rendiconti dell' Accademia Nazionale dei Lincei* (1958) 61-89.

———— 'Quelques remarques sur le style des constitutions de Constantin', *Mélanges Lévy-Bruhl* (1959) 325-34.

———— 'Il problema del testo delle costituzioni imperiali', *Atti II Congr. Intern soc. ital. del diritto*, vol. II (Firenze, 1971) 821-1097.

———— 'Sul contenuto del Codice Teodosiano', *BIDR* 3rd series 23 (1981) 85-124.

———— 'Le sette costituzioni di Valentiniano e Valente contenute nella *Consultatio*', *BIDR* 3rd series 24 (1982) 171-204.

VOSS, W.E., 'Juristen und Rhetoren als Schöpfer der Novellen Theodosius II', in K. Luig and D. Liebs (edd)., *Das Profil des Juristen in der europäischen Tradition* (Ebelsbach, 1980) 199-256.

———— *Recht und Rhetorik in den Kaisergesetzen der Spätantike* (Frankfurt am Main 1982).

———— review of the re-edition of *Zeitfolge*, *ZSS RA* 106 (1989) 632-45.

WALLACE-HADRILL, A., 'Family and Inheritance in the Augustan Marriage Laws', *PCPhS* 207 (1981) 58-80.

WALLACE-HADRILL, J.M., *The Long-Haired Kings* (London, 1962).

WATSON, A., *The Law of Persons in the Later Roman Republic* (Oxford, 1967).

────── *Roman Private Law around 200 BC* (Oxford, 1971).

WEAVER, P.R.C., *Familia Caesaris* (1972).

WEBER, W., 'Otto Seeck', *Encyclopedia of the Social Sciences*, vol. 13 (London, 1934) 642.

WENGER, L., *Die Quellen des römischen Rechts* (Österreichische Akademie der Wissenschaften, Denkschr. der Gesamtakademie, Band 2; Wien, 1953).

WHITMAN, J.Q., *The Legacy of Roman Law in the German Romantic Era* (Princeton, 1990).

WICKERT, L., *Theodor Mommsen. Eine Biographie*, vols. I, III, IV (Frankfurt, 1959, 1969, 1980).

WIEACKER, F., *Vulgarismus und Klassizismus im Recht der Spätantike* (Heidelberg, 1955).

────── *Allgemeine Zustände und Rechtzustände gegen Ende des Weströmischen Reiches, IRMAE* 1.2 a (Milan, 1963).

────── *Römische Rechtsgeschichte* (Munich, 1988).

WILLIAMS, R., *Arius: Heresy and Tradition* (London, 1987).

WILLIAMSON, C., 'Monuments of Bronze: Roman legal documents on bronze tablets', *Classical Antiquity* 6.1 (1987) 160-83.

WINKELMANN, F., 'Prosopographia Imperii Romani saec. IV, V, VI', in J. Irmscher, ed., *Adolf Harnack und der Fortschritt in der Altertumswissenschaft; zu seinem 50. Todestag* (Berlin, 1981), 29-34.

WITTE, C., *de Guilelmi Malmesburiensis codice legis Romanae Visigothorum* (Bratislava, 1831).

WOOD, I.N., 'Gregory of Tours and Clovis', *Revue Belge de Philologie et d'Histoire* 63 (1985) 249-72.

────── Disputes in Late Fifth and Sixth-century Gaul: Some Problems', in W. Davies and P. Fouracre, *The Settlement of Disputes in Early Medieval Europe* (Cambridge, 1986) 7-22.

────── 'Administration, Law and Culture in Merovingian Gaul', in R. McKitterick, *The Uses of Literacy in Early Medieval Europe* (Cambridge, 1990) 63-81.

────── 'Ethnicity and the Ethnogenesis of the Burgundians', in H. Wolfram and W. Pohl, *Typen der Ethnogenese und besonderer Berücksichtingung der Bayern* (Vienna, 1990). 53-69

WORMALD, P., 'The Decline of the Roman Empire and the Survival of its Aristocracy', *JRS* 66 (1976) 217-26.

────── '*Lex Scripta* and *Verbum Regis:* Legislation and Germanic Kingship from Euric to Cnut', in P.H. Sawyer and I.N. Wood, *Early Medieval Kingship* (Leeds, 1977) 105-38.

de WRETSCHKO, A., 'De usu Breviarii Alariciani forensi et scholastico per Hispaniam, Galliam, Italiam regionesque vicinas', in Mommsen, *CTh*, pp. cccvii-ccclx.

WURM, H., *Studien und Texte zur Dekretalensammlung des Dionysius Exiguus*, Kanonistische Studien und Texte 16 (Bonn, 1939).

Index